South Africa

CIVILIZATIONS IN CONFLICT

South Africa

CIVILIZATIONS IN CONFLICT

JIM HOAGLAND

A Washington Post Book

HOUGHTON MIFFLIN COMPANY BOSTON

1972

TO GRETCHEN
who persisted

Acknowledgments

WHAT FOLLOWS is a journalist's attempt to sketch some of the important realities of Southern Africa today and to examine some of the implications those realities suggest for racial conflict in general. It is not intended as a polemic, nor as an academic study, but as an account that tries to make the complexities of that region more accessible to a larger number of people. Historical detail, which is drawn from published and easily available sources listed in the bibliography, is limited to that which is immediately relevant to Southern Africa today.

This book originated in a series of articles I wrote for the Washington *Post* in 1970 and 1971. It would not exist at all except for the encouragement, patience, and help of a number of people at the *Post.* Chief among them are Executive Editor Benjamin C. Bradlee, Managing Editor Howard Simons, Philip Foisie, John W. Anderson, and a host of other colleagues on the Foreign Desk. To them all, my thanks.

I would also like to acknowledge my great debt to Professor Julius Lewin of South Africa, whose published works and invigorating guest lectures at Columbia University in 1969 greatly stirred my interest in his country. Professor Lewin and Stanley Meisler, Africa correspondent for the Los Angeles *Times*, have read portions of the manuscript and have made helpful suggestions. A number of colleagues throughout Southern Africa gave much in the way of hospitality and expert advice during my visits there. John Jordi, editor of the *Star* of Johannesburg, especially demonstrated that the reports of the warm hospitality of South Africans are not exaggerated. None of the above named should be saddled with the responsibility for the conclusions drawn and facts recited herein, however. They are friends, not accomplices.

Finally, there are a great number of Southern Africans, white, black, and brown, who gave generously of their time and thoughts. I have attempted to let them tell their own story in their own words as much as possible. Thus the book relies heavily on quotations from conversations and interviews. Because of the unhappy situation in their region, however, it has often been necessary to omit their names, just as it is necessary to omit some names from these acknowledgments. But they are not forgotten.

JIM HOAGLAND

Contents

Maps

Introduction

"Then the Lord planted a new nation at the Southern tip of Africa . . . (T)his people was to stand on the verge of being wiped out in many cases and yet was to be saved in a wonderful manner . . .

"From the political clashes of this new nation, its special characteristics will become apparent – its striving for freedom and race purity."

Geskiedenis vir Standerd 6, a primary school textbook
for Afrikaans-speaking children in South Africa.

THAT NATION endures. More than two million strong, it is the white nation of the Afrikaner. Its survival into the closing third of the twentieth century has frozen the world's second largest continent in time and psychology, as Africa waits restlessly and insecurely for an end to white domination on its shores, a resolution of what William P. Rogers, U.S. Secretary of State, has called "the unfinished business of the emergence of Africa." Black Africa to the north diverts much of the moral and political energy it needs to build its own fragile states to the problem of ending that white rule, and world bodies such as the United Nations are regularly convulsed by the need to become involved there, at least rhetorically.

Some independent Black African countries see the Afrikaner

nation as a white peril, a strategic beachhead from which the Western world will launch a new offensive to reimpose direct control over Africa in different forms. Much of the Western world views the white South African minority as part of a last outpost, a remnant of a dying white colonialism in Africa that stubbornly refuses for the moment to abide by the inevitable sweep of history and African nationalism. The white South Africans, however, regard themselves as a first outpost. They represent white civilization in miniature, surrounded by a numerically greater nonwhite world but able to monopolize the wealth and technology of weapons and remain in power. They are in their own view fighting the White Man's Battle, in its first and for them most crucial phase.

Such are the sweeping and conflicting visions conjured up by the continuing rule of the Afrikaners and their 1,500,000 white English-speaking countrymen in South Africa, the half-million Portuguese in Portuguese Africa, and the one-quarter million white settlers in Rhodesia. Together, they continue to dominate thirty-five million Africans a decade after the winds of change were supposed to have swept the whites back into the sea, from whence they first came 300 years ago.

Instead, white nationalism has entrenched itself more firmly than ever at the southern corner of the continent. In South Africa, the key to the region, the chances for a successful black revolt seem to have grown more distant with each passing year since the threat of an internal explosion was overcome in 1960. By the end of the decade, one of the country's most distinguished educators could paraphrase Chesterton on nineteenth-century England to say that "the most important event of the twentieth century for Africa will be the revolution that did not happen." South Africa's revolution was the one that receded; its return remains problematic at present. A counterrevolution was mounted in the 1960s by a radical right-wing government of whites. The view of Afrikaners on race may outwardly appear to resemble those of the conservative societies of the American South or neighboring Rhodesia, where officially sanctioned racial discrimination has also been a political mainstay, but in fact the Afrikaners are profoundly different. The world confronts in the South African power structure a radical force.

In that same tense decade, South Africa experienced one of the highest rates of economic growth in the world. Many calculations place South Africa's 7 to 8 per cent annual real economic growth second only to Japan's among developed countries. South Africa's mines produced record amounts of the gold and other valuable minerals it sells abroad, its factories boomed as domestic production and consumption rose sharply, and foreign investors rushed to pour more capital into the country. American businessmen, apparently ignoring the State Department's view that South Africa's "firm repression of African nationalism can lead only to disaster for all its people," have placed about $1 billion of investment in South Africa and given America a major stake in what happens there. British investment is three times as much.

This book is an attempt to examine the durability and exercise of white power in Southern Africa, where European settlers have taken the country on a significantly different course than they did in North America or Australia, the region's two historical siblings. The time focus is 1970 and 1971, years of significant change for Southern Africa, perhaps more accurately, years in which the forces that had been building during the previous decade, and which will determine the course of events in the coming one, could be seen most clearly. As the new decade began, there was a rebirth of black political activity in South Africa and Rhodesia which, while modest in scale in relation to the monopoly the whites continued to hold on power, held out the promise of an end to the static recent past. This account is a largely descriptive one that allows themes to emerge and that perhaps will offer some insights into the region's deep human conflicts, the subject of much emotional debate and rhetoric but too little dispassionate reporting.

NEW PROBLEMS, OLD SOLUTIONS

Surveying the coming one hundred years, W. E. B. Du Bois wrote in 1900 that "The problem of the Twentieth Century is the problem of the color line." There is still a good chance that he will be proven correct for the world as a whole if the differences between white and nonwhite (or colored and noncolored) peoples continue to diverge in the next three decades. In Southern Africa, his prophecy has already born bitter fruit. A centuries-old struggle there that contained important tribal/national elements has been transformed in the last generation into an exclusively racial one, as the urbanization and industrialization of South Africa helped give rise to the ideology of apartheid and the awakening of African nationalism was brutally repressed by the whites.

Men form themselves into extrafamilial groups at first to protect the resources they need for survival; later they expand these groups to gain and protect privilege as the horizons of their societies widen. Horizons are expanded through the stages of tribe, nation, and then country. The two widest social categorizations of men — that of race and that of class — are the two most directly concerned with the protection of privilege. All these stages of social and political evolution continue to be important in Southern Africa today. They are in deep conflict all across the region of two million square miles, forty million people, and immense mineral wealth.

Two-thirds the size of the United States and as geographically diverse, Southern Africa contains only one-sixth as many people. But it is a kaleidoscope of populations. There are several hundred tribes, a few identifiable ethnic nations such as the white Afrikaners and the black Zulu, and two groups that are members of world civilizations — the English-speaking settlers of South Africa and Rhodesia and the Portuguese. A fourth imperial European power, Germany, has disappeared from the area, but has left its imprint. The conflicts of these strong-willed, grasping peoples have turned Southern Africa into a crazy quilt of jumbled societies, and the sorting out of them that is beginning is the cause for much of the region's current agony. These peoples have fought each other for several centuries for more of the land's riches, but they have fought even harder to be free from the domination of each other. They have all failed at one time or another, and in the last generation they have all failed simultaneously (if in different ways) as the essential nature of their struggles has become different and infinitely more dangerous for them all.

Southern Africa's most intense struggles of the past have been essentially powered by tribal or nationalistic rivalries in which whites fought whites and blacks fought blacks. The military regiments organized by the greatest African warrior of modern history, the Zulu chief Shaka, killed many more Africans than they did whites; the bitterest and most costly struggle the Afrikaners have ever waged was against the British imperial army; the Portuguese have traditionally had more to fear from British designs on their territory than from African uprisings. White and black conflict has also been bitter, but intraracial violence has been at least as significant if not more so.

Although many outsiders think of South Africa as two great monolithic population groups facing each other, the country is in fact one of the world's greatest ethnic jumbles. The country lies at the tip of the continent and was the last area to be penetrated by the great African migrations that moved across the continent from east to west, and then north to south. African tribes moved under the pressures of the drying out of the areas around the Sahara, invasions from the Arab Middle East, and local tribal disruptions. Exactly when the migrating Bantu tribes arrived in South Africa is a fiercely controversial question, since the white Afrikaners claim they reached the interior prior to or at the same time as the black tribes moving down from the north, in the seventeenth and eighteenth centuries. (A recent authoritative work, *The Oxford History of South Africa Volume I*, edited by Monica Wilson and Leonard Thompson, presents a convincing case that Bantu-speaking tribesmen were probably in the region at least as early as the eleventh century.)

Given the present power realities, the debate over a historic moral claim to the land of South Africa has a slightly nostalgic and theoretical air. What is certain is that the white settlers from Europe and the Bantu squeezed between them and virtually eliminated the original inhabitants of the territory, the yellow-skinned herders who were called the Hottentots and primitive hunters, the Bushmen. The Dutch settlers who arrived in the middle of the seventeenth century were the first permanent European settlers in Africa. They began to arrive when African settlement of the region was still in a state of flux and indigenous patterns of social organization were just coming into being.

Both white and black were at the end of the migration route in Southern Africa, and they faced each other to begin the struggle that has still not been resolved. But the arrival in South Africa of a second European nation, Britain, created more fragmentation of purposes and peoples, as the British fought both the Dutch and the Africans. Gradually, the British immigrants and their children began to identify themselves with the new country of South Africa and began to think of themselves not as British, but as English-speaking South Africans.

African social structures collapsed under the pressures of the white military campaigns and the competition for the land. The Zulu, welded into a nation by Shaka, were fragmented into small, scattered tribal groupings separated by white occupation. The white conquest arrested the evolution of African tribes into broader nations, but it reinforced the nationalisms the two white groups had imported from Europe.

This recurring conflict of tribe and nation and the continuing great disparity between their levels of development have created an Uncommon Society within the borders of a convenient geographic unit known as South Africa. This is a self-evident truth to most white South Africans, who see the economic, social, and political structures of the country rising from their efforts alone. They assert they have no common heritage or culture with the black men that the rest of the world mistakenly insists are their countrymen and who therefore deserve an equal opportunity to share in the society's benefits. This common society does not exist for the whites. For much of this century, the two main white groups have had precious little in common among themselves, practicing voluntary apartheid in their schools, churches, and social relationships.

In a predominantly rural country, where African tribes occupied clearly defined territory and managed their own tribal affairs, the Uncommon Society concept had tremendous force, and there was little outcry about customs and legislation that enforced the differentiation, no more than when Indians were restricted to reservations in America. But at the middle of the twentieth century, South Africans like many other peoples became aware that their country was undergoing a dramatic and important change. The forces of urbanization and industrialization, which pulled both the rural white and rural African into the cities and into similar environments, were beginning to forge a Common Society. Both the Afrikaner and the African were being detribalized, although the former at a much greater rate and earlier than the latter. The city's similar systems of education and economic structures and the need for a common language of business and commerce were slowly breaking down the natural lines of separation. Urban Africans were becoming a New Tribe, with the potential to evolve into a New Nation that would outnumber the whites.

As this was occurring, black countries to the north were being given self-government and promises of independence. They had a chance to run their own affairs within modern structures of government transposed from the Western world. The white man in South Africa suddenly perceived, or perhaps got around to admitting to himself, that the difference in development of white South Africans and black South Africans was conditioned more by environment and opportunity than by the color of skin chosen by God. For a white minority, even one as large and as powerful as the one in South Africa had grown, this presented an unacceptable threat.

The response was apartheid — "apartness." At first it was a simple legalistic approach to restoring the separation of the races within the urban areas, where racial ghettos were created by law and facilities and privileges were reserved by whites. Then apartheid was expanded into a grand design to restore separation on a much greater level, psychologically if not territorially as it promised. African tribal structures were suddenly praised as the bases for building new independent African nations, in which blacks could devise their own society and practice their own rights. Africans were encouraged — then coerced — into returning to the tribal areas. The insistence of the white government that Africans could attain their rights only through the tribal structures gave rise to the suspicion, however, that what was really involved was an attempt to preserve the political and ethnic fragmentation of the African population, which had permitted the whites to win the initial struggles against Africans. The aim was to arrest again development beyond tribalism, skeptics said.

Like all grand solutions, ranging from the United Nations to sex education to Richard Nixon's 1971 discovery of China, apartheid is drawn to solve problems of the past. Perceived only after they have slipped by us, these problems have grown into something quite different. Grand apartheid might be an effective response if South Africa's problems today were ones of conflicting localized nationalisms (although to work, apartheid's division of territory would have to be altered from the whites' magic 87-13 formula, which gives 87 per cent of the country to the 17 per cent white population and only 13 per cent to the Africans).

Over the last two decades, however, the conflict has been transformed into an openly racial one. The Afrikaners have implicitly acknowledged this in dropping their traditional isolationist stance toward the English-speaking whites of South Africa and appealing to them to join in a "broad new South African nationalism" that has only one criterion — a white skin. Blacks in South Africa are kept off buses or out of hospitals or at low-paying job levels not because they are Xhosa or Zulu nationals, but because they are black.

Two guerrilla wars have erupted next door to South Africa in Portuguese Africa, aligning blacks on one side and all the whites — Portuguese, South Africans, and Rhodesians — on the other.

Rhodesia is increasingly turning toward apartheid, a doctrine that equates white supremacy and white privilege with a way of life that must be protected. This polarization on racial lines indicates a racial resolution of the conflict, that is, white power continued, or black power arisen and triumphant. Multiracialism — an equitable sharing of economic and political power among races who actively cooperate with each other in a unitary system of government for the common good — is no longer a feasible alternative in Southern Africa.[1] A possible exception is the Portuguese territory of Angola, although even there it is highly unlikely. Apartheid is forging a counterapartheid across the region.

THE OTHER AMERICANS

That is the quasi-theoretical burden of this book, which deals in theory only to a limited degree. It depends more on detail and incident to explain South Africa than upon immutable truths. There is perhaps more to be learned about South Africa and apartheid from cases like the one of the banned Beethoven Bantu than from vast stores of theoretical writings, propaganda materials, and mellifluous speeches.

The South African Broadcasting Corporation organized a musical competition to commemorate the two-hundredth anniversary of Beethoven's birthday, which fell in 1970. A string quartet composed of Bantu (as Africans are officially known in South Africa) entered the contest, but the Corporation barred them from playing Beethoven on the contest broadcast when it was discov-

[1] The use of the term "multiracialism" throughout this book is normally in this sense, which emphasizes the political aspects of racial cooperation and the resulting division of resources and benefits. It is distinct from nonracialism, which implies that governments and individuals do not make significant differentiations (or at least discriminations) on the basis of race. Multiracialism is more positive than that. It also differs from the ordinary usage of integration, which puts a certain stress on assimilation and social aspects of racial contact. Apartheid intends to destroy or severely limit all three, all of which involve the individual's freedom to choose to associate or not associate with anyone of other races. Multiracialism implies a clear recognition of racial differences, but a willingness to use those differences as a basis for sharing rather than hoarding.

ered that they were Africans. "Different races perform best in their own idoms," explained a public relations officer at the network when asked about the rejection of the entry.

The official rationale for keeping Africans out of white facilities and institutions that range from rest rooms to Parliament is that the blacks are so different, so unique, that they cannot, should not, and do not want to assimilate to Western ways. Beethoven is one of the highest expressions of the art form of Western civilization, the mystical set of values that white South Africans assert they protect by continuing to exist. To allow four urbanized (they were from Johannesburg) young Africans to play Beethoven, and perhaps play it well, would do grievous damage to South Africa's elaborately constructed theory of human relations. "The white South African says that Western civilization will be preserved by him and no one else," Knowledge Guzana, an articulate and well-educated African lawyer, told me. "The African is moving away from tribalism and his aspirations are with the modern world. But the whites for their own power reasons are attempting to shove him back into the tribe."

The Afrikaner has a major stake in casting himself in the role of the guardian of Western civilization in a threatening world. It serves not only to bolster morale and discipline at home within the white population, but seeks to gain support from the other white or white-dominated nations of the world. This was a support that the Afrikaner once counted on automatically and usually received. But Adolf Hitler gave racism as well as Fascism a bad name. Nonwhite countries gained independence and became apparent factors in world politics. Other governments began to shrink away from officially condoning racial prejudice, whatever actual practices within their countries were. This change came while South Africa was marching in the other direction to the tune of apartheid. The South Africans were stunned, then puzzled, and finally angered by the criticisms of their racial policies by other white countries. They were, in their own view at least, merely doing what white men had always done. They had not changed at all; it was their new critics who were being inconsistent. And al-

though it falls outside the scope of this book, it is helpful in understanding white South Africa, and perhaps America, Australia, and
other lands wrenched away from indigenous peoples, to acknowledge at this point that the South Africans are largely right. The
reaction of white South Africa to its problems today is a reaction
of European settlers, caught in a unique historical situation.[2]

New England and South Africa were initially settled about the
same time and by the same two main European nations, the
Dutch and the English, after Iberian expeditions had probed both
continents' coastlines. The patterns quickly diverged, as the
Dutch were frozen out of America by the English, but went on to
dominate the tiny white settlement in South Africa.

Portuguese navigators were apparently the first Europeans to
reach the southern tip of Africa. Bartholomeu Dias rounded the
Cape of Good Hope in 1488. Ten years later Vasco da Gama
rounded the Cape and sighted the eastern shore of Africa. On
Christmas Day, he named Natal, the Indian Ocean province of
South Africa. Da Gama hurried past Africa, however, on his way
to the fabled riches of India.

For the next 100 years, the Indian Ocean trade was the private
preserve of the Portuguese, who preferred to build up the better
natural harbors on the southwestern and southeastern flanks of
Africa than to implant themselves at the tip. The Portuguese Empire went into eclipse with the annexation of Portugal by Spain at
the end of the sixteenth century, at the same time that the Dutch
commercial fleet began sailing around the Cape and on to Java.
In Amsterdam the Dutch East India Company was formed in
1602 to direct this lucrative trade, and the Dutch soon replaced
the Portuguese as masters of the Eastern trade. A refreshment station, a sort of halfway house between Europe and Java where food
could be grown and animals raised, was needed and the Dutch decided that the Cape of Good Hope was the best spot to land farmers.

---

[2] This does not mean to suggest that racism is a unique trait of white populations around
the world. There is too much empirical evidence available in Africa and Asia to the contrary.

According to tradition, the lookout on Jan van Riebeeck's ship sighted the crest of Cape Town's Table Mountain at 2:30 P.M. on April 5, 1652. Van Riebeeck, a captain for the Dutch East India Company, had brought three ships of company employees and instructions to settle only enough territory for farms to provide the Company's ships with fresh meat, vegetables, and fruit. The Dutch came not to bring civilization, nor to take slaves, but for commerce. The settlement gradually grew as the Company found it needed more soldiers to protect the farmers and their cattle against the Hottentots and the Bushmen and more farmers to grow more food. Immigration of "burghers," or farmers who were granted land, was for a time encouraged. Slaves were imported into the settlement from Madagascar and the East Indies, since it was against Company policy to disturb the local tribes and also since it was extraordinarily difficult to turn the elusive and primitive Hottentots and Bushmen into slaves.

There were only 600 Dutch landholders farming on the Cape three decades after van Riebeeck had landed. Economic opportunities were limited by the Company's strict rules, based on its desire to retain a monopoly on all trade. The Dutch were forbidden to trade with the Hottentots and warned to have as little contact as possible with them. Both prohibitions were apparently broken with regularity.

In 1689, several hundred French Huguenots who had originally taken refuge in Holland arrived at the Cape. German Protestant immigrants also came to the settlement. Calvinism and common habits brought these groups together in a few generations. Eventually they were to develop a hybrid language, a rough and unsophisticated tongue known as Afrikaans — the African language of white men. It resembled Flemish, but was identifiable as a separate tongue. Their word for farmer was Boer, and so they called themselves.

Chafing under the restrictions of the Dutch Company, the Boers pushed their farms outside the limits of the Cape settlement. Cattle grazing and hunting extended their frontier further into the dry, riverless interior. Those in the vanguard of pushing the fron-

tier forward were the Trekboers — the traveling farmers. The
Company lost control over the Boer expansion. Over the next
century, they pushed deeper into South Africa and farther away
from Europe. "In the long quietude of the eighteenth century the
Boer race was formed," C. W. de Kiewiet has written in perhaps
the most quoted sentence in South African history. "In the vast,
unmysterious, thirsty landscape of the interior lay the true center
of South African settlement." [3] During that century, the white
population increased to only 20,000. There were perhaps an equal
number of slaves in the colony.

But in the final years of the century, the Dutch East India Company slid into bankruptcy as the Dutch Empire went into a sharp
decline. Troops were withdrawn from the Cape settlement to cut
expenses, and trade dropped for the farmers as ships came less
and less frequently. In 1795, the British occupied the Cape,
largely to keep the territory and its command of the sea lanes to
the East out of the hands of the French. It was reclaimed by the
Dutch, with British acquiescence in 1803, but in 1806 the British
established themselves as rulers of the Cape once and for all, or so
they thought. The Cape became a British colony, with an almost
entirely Dutch settler population.

Few Englishmen were willing to try their luck and settle there in
the first years of British occupation. Instead, soldiers and missionaries came. Dr. John Philip of the London Missionary Society arrived in 1819. He was largely responsible for freeing the Hottentots and the mulatto population in 1828 from the requirement of
carrying passes. Otherwise they would have been arrested as va-
grants and forced into labor for the whites. Philip also helped persuade London to abolish slavery in the Colony in 1834. These reforms made Philip one of the most hated men in Boer history.
They deprived the Boers of their primary source of labor for the
vast farms they had claimed and threatened to give men of color
the appearance of equality with whites. Philip's reforms added
greatly to the list of grievances the Boers felt they already had

[3] *A History of South Africa, Social & Economic,* Oxford University Press, 1957.

against the autocratic British administration of Cape Town, and they decided to rid themselves of British control. They organized the Great Trek. Harassed by the British at their rear, and blocked from moving along the coast by the thick concentration of African tribes there, the Boers gathered together covered wagons and oxen and poured into the center of South Africa in a movement that the South Africans compare to the pioneer movement across the Western United States.

Between 1836 and 1846, perhaps 10,000 men, women, and children climbed aboard ox wagons and left the Cape Colony. Many left as a form of rebellion against British authority, but others, facing agricultural ruin because of four years of drought, went into the interior in search of new land. Behind them they left 30,000 Europeans and mulattos.

They moved in waves rather than one steady stream, and they soon collided with the African tribes who were seeking the same land for cattle grazing, water holes, and farming. Battles erupted along the white line of immigration. To protect themselves, the farmers used their wagons as movable fortresses. Ox wagons were formed into a square, their wheels locked together with chains and the spaces between stuffed with whatever materials were handy. This was the *laager,* the Boer fort into which the entire group gathered at signs of danger. Only when the leaders of the group considered the danger past was the laager split and travel resumed. The laager and the rifle were the essentials of Boer security.

The earlier expansion inland from the Cape had already brought the Boers into contact with the Bantu tribes who had advanced as far south as the Fish River, near what is today Port Elizabeth. The similarity of their economic aims — land and cattle — made conflict inevitable. It exploded in 1799 into the first Kaffir[4] War, the first of a long series of frontier clashes between white and black that continued into the last part of the nineteenth century.

---

[4] The word kaffir is originally an Arabic term used for infidels. It has been adopted throughout Southern Africa as a racially derogatory term for blacks. It is usually translated in the American idom as "nigger."

In the years preceding the Great Trek, a black South African nation was also expanding into the interior. The Zulu nation was being assembled by the recklessly brave and bloodthirsty warrior king Shaka. Shaka welded tribes together in a larger ethnic unit through military conquest and through his use of military regiments as a form of early political organization. Tribes who opposed Shaka's regiments were defeated, then assimilated or driven away, as the Mfecane, the great period of African tribal warfare, reached its peak between 1817 and 1828. Shaka was assassinated by his half brother Dingaan, who became Zulu king.

Shaka made friends with the few British traders who ventured into the area around Natal, and Dingaan continued his policy of welcoming the emissaries the British administration in Cape Town sent. But the Boers arrived in Natal in November 1837 and demanded that Dingaan cede territory to them. The Zulu king temporized. The Boers finally sent a mission to Dingaan's camp in February to obtain a charter granting Natal to them. Dingaan signed the charter to put the whites at ease and then had them murdered. His regiments attacked Boer encampments in Natal, but the laagers beat off the attacks. The Boers gradually assembled force for a counterattack, and on December 16, 1838, they decisively defeated the Zulu regiments at Blood River. The Battle of Blood River did not destroy the Zulu kingdom, but for the Boers it was the sign of God's will that they should conquer the land. After Blood River they never felt that their expansion across the country was in doubt, although it would at times be greatly retarded by the Africans and the British.

It was the British army that eventually broke the major African tribes in South Africa, the Zulu and the Xhosa. In 1856, a Xhosa witch doctor named Mhlakaza interpreted a vision seen by a young girl as a prophecy. In February of the following year, dead Xhosa chiefs and warriors would arise and help drive the white man back into the sea — if Africans slaughtered all their cattle and destroyed their grain as an act of faith. Then two suns would arise on the fateful morning and a hurricane would sweep the white man away. The tribesmen obeyed the witch doctor's instructions and starvation spread across the Xhosa, destroying them as a fighting nation. In one area, the population was reduced from 100,000 to 37,000 within a year. The day for the suns and the hurricane came and went, and the white man's advance continued.

The Xhosa witch doctor was not the last opponent to underestimate greatly the tenacity of the white man in South Africa. Over the past few decades, many people seemed to have been still waiting for the double suns and the hurricane, while the Afrikaner went about building up stronger security machinery and the vast, powerful bureaucracy that reaches into the most intimate corner of the lives of everyone in South Africa who has any contact, on whatever level, with persons of another race. Pressures that range from polite condemnations in world forums to guerrilla warfare have failed to shake the white grip across Southern Africa. Today's honorary witch doctors in Addis Ababa, New York, and London incant phrases about the evils of apartheid and colonialism and then wonder why there is no collapse.

By 1970, apartheid was a generation old in South Africa, but it was still poorly understood abroad and at home. By 1980, according to Pretoria bureaucrats, it is supposed to be in place, as Bantu homelands begin their march to independence and the notion that a black man can be a citizen of the White Fortress South Africa becomes a thing of the past. Much of the first part of this book deals with the origins of apartheid, its development from a pragmatic policy of prejudice in 1948 into a grand ideology that has acquired a political momentum of its own and the effects apartheid has had on the diverse populations within South Africa.

The second part examines South Africa's links to its white allies in the region and the alternative approaches they appear to offer for the racial problem that is at the heart of the South African dilemma. South Africa's campaign to win friends in black Africa and the outside world are also considered.

A few final notes of explanation and qualification need to be added before passing on to a statistical setting of the South African scene.

Where figures given in South African rand have been converted to dollars for the reader's convenience, the conversion has been at the predevaluation 1971 rate of 1 rand for $1.40.

One of my operating assumptions is my belief in the importance of the interaction of national character with other historical factors. The fact that it was the Dutch who settled the interior of South Africa, and not the Portuguese or English, has made a significant difference in the way that the country has developed, although the essential condition of white-minority rule over a black majority would undoubtedly still be the end result because of considerations even more compelling than national character. There is an attempt in the book where possible to draw generalizations about the factors that shape a national or ethnic characteristic or attitude. I have tried not to turn this into a license for unbridled generalizations of the "All Americans drive big cars" kind. Instead, the quest has been for the type of information that enables one to conclude, "Because of the greater distances of their country, the lower costs of oil and gasoline, and the availability of metals and technology, Americans build and drive cars that are considered large by the standards of most of the peoples of the world." However often I have used shorthand to get this type of idea across, this is the thought that lies behind the generalization. In any event, it can be argued that the deep conservatism and conformity of Afrikaner society and the racial and group stereotyping of all of South Africa's peoples make generalizations about them inevitable, whether from themselves or outsiders.

By and large there are no heroes in this book, but identifiable villains are also in short supply. Most of the people I met demonstrated many of the human strengths and virtues, foibles and faults, of people anywhere in the world, and I have recorded a scattering of each. Adjectives have been avoided when dealing with the more controversial actions of governments and individuals. In most cases, those actions speak loudly for themselves.

The white rulers and their communities are discussed at greater length than are the black communities. That is partly because I am attempting to deal with power realities, and at the moment it is the whites who have power. But also, it is because a white visitor operating in white-ruled Southern Africa has great difficulty in determining exactly what is going on behind the walls that have been built around the black populations. Unlike a number of others, conservatives and liberals, who have written on this subject in recent years, I do not assert that I know what is really going on in the black communities. They may be laughing and dancing and happy, as the white governments suggest, or they may be on the threshold of a successful revolution, as the guerrilla movements suggest. My own impressions do not tally with either suggestion. All I can do is report those impressions and admit that they are not as complete as I would like them to be.

Finally there is little discussion here of the international aspects of the dispute over Rhodesia's Unilateral Declaration of Independence from Britain. My vantage point is too close to the ground in Africa to permit a good view of those aspects, and they have been covered thoroughly elsewhere. Much the same is true of the continuing World Court and United Nations involvement in the disputed territory of South West Africa, a largely desert wasteland on South Africa's western flank, which I was unable to visit. A number of observers have argued that South West Africa could prove to be South Africa's Achilles' heel. The international dispute provides a better case — or pretext — for an international intervention there than in the rest of the country. (The uncharacteristically strong American position on South West Africa in the United Nations led many South African whites to fear at one time that the United States might even take the lead in a display of force to free the territory from Pretoria's grasp — a fear now realized to have been greatly exaggerated.)

South West Africa conceivably could be a wedge for a big power or international strike at South Africa. But I don't think it is likely to be so in the next decade, and in any event the target is no longer South West Africa. The important target has become the complete collapse of the white South African government. The course of events in South West Africa in the coming few years depends on the power situation in Pretoria, not vice versa.

THE SETTING

South Africa occupies a territory of 472,550 square miles, which makes it a little larger than the geographic unit formed by the states of Texas, New Mexico, and Oklahoma. Most of the country lies well south of the tropics, and the plateau land of the interior also makes the climate temperate. Johannesburg's winters can be chill and sharp, and frosts are widespread across the country. The plateau land ranges from 1000 feet to 6000 feet in altitude, with an average height being perhaps 4000 feet. Rainfall is uncertain throughout most of the interior, and in the south and west the scrub country shades into vast desert lands that belong to the areas known as the Kalahari and the Karoo. Mountain ranges that climb up to 10,000 feet break up the edges of the plateau, partially separating the interior from the 1800-mile South African coastline, which is marked by a coastal belt varying in width from three to thirty miles. The coast is the only part of the country that can depend on regular rainfall.

South Africa has no navigable rivers. The two most important are the Orange River, which stretches nearly across the country from the Atlantic to the Indian Oceans, and which has an important tributary in the Vaal River, and the Limpopo, which forms the border with Rhodesia and flows out to the Indian Ocean through Mozambique.

South Africa's ties to the outside world are much more direct than most people suspect. The chances are about 40 per cent that the diamond an American bride wears comes from South Africa and about 85 per cent that it was originally marketed by De Beers, a South African firm that is one of the world's greatest monopolies. The gold of her wedding ring almost certainly was mined in South Africa. That country's fifty to sixty gold mines produce 75 per cent of all gold mined in non-Communist countries. There is a very real connection between the executive of the International Monetary Fund who sits in an air-conditioned office in Washington working with world monetary exchange rates that are all backed by gold and the black miner operating a jackhammer drill

PART I

INSIDE THE LAAGER

PRELUDE

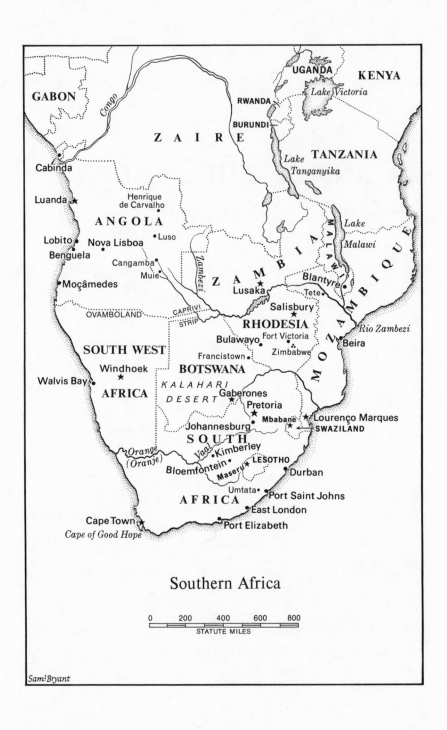

Southern Africa

0　　200　　400　　600　　800
STATUTE MILES

Sam!Bryant

SUNDAY IS THE BEST DAY to see modern South Africa. It is the only day on which the tensions between its peoples seem to recede, as they separate and briefly enclose themselves inside the worlds that apartheid would sever completely, if it could. It can't. On Monday the need for money, for goods, and for human contact — even if that contact is built around hatred or humiliation — pulls them back together again.

Excelsior is a small frontierlike town in the Orange Free State. Afrikaner farmers and their families rise early in the morning, as they do every other day of the week. Soon they are riding or trekking toward the spire of the sandstone Dutch Reformed Church, which dominates the dirt roads of the town and rolling farmland around it.

About 500 of Excelsior's 700 whites, almost all of whom are Afrikaners, live in the town. The rest are scattered, far apart, on the large farms. Two thousand Africans also live around Excelsior, either in a fenced-in location or in small clusters of huts on the white farms, where they work. None of the Africans are going to the "white man's church" on our typical Sunday morning.

The Afrikaner, wearing the dark, ill-fitting suit that he dons once a week, returns home after church. Later he may call on a neighbor, who will greet him or any other white man who happens by with an overwhelming hospitality, huge quantities of food, and good cheer. Or the Afrikaner may remain at home, reading the family Bible, the small regional Afrikaans-language newspaper, or a slightly popularized Afrikaans novel about the Boer War. He will, in any event, do nothing to break Sunday Observance, which forbids any frivolous undertakings or entertainment on the Sabbath. Even hunting, his favorite pastime, is forgotten on Sunday in Excelsior.

The family Bible is the key document in the Afrikaner household. Many of their Bibles contain blank pages at the back for listing all the members of the family. If a kinsman does something to disgrace the clan, the page is ripped out, the most serious form of excommunication in Afrikanerdom. Here in Excelsior, it is likely that 1971 saw a record number of Bibles thus mutilated.

Somehow, in spite of apartheid's theories and Afrikanerdom's strict codes, five respectable farmers in Excelsior were charged with having had sexual relations with fourteen African women (over several years). If convicted under the Immorality Act, which prohibits sex across the color line, the farmers (and the women) could conceivably have gone to jail for seven years.

After much unfavorable publicity, and the surfacing of suggestions that the defense would claim in court that the African women had been beaten by police to get confessions, the charges against four of the farmers were dropped. But the matter would remain alive in Excelsior for a long time.

"For [the Afrikaner] it is as if the farmers had been suspected of raping their sheep," commented Colin Smith, a perceptive correspondent of the *Observer* of London. "In a South African court a first offender on a morals charge usually gets a suspended prison sentence. The real punishment is left to his friends and neighbors." This was not the case for the fifth accused. He committed suicide before the charges were dropped. People in Excelsior took it as an admission that he had slept with a black woman.

Pretoria's sprouting concrete and glass office buildings and modern shopping arcades happily do not obscure its rural origins and graces. The Dutch Reformed Churches here have been hemmed in by the new commercial and government edifices and no longer dominate the horizon, but at Pretoria's center is preserved a large oasis of green, a park dominated by an imposing stone statue: Oom Paul Kruger, the most revered of Afrikaners. This jumbled cityscape with a constant heart is an easy symbol, just the kind that John Barth in *The Floating Opera* warns writers to avoid. But it may be useful as we consider the urban Afrikaner who, in the course of the last seven decades, has come to represent three quarters of all Afrikanerdom.

Our cardboard cutout of an urban Afrikaner is a young married architect. His wife is a pretty blond English-speaker who occasionally models for local fashion advertisements. The husband usually takes their two small children to the Dutch Reformed Church two or three times a month, and the wife accompanies them perhaps twice. Too many questions are raised if they miss doing this too often. But on this Sunday, they sleep late and skip church. They have been to a late dinner party on Saturday night, at which heroic amounts of whiskey were consumed. The wife, who speaks Afrikaans but almost always talks to her husband in English, is slightly cross with him this morning for having spent most of the party in flirtation with other women. But it is an indulgent irritation, as a mother shows toward a youngster who had committed an entirely normal and predictable misdeed.

The husband's Afrikaans Sunday newspaper is *Die Beeld*, which, although it is also tied directly to the ruling National Party, will occasionally voice doubts about some aspects of government policy. He may also receive *Die Transvaler*, if he wants to keep up with the voice of conservative Afrikanerdom and with what the older bureaucrats who inhabit his neighborhood are thinking. But the only paper he devotes much time to is the English-language *The Sunday Times*. He disregards most of the political news, as he is firmly convinced that the English-language press distorts politics. He turns instead to the entertainment section, the comic strips, and the in-depth economic reporting that the Afrikaans papers lack.

Sunday afternoon does not present any great range of choices in Pretoria, either. There is no television to watch because the government, fearing its impact on South African society, has banned it until at least 1974. Cinemas are closed, too. The young Afrikaner may read a modern Afrikaans novel, one by André Brink or Etienne Leroux, that will tangentially raise the question of the country's racial problems without dissecting them. Or he may drop in on one of Pretoria's many young civil servants who work for the central government to talk politics — which means debating whether apartheid is or is not working.

This Sunday in South Africa is an April one. It is too chilly, then, for the English-speaking businessman living in one of the affluent northern suburbs of Johannesburg to use the swimming pool in his backyard. So before lunch he and a friend enjoy a quick game of tennis on the court in the front yard.

English-speaking white South Africans are fond of saying that they live like Americans. They do, only much better. On $20,000 to $30,000 a year, a thirty-five-year-old sales representative such as the one we are visiting, who works for an international firm, will have not only the swimming pool, tennis court, ranch house in the suburbs, and two American-style compact cars, but also two or three black servants. After Beverly Hills, Johannesburg is thought to have the greatest concentration of swimming pools in the world.

Per capita, South African whites also have more guns (a fourteen-year-old can obtain a license and South Africa's 3,800,000 whites have more than 1,500,000 firearms), heart attacks, and suicides than just about anybody else in the world, except perhaps Americans. Interestingly, South African blacks do not have many guns, heart attacks, or suicides, statistics indicate. Nobody seems quite sure what the implications of all this are.

Affluence, black servants to do the work, temperate climate, and Sunday blue laws add up to a sports-crazy people. Sunday is tennis and /or swimming, or perhaps riding. English-speakers are known to schedule their vacations around important rugby and cricket series. Sports, participatory and spectator, are a national white mania, along with politics.

Lunch on this Sunday is a barbecue of tasty beef sausages and steak accompanied by excellent red wine from the Cape. Talk about race, the inevitable subject, is more direct and relaxed. The English-speakers have not personally drawn the apartheid line and are not as defensive as the Afrikaners. "If I could have some kind of guarantee that my job and position here would be safe, then I wouldn't mind giving educated Africans political rights," the English-speaker says. "But nobody has been able to come up with a guarantee, and that is why we don't fight all that hard for change." He is considered by his associates as quite liberal on race, in South African terms.

Fifteen miles away lies Soweto, a black township of 700,000 Africans. Sunday is recovery day here from a week of shuttling back and forth between Johannesburg, where Africans work, and Soweto, where they live. They may not go to Johannesburg on Sunday (unless they have a job that requires it), and it is against the law for whites to go to Soweto on the weekend. ("I don't know if the government keeps whites out at night and weekends because they don't want us to see what is going on, or because they are afraid we will get killed," a white South African journalist told me.)

If the African glances at *his* weekend newspaper, he will see a reflection of his life in Soweto in the headlines, which are likely to concern murder or other violence. The frustrations built up in the segregated society explode here in Soweto, which has one of the highest murder rates in the world (although, as I said, not suicide). Sunday morning at the massive Baragwanath Hospital, which the government proudly says is perhaps the largest in the Southern Hemisphere and is all for the natives, means the rush of the weekend is slowing down, and the emergency ward is less crowded with the crying, bleeding people who sometimes still have a knife, or an ice pick, imbedded in their bodies or skulls when they stagger in through the door. (Violence pervades all of South Africa, not just Soweto. The country has one-tenth as many people as the United States, but 60 per cent as many deaths caused by criminal acts of violence. The United States records between 15,000 and 16,000 criminal homicides a year; South Africa has more than half that many.)

Sunday keeps the blue and white bus, which brings white tourists through Soweto five days a week, from plying the streets with their white guides telling the white passengers how well cared for and happy the natives in Soweto are. The shebeens, the Soweto versions of the speakeasy, are slowly coming back to life in the late afternoon. Almost every block in Soweto has one. Although prices for a drink are higher and there is always the danger of arrest, many Africans prefer them to the government-sponsored beer halls. That is the extent of visible rebellion in Soweto these days.

Oswald Joseph Mtshali, a thirty-one-year-old Soweto resident, has in a short time established himself as a major poet in South Africa. His first book, *Sounds of a Cowhide Drum,* published in 1971, went through its first printing in a few weeks. One day in his existence is described in "Always a Suspect":

> I get up in the morning
> and dress up like a gentleman —
> A white shirt a tie and a suit.
> I walk into the street
> to be met by a man
> who tells me "to produce."
> I show him
> the document of my existence
> to be scrutinized and given the nod.

. . . .

> I trudge the city pavements
> side by side with "madam"
> who shifts her handbag
> from my side to the other,
> and looks at me with eyes that say
> "Ha! Ha! I know who you are;
> beneath those fine clothes
> ticks the heart of a thief." [1]

[1] *Sounds of a Cowhide Drum* by Oswald Joseph Mtshali. Reprinted with the permission of The Third Press–Joseph Okpaku Publishing Company, Inc., New York.

Nadine Gordimer, one of South Africa's most gifted white writers, calls Mtshali a new voice for Africa, that of the urban underprivileged black, of the "dead-end elite" apartheid has created. The jacket of the South African edition of his slender book of poems tells us even more about him: "Mtshali is married, lives in Soweto and works as a messenger."

The mists settle in around Cape Town in April and on a Sunday evening, as the sun fades, a ghostly fog spills over the mountains and hills that form a protective bowl at the city's back. The fog slithers down the hill and about halfway to the bottom penetrates into District Six. For decades, District Six has been the home of about 30,000 people. Nobody is sure exactly how many residents it has; District Six is not a precise geographical term. It has, like Harlem, or Soho, or Pigalle, been used more often to describe a condition than a certain area. It has been a spiritual homeland to perhaps two million South African Coloreds, the mulattos who some place along the line have had white and black ancestors but under apartheid can claim neither. They are classified as nonwhites, of a special category.

In the Sunday night fog, the remarkable women of District Six, who frequently hold down one or two jobs in addition to running a home, gather in the combination corner stores–cafés that dot the slum area's street corners. Their frequently bulky frames are outlined in the yellow glow of the lights as they stand and chat for hours beneath hanging bags of South Africa's giant oranges.

The social diseases of any bad slum — shabby housing, crime, filth, and poverty — are written across the face of District Six. But so is a special élan, an easygoing vitality and spirit, because here, at least, Coloreds owned property and established their own enclave. "In the summer you could go through District Six and think you were in Italy. All the windows would be open and you could hear singing and laughing," says W. J. M. van Heerden, a white man who represented the Coloreds in Parliament once.

But the song of District Six at the beginning of the 1970s was one of sorrow and bitterness. Apartheid, which had stamped out representation for Coloreds in Parliament, had also condemned District Six to extinction. The Coloreds were being given one-way tickets out of town and sent to live twenty miles away, on the windswept Cape Flats. District Six is to become a white housing area.

The Coloreds are the in-betweens. They do not have to carry passbooks, they can have political parties and unions, and they can legally qualify for more skilled jobs than Africans. But they are not allowed on white beaches or buses, or in white schools or cemeteries. They are the most dispossessed and vulnerable of all of South Africa's human creatures, for they have no distinct culture, race, or language. Apartheid demands that everyone should have these.

But they are two million anomalies, two million problems for apartheid's planners, two million products of racial crime, two million anguished, hard-drinking, melancholy people.

Sunday night is a quiet moment for all of South Africa's peoples. They do not even have television, or a movie, to distract them from the thought that tomorrow, they will be in collision once again.

Chapter One

The Roots of White Power

JOHANNESBURG is Africa's mightiest and richest city. Skyscraper windows glitter in the luminous, liquid sunshine that flows through the city on April afternoons, as autumn traverses the Southern Hemisphere. Cool winds begin to blow across and stir dust from the giant yellow and green hills of earth and ore brought to the surface and dumped seventy years ago as men dug deeper for the gold buried in the ridges Johannesburg straddles. A bustling city of steel and concrete has grown around those hills of discarded earth.

It is not a city that South Africa's ruling group, the Afrikaners, always feel comfortable in, however. It is on their land, but it is a city built by the money of the English and the labor of black South Africans. Many Afrikaners prefer their Pretoria, forty miles to the north, the administrative capital of the Republic of South Africa; or Bloemfontein, a more rustic town that is the country's judicial capital; or even Cape Town, the seat of Parliament, where English and Dutch influences mingle in one of the world's most beautiful settings for a city. They distrust Johannesburg's worldliness, and its richness.

Some Afrikaners caustically refer to Johannesburg as "Jewburg" instead of the usual nickname "Joberg" referring to the prominence of Jewish merchants and businessmen in the city's flourishing commerce. Far more unsettling for them is the pervasive awareness of the presence on Johannesburg's outskirts of a sprawling housing compound containing nearly 700,000 Africans — the most urbanized, frustrated, and important group within South Africa's black mass.

Some of the uneasiness and distrust seemed apparent as the Afrikaners began to gather on an April evening in 1970 in Johannesburg's cavernous City Hall auditorium. The hall is usually identified with the English-speaking political opposition, which the Afrikaner was once taught to consider as his second greatest enemy, just after the black man.

But for this night, the hall had been turned over to the Afrikaners' own National Party for one of its final campaign rallies in the hard-fought parliamentary elections. Slowly the apprehension dissolved as more Afrikaners, 4000 in all, filed into the auditorium. Gradually the crowded hall was transformed into a laager in enemy territory as the white tribe that rules one of the world's most industrialized and affluent countries journeyed, psychologically, back to its frontier origins, in search of renewed strength for a never-ending battle.

The rally was my introduction to the Afrikaners, strongest and most domineering tribe in Africa, which I was covering from the recently independent country of Kenya for the *Washington Post.*

When I had arrived, a few days before the Nationalist rally in Johannesburg, a Ministry of Information official told me that it was unfortunate I had chosen election time to come. "One never gets the true picture of a country during a campaign," the Afrikaner bureaucrat said. I disagreed. Campaigns of course exacerbate divisions and bring to the surface the electorate's fears and hopes, writ much larger than usual. But watching the country's leaders respond to these hopes and fears sometimes provides more insight into a country's government, and ultimately the people, than dozens of official interviews and reams of statistics.

Prime Minister Balthazar John Vorster, who was on his way from Pretoria to speak to the rally, had called this election six months earlier, although his National Party still had a year left on the one-sided five-year mandate it had gained in the 1966 elections. "We cannot let the world get the idea that South Africa has an unstable government," Vorster had explained in announcing the surprise election.

He spoke as the leader of a party that had been in complete

control of South Africa for twenty-one years and which was certain beyond doubt to obtain another resounding endorsement from the all-white electorate of two million voters. Yet John Vorster was running hard in this last election campaign week in 1970, and he was running a bit scared.

The strength in South Africa's electorate is not with the owners of the gold mines or expansive farms that symbolize South Africa to much of the outside world. It lies instead with the white working class of the cities and the small farmers of the interior flatlands. The influence of these farmers is much greater than their numbers because of the overrepresentation of rural areas in Parliament. White political power in South Africa is wielded not by those whom apartheid enriches, but by those whom it protects.

A handful of men, labeled ultrarightists in the context of South Africa's narrow political spectrum, had challenged Vorster for the allegiance of these conservative-minded people. These Afrikaners had accused Vorster of being a "weak, opportunistic and vacillating" leader in an anonymous letter they had distributed within the National Party hierarchy; they said Vorster was going soft on segregation and not keeping the African in his place. Vorster reacted by driving them out of the party and called the 1970 election in order to crush this splinter faction before it gained strength. His foes then accused him of allowing himself to be seduced by the dangerous English-speakers in the white population and opening Afrikanerdom to dangerous influences.

This is a highly charged issue in Afrikaner politics. Twice before in the century breakaway groups had preached Afrikaner purity and rejected cooperation with the English-speakers. They had eventually taken the government away from Afrikaner leaders who favored cooperation with the English. What worried John Vorster was not instability in the government, or even in the National Party. What he had had in mind when he called the election was instability within Afrikanerdom, the collective soul of the Afrikaners. The election campaign, which had been corrosive and punctuated by violence, unruly meetings, and much racist demogoguery, had gradually taken on the air of a holy war between

Afrikaner politicians for the spirit and mind of their white tribesmen. The setting for John Vorster's speech in the Johannesburg
City Hall underscored that.

Orange pennants bearing the names of dead Afrikaner prime
ministers fluttered overhead on cords, and replicas of the curved
powderhorns the Trekkers depended on for ammunition hung
from the walls. The powderhorn, rather than a donkey or an elephant, had become the symbol of the National Party. Schoolgirls
wearing the green and gray hoop skirts of the pioneer women who
went on the Treks lined the aisle as usherettes.

Vorster's cabinet, local party officials, and candidates had already assembled on stage. Connie Mulder, the Minister of Social
Welfare, Information and Immigration, who could have more
easily passed as a relatively dapper, attractive butter and egg
salesman from Minnesota, led the crowd in singing hymns and
Afrikaner folk songs relating Boer battles with the British and
Africans.

The crowd was composed of family groups. Vorster's speech
had drawn an audience one third of which seemed to be well
under the South African voting age of eighteen years. Young
boys, all wearing blue or green blazers from different schools,
would sit through an evening of political rhetoric in seemingly
rapt attention. Those that did not would be nudged sharply by
one of their parents.

A slightly smiling, determined-looking Vorster strode into the
rear of the hall and made his way along the aisle marked out by
the young hoop-skirted girls. A tumult rose from the crowd as he
walked forward. In the far balconies, it sounded as though people
were singing an Afrikaans campaign song that had been written
about Vorster:

> Have you heard of our champion/our hero
>   and friend John Vorster?
> He was interned because he wanted to protest/
>   against a war that didn't concern us.
> Vorster, Vorster/our Vorster is still fighting/
> Even if he is scorned/even if he is hated/
> His enemy is always late/His enemy is always late.

But it was difficult to be certain. Journalists from the city's English-language newspapers, clustered around a long table just below the stage, stood uneasily and self-consciously for Vorster's entrance. Vorster, although head of government as Prime Minister, was not a head of state and it was not necessary to stand for him. Journalists from the Afrikaans press working at the same table were also on their feet, joining the clapping and hurrahs.

A Dutch Reformed Church minister droned through a lengthy opening prayer. The Nationalist politicians on stage did not just close their eyes in a religious tribute. They clenched them shut tightly, contorting their features in a display of devotion that would not be open to question. For the Afrikaner, whose Calvinism was nurtured in isolation for more than a century, God is not Love, but Power. Politics and governing are exercises of religion. Like voting, they are to be reserved for God's chosen, which, in the case of South Africa, means the whites.

Beside Vorster and the other politicians stood their wives. Dressed for the most part in black or gray, they too looked to be in their fifties or sixties. Unlike their men, however, they had not let their features go soft and puffy in the offices of Pretoria. The women had retained the pinched leanness one would expect of frontier folk. Hardness, discipline, and drive were etched on the faces of these women.

Vorster sat and listened as Ben Schoeman, a sleepy-eyed but vitriolic tribal elder, warmed up the crowd for him. Schoeman, and not Vorster, might have become Prime Minister in 1966 had it not been for the fact that some members of his family had not belonged to the majority denomination of the Dutch Reformed Church. That at least is one explanation for his defeat in the party caucus that had to choose a Prime Minister in the wake of Hendrik Verwoerd's assassination by an insane man working as a messenger in Parliament in Cape Town.

By 1970 Schoeman had come to accept that he was too old ever to be Prime Minister. A member of the cabinet since 1948, he had become Vorster's Minister of Transport and the second strongest man in the government.

Schoeman devoted much of his speech to berating the country's English-language newspapers, which he described as "part of the long-haired scum that wants to tear down South Africa." The newspapers, which had often criticized the way apartheid was being implemented, "are anti-South African. They are leftist and liberal," Schoeman said, causing journalists at the bench to squirm. "They would sooner see a black government here than a white National government."

Vorster began quietly, clasping his hands piously in front of his round torso. Even in delivering some of the small jokes that have drawn the fire of the extremists in this campaign, he managed to look stern, at times bullying, at others lecturing. He had to combat the image the ultras were spreading of him as being a leader whose flexibility showed signs of fatal weakness. Slowly an anger that was real and not simulated for the rally built as he talked about the HNP, the Herstigte (Reconstituted, or Purified) National Party, as the breakaway Afrikaners called themselves. Their insult, more than six months old, was still rankling.

"They say I'm weak, and I'm a dictator. You ever heard of a weak dictator?" The audience roared appreciatively and repeated the roar a few minutes later when Vorster noted that the rightists "are talking like the Communists now" because they had accused him of tapping their phones.

The first part of the speech was in Afrikaans. Later, Vorster switched to English and repeated the appeals he had been making for English-speaking South Africans to support the National Party. He coupled these with explicit urgings to the Afrikaner nation to accept this help from the once hated English. "There is one luxury we cannot afford — that is a fight between English-speaker and Afrikaner. We have reached the crossroads. Circumstances demand that we work together." Having begun this part of his speech as a champion of the blending of the two once conflicting white nationalisms into a racial nation strong enough to withstand the pressures focused on South Africa, Vorster now circled back toward the laager. Anyone who expected him or other Afrikaners to give up any of their national identity or culture as

Afrikaners "can go to a place that is not so cool." He roundly condemned English-speaking "liberals," a word he pronounced with disgust, and reopened Schoeman's attack on the press. "They don't have the guts" to tell the truth, Vorster snarled, as the delighted crowd shouted agreement.

Vorster's scorn reached its peak as he reminded the crowd that there was a political group in South Africa, the small Progressive Party, that advocated allowing a tiny number of Africans with high incomes and advanced education to vote. The Progressives, who had one member in Parliament, argued that this would lower racial tension and prevent what would otherwise be an inevitable black uprising. "They want us to commit suicide because they are afraid somebody is going to murder us," Vorster said in one of the most concise summaries I was to hear of the Afrikaner's rejection of even token integration.

His virtuoso performance at the rally may have provided another important key to unlocking the riddle of the Afrikaner. In the question and answer period that follows political rallies in South Africa, an antagonistic questioner asked Vorster why he had ordered a judicial inquiry into the affairs of the HNP, after the breakaway group had begun making embarrassing charges about Vorster's use of the security network that envelops the country. The Prime Minister rocked back on his heels, heaved his eyebrows upward, and said inquiries should not bother his opponents. "You ever heard of a man who tells the truth being embarrassed?" he wanted to know. It was a question from another time, a rural past in which the Afrikaner had known and trusted all his neighbors. Here was a clear expression of the Calvinistic belief that only good men are chosen in God's nation to wield power, and therefore power will not be abused. Honest men have nothing to fear. The Afrikaner will do the right thing.

A few days later, South Africa went to the polls for the fifteenth time since it had been shaped as a modern nation in 1910. The voting itself provided no suspense. Vorster's "Nats" would win. He had predicted that the party would increase the 126 seats it had won in the 1966 balloting for the 166-member House of Assembly, the all-important chamber of South Africa's Parliament. The United Party's thirty-nine seats would shrink, and perhaps Helen Suzman, the lady liberal who was the Progressive Party's only member of Parliament, would be defeated, the Nationalists predicted.

Late in the afternoon on election day, I ran into Willem, a young Afrikaner civil servant whom I had come to know partly by chance a few days earlier. We had a cup of tea (alcohol sales were banned on election day, even for the Africans, who couldn't vote) and talked about the voting. "There's no question about my voting for another party," he said. "None of us could do *that*. But I'm certainly not going to vote for that lot that is running our party now. The campaign has been a disgrace. I hope enough of us stay away so they get the message that they cannot go on handling things this way."

Willem's words were heresy to the laager discipline that has guided Afrikaners through the dangers of South Africa. They were against the teaching of many Dutch Reformed Church ministers who suggest to their congregations that to fail to vote Nationalist on an election day is a minor sin as well as a dereliction of duty to the Afrikaner nation. I wondered if Willem was only striking a liberal pose for a visiting correspondent. In any event, I doubted that his views would prove to be very representative, even of young, well-educated Afrikaners.

But early the following morning I reconsidered as the final results came in. Vorster had made good on his promise to obliterate the far right HNP, which managed to attract only 53,000 voters away from the Nationalists. Every one of the HNP candidates was defeated. But Vorster, intent on the right, was caught off balance at the center. The United Party of the English-speakers, whom he had been trying to woo, wrested eight seats away from the Nationalists. Most of the changes came in urban areas, where the United Party also significantly reduced the margin of victory in a number of districts the Nationalists had won with ease in 1966. Mrs. Suzman tripled her margin of victory, and the Progressives came within an inch of electing a second member of Parliament.

In terms of votes in Parliament, the Nationalist losses were insignificant. They still had more than a two to one edge in forming the government. But the effect in South Africa was electric. There, events that are ripples elsewhere can take on the proportions of tidal waves. These were the first losses the Nationalists had suffered since coming to power in 1948, when they introduced apartheid as the all-purpose answer to South Africa's enormous problems. From 1948 through 1966, they had successively added seats to their parliamentary majority. Now, John Vorster had presided over a small erosion. In modern South African political history, such a small erosion has invariably signaled the beginning of the gradual fall of ruling political parties. "This is the first election morning in twenty-two years that I haven't felt like shooting myself," a white South African journalist told me happily.

South African political scientists analyzed the results as a shift of about 4 per cent away from the National Party. (About 75 per cent of the electorate had voted. The Nats gained 54.8 per cent of the votes cast, the United Party 37.5, the Progressives 3.4, the HNP 3.5.) The consensus of the analysts was that Vorster's bid for new English-speaking support had failed. The rough campaign tactics appeared to have driven some recent Nationalist converts back to the United Party. Secondly, a surprising number of urban young Afrikaners like Willem had refused to register or to cast their ballot. In the context of Afrikaner politics, not voting is an act of defiance, not one of omission. For the first time, apparently, the National Party had conducted the campaign in an idiom that many of its young could not, or would not, understand. It was perhaps a tiny sign that an age was changing and that the Afrikaner leaders were falling behind in a race with historical change. Time, which has alternately conspired with and against the Afrikaner, was pressing him once again.

TIME AND THE SETTLER

Time and change provide the essential framework for looking at the Afrikaner and the systems that he has built to preserve white power in Africa. There are other pieces we have to fit into the jig-saw puzzle representation of the Afrikaner we are confecting: land, to which he has had an almost mystical attachment; poverty, which he has conquered but still remembers; religion, which has provided him with a necessary vision of the black man as fit only for labor; and finally the quest he has carried out for centuries. It is a quest for definition of himself and others. But all of these pro-ceed from the relationship between time and the Afrikaner. The single most significant comment ever made about the Afrikaners comes from one of their academics, F. J. Van Jaarsveld: "We got stuck in history."

Black Africa, and much of the rest of the world, tends to look on the Afrikaner as being stuck in time in the sense of being a remnant of European colonialism in Africa, which should have been swept away shortly after the British, French, and Belgians surrendered political control of their colonies. This is a largely false vision. It helps explain why the methods chosen to seek an end to white minority rule in South Africa have largely failed. The methods were shaped to defeat a different kind of white peo-ple.

The Afrikaner is a unique historical and sociological phenome-non. He is the settler who got lost, and who has now re-emerged in a changed world. Unable to destroy the indigenous society as the whites who settled in America and Australia did, he cut him-self off in the interior of his new land and built a society beside that of the native. The modern Afrikaner is paying for the inef-ficiency of his settler forefathers.

The other perspective from which one should view the Afri-kaner is to juxtapose him with the other tribes of Africa who are also trapped in time, although in a different way. Colonialism pushed African tribes inside boundaries drawn by Europeans with little comprehension of Africa. At the beginning of the last dec-ade, the Europeans withdrew their direct political control and re-sponsibility, but left the artificial "national" structures they had imposed. It was up to the black elites they had formed to try to fill those structures with a new nationalism. Some of those elites suc-

ceeded surprisingly well, but many failed spectacularly and disas-
trously, as the different historical stages of tribe and nation-state
came into conflict in country after country.

Tribalism tends to be a constricting, or at best static force. Nation-building is an expansive process that involves a redefining of
group obligations and rights. Essentially, tribalism in white,
black, or brown societies has been based on a narrowing of
human horizons. It has been a seeking of the most efficient possible group in situations in which resources or opportunities are extremely limited. The group has to be large enough to obtain
and/or protect those resources and small enough to exist from the
resources. The group must also be of a size, or a nature, so that
obligations and prerogatives are clearly understood and fulfilled.
Trust is the cement of the tribe. In many circumstances, these
conditions are most efficiently defined in terms of blood relationships. The family and extended family are the nucleus for tribalism. But the availability of resources and the external threat to
them are perhaps the dominant influences on determining how far
the family is to extend. Increasing affluence, accompanied by a
perceptible increase in the distribution of resources, should in
theory diminish the pull of tribal units. It should mark the critical
part of the transition from a tribal social organization to that of a
nation. This is a transition that few African countries have made,
partly because of their crippling lack of resources. Many of them
continued to be run as tribal states a decade after independence.
But after a long and difficult ascent to power, the Afrikaner feels
the full effects of affluence and urban growth, which threaten to
affect his tribal identity and eliminate the positions of power held
by the tribal elders.

To describe the Afrikaners as a tribe at one stage of recent history is to make a minor historical judgment in their favor, since
they argue they are a permanent part of the African scene even
though their skins are white. But it is a necessary term of reference for those interested in both white- and black-ruled Africa.
The Afrikaners have used the government as a tribal instrument
since they gained complete control of it in 1948, much as the Kikuyu have in Kenya or the Sara in Chad. And the history of their

ascent to power contains patterns of development that the Ibos of Nigeria, who formed educational and economic unions to advance their tribesmen, would immediately recognize. But the Afrikaners have also gone on to develop their social and political organizations in accordance with modern territorial as well as ethnic imperatives. They consciously accept the place of their territory in the nation-state system in dealing with the outside world. This is another mark of transition from tribe to nation, which the Afrikaners have largely, but not completely, achieved.

As South Africa's greatest historian, C. W. de Kiewiet, has suggested, two factors dominated the formation of the Afrikaner tribe and thus of white South Africa. They were the failure of the white settlement begun by van Riebeeck to draw significant numbers of new white immigrants from Europe and the isolationist temper of the white settlers who did come.

South Africa was an economic backwater in the first two centuries of its existence and could not compete with the attraction of North America and Australia for European immigrants. The white settlement never developed the population pressure and depth that pushed a steady line of settlers across the United States, sweeping the Red Indian population away before it. The population influx needed to build a "new world" society in Africa did not come until the end of the nineteenth century when diamonds and gold were discovered and a flood of whites poured in. White South Africans have in some respects faced the problems of organizing society in the last seventy years that Americans and other white immigrant societies faced two centuries ago. Having "solved" their own native problems, America and Australia and other countries can now demand that South Africa show a little morality in such a process.

Although estimates vary greatly, it is possible to suggest that there were in 1700 one million Indians in the area that is now the United States and perhaps one million indigenous Africans in the area of what is now South Africa, Botswana, Lesotho, and Swaziland, with the latter estimate being even rougher than the former. In the United States in that year, the white population was perhaps 250,000 — a figure that South Africa, then with only a few thousand white settlers, would not reach until 170 years later, after the mineral discoveries.

At the time of the Great Trek, in 1836, about 40,000 non-Africans lived in South Africa. There were 13,000,000 whites in the United States. The Boers and the British army campaigns subdued the Africans but could never really decimate them. And African civilization proved to be much more flexible than that of the American Indian. After losing battles to the Boer, the African would go to work on his farm or just fade from sight on another plot of land. The Indians stood and fought and by 1860 had been reduced to perhaps 50,000 by the bloody sweep west.

The Dutch settlers who stayed on the Cape in 1835 had occasional contact with the outside world through passing ships and with the British, who were beginning to settle in the Cape area. They became known as the Cape Dutch, or Cape Afrikaner, and to this day are regarded as less intransigent on race and politics than the descendants of the Afrikaners who trekked inward, to the hinterland to isolation.

These Voortrekkers remained by and large cut off. Unlike the Europeans moving into the forests of America at that time, the South African pioneers did not automatically establish transportation and trade routes with the coast settlement as they went. They had fled Europe and they had undertaken the Great Trek partly to escape the interference of the British, who had cut off their supply of black labor by abolishing slavery. They wanted to be left alone. De Kiewiet's "quietude" of the eighteenth century for the Dutch in Africa turned into almost complete isolation in the first half of the nineteenth century.

The most important contact the Boers had in that period was with the African tribes they found moving into their path as they pushed into the interior. Their continual clashes with the blacks ranged from great punitive campaigns, like the battle of Blood River, to the much more frequent ad hoc ones with minor goals — cattle, grazing land, water holes, or land occupation rights. These clashes, much like the ones that are still fought in parts of

Africa today where land is poorly demarcated, shaped many of the tribal aspects of Afrikaner society.

Within their settlements, which had spread up to the Limpopo River, the Boers set up their own Afrikaans-language schools and local governing councils. Both of these institutions were under the pervasive influence of the only lettered men in the communities, the ministers of the Dutch Reformed Church. The Church had come ashore from Holland with van Riebeeck and the settlers he had brought, who were told that they were serving Divine Will by working for the Dutch East India Company's interest. Predestination, a belief that they had been chosen as God's elite to settle a heathen land, was one of the few forces strong enough to drive settlers into the dry, uncharted interior of South Africa. The belief, embodied in their interpretation of the Bible, was essential to their survival. The Church, too, became cut off from the outside world, and its dogma was hardened by the conflicts in the lonely interior. The vision cast by Dutch Reformed ministers of the African as a hewer of wood and drawer of water was useful for the Boers who settled land and then put the Africans to work on it.

Faced with a need for common defense against the African tribes to the north of them and the British to the south of the Orange River, the Afrikaners established a simple governmental machine that knitted their settlements together under a rudimentary, frontier constitution. By 1854, the British had decided to limit their own responsibility beyond the Cape Colony and agreed to recognize the sovereignty of two Boer republics in the interior. One was located between the Orange and Vaal Rivers and was known as the Orange Free State. The other, across the Vaal, became the Transvaal. Sharing a territory about the size of the state of California, the two Boer republics had a total white population of less than 40,000. The white population of the Cape and Natal colonies was less than 100,000.

Each republic had an elected Volksraad, or Legislative Assembly modeled on European lines, but they were undoubtedly more democratic than most European assemblies of the day. The republics were so small that every Boer's vote counted and was valued. The African tribesmen who lived within the boundaries of the republics had no more say in white affairs than American Indians did in Plymouth town meetings, or within Fort Sill in Oklahoma.

The Boers established huge, inefficient farms and depended on untrained African laborers to work them. A number of historians have underlined the lassitude that gripped the Boer settlements and the noticeable refusal of the Boers to do any manual work. Many of them became lazy and largely unsuited for economic competition.

The Boer's treasured isolation was shattered with the discovery in 1867 of an oddly shaped, glittering stone on the banks of the Orange River. It was a diamond, and there were many more in fields around Kimberley, on the border of the area claimed by the Orange Free State. English settlers rushed into the area from the Cape, and then from England, and established a pocket republic of their own. Britain backed their claim to the land and eventually annexed it as part of the Cape Colony. To the dismay of the Boers, the British economic settlement drew as many as 100,000 tribal Africans over the next decade to work the deep shafts being dug in the hunt for diamonds. South Africa's industrial demand for black labor had begun.

Both of these worrisome trends, increased English settler migration and the drawing of Africans out of their disorganized and disrupted tribal societies into a quasi-monetary society, were accelerated by the discovery of large gold fields in 1886 in the Transvaal. British and Boer again disputed control of the land, and British capital, settlers, and troops secured a hold over the area. Africans streamed into the camps looking for work.

All of this was happening about the time Cecil Rhodes was sealing off the routes that could have been used for Boer treks to the north and west. Rhodes implanted British control in the areas that are today Rhodesia and Botswana. Gold and Rhodes added up to disaster for the Boer nation, as the crusty, granitelike Paul Kruger, President of the Transvaal, correctly foresaw. He advised the Boers to "Pray to God, as I am doing, that the curse connected with its coming may not again overshadow our dear land. Every ounce of gold taken from the bowels of our soil will yet have to be weighed against rivers of tears, and the like blood of thousands of our comrades in the defence of that same soil from the lust of others, yearning for it solely because it has the yellow metal in abundance." [1]

But Kruger's way of life was not to be spared. The high ridges of the Transvaal were soon aswarm with gold prospectors and then miners. Along the Witwatersrand, as the series of ridges came to be known, gold fields stretching sixty miles were developed. A foreign enclave, inhabited by brawling, hard-drinking English miners and adventurers, sprang up on the "Rand." To the whites it was Johannesburg, and to the Africans it was Egoli — the City of Gold. Within a few years, South Africa became the world's largest producer of gold.

The mining camps gave a significant boost to the Afrikaners' economy, as for the first time they had a nearby market for their agricultural produce. They also levied tariff and customs duties on the miners. But, as Kruger had foreseen, this economic advance brought problems. The English settlers, sure that Kruger would refuse, petitioned him for the right to vote and to have a say in the affairs of the Transvaal. Kruger refused, in his words, to "hand my country over to strangers."

The economic attractiveness of South Africa coincided with a shift in mood in Britain. Advancing political control over other areas of Africa, the British were no longer reluctant to extend their responsibilities in South Africa. The friction between the Boers and the English settlers in the Transvaal, which had already flared into skirmishing in 1880, exploded into full-scale war in 1889. This was the conflict known to the outside world as the Boer War. To the Afrikaners, it is still known as "The War for South African Independence." The farmers united to wage a guerrilla war against British imperialism. This and the 1880 violence form the basis for the Afrikaners' claim to have been the first effective anticolonial people in Africa.

[1] John Fisher, The Afrikaners (International Publishers Service, 1971), p. 137.

It took the better-equipped, better-trained, and much more numerous British troops (estimated to have been between 300,000 to 400,000 men, against a Boer force one-fourth that size) two years to defeat the Boers. The British scorched the earth as they moved through the Boer republics and devastated the large Afrikaner farms. The Boers were to say later that 26,000 of their people died in British concentration camps and 3800 were killed in battle. This was the decisive twist in the birth of the modern Afrikaner nation. It completed the Afrikaner's hatred of the English-speaking whites who had pursued them first to the coast, then to the interior, and now into their very homes.

The war's destructiveness gave a new urgency to a new Afrikaner trek that had been developing. Despite the attachment to the land that had been one of the central definitions of his being, the Afrikaner was being squeezed into the English-controlled cities. Droughts had continued to rob the land of its fertility, the inefficient farming methods the Boers and Africans used had further eroded it, and the complex inheritance system of the Afrikaners had fragmented land into units that were no longer economically feasible for a white man to farm.

BUILDING A NATION

In the cities and mining camps the Afrikaners were ridiculed by the British for their poverty, their country ways, and their language. In the first two decades of this century the Afrikaners were treated like unskilled immigrants in their own country.

They watched as English capitalists gave jobs they sought to black men. The blacks may have spoken English better than the Afrikaners or have been willing to work more cheaply. But for a white man to employ them when other whites needed work was incomprehensible to the Afrikaner, who only saw Africans as the people he had defeated in battle and then taught to hew wood and draw water. "The Afrikaners never forgave either the English-speakers or the Africans for that," an English-speaking academic told me.

A South African economist, J. L. Sadie of Stellenbosch University, described the Afrikaners just after the turn of the century as "people who felt themselves kicked around, trampled upon, and humiliated." They were also poor. By 1930, there were at least 300,000 "very poor" whites in South Africa, a special study found. Most of them were Afrikaners. This was the only large poor white class that has ever existed in Africa. But it was more than a class; it was still a Teutonic tribe. It possessed institutions, a single and unique language, and the ability to impose obligations on its members. The horizon of the Afrikaner was sufficiently narrow to enable him to reorganize to win the peace after having lost the war.

There followed for the Afrikaner a process that is today called "nation-building" when it is attempted by brown and black peoples newly emerging from colonial control. In this case, the Afrikaner tribe was to evolve, in its own terms at least, into a nation, as a reaction against control by other whites: the English-speakers. Later, after 1948, as they gained a greater share of South Africa's affluence, another shift would begin to occur as the need for national identification became less urgent than that of racial identification. The Afrikaner's own experience with the evolving nature of the forces of tribe-nation-race have been a decisive influence on the shaping of theoretical apartheid, which would arrest the development of Africans at the tribal stage. (In practice, the day-to-day discrimination of apartheid has, however, probably greatly speeded the evolution of black South Africa's national and racial consciousness, as we shall see presently.)

Although they had to go to work for the English, the Afrikaners refused to be absorbed into English society and institutions. They kept their own schools and churches and formed new economic and political institutions to advance Afrikaner interests in the changed political and economic situation the forming of the Union of South Africa in 1910 brought. From, and by, these institutions was the Afrikaner nation knit.

The National Party was the first important post-Union Afrikaner institution to be formed. It was founded in 1913 by Boer

War general J. B. M. Hertzog, who argued that Afrikaner interests could only be protected by Afrikaners. Another Boer War general, Louis Botha, had agreed to cooperate with the English. His coalition Afrikaner–English-speaker South Africa Party formed the first Union government. Later Afrikaner Jan Smuts followed Botha and became South Africa's greatest political figure and leading proponent of Afrikaner–English-speaker political unity.

Isolation or cooperation? This has been the fundamental and recurring schism in Afrikaner politics. In 1924, Hertzog, tired of the wilderness, made an election pact with the predominately English-speaking Labour Party and formed the Pact government. This provoked the 1934 break by D. F. Malan, who was disheartened by Hertzog's refusal to move away from the British. Malan formed the "Purified National Party" (purified of non-Afrikaner elements). This was the party that came to power in 1948 to complete the Afrikaner dream of ruling absolutely and alone. This was the party that encased the purity of Afrikaner political rule in apartheid.

British attempts in the period after the Boer War to suppress culturally the use of Afrikaans in schools served only to fan the flames of Afrikaner cultural nationalism. Much as white settlers looked on Swahili in East Africa as a kitchen language so the English in South Africa looked on Afrikaans, which was then a rough, archaic language, largely unwritten. A major step in the acceptance of the Afrikaner nationality as a viable concept came in 1916 when Afrikaans was placed on a footing with Dutch in the Dutch Reformed Church of South Africa. Newspapers had also begun to be published in Afrikaans, and Parliament accepted it as an official language. In 1933, the Bible was published in Afrikaans for the first time.

The most traumatic transition was the economic one. It has produced deep conflicts within the Afrikaner nation that are still unresolved. The Afrikaner discovered the large capitalist system built on the profit motive much later than most white men. The isolated farmer's innate distrust of the economic competition that capitalism requires was pitted against his desire to increase his

own economic power. This transition perhaps more than anything else reflects the uneven development that has "stuck" the
Afrikaner nation in history.

"The Afrikaner missed the lessons of the nineteenth century
about liberalism and equality in the solitude of his farms," Professor Julius Lewin, an English-speaking South African, says. "He
emerged into the twentieth century as a modern man, wearing that
label because he knows how to make money."

In the cities, the Afrikaners began to insist that clerks speak to
them in Afrikaans. If not, they would shop elsewhere. An Afrikaner cultural organization known as F.A.K. (Federasie van Afri-
kaanse Kultuurvereninigings, or Federation of United Afrikaans
Culture) exhorted Afrikaners to insist on service in their own language in all business transactions.

As the Afrikaners accumulated cash, they put it into their own
shops, which they patronized exclusively. Then came their own
insurance firms, and their bank, Volksas, to compete with the British Barclays and Standard, which dominated the finance field. As
Afrikaners gained control over municipal councils and other local
governing bodies, they shifted the councils' banking accounts to
Volksas. A major Volksas client was the Dutch Reformed
Church.

The Federal People's Investment Company (Federale Volksbeleggings) was formed to channel the money being spun off from
these Afrikaner enterprises into new ones. The profits also helped
bolster Afrikaans-language metropolitan daily newspapers and
new Afrikaner universities. As other African tribes were to do
decades later, the Afrikaners set out to "redress the imbalance" by
acquiring education, and political control, as the access to
affluence.

Despite these strides, at the beginning of World War II, the
Afrikaners continued to play an insignificant role in the economic
and administrative life of South Africa. J. L. Sadie's studies show
that the Afrikaners, then almost half of the country's two million
whites, controlled less than 10 per cent of South Africa's trade and
commerce, less than 1 per cent of the vitally important mining in-

dustry, and less than 1 per cent of senior managerial positions. No more than 20 per cent of the country's physicians were Afrikaners.

The only area the Afrikaners made significant progress in was the poorly paid state bureaucracy. The 1946 South African census indicated that Afrikaners had become 79 per cent of the police force, 71 per cent of the government transport drivers, and 55 per cent of the lower ranges of the civil service. Afrikaner males also predominated in nonuniversity teaching.

Despite the continuing drift to the city by the Afrikaners (they became the urban white majority in the middle of the nineteen forties), they still controlled 80 per cent of the country's farms. And by 1948 the Afrikaners, who had a higher birthrate than the English-speaking whites, had become a statistical majority within the white minority. Their political victory over the English-speakers was inevitable, if they could be held together as an ethnic political bloc. In 1948, they were.

Deserting a coalition Afrikaner–English-speaking party that had led them into both world wars on the side of the British against a German nation that many Afrikaners sympathized with, the Afrikaners united to give the National Party at least 70 per cent of their vote and gave the Nationalists a thin margin of victory.[2]

The open connection between the rise of Afrikaner political and economic fortunes that followed the 1948 election weighs heavily not only on Afrikaner–English-speaker relations but also on white-black rivalries. One theme that runs through the more moderate remarks of Afrikaners is the fear that the Africans will follow precisely in their footsteps unless strong controls are used against them. "We must avoid creating the impression in the African population [that] the only way to gather economic benefits is through political power," Professor Sadie said at one point during a lengthy discussion. It was easy for me to see how the African

[2] The Nationalists in fact did not receive a majority of the votes cast, but did gain a working parliamentary majority of five seats.

population might get that idea. It is also easy to understand why the Afrikaner fears that the blacks would wield political power for economic ends as harshly as has the Afrikaner. "The black man is no different from us in that respect," several Afrikaners said to me, though not always in these exact words. "He would vote for blacks because they are black, then kick us out of jobs and give them to blacks. Why should he be any different? And why should we go along with that?"

After their political victory, the Afrikaners gradually purged English-speakers from the top jobs in the police and military establishments and from the civil service. It was not just a case of spoils for the victors, many English-speakers concluded. They were considered "unreliable" on the racial and republic issues that were the touchstones of Afrikaner politics. They were from the wrong tribe. The Afrikaners still longed to re-establish a republic outside the British Commonwealth, even if it cost them economic advantages the Commonwealth brought.

Moreover, the closely knit ties between the Afrikaner politicians and the economic institutions of Afrikanerdom provided a solid base for the Afrikaner entrepreneurial takeoff that followed, as the Afrikaners moved to "redress the imbalance."

One vision of the Afrikaner's rise was given to me by T. F. Muller, one of South Africa's most important Afrikaner businessmen, in his Johannesburg office. Muller, managing director of a rapidly growing financial enterprise known as Federale Mynbou/General Mining Group, and brother of Foreign Minister Hilgard Muller, explained that "The Afrikaner people came from sound basic stock: Dutch, French, from the Continent. There was no reason why they should not be as economically important as anyone else. The biggest driving force of the Afrikaner has been his ambition, the desire to overcome the slights that had been shown him."

In the twenty years that followed the 1948 election, they moved a long way toward that goal. The Afrikaner had built up his share of control in the mining industry to 20 per cent. In 1968, he had 44 per cent of all government jobs, a figure that Professor Sadie estimated was double the pre-1948 figure. Afrikaners were getting

44.7 per cent of the national income earned by whites, compared to their 39 per cent share in 1955. The crucial trends continue up. By the end of the century, according to Sadie's predictions, Afrikaners will control 50 per cent of the country's commerce and trade, an area they were completely shut out of as late as 1930.

And they will continue to own 80 per cent of the farms in the year 2000, if there is still a white South Africa then.

Muller, an urbane executive, is a good example of the transitional Afrikaner business leader. Born in 1916 on a farm in the western Transvaal, he went to the university to become a mining engineer. He worked his way up through the hierarchy of technical and managerial mining jobs, and in 1957 he joined a small company called Federale Mynbou Beperk. It had been formed by Afrikaner businessmen to drive a wedge into the English-speaker's last complete business stronghold, the gold fields, which were run by seven groups of associated companies, all controlled by English-speakers.

Federale Mynbou was one of the spokes radiating from the hub of the Federal People's Investment Company (Federale Volksbeleggings). Muller quickly became the general manager of Mynbou, which had a few coal mines that produced about 100,000 tons a month. The company received a government agency contract that tripled its sales and shortly led to the company's becoming the biggest supplier to the governmental Electricity Supply Commission. Muller's company soon acquired enough capital, expertise, and leverage within the mining industry to buy out the English-speakers who controlled General Mining, one of seven traditional "houses," in 1964.

Muller is still identified with national Afrikaner economic interests. The new breed of Afrikaner entrepreneur that is emerging as a result of the economic boom of South Africa in the last two decades sees business primarily as a means to profits instead of ethnic advancement. Efficiency is a better drawing card than nationalism, they say, at least implicitly.

THE NEW BREED

"You cannot classify business as Afrikaner and English anymore," Jan Marais, the energetic and very American-oriented chairman of South Africa's Trust Bank, said as we sat in his lavishly decorated Cape Town office. Marais, who had ducked out of one meeting to chat with me and who was on his way to another one immediately afterward, kept relighting one of the largest cigars I had ever seen. He wore a silk tie, unmistakably Dior. "Both groups no longer look inward. We've discarded that inward philosophy and are moving toward a broad South African nationalism. Afrikanerdom is in continuous change and development, like every other people."

The Trust Bank began in 1954, as an offshoot of the Afrikaner financial complex. Its recent spectacular growth seemed to have stemmed from the hard-sell, one-stop retail banking approach that Marais has used and which has jarred the staid and unimaginative South African banking establishment. (By 1969, the Trust Bank had combined assets of more than three quarters of a billion dollars, an impressive total for a young South African bank.) Miniskirted girls ushered customers into comfortable chairs in his Cape Town banks. The customers listened to tape-recorded music systems while the girls flounced off to cash checks or make deposits. Marais proudly pointed out to me that there were no segregated waiting lines in his Cape Town banks. Mulatto and white customers were peacefully waiting their turns to be served.

It was the kind of scene that left Dr. Albert Hertzog, a diminutive, acid-tongued seventy-year-old Afrikaner tribalist, fuming all that year. Afrikaner businessmen seemed to have become more attached to the idea of making money for money's sake, despite Paul Kruger's injunctions about not confusing money and gold with important things, like white supremacy, land, and keeping political control of the Afrikaner nation completely in Afrikaner hands.

The failure to keep unabashed capitalism at arm's length was producing an enlargement of class structures, elites, and status consciousness within the Afrikaner society that had to remain sternly puritanical, agrarian-oriented, and essentially classless if it was to survive, Hertzog said. A physician, a former Cabinet minister under Vorster, and son of the general who founded the National Party, Hertzog led the HNP extremists out of the party and thus for Vorster out of the laager. Renegade Afrikaners had to be destroyed.

Vorster attempted to portray the Hertzog challenge not so much as an attack on him as a leader, but as an attack on the National Party. Here was a small band of men, he said, whose divisiveness would destroy one of Afrikanerdom's central institutions, the National Party. What appeared to be happening, however, was more of a battle among the all-important Afrikaner institutions that, until the nineteen sixties, had viewed their interests as identical. According to reports gathered by South African newsmen, the Hertzog group had strong support from the ministers and elders in the Dutch Reformed Church, from the Afrikaner labor unions most fearful of African competition, and from the Broederbond, the secret society of Afrikaner's most influential men. The party leaders, however, tended to see their interests coinciding more and more with those of the new Afrikaner business community. While most of their words tried to obscure that, the pattern of actions by the party leaders made it clear in the first two years of this decade that such was the case.

The Hertzog group and its sympathizers had come to be called the Verkramptes, or the "enclosed ones" in Afrikaans. Their vision of the laager was an exceedingly narrow one. Television was an international liberal conspiracy that had no place in South Africa. Jobs traditionally held by white men should not be given to blacks under any circumstances, even if there were no whites to fill the jobs. Racial purity was more important than economic progress. And so on. Their rigid and unquestioning rejection of change was a pure expression of the almost irrational conservatism that has marked South African society for so long.

The Verkrampte revolt was a strong reaction to what they saw as the increasing influence of their ideological opposites within

Afrikanerdom, who were called the Verligtes, or "enlightened ones." The Verligtes felt that the laager could best be protected by an apparent extension, accepting the English as white allies against a black peril, while devising and implementing ways to improve treatment of the blacks and reduce that peril. Economic expansion was important to this. It would continue to give the African majority enough of a stake in the existing system to head off revolution. Anton Rupert, one of the leading Verligte businessmen, often said of the Africans: "If they don't eat, we don't sleep."

Rupert, like Marais, is a Cape Afrikaner businessman. His Rembrandt Corporation manufactures cigarettes in more than two hundred fifty factories in sixteen countries. Rupert does a lot of business with black Africans outside South Africa, and it is in his interests to diminish the friction between white and black Africa. As a result of his interest in black African markets, he has been one of the leaders in shaping the "outward policy," which calls for good relations between independent black-ruled countries and South Africa. This is the policy that led to the strange spectacle of John Vorster having an African to lunch, when he invited the Prime Minister of Lesotho to visit South Africa in 1967.

Rupert has served without compensation as financial adviser to Lesotho. Vorster's sitting down with the Prime Minister of that small enclave convinced the men who were to become the HNP leaders that the destruction of white South Africa by the dangerous new concern for money was imminent.

The development of the Verligtes signaled the arrival of men with new economic interests within Afrikanerdom. They allied themselves with a few leading Afrikaner academics and editors to articulate an alternative to the government's rigid and often brutal implementation of apartheid, which had been sold to Afrikanerdom as a moral solution to the race problem. Vorster did not accept the Verligte articulation, but he did seem to be aiming for a synthesis of party interests and the new economic interests of Afrikanerdom, rather than clinging to the older, more conservative institutions. This required him to perform a delicate balancing act that in itself contributed to the pace of change. The man who headed South Africa's government at the beginning of the third decade of apartheid showed a flexibility in leadership that was discomforting and even disorienting to many Afrikaners, who were accustomed to dogmatic, strong-willed, and disciplinarian leaders, soldiers like the first Hertzog, or preachers like Malan and Vorster's predecessor, the great cold intellectual Hendrik Verwoerd.

South Africa has a ceremonial State President. Power rests with the Prime Minister, chosen by the majority party caucus in Parliament. The National Party's Parliament group is dominated by conservative farmers and lawyers from the Transvaal and Orange Free State. Their man becomes Prime Minister. They continue to harbor a distrust for the "dangerously liberal" Cape Afrikaners, who are not sufficiently doctrinaire on race. When they elected him in 1966, the caucus had no reason to fear that John Vorster would be dangerously liberal on anything, even though he had been born in the Cape Province.

But history, which is not likely to accuse him of greatness, had asked Vorster to play a variety of roles, and he had always willingly done so. Unlike the steel-souled Verwoerd, Vorster tried to ride the currents of South African politics, rather than create them. A man of ponderous fleshy chins, baggy dark suits, an ever-present cigarette in his cupped hand, Vorster would have been a good congressman from Kansas City twenty-five years ago, or South Carolina ten years ago. Instead, he was chosen in 1966 to ride the back of one of the world's great racial tigers.

Born in 1915, the thirteenth child of a poor family (thirteen remains his favored number), in the Cape Province, Vorster studied arts and law at Stellenbosch University.

As Britain moved toward World War II, Vorster joined those Afrikaners who openly opposed South Africa's fighting for the British against Germany. The Afrikaner calculation was that a Nazi victory would make it easier for them to establish a republic outside the British Commonwealth. Some of their leaders also frankly said that a victory by Hitler would greatly lessen outside pressure on white South Africans on the racial situation. And there was of course the lingering hatred of the British from the Boer War.

Vorster was interned by Jan Smuts' government for subversive activities and war protest in 1942. Released in 1944, he resumed his law practice. But, as a notable American politician was to do later after suffering a humiliating experience, Vorster trekked across country to another and better political base. He began to rebuild his fortunes in the Transvaal. He moved from a fringe Afrikaner party into the National Party and was elected to Parliament in 1953, where he quickly displayed a skill and zest for party infighting that led to his being named Deputy Minister of Education in 1958. Three years later, as the crackdown on black political parties and white liberals grew rougher after Sharpeville, he was made Verwoerd's Minister of Justice.

He developed an image of efficiency, ruthlessness, and dedication to apartheid so clear that he was the natural choice to become Prime Minister in the period of shock and fear that followed the assassination of Verwoerd.

Shortly after taking power, Vorster began a remarkable public metamorphosis that paralleled, either consciously or otherwise, many of the changes that were taking place in Afrikanerdom, which was also seeking a more benign, sophisticated, and "modern" image. Balthazar Johannes, as he was born, became the less heavy and sinister (at least to non-Afrikaner ears) John, or just B.J. Newspapermen were rated by the government as friendly or hostile depending on whether they used John or Balthazar in their stories about Vorster. Vorster's golf game became a topic of conversation in the way Eisenhower's once had for Americans. He told jokes in his speeches (eighty-three in one speech alone, the HNP reminded a public accustomed to devout politicians). He pushed the outward policy. He offered a politics of expanding the laager to include all right-thinking whites, Afrikaner or English-speaker.

On race, Vorster followed the sophisticated, double-level approach that Verwoerd had pioneered. He did not make racist appeals. He did not have to. His audiences understood him when he said that Africans were equal and should have "their freedoms in their areas." He had spelled it out at the campaign meeting in Johannesburg: "We whites in this country have the right to maintain our white identity in all circumstances . . . Black people are also creatures of God. They are entitled to political rights, but only in their own areas. It is good and it is right that it is so . . . The moral basis of my argument is to say to them, 'Go look for it [freedom] in your own area, among your own people, not over my people and not in my Parliament.' "

It became clear in the 1970 campaign that Vorster was not sure that he had the Afrikaner electorate and the National Party rank and file with him on this softer approach. His subsequent performance increased the suspicion among many South Africa watchers that his new-found flexibility had been designed largely for external consumption, to make it easier for South Africa to find friends in the West, rather than to seek change at home. Vorster ran a rough campaign, permitting his Cabinet ministers to try to "out-nigger" the HNP, as George Wallace might put it. The Verligte voices faded during the campaign, drowned by the rancorous cries of the party machine.

For here was part of the paradox created by the unprecedented conflict of institutions within Afrikanerdom that seemed to be occurring. The new roles opening to Afrikaners in the economy had brought at least a superficially liberalizing trend in that area. But the economic growth also drained off much of the talent that might otherwise have been able to produce changes within the Afrikaner political body.

"You can't run the country from board rooms in Cape Town," a young Afrikaner newsman who supports the Verligtes said. "You have to run it from Pretoria. Politics, or the church, or both, have always been the home of the bright young Afrikaners. Now they go into business and all they influence are dividends for shareholders. The government meantime is composed of party hacks who make the decisions that count," he told me pessimistically.

Piet Cillié, editor of the Afrikaans-language Cape Town newspaper *Die Burger*, is considered to have been one of the architects of the Verligte approach. Visiting colleagues always seek out Cillié to hear his appraisal of current trends, since his and all other Afrikaner newspapers are directly tied to the National Party. Cillié is much more articulate on what the government is doing than any of the government officials are themselves. (He is also much better company.) "The party could crush the Verligtes any time," he told me just after the campaign had ended. "Any power the Verligtes have here is highly ephemeral. The fact is there aren't any Verligtes within the party itself. The important thing about the elections was that the conservative establishment protected us."

The 1970 election results were the most visible sign yet given of the ferment within Afrikanerdom that I had heard a great deal about. The Verligtes seized on the results as proof that the National Party was lagging behind. By 1970, almost 75 per cent of the white Afrikaans-speaking population was living in the cities. Their fear of direct economic competition had lessened as they became increasingly the skilled and white collar workers, instead of the immigrant class from the farms. The young were becoming less parochial, the Verligtes said. The strict rules of Afrikanerdom, devised for the rural and intensely religious society of Excelsior, are running into increasing conflict with the new Afrikaner environments of Pretoria and Johannesburg. A lively and cosmopolitan city six days of the week, Johannesburg becomes a silent, absurd anachronism at Saturday midnight, as Paul Kruger's 1896 ban on Sunday entertainment shuts the city down.

"The highly structured and controlled rural world of the Afrikaner is disappearing," the Reverend C. F. Beyers Naudé, an Afrikaner clergyman whose liberal views have alienated him from his Dutch Reformed Church colleagues, told me in Johannesburg. "The Afrikaner senses there are forces at work that he doesn't understand, and that the Church doesn't help him understand. There is much confusion, and insecurity, among young urban Afrikaners. The whole moral outlook of the Afrikaner is built around the church and Sunday Observance. Yet, it just doesn't fit in a big city like this."

Despite this optimism, however, most Afrikaner institutions remained under the firm control of men hostile to change. The need of Afrikaners for those institutions was also greater than was generally recognized. More than with most tribes or nations, institutions provide the Afrikaner with his vision of himself and in many ways with his definition.

Conformity is the end product of Afrikaner institutions. Doubt is a luxury that the Afrikaner nation cannot afford, I was told repeatedly by Afrikaners. Dissent within the community seemed to be a treachery that had to be punished before it spread. The physical hardships and perils the Afrikaner nation has faced, and continues to face in the midst of the 15,000,000 Africans they have subjugated, accounts to a great degree for the innate insecurity the Afrikaner seems to feel. But there is also a psychological insecurity within the Afrikaner, a kind of continuing identity crisis that lies so close to the surface that self-doubt could destroy the Afrikaner nation.

The Afrikaner cannot afford to risk giving up any control over his institutions, for they are his link to his identity. That is the meaning of John Vorster's words — "They want us to commit suicide because somebody is going to murder us" — and perhaps of a puzzling comment that I heard several times, best expressed by the Reverend Willem A. Landman, spokesman for the Dutch Reformed Church: "You can't reverse integration. If we start it and find that it doesn't work, we can't go back to segregation. If we find that apartheid doesn't work, however, we can always go on to integration." (He added quickly that apartheid would work.)

The way in which the Afrikaner has chosen to define himself is an insecurity-producing contradiction even in his own terms: a white African. Few other peoples have as distinct a need to assert or withhold their collective identity so insistently as the Afrikaners. The American-ness of an American is pretty well taken for granted, by himself and others, even should he disagree with the government or do worse. Lee Harvey Oswald is considered by his countrymen to have been American. Yet I found Afrikaners who told me that Jan Smuts should not be considered an Afrikaner Prime Minister, because of his record of cooperation with the English. The Reverend Beyers Naudé found that after he spoke out against apartheid, he was forced to resign from his job and was also ostracized from the Afrikaner community. "They view me as a heretic and a non-Afrikaner now," he said. Another example is W. J. M. van Heerden, a prominent member of the Progressive Party and an ethnic Afrikaner. "Opposing apartheid is worse than murder to some Afrikaners," he said. "You endanger the nation by refusing to conform."

To question apartheid, the modern expression of the Afrikaner's mission, is in a very real sense to question the Afrikaner's identity and his right to exist. His view of his historical mission is the key to his identity, his behavior pattern, and to white rule in South Africa today. Acceptance of the mission is the dividing line among those who speak the Afrikaans language or have Dutch heritage or who otherwise might qualify as Afrikaners.

Dr. Gert Scholtz, editor of the Afrikaans newspaper *Die Transvaler*, told *New York Times* correspondent Joseph Lelyveld in 1966 that a nation "is a spiritual entity. If you don't subscribe to its principles, you belong to another group."

To ostracize in Afrikaans literally means to cast out into the wilderness, where the dissident will not weaken the frontier fort and where he will perish. The casting out is accomplished by cutting the dissident off from the Afrikaner institutions.

THE AFRIKANER'S MISSION

The view of the mission is best seen from a rising wooded hill outside Pretoria. There stands the massive Voortrekker Monument, a soaring mausoleumlike structure that is adorned by friezes depicting the Boer trekkers battling, killing, and defeating the Zulus at Blood River. Outside, standing guard with muskets at the four corners, are alabaster-white, fifty-foot-high statues of the pioneers. As the young Englishman who took me around the monument told me, "There hardly seems to be an Afrikaner monument without guns." A few miles away in the center of Pretoria stone riflemen encircle the pugnacious statue of Paul Kruger.

"The Afrikaner's history is violence," the young English-speaker insisted, "violence and strength, and they are the only things he respects. The Africans understand him better than other white men do. They know that anything they get from the Afrikaner will have to be paid for in blood — mostly theirs, but also his."

That is not at all how the Afrikaners see their past, or their future. For them the key figure of this monument, which is the Afrikaner's statue of liberty, is the statue in front of the main entrance. A bronze voortrekker mother protects a small girl and boy. The official Monument Guide, originally written in 1954 and reprinted in 1969, describes the statue:

"The place of honor has been given to the woman because it was she who ensured the success of the Great Trek and thus brought civilization into the interior of South Africa. She made everything possible by trekking with her husband. Her courage and enterprise founded a white civilization in the interior of the black continent.

"Black wildebeest have been hewn into the wall on either side of this figure of a woman. This representation is given here because it is said that the evening after Piet Retief had signed the treaty with Dingaan, there was considerable noise outside the Zulu Chief's kraal. Replying to an inquiry by Retief, Dingaan is supposed to have said: 'That is my regiment of wildebeest.' Later this selfsame regiment massacred Piet Retief and his fellow trekkers.

"The statue of the Voortrekker Mother and her children symbolizes white civilization while the black wildebeest portray the ever threatening dangers of Africa. The determined attitude and triumphant expression on the woman's face while confidently gazing into the future, and the retreating attitude of the wildebeest, suggest that the dangers are receding and the victory of civilization is an accomplished fact."

That the Afrikaner is in South Africa is the choice of God. The others have wandered into the land to which he was sent. They are there to serve him; he is there to bring them into contact with civilization. Whoever opposes him opposes God's will, is therefore Godless, and latterly is therefore Communist or equally villainous.

Partly from conviction, partly from convenience, the Afrikaner has found that it is his mission to found and preserve a white nation in Africa.

Nonwhites cannot possibly have any role in a mission so defined, except to help the whites build the nation as the whites envision it and to accept those rewards that the existence of a white society can give them. ("Give" is a key word in South Africa's race relations. The whites are always "giving" blacks freedom, or material rewards, or whatever.) This concept of mission was for me perhaps the fundamental difference between white supremacy in South Africa and the concept of white supremacy I had known in South Carolina, where I was born and educated. Whites in South Carolina were never really concerned about "serving" blacks. The Afrikaner becomes superior through the belief in his mission (although he may not personally do much to advance the mission, except by merely existing). That is the difference between him and the African, and even other white men; that is his definition.

There can be no question of his participating in a "multiracial" nation. To him, that is the much greater contradiction in terms than "white African." The only question that is open is how he is to define the white nation. That is the philosophical intent of apartheid, which is to lead to a spiritual, if not physical, partition of South Africa. It is in this area that the most liberal of the Verligtes are working, by seeking a definition of a white nation that provides Africans a more equitable place within the country of South Africa. An Afrikaner who accepts the idea of a multiracial nation opts out of the Afrikaner nation.

This is the great chasm that separates the Afrikaner from much of the rest of the world. It is formed largely by the outsider's skep-

ticism that the Afrikaner can continue to believe that he is fulfill-
ing God's will by keeping Africans away from the ballot box, out
of skilled jobs, and out of cities. The outsider looks at the sophisticated economic and political systems of white South Africa and
assumes that their modernity is similarly reflected in modern secularized thinking on race relations and other points of morality and
sociology. The protestation of religious motives, service to others,
and acting in the interests of the African must be hypocritical cant
designed to deceive him, the outsider concludes.

But the main deception involved is not that of others, but a necessary one of the Afrikaner himself. "Once a ruling class loses
faith in itself, once it becomes cynical, then it faces a pre-revolu-
tionary situation," Piet Cillié told me, with a trace of sorrow in his
voice. "If we lose faith, we've had it. If we lose faith in our solutions, we've had it."

Because of the powerful control the Afrikaner nation exercises
over ideas, it can keep the sense of mission (and thus identity)
alive. It is over the institutions of ideas — the church, the schools,
the press, and literature and media — that the tightest, most conservative controls are placed by the Afrikaner power structure.
That this goes so largely unquestioned within the Afrikaner community is a sign of the remarkable success of the Afrikaner government in maintaining its theocratic aura.

"To the Afrikaner, the state is created by Providence, and or-
dained and blessed by the Supreme Being, to run the country,"
Professor N. J. J. Olivier, a member of the faculty at Stellenbosch
University, said to me one day as he discussed his people. "With
his rural background and his Calvinistic belief that only good men
obtain power, the Afrikaner assumes there will be no abuse from
the state."

Many of the Afrikaners I met on my six-week journey across
South Africa seemed genuinely puzzled, and hurt, that the outside
world is so critical of them for having drawn up the grand design
of apartheid, which intends to resettle the country's African population onto barren "homelands" without letting the Africans have
any say on it. "We know we are doing the right thing," they said

insistently. It also seemed a matter of routine to many of them that the Afrikaner-controlled Parliament had given the Afrikaner-controlled police force the authority to arrest anyone, any time, without giving any reasons or even public notice, and to hold them indefinitely. No innocent man would be arrested.

That was the message that was delivered to them, at least by implication, each Sunday by the Dutch Reformed Church ministers, who were so vital in organizing Afrikaner communities in the nineteenth century, and whose importance continues today. In few other countries has the small-town minister retained the influence that he has in South Africa.

Fifty-two per cent of South Africa's total white population belong to the three denominations of the Dutch Reformed Church. "Only eight per cent of the Afrikaner nation has gone astray," the Reverend Mr. Landman said with unconcealed satisfaction as we talked in his study in Cape Town. One of the D.R.C. denominations is a highly conservative group that has declined even to sing hymns, since they are too frivolous. This church has about 4 per cent of the whites. Another denomination, which is noted for its liberalism because it does not attempt to justify apartheid with scripture, has about 6 per cent of the white population. (To define the position of that denomination, Mr. Landman explained that "they support the government's policies without doing anything.") Mr. Landman's denomination, known as the Nederduitse Gereformeerde Kerk in Afrikaans and the body that is generally meant when there is a reference to the Dutch Reformed Church, is by far the largest of the three. In all, they have more than 1,500,000 white members.

Mr. Landman proudly told me that the Church had played a major role in the shaping of separate development, as apartheid is called in polite conversation these days. In 1857, the British administration sent a Scot minister to a town called Stockenstroom, in the Eastern Cape. He held integrated services, not unusual at the time. But he also used a common communion cup, which upset the fifty Boers in his congregation. They demanded a separate communion service. "There will be no division at the table of the Lord," the minister is supposed to have said. "Well, you have the table, but we'll bring our own cup," the Boers replied. The squabble was settled by them pulling out and forming their own all-white congregation. Since then, Afrikaners have maintained their preference for separate facilities.

The Dutch Reformed Church has established separate "daughter" churches for mulattos and Africans. The white priests who work in these churches are still often called missionaries. The Church is strong among mulattos. Almost half a million, or 25 per cent of the mulatto population, belong to the D.R.C. daughter churches. Half a million Africans, or about 3 per cent of the black population, belong.

Each Dutch Reformed parish is limited to about 700 adherents, and the parish is divided into wards composed of twenty to thirty families supervised by an elder and a deacon who are usually in constant contact with the minister. The minister is likely to head the local school committee, which has broad powers in hiring teachers and suggesting curriculum. This influence extends up to universities. Two of the four Afrikaans-language full universities have in recent years refused to teach the theory of evolution because it conflicted with D.R.C. doctrine.

(At other levels, the government can intervene directly "to eliminate teachers who endorse the dangerous proposition that all men are equal," Professor Lewin had told me. It is illegal for whites to teach Africans without a permit, as Lewin discovered when he was visited by police after volunteering to teach some black youths to read in a makeshift school in his garage.)

Dutch Reformed Church ministers also are prominent in the Broederbond (Brotherhood). The Reverend Beyers Naudé, who was in the Bond at one time, puts the D.R.C. membership at about 500, out of a total 8000. The membership of the Bond is thought to include most important, "right-thinking" Afrikaners, including the Prime Minister, his Cabinet, and perhaps three quarters of the members of Parliament.

It is South Africa's only secret organization (the government otherwise enforces the law banning such groups) and information about it is difficult to evaluate. Orthodox Afrikaners will compare it to the Masons and refuse to say anything else about it. The information that has come to light comes from bitter breakaways, like the Reverend Beyers Naudé.

The Bond apparently has structures paralleling the government and party machineries. It ties the Afrikaner religious, cultural, political, and financial institutions into a strong monolith and seems to be a body designed to enforce discipline on the community. There are detailed accounts of gruesome initiation ceremonies, which seem to resemble Kikuyu oathing practices in Kenya, although it is difficult to judge their accuracy. The Bond is dominated by the most conservative members of Afrikanerdom. Its head in 1970 was thought to be the Chairman of the South African Broadcasting Corporation, Piet Meyer, one of the few South African officials who has never attempted to play down his World War II affection for the Nazis. Lelyveld of the *New York Times*, who chooses his words with care, referred to Meyer as a neo-Nazi. In any event, his tastes are conservative. Meyer's Broadcasting Corporation banned the Beatles from the air completely after John Lennon had compared their popularity to that of Jesus Christ. The ban was lifted in 1971, only after the Beatles had disbanded.

Meyer didn't have to worry about banning them from television, since there was no television in South Africa. It was illegal to own a television set. While some poverty-stricken countries to the north plowed ahead with building television networks to prove their national status (and then filled the air time with inexpensive, tired reruns of Lucy and Maxwell Smart), South Africans remained in the dark. A group of them flew to London in 1969 just to watch the televised landing on the moon of American astronauts. Finally, the public demand became an issue that Vorster was afraid would cost the National Party support, and an intention was announced in 1971 to have a television network in operation by the mid-1970s. Many were still skeptical, however, that the government meant it.

The man who occupied the key chair in the drive to keep South

Africa white by keeping it clean at the beginning of the nineteen seventies was J. J. Kruger, a silver-haired, deliberative Afrikaner in his early sixties, who was the government's chief censor. Kruger put aside a French magazine that had just arrived to talk to me in his Cape Town office. From the wall stared a framed picture of General Christiaan de Wet, a Boer War hero to whom Kruger is related. The censor also conceded a "humble relationship" to Paul Kruger.

"The sweet moan" was worrying Kruger that day. He described it as the biggest threat facing South Africa and indicated that the permissive society, not black revolt, was the main danger his nation faced. "This sex wave that is engulfing the rest of Western civilization is not for us. We are religious and conservative people. The people don't want the sweet moan of pornography."

Kruger was perhaps the Quintessential Sophisticated Afrikaner for me. Born in Bloemfontein, which is considered the spiritual home of Afrikanerdom, he worked on *Die Burger*. He succeeded Verwoerd as editor of *Die Transvaler* when Verwoerd became Prime Minister and was cultural adviser to the national broadcasting corporation. He is a devout member of the Dutch Reformed Church, of course, and he once lived in Holland. During our conversation, he puffed on a lidded pipe. He spent much time telling me how the Afrikaans language was being corrupted by young Afrikaners who were mixing English slang into it.

The Publications Control Board had been established in 1963 in an effort to systematize the somewhat haphazard censorship that had preceded it. The Board had the power to ban any publication except newspapers. (The press exercised a loose form of self-censorship under a press council, which wasn't really needed. The Afrikaans newspapers were all controlled by the National Party and would not be troublesome. The English-speaking press was a sharp critic of the government, which could afford to ignore it because Afrikaners tended not to believe what they read in English papers anyway. Newspapers designed for black and mulatto readers were frightened, and circumspect.) The Board could also ban any phonograph record, or an "object," if there was a complaint from the public. The Board screened and had to approve every film that was to be shown in South Africa.

In 1969, Kruger said, he and the ten other board members had been forced to decide that South Africans should not read 622 books, magazines, and pamphlets. They ranged from *Playboy* to Karl Marx. There were forty-six films completely banned. Among the records unfit for South Africa was the cast album for *Hair*. The Board kept black South Africans from seeing more than 100 films passed for whites and cleared expensive hardback editions of books on politics and sex while banning the cheap paperback editions that might have been within the price range of Africans.

Kruger said the increasing frankness of movies — and sexy movies appeared to be as popular with Afrikaners as the rest of the world in 1970 — made film screening the hardest part of his job. Sex, violence, and "objectionable intermingling of the races" were the three main troublesome subjects. It took seven sessions for the Board to chop *The Wild Bunch* down to South African size. *Bonnie and Clyde*, another film of stylized bloodiness, was banned completely. So were *Easy Rider* (although Kruger could not recall what the film was about) and *Belle de Jour*. (That one Kruger recalled. "Two thirds of that takes place in a brothel. We weren't about to pass it.") *The Graduate* made it into South Africa after two years of rejection, but it was slashed. Dustin Hoffman was not allowed to say incredulously, "Mrs. Robinson, you're trying to seduce me." And Sidney Poitier did not come to dinner in South Africa. "Social integration is not allowed here, and it cannot be allowed on films," Kruger said.

"Why don't they make more films like *True Grit?*" Kruger asked me. "That was a splendid film, and we could pass it right away. Rolling grass, and a good fellow like John Wayne." I gathered that Kruger looked on John Wayne as a sort of honorary Afrikaner.

More than 12,000 books have at various times been banned in South Africa. Books mentioning revolt, socialism, or black in their titles did not make it. Virtually every important African thinker was banned. So were Steinbeck's *The Wayward Bus*, Roth's *Portnoy's Complaint*, Sartre's *Age of Reason*, and a book called *Gene Autry and Champion*. Mona de Beer, a South African who researched censorship of books, felt that any author whose name ended in "ov" was in trouble. She counted twelve authors banned, including Alivmov, Nabokov, Sholokhov, and the government's spelling of "Krushcheov."

Kruger tried to add some sophistication to the Board's often Pavlovian banning. *Candide*, for example, was rescued from the banned list, after somebody looked behind the title, as was Anna Sewell's *Black Beauty*. Some titles are not so lucky, however. When the Board discovered that the banned *Bed Bait* by Robert Devlin was actually entitled *Red Bait*, it decided the ban applied anyway. Or perhaps more so.

The slightly madcap air to some of South Africa's censorship does not obscure the severely inhibiting impact it has on South African society. Serious writers like Nadine Gordimer see their work banned in their own country. Young writers find publishers reluctant to take chances on anything that may be controversial, and printers, fearing prosecution, often refuse to produce books that are critical of the government's race policies.

André Brink, a novelist and professor of literature, asserts that one of his books was accepted by a publisher on literary merit and then returned after the publisher's lawyers read the manuscript. Brink is a young Afrikaner who belongs to "Die Sestigers." The Afrikaans term means "The Sixtiers" and applies to writers who try to write realistically about the last decade and its impact on Afrikaners.

"The work of the Sixtiers may be tame by outside standards, but it is a remarkable departure for Afrikaans literature," says Tertius Myburgh, an Afrikaner newspaper editor who has followed the movement closely. "From a superpatriotic, Russian-like glorifying of the past and Calvinistic virtues, we have come now to books where the characters copulate and use four-letter words."

Brink, however, termed the Sixtiers movement "a safe revolt. It knows how far it can go. It attacks religious and moral taboos because they are not so vital to the Afrikaner mind as political taboos . . .''

In a paper written for the anti-apartheid Christian Institute, Brink suggested that one of the keys to change would be the deliberate courting of censorship by more progressive Afrikaner authors. There had obviously been a reluctance by the censors to strike against Afrikaners writing, but Brink advocated a showdown as a method for increasing the ferment in Afrikanerdom.

I asked Kruger about all the reports of ferment, of Afrikanerdom reforming itself.

"Only about three per cent of our youth is affected by these superficial signs of change," he replied. "But ninety-seven per cent is as sound as gold. Inwardly there is nothing wrong with them and we know we can count on them in the future."

"But I don't know about the rest of the world. I wish they would remember that sex is as old as Adam and stop all this dirty stuff. It could destroy Western civilization."

POSTSCRIPT

There are a number of things about the Afrikaner that I have not explored here that may be important. One is his external grayness. At least for the urban Afrikaner, as he ages he seems to become inevitably grayer. His hair is gray, his short, clipped mustache is gray, his mood to strangers to whom he is not introduced has the same metallic quality. The Afrikaner is not white, as he proclaims, or even pink, as most Americans are. He is gray.

Another characteristic that I haven't gone into is the Afrikaner's fascination with verbal sounds and names. Afrikaners that I met continually repeated my name in the course of our conversations. I thought at first that this might be a peculiar case, since my name could resemble an ancient Dutch one. But checking with many visitors convinced me that Jim Smith would have received almost the same scrutiny. Older Afrikaners linger over surnames, carefully inspecting them as they say them, and then invariably ask about the national origin. The quest for self-identification may be a strong influence on this.

Finally, I would think that any serious future attempt at examining the Afrikaner will have to come to grips with the way in which he expresses his sexuality, a subject that existing literature ignores. There is a virility in the society that is quickly apparent, and on the surface at least it seems to exceed that of many other societies. This is usually viewed in the context of the color bar and the Immorality Act. The conclusion often is that the Afrikaner is greatly attracted to interracial sex because it is forbidden fruit. This is probably inexact. My own impression is that the Afrikaner is greatly attracted to sex, period. Too much is read into the instances of interracial sex involving Afrikaners, and not enough attention given to his more generalized randiness. (Actually, my wife called this to my attention after we had been to dinner in the homes of several Afrikaners, who made passes at her, ranging from discreet to not so discreet, over the course of the evenings. When the Rand *Daily Mail* published the results of a poll suggesting that seven out of ten Afrikaner husbands proudly owned up to having committed adultery, I was prepared to accept its findings in a general way, although the sampling was too small to be authoritative.) A serious study will help complete the still roughly sketched picture of the toughest, most dedicated white man Africa has known, for I found one of the most incisive ways in which Afrikaners define themselves in relationship to the other ethnic groups in South Africa involved sex. This was an Afrikaner's answer to my question on why so many mulattos had Afrikaner names: "Why, no sensible Zulu woman is going to bed with a bloody Englishman, is she?"

Chapter Two

Losing the Peace

UNLIKE THE AFRIKANERS, the 1,500,000 white South Africans who call themselves English-speakers belong to a world culture. Their language, their religion, their traditions are comfortably familiar to the resident of New York or Sydney. Their identification goes well beyond that of the tribe and for a long time stretched beyond that of the nation. There was an Empire, and then a Commonwealth, that linked them to similar men throughout the world. They have never felt their backs to the wall, as the Afrikaners have. They have not feared that a distinct way of life or religious creed would come to an end if they did not take a harsh line with the Africans. They did not see themselves, or their society, reflected in the African and were therefore confident of their ability to dominate him. They have not been driven by the desperate need for unity and nationalism that has built Afrikanerdom.

Comfortable with the class-structured society that they could manipulate through their economic domination in the country, the English tended to assume or perhaps hope that the fiercely democratic and agrarian tradition of the Boer would fade away and the country would be managed rationally by economic classes and interests, rather than by government hierarchy. Since 1948, however, that assumption has proven to be woefully wrong, and the English-speakers have paid a price for it.

In 1961, the Afrikaners forced the English-speakers to cut the psychological umbilical cord with Britain by withdrawing South Africa from the Commonwealth. The decade that followed was not a happy one for English-speakers like the businessman who took me to lunch in his club in Cape Town.

The club (I had not been told its name, and it seemed impudent to ask, since my host assumed I would know automatically) was part of the shrinking enclave the British Empire maintained in Cape Town. Cheese followed the dessert, *Punch* lay on the reading room table, and Lord Charles Somerset gazed down suspiciously as I signed the guest register near the club's entrance. The somber portrait of Lord Charles, the first English governor of the Cape, dominated the studied bareness of a world in which English gentlemen gather without their ladies.

"A lot of us retreated into clubs like this in the past nine years, trying to pretend that things were the same," my host said as the conversation turned to present-day British-Boer relations. "But of course things have changed. People keep talking about us finding a new identity as South Africans. There's something to it, but the really basic thing is that we are losing our distinct values, and identity, just like we lost our hold on the country."

By 1970, the political effectiveness of the English-speakers had been cut to zero. Their once unquestioned economic dominance had been whittled away as the Afrikaners consolidated their rise. And many of the brightest of their sons and daughters were choosing to live abroad rather than face the rising pressures that operate on the white subminority within South Africa's white minority.

As a result, many English-speakers were beginning to show signs of despondency and doubt about their role in the country. Guy Butler, one of the country's leading writers, told an academic conference on South African literature in July 1969 that members of his group "feel a lack of purpose, of direction; they want to feel they belong, and they are afraid of belonging; they don't know what they want to belong to."

English-speakers were being written off as a meaningful force for change at a time when change seemed possible. Unfortunately, South Africa's predicament today is as much a result of the failure of the English-speakers as the success of the Afrikaners. The liberalism once so strongly voiced by English-speakers who supported multiracialism in South Africa has appreciably diminished in the last decade. It has been snuffed out among blacks and whites alike, leaving the field to white supremacy and whatever black supremacy movement may be developing behind the walls of silence and frustration that have been built around the country's Africans.

Some English-speakers feel that their group has never understood the country they live in. Professor Julius Lewin, formerly a lecturer at Witwatersrand University in Johannesburg, told me:

"The English-speakers have failed because they failed to understand either the white nationalism of the Afrikaner, or the black nationalism of the African. The English are embarrassed by nationalism because it is so emotional and un-English. They see no need for it. So they devoted themselves to the business of doing business, while the Afrikaners devoted themselves to taking over the country."

The suggestion is not that the English-speaker loves South Africa any less, or is less patriotic, than the Afrikaner. That is not accurate. What is important is to recognize the difference in the way the two groups have seen, and continue to see, their roles in the country.

Migration from Great Britain to South Africa began on a modest scale in 1817 with the arrival of a few hundred Scots artisans. But America was exerting a much stronger pull on those ready to quit Europe. Population growth among English-speakers was slow.

The first major influx came in 1820, when 5000 English settlers arrived in Port Elizabeth on the eastern Cape, beginning a pattern that was to remain constant over the next few decades. The English settled around cities along the coast, while the Afrikaners gradually contracted back into the interior. To secure their settlements, the English moved along the coast by military conquest. Political annexation of the conquered area followed. To the British this arrangement included the African tribes they had defeated in battle or had made treaties with. The Afrikaners settled, took land, and defended it. They drove the Africans out and never considered them a part of their settlements, except as occasional laborers.

By 1860 there were still only about 40,000 to 50,000 English settlers, while the white Afrikaans-speaking population was probably in the neighborhood of 100,000. But the English accounted for most of the country's trade and commerce, which centered around wool that was shipped off to England.

The discovery of gold and diamonds changed this. Tens of thousands of immigrants poured into South Africa to start what Leo Marquard has called the "minerals Trek." They built up Johannesburg and Kimberley. Unlike the Boers, they were able to gather from abroad, where the industrial age was in full swing, the capital needed to exploit the mineral discoveries. Soon they developed a financial infrastructure of banking, finance, and commerce that was largely alien to the Boers' agricultural life.

The mineral discoveries also fired the imagination of financiers like Cecil Rhodes, who developed the tradition of the hard-driving, unscrupulous English entrepreneur. The gold rush made the rich richer and the adventuresome more adventuresome. The result was the Boer War.

As Vietnam was to do with another powerful nation later in the twentieth century, the Boer struggle wore out the British, morally if not physically. Concentration camps in which thousands of Afrikaner women and children died and the scorched earth of Boer farms gave imperialism a bad name with much of the British public. By 1902 the victorious British were almost as eager to sign a peace treaty as the vanquished Boers.

London wanted to limit its direct responsibility and prevent a resumption of the fighting between Boer and English-speaker. Having secured their economic position, the British were now prepared to make what appeared to be insignificant concessions to the Afrikaners on a political structure that would be within the British Empire. The cost of these concessions, which revolved around rights for the Africans, has been enormous for modern South Africa. The erosion of the more tolerant English stance on the country's racial problems began almost immediately after their victory in the Boer War.

The two defeated Boer republics became crown colonies, along with the Cape Colony and Natal, the other British crown colony located around Durban. The Boers were shortly given self-governing status, however. In 1908 the leaders of the four colonies met in a national convention to discuss union, and two years later the Union of South Africa came into being. Four provincial councils would govern local matters, including education. A Union Parliament would be sovereign over the four provinces. The rural areas, and especially the Transvaal, received a disproportionate number of seats because of the argument that the population in the boom towns was less permanent.

The major conflict involved voting rights and illustrated the different approaches of the two white nations at the tip of the black continent. In the Cape, society was organized along class lines. African and Colored males could vote if they earned a certain income and had education. Few did in the Cape, and almost none did in the more insular, race-conscious Natal province. In the Boer territories, all white males had the franchise. No African had ever voted there, and the Boers vowed that none ever would. Their leaders were intransigent, and the English-speakers agreed to a compromise. The Cape kept nonwhites on its roll of voters, but agreed that only whites would sit in the Union Parliament. (In 1936, a special limited voting roll was set up for Africans, and by 1959 the Afrikaner government had succeeded in completely abolishing any hint of national representation for blacks.)

In the conciliatory mood of 1910, London arranged to appoint as the Union's first Prime Minister Louis Botha, the Afrikaner who stood for cooperation between his people and the English-speakers. Botha organized the first general election. His South Africa Party won and he continued as Prime Minister.

All of South Africa's Prime Ministers since have been Afrikaners, although some of them have belonged to or depended on parties that included English-speaking supporters. The English-speakers have not developed any outstanding political leader of their own. As a group, they have shown little interest in participatory politics, preferring to run the country's commerce while the Afrikaners took over the political chores.

Partly as a result of this, the 1948 National Party victory gave the Afrikaner the chance to remake the nation in his political and racial image.

One of the main drives of Afrikaner nationalism after the Boer War was to detach the Union from the British Commonwealth and make it a republic. Direct British intervention in South African affairs quickly faded after the union of the colonies, but the Afrikaners did not like even the ceremonial tie. As decolonization began elsewhere in Africa, the Afrikaners saw a new chance and made the most of it.

In January 1960 Verwoerd called for a referendum on making the country a republic. One month later, then British Prime Minister Harold Macmillan surprised the world, and his white South African hosts, by delivering his "winds of change" speech to the Cape Town Parliament. He advised the white South African power elite that African nationalism was a fact of life that they would have to come to terms with. However accurate Macmillan's view, it did not win any friends for the British establishment in South Africa. One month after that, the shooting at Sharpeville[1] traumatized South African whites, and the winds began to blow the other way. In October, white South Africans voted against staying in the Commonwealth and the Union became the Republic of South Africa on May 31, 1961. The action ended any confusion about what white English-speaking South Africans should be called. They no longer could be viewed as "British."

UNION TO REPUBLIC

In a number of visible aspects, the change from Union to Republic did not seem to be a drastic one. South Africa continued to receive preferential trade treatment from Britain, the United Kingdom's 55 per cent share of foreign investment in South Africa was unaffected, and, perhaps most importantly, the outward shape of the South African government remained unchanged.

[1] See page 132–133 for a detailed account.

This was an important factor to the English-speakers, many of whom seem to have lived under a series of illusions about the nature of power in South Africa. This began with Union, when the British Crown was theoretically the ultimate power, although in fact the country quickly became entirely self-governing. There is still something of a hangover of this today, even after the Commonwealth break.

"The Nationalist Government has been very intelligent in maintaining many forms of a Westminster-style Parliament. Most English-speaking South Africans assume, unthinkingly, that if a parliamentary government is functioning, all must be well." That is the view of C. O. Gardner, lecturer in English literature at the University of Natal, writing in the *Financial Times* of London.

Leaving the Commonwealth was the beginning of the ending of the illusions, however. Britain's role in the decolonization rolling across the rest of the continent was an embarrassment for the English-speakers. The cases of Kenya and Rhodesia especially heightened the feeling of alienation from Britain. "From being an appendage of the British nation, they have changed into South Africans," J. L. Sadie observed toward the end of the decade in writing about the English-speakers. "This has greatly accelerated during the past few years as most of the English-speaking section formed the impression that Britain was selling the white man in Africa down the river."

Sharpeville and its aftermath accelerated another trend — apartheid's transformation of the clash of nationalisms into the much broader one of races. This is the process that South Africans are actually describing when they speak of the two white groups coming together into a "broad South African nationalism." It is the English-speakers who are making most of the concessions for that coming together. Unable to impose their values and tempering influence on the volatile Afrikaner and African, they have tended to accept increasingly Afrikaner attitudes on politics and race, or, more likely, just to fall silent and enjoy a comfortable living while the Afrikaner worries about politics and ideology.

On a chill May Sunday afternoon in Cape Town I listened to two English-speakers, both with impeccable liberal credentials, in South African eyes at any rate, talk about the military training their sons were then receiving. They were discomforted by the rigid right-wing political ideology the Afrikaner instructors were giving the youths. But one went on to say, "Oh, yes, if the United Nations tried to come here, or other African countries tried anything, or there was an uprising, the boys would fight to save this government. So would we. We'd like to see some peaceful change but we will not accept those things." Then, more thoughtfully, he said, "You know, I'm not sure I would have said that fifteen years ago. Something's happened in that time."

What had happened in those years was the culmination of the wearing down of the Cape Colony liberal traditions that had begun with the compromise at union. On point after point involving race, the Afrikaners, steeled by their sense of mission, refused to give an inch. The English-speakers, either to gain economic advantage or because they felt they would eventually prevail over the Afrikaners, yielded. This not only progressively weakened their position vis-à-vis the Afrikaners, who became increasingly the protectors of the system, it led to the destruction of multiracialism.

Blacks tend to blame most of their present misery on the "Dutchman." But among South Africa's Coloreds and citizens of Indian descent, who have had more contact with the English than the Africans have, there seems to be an especially keen disappointment at the English failure to stem the outpouring of racial legislation since 1948. In some cases it almost amounts to a feeling of betrayal, as the class attitudes that allowed a few nonwhites into the good graces of Cape Colony society have given way to the harsh lines of apartheid.

"We used to think the English were more fair-minded," a long-time political leader of the Colored community said in Cape Town. "Now we see that they are not a damn bit better. The hell with a whole bunch of white men." A more thoughtful assessment was given me in Durban by Fatima Meer, a sociologist whose family, like many others, migrated from India to Natal in the nineteenth century: "The English-speaker hasn't had the nerve, nor the foresight, to develop his prejudice into an ideology. That has been the trump card of the Afrikaner. The Afrikaner's ideology of race makes it possible for him to say, 'I'm discriminating and it's all right because it is God's will.' The English-speaker tells us, 'I'm discriminating and it's bad, but I'm in a tough spot, you see. What else can I do?' "

Mrs. Meer, who has had to live under a number of government restrictions because of her outspoken opposition to apartheid, pointed out that the United Party introduced the legislation in 1946 that forced Indians to live in segregated areas.

Afrikaners say that the English have not developed a visible hard line on race only because they don't need to. "All we have to do to the English is call them and they come running," John Vorster is supposed to have told a friend in private once, as he made a beckoning motion with his hand. "And when they get close enough," he said, smiling and closing his hand into a fist, "we clout them on the chops. And they take it because Corporal van der Merwe [the symbolic Afrikaner] is the only thing that protects them from the blacks."

I could not authenticate the story. But it was told by an important Afrikaner, in a position to know the truth of the matter, to an important English-speaking businessman, who does not sympathize with the National Party. That in itself reveals a great deal about the attitudes of the two groups.

Afrikaners delight in, and firmly believe, another analysis of the English-speaker's politics: "They talk Progressive Party [a small, relatively liberal group], vote United Party, and thank God every night for the National Party."

Although most of the dissent against apartheid has come from the English-speaking community, it has come from a very small number of people and organizations. There seems to be little question that the great majority of English-speakers agree with Afrikaners on the need for white domination; the only question is the form it will take. That is the only issue debated between the organized political parties in South Africa today.

The United Party is the voice of the English-speakers in Parliament and depends on them for its support. The U.P. would have been invented by the Nationalist government if it had not already existed. It keeps alive the theory of opposition without offering any alternative to apartheid. Its existence helps obscure the fact that political opposition on important questions — that is, race — is totally ineffective and irrelevant to Afrikaner aims.

Once a successful coalition of Afrikaners and English-speakers, the United Party was deserted by the Afrikaners in the wake of World War II. After more than two decades in the political wilderness, it has become a weak shell thrown up around policies that project little more than a fuzzy shadow of apartheid. The United Party would enforce segregation less harshly, particularly in the economic sphere, if it were to come to power. Conceivably it might even revive some of the token multiracialism that the Nationalists have crushed. But essentially, the stand of the leaders of the United Party, and the majority of English-speakers, has not altered substantially since Alfred Milner, Governor of the Cape Colony, said at the end of the last century: "The ultimate end is a self-governing white community, supported by well-treated and justly governed black labor." That is still about the best Africans can hope for from the country's second largest political party.

The Progressive Party is the most liberal political organization functioning in South Africa today, and its success in winning representation in Parliament is an accurate reflection of the strength of liberalism in South Africa. The Progressives managed to win one seat in Parliament in the first decade of its existence. This was captured by Helen Suzman, the articulate, tireless liberal whose stinging verbal attacks on the follies of apartheid have enlivened Parliament as nothing else has. It is largely Mrs. Suzman's effectiveness, and the publicity she has obtained outside South Africa, that has caused the Nationalists to devote an inordinate amount of their time to warning about the dangerous pink liberals of the Progressive Party.

In fact, the Progressive program is a clear expression of the English aristocratic tradition transposed into a modern society. The Progressives would revive the Cape Colony–style franchise with income and education qualifications for all voters. This would continue white domination in South Africa into the distant future. The Progressive argument to the white electorate at voting time is that only such a program will prolong white rule, by easing the frustrations of the black majority, which will otherwise inevitably explode, bringing down white rule.

This is an untenable political argument for South Africa now that apartheid has carved it into discernible white and black political spheres that increasingly have little to do with each other. Neither whites nor blacks are any longer interested in gradualism, and not really in multiracialism. Whites have become convinced in the past decade that they can continue to rule the black majority indefinitely and almost as harshly as they choose. The explosion may come, but the elaborate security apparatus Pretoria has built will control it and direct it against the Africans. And the kind of appeal the Progressives have been making in itself reinforces the fear of the whites and produces more of a determination to keep Africans in line.

The Progressive Party was an integrated body until 1968, when the Nationalists passed the Prohibition of Political Interference Act, which outlawed racially mixed political parties. The Progressives opposed the law, but swallowed it when it was passed and continued as an all-white party.

The Liberal Party, the only organized body then advocating universal suffrage and complete removal of racial segregation, disbanded rather than accept the principle of segregated political parties. Politically, the loss of the party was insignificant. It had fewer than 4000 members at its demise. But it had served as a platform for writer Alan Paton and other vocal English-speaking liberals and had provided one of few areas of racial contact left in the country.

The Progressive Party, the English-language press and universities, a handful of social and educational organizations, and the churches of the English-speaking minority now provide the only important organized dissent that is voiced in South Africa.

In varying degrees and with different tactics, they oppose apartheid and the erosion of law that has occurred for both blacks and whites under Nationalist rule. They are offended by the crudeness with which the Afrikaners have carried out white domination, a crudeness that many English-speakers do not feel is necessary.

There are two ways of looking at the English-speakers' channels of dissent. One is to dismiss them as ineffective, extraneous parts of the white power structure. The other is to consider what South Africa would be like today if they did not exist. Their presence has certainly served to moderate some of the worst features of Nationalist rule and apartheid. On a case by case basis, Mrs. Suzman's sharp denunciations in Parliament or the exposés in the English-language press do improve conditions for an African family, an entire village, or prisoners in jail.

But dissent has been unable to promote any fundamental change within the power elite, the Afrikaners, who have sealed themselves off in their own institutions from any debilitating influence on race.

This is best seen in the pattern of newspaper circulation in the country. Many Afrikaners read the English-language press, but seem to discount automatically the editorial criticisms of apartheid and the "political slant" of the news columns. They have been taught to regard it as a foreign press, not a South African one.

Daily circulation of all newspapers in South Africa in 1970 was about 960,000. Of those, the fourteen English-language daily papers sold 750,000 copies. The six Afrikaans dailies accounted for only 210,000 sales.

The editorial standards of the English-language press are remarkably high — much higher than those of the Afrikaans press. The English papers have wider, more analytical, and better-written news coverage, and an interesting collection of bikini-clad South African blondes that are regularly featured in cheesecake sections.

The Johannesburg and Cape Town dailies are easily the best newspapers in Africa and compare favorably with their American and English counterparts. Johannesburg's *Star* has a daily circulation of nearly 180,000. The Rand *Daily Mail*, Johannesburg's morning newspaper, sells about 125,000 copies. The *Mail*'s Sunday sister, the *Sunday Times*, is the country's biggest seller — 444,000 copies each week.

The *Star*'s editorials tend to fall just right of the Progressive Party's politics. Its editorial writers consciously set out to establish credibility with the Afrikaners by concentrating more on the inefficiency and absurdities of apartheid instead of continually raising it as a moral issue. The *Mail*, on the other hand, has established a high moral tone in the debate on apartheid and is probably the most persistent, best-informed daily critic of the South African government in the world today. It has a tradition of strongly opinionated editors who are given a relatively free hand by the newspaper's owners.

The *Star* and seven other English dailies are owned by the Argus syndicate, while The *Mail*, two other dailies, and two Sunday newspapers belong to South African Associated Newspapers, which also owns half of the country's leading weekly magazine, the *Financial Mail*. Both syndicates were formed by mining companies, and the concern of the mine owners with rationalizing apartheid's economic controls is reflected in the approaches of the newspapers.

Every indication is that the owners rarely interfere with the functioning of the English-language press. The government does, however. The indirect pressures it can bring make editing a South African newspaper akin to "walking through a minefield blindfolded," as one South African newsman has noted. There are laws against quoting anyone that the government lists as banned and laws against divulging police matters that the police might consider embarrassing. If there is not a specific law at hand, the government gets an easily obtainable injunction from its magistrates to halt publication of any story it does not like. It uses the power sparingly, but the shadow of it hangs over all newspapers in South

Africa each day, as does the example of the prosecution and conviction of Lawrence Gandar, editor of the Rand *Daily Mail*, for publishing in 1965 a series of articles detailing accusations of brutality and bad conditions in South Africa's prisons that the government later claimed were false. Gandar and Benjamin Pogrund, the reporter who wrote the articles, were given light fines, but the costs the newspaper had incurred in defending the drawn-out case, tried in 1968, constituted the real punishment. After the trial, Gandar went to England. Pogrund remained at the *Mail* and was periodically harassed and arrested by the security police throughout the next two years.

CHURCH AND STATE

The diversity of opinion and tradition that exists in the English-speaking community, in contrast to the tribal solidarity of the Afrikaners, continues into religion. While almost all English-speaking whites are professing Christians, few of them are as openly fervent on the subject as their Afrikaner compatriots. While 85 per cent of the Afrikaners belong to a single denomination within the Dutch Reformed Church, English-speakers are scattered among the Anglican, Methodist, Roman Catholic, and Presbyterian churches.

The Anglicans, who have twice as many members as the Methodists, have only about 30 per cent of the English-speaking population. There are seven other sizable Christian denominations in South Africa.

The English-speaking churches, to greater and lesser degrees, have opposed apartheid and the Nationalist government's repression of liberal dissent. But most clergymen who have endorsed multiracialism from the pulpit have found it difficult to get their congregations to practice it, even in church on Sunday. They are also vulnerable to the government's retaliations against critics of apartheid, as the arrest and prosecution of the Very Reverend Gonville ffrench-Beytagh, the Anglican Dean of Johannesburg, demonstrated in 1971. He was sentenced to five years in prison on charges that amounted to having contacts with and sympathizing with African nationalists. The conviction was overturned on appeal, but the Dean felt sufficiently intimidated to leave South Africa for good.

Local churchmen also felt the repercussions of the World Council of Churches' decision in 1970 to donate $200,000 to anti-Portuguese guerrilla movements. More than twenty-five foreign churchmen were expelled from the country in the three months after the announcement, and church groups were raided by security police. Prime Minister Vorster told the English-speaking churches that they would have to quit the Council, or "action would be taken against them." The churches refused, but they quickly condemned "contributions to terrorists."

The pattern of English-speaking churches — organizational condemnation of apartheid, with widespread individual acceptance of it — has been reversed by the country's 120,000 Jews. Organized Jewry has never taken a public stand on apartheid, but individual Jews have been at the forefront in keeping dissent alive in South Africa in the last two decades.

The Jews were a major part of the influx into the cities that grew up around the gold and diamond fields. They came from Germany, Eastern Europe, and especially Russia to escape persecution. A second, smaller wave came in the middle 1930s, as German Jews fled from Nazi rule. From 1933 through 1936, 3617 Jews immigrated to South Africa.

Led by Nationalist Party leaders who warned that the rising influx of Jews was causing "nervousness among all sections of the population" because they were getting the best jobs in business, Parliament enacted a curb on Jewish immigration in 1937.

South Africa's Jews are generally recognized, however, as having made major contributions to the development of the country. They have added much to the cosmopolitan air of Johannesburg and have played key roles in building up the commercial and financial infrastructure of South Africa. Immigrant Jews were among the most important early financiers in the country. Sir Ernest Oppenheimer, one of the two most important financiers in South Africa's history, came from a German-Jewish merchant family.

South African Jews make up the world's tenth largest Jewish community. About half of them live in Johannesburg. Culturally and politically they have always identified with the English-speakers. The country's Board of Deputies, the highest official body of Jewry, openly supported the United Party in the crucial 1948 election.

But after his victory, Prime Minister Malan publicly declared that the National Party was not anti-Semitic and promised to keep the issue out of politics if the Board would. To the dismay of liberal Jews (but, one gathers, to the relief of many of the community) the Board accepted the arrangement and has never issued an official statement on apartheid.

"As individuals, some of us do what we can. We know too well what institutionalized prejudice and violence can do to a society," one of the Board members told me. "But as a group we're too vulnerable. We can't afford to shed our protective coloration."

Recently, events have tended to underline that vulnerability. In 1966 and 1967, young German immigrants provoked clashes with Jews and proudly celebrated Hitler's birthday by painting swastikas on synagogues in Johannesburg. More ominous, perhaps, was a speech made in August 1968 by Minister of Interior and Police S. L. Muller, who accused Jewish students of whipping up university demonstrations against the government.

"The people who are leading the protests are foreign students . . . and a whole group of people with Jewish surnames," Muller said. "I want to tell the Jewish community that the time has arrived for it to adopt an attitude towards the behavior of these students. I don't have feelings against the Jewish community. Many of my best friends are Jews . . ."

In 1970 such tactics continued. "The South African security police make a special point of letting us know that Vorster doesn't like what our young people are doing," the Board of Deputies member said. He asserted that even the Board had been infiltrated by police informants.

Israel created a new furor in South Africa in May 1971 by announcing a $2800 donation to the Organization of African Unity's Liberation Committee, which finances the guerrilla movements trying to dislodge white rule in Southern Africa. The Israelis subsequently said the donation was intended only for medical and educational help, and the OAU, which has eight Arab governments among its forty-one members, balked at accepting any Israeli help anyway. The offer was quietly allowed to lapse.

But the South African government had quickly retaliated by freezing the large contributions South African Jews had been sending to Israel. Donations, variously estimated to range between 10 and 15 million dollars a year since 1967, had been partially exempt from South Africa's tight foreign transfer controls.

Jews immediately rushed into print with letters in the Johannesburg press deploring the Israeli action and proclaiming their loyalty to South Africa.

There seems to be almost no visible officially inspired anti-Semitism in South Africa today, however. "We can't afford it," an Afrikaner with influence in the government said over lunch one day. "It would be the cherry on the cake. It would be all the world would need to brand us . . . And most of us wouldn't stand for it, anyway. It isn't right."

Helen Suzman, the leading liberal voice in Parliament and a Jewess, describes anti-Semitism in South Africa "as more an English kind of thing. They develop it as a social prejudice in their clubs and private schools. The Afrikaner is more egalitarian than that — as long as you're white."

She does receive crank letters from Afrikaner farmers at times. But she noted in 1970 that the thinly veiled offers she used to receive from the National Party leaders during parliamentary debate to go to Israel if she didn't like South Africa, and the National Party press cartoons showing her not only with horns and a pitchfork but also with a prominent curling nose, have declined in recent years.

In the 1970 elections, much of her campaign work was done by the kind of young Jewish students S. L. Muller is keeping his eye on. Some of them are impatient with the refusal of the Board of Deputies to condemn apartheid, as some Christian churches have done.

"The Jewish establishment doesn't see that as soon as the Nationalists think they don't need white unity, we will be next on the list to be herded away into our ghetto," one of them told me. My own feeling was that even if the Afrikaners wanted to strike at the Jews (and I found no evidence of it), they are not likely to do so any time in the foreseeable future. The demands of white unity will continue to be too great, and the analogy of the Israeli struggle against the Arabs is too useful to Afrikaners to be given up easily.

South Africa was one of the first states to recognize Israel, and Malan became the first foreign chief of government to visit Israel in 1948. Although Israel recalled her ambassador in 1964, as black African pressure mounted, diplomatic relations continue smoothly at the chargé d'affaire level.

To Afrikaners, the parallels are as obvious as they are embarrassing to the Israelis. They and the Israelis are essentially white, Europeanized peoples who have carved their own nations out of a land inhabited by hostile, non-European majorities that would destroy the two nations if the Afrikaners, and the Israelis, listened to the United Nations and depended on world opinion. Their religions are similar, each being a "chosen people." Israel, to the Nationalist government, is the other Western outpost in the Third World. The 1967 victory of the outnumbered but technologically superior Israeli forces over the Arabs gave the South African whites a tremendous boost in morale.[2]

[2] C. L. Sulzburger, the astute foreign affairs columnist for the *New York Times*, reported in 1971 from Johannesburg that the Israeli 1967 tactics are given major attention in South Africa's military maneuver schools. He noted that South Africa has been licensed to manufacture the Uzi submachine gun, invented by the Israelis. Sulzburger, a serious and important journalist, reported "unconfirmable rumors" that a South African mission flew to Israel during the Six Day War to study tactics and that the Israelis passed on to the South Africans secret plans of the French Mirage fighter engine they had secured in Switzerland.

BUSINESSMEN AND BUREAUCRATS

Perhaps the greatest shock of the past decade for the English-speakers was their discovery that they were unable to use the financial and commercial base they had built as a counterpoise to Afrikaner political power. This is partly because until now there has been no essential conflict between apartheid and the pursuit of making money in South Africa. There have been inconveniences, but still plenty of profits.

But it is also due to the Afrikaner's willingness to defy standard principles of economics to further his racial ideology. Most English-speakers sat by as the Afrikaner state built a vast bureaucratic and legal machine to enforce apartheid and control the blacks. Liberty and freedom of action were indeed divisible in South Africa along racial lines. It has only been in the last few years that English businessmen, the only important alternative source of white influence in South Africa, have found that they, too, have become vulnerable to the machine and have more reason than ever to be kindly disposed to the government that brought them apartheid.

This message was driven home to them during the 1970 campaign, especially by a clash that for many symbolized the course that relations between the South African nations of Briton and Boer have taken in this part of their history. It was, for many, a clash between Hoggenheimer and van der Merwe, the two ethnic stereotypes of South Africa's white groups.

Hoggenheimer is the cartoon character much used by the Nationalist press to bait the English-speakers. He is the corpulent, consummate capitalist, ready to sell out his race for a few more dollars, even though he is already rich. For the English, van der Merwe is the archetypal Afrikaner: a dumb, crude farmer or government bureaucrat obsessed by race. Both seemed to come to life in 1970 when John Vorster's Minister of Health, Mines, and Planning, Carel de Wet, decided to flex his muscles against Harry Oppenheimer, one of the world's richest and most important businessmen.

Oppenheimer is Mr. Mining. His De Beers company handles 80 to 85 per cent of all the diamonds sold in the world, and his Anglo-American group provides one third of all the world's gold mined outside the Communist bloc. Oppenheimer also controls an industrial empire. His family's personal fortune is thought to be in the neighborhood of $300 million, and the combined assets of his companies ten times that figure. He is, in short, to South Africa what General Motors is to the United States. His companies pay well over $150 million a year in taxes to the South African government. In his sixties, Oppenheimer, a soft-spoken, pleasant man, has become the Afrikaner's "Randlord" par excellence.

Oppenheimer also illustrates, on a grand scale, many of the contradictions within English-speaking society. He is a member of and major contributor to the Progressive Party. He has frequently criticized apartheid, especially in terms of its stifling effect on the economy. He has called for a more just society.

Yet the wages his companies paid Africans were not appreciably higher than those paid by companies devoted to apartheid. Many of his actions strengthened the economy and therefore made the government more stable. His African Explosives company made a major portion of South Africa's domestically manufactured munitions. Colin Legum, in *South Africa: Crisis for the West*, has given a detailed analysis of the "bewildering ambiguities" that a major businessman like Oppenheimer necessarily faces when he speaks out against a system on which he depends for an enormous economic gain.

De Wet, a former minister of Parliament who had also served as South Africa's ambassador to London, was an apartheid superhawk. He controlled the Physical Planning Act, a 1967 law the National Party had pushed through Parliament that enabled the government to freeze the number of Africans employed in major industrial areas. The purpose of the law, the government assured the English-speakers, was to shift African workers out of white areas by persuading companies to relocate instead of expand. It seemed to have little effect at first, as companies continued to expand by routinely applying for and receiving exemptions to the law.

But in April 1970, toward the end of the campaign, de Wet startled the financial community by publicly warning Oppenheimer to stop criticizing apartheid. Unless Oppenheimer endorsed government policy within twenty-four hours, de Wet told newsmen, he would make sure the mining king would become "acquainted with government policy in a tangible way." De Wet said that he would treat applications from Oppenheimer's firms for more African labor "with the greatest suspicion."

Oppenheimer, then abroad on a business trip, declined to comply with de Wet's order. After the bitter election campaign ended, the matter was allowed to drop. But the point had been made. The arsenal of apartheid legislation was broad enough to allow the government to seek out any number of targets. Not only black revolutionaries, or white liberal political activists, but also white businessmen might be asked to give up some rights to further apartheid. It was a sobering realization, but one that probably had come too late. The *Financial Mail*, South Africa's equivalent of *Business Week* magazine, entitled its account of the incident, "Oppenheimer today, you tomorrow." It wondered if the government would stop at threatening to take away African labor from businessmen who disagreed with apartheid. There were also passports that could be removed, as well as just about any other right.

Except for a brave, praiseworthy, and too small minority among them, South Africa's English-speakers have not been deeply concerned with the Afrikaner's drive to destroy whatever stands in the way of his racial ideology. Apartheid has presented no essential conflict with what they perceive as their interests. Now, with the changing nature of the economy, it may. And it may be too late for the English-speakers to do much about it.

Chapter Three

The New Tribe

Men shorn
of all human honor
like sheep after shearing,
bleating at the blistering wind,
"Go away! Cold wind! Go away!
Can't you see we are naked?" [1]

"THEY DO EVERYTHING they can to make us invisible, to get us out of sight and out of mind, and to pretend we are not persons," an African journalist told me one morning as we stood on a railway bridge overlooking Johannesburg's central railroad station. "For the whites to see this marching river of people would be a trauma. It would frighten them silly." He spoke of the black workers who were beginning to pour into Johannesburg for the day.

It was after 6 A.M. and Johannesburg had belonged almost exclusively to the whites for about eight hours. I had walked over to the bridge at my colleague's suggestion. Dawn was sliding softly up the ridges that break around Johannesburg and was probing the quiet canyons between the clean, new skyscrapers of the center city as I left the President Hotel, an expensive and cloyingly posh establishment. The bridge, a few blocks away, was deserted and quiet as I arrived.

The hum began a few minutes later, far away, but rolling toward town, growing, suddenly becoming a roar of hurtling steel and iron as the trains from Soweto began to arrive and Johannes-

[1] Oswald Joseph Mtshali, *Sounds of a Cowhide Drum.*

burg started its descent back into the uneasy black-white division of the day after having been white-by-night.

A swirling mass of black men and women exploded out of their separate trains across their separate station platforms and up their separate stairways, out into the city streets that are off limits to them each night after 10 P.M. In these morning hours the eleven-car trains will make two hundred trips from Soweto to bring 213,000 African workers into the city where they earn, and spend, their money. In the early evening, the same 213,000 persons will crowd back into the same cars to be shuttled back to Soweto, where they sleep, drink, and occasionally kill each other.

My colleague soon arrived and we strolled into the black tide that was filling the streets with the rush of feet and a conglomerate buzzing of tongues. The clicking sounds of the Xhosa tribal language mingled with the gutteral Afrikaans. At this hour, there were no other whites around the nonwhite exit (it was illegal for me, or any other white, to enter the nonwhite part of the station). Only a few white policemen moved through the crowd to check passbooks. I was carried along in the black surge. I soon felt the apprehension of a lone white man, the fear that white South Africans must carry with them, at least subliminally, every day of their lives. But I was not challenged; indeed, I was not even looked at. The Africans, hurrying to work, kept their eyes toward the pavement, just as, it seemed to me, they always do when in Johannesburg. My white South African friends said this was not so.

Officially, none of these black people who surrounded me were Africans. They were Bantu (singular or plural). To call them African would cast doubt on the whites' claim to have arrived in South Africa before the black tribes that were migrating from the north. It would be confusing, too. The Afrikaners had pre-empted the term in Afrikaans for themselves. "Native" and "kaffir" had fallen into disuse, officially, as those words might cause the outside world to think South Africans prejudiced. Thus, Bantu, a nicely neutral word, had been designated by the government as the correct term for South Africa's black and dark brown residents.

Unable to agree even on what they should be called, white South Africa and much of the rest of the world spend an enormous amount of time and energy debating whether these people are happy or miserable, well fed or hungry, ready to revolt or grateful to the white man for all that is being done for them. The debate is conducted in an almost complete vacuum, for outsiders rarely get a chance to ask the Africans, and white South Africa rarely bothers. Each side thinks it already knows the answers. It is two dogs fighting over a bone, and the bone has nothing to say about it, to paraphrase a comment one black South African made to me.

South Africa's fifteen million blacks are the most scrutinized, but perhaps least known, people on this continent. The United Nations constantly frets about them. They have acquired champions in the United States Congress. Most of the rest of the world, when it thinks about South Africa, wonders how much longer it will be before these blacks rise up to smite, and overthrow, their white masters. That, to a large number of people, is the only question worth asking about South Africa.

On the surface at least, the prospect of a black revolution seemed to be growing dimmer with each passing year as the nineteen seventies began. South Africa's blacks seemed to an outsider leaderless, frightened, divided, and, although few people on the outside seemed to recognize it, extremely vulnerable to a number of different pressures that the white government skillfully exerted on them. Waving both a heavy stick and an elusive carrot of economic progress that kept them running, the white regime was carrying out an efficient divide-and-rule campaign against the black mass that surrounded it.

This black population was what Helen Suzman called "the great silenced majority." No one could claim to speak for it, and no one really seemed to know what was going on within the black community. Black political leadership — radical, moderate, or conservative — had been completely smashed in the nineteen sixties. The people who, thirty, twenty, or even twelve years before, could have spoken for the community had ended in jail, in exile, or in deep, lonely despair, as one of their white friends has said. The silenced Africans of the late sixties seemed to have lost a generation of leaders in less than a decade. Albert Luthuli, Nelson Mandela, and Walter Sisulu were contemporaries of, or younger than, Jomo Kenyatta, Kwame Nkrumah, and Moise Tshombe. The accomplishments of the latter three men are a part of modern Africa, part of a stream of political continuity. Yet, when I arrived in South Africa, it seemed as if Luthuli, Mandela, and Sisulu were perceived dimly, as if they belonged to another time, long past and long lost. These men, potential symbols of unity, had been removed, and the division of black South Africa accelerated in the past decade.

The assumption that the blacks would overcome the whites in a battle because of their superior numbers is a dangerously facile one, based on the misleading statistic that blacks outnumber whites nearly four to one in South Africa. The black population is actually divided into three large geographic slices.

About 40 per cent of the African population — mostly women, children, and old men — have been left behind or shipped back to the "homelands," which are often remote, inaccessible tribal reservations where they are watched over by black chiefs appointed and paid by the white government. These are people not needed by the white man's economy. They have little education, little money, and little chance of striking at the white man.

Another 24 per cent of the African population lives and works on white farms. Blacks greatly outnumber the whites on these farms, but they are cut off from the outside world, and each other, and often lead an almost semifeudal existence. They are perhaps the most invisible of all of South Africa's blacks. Education, politics, newspapers are all words largely without meaning for them. Farmers, who can get cheap convict labor, get by with paying regular workers five or six dollars a month. If the farmer desires, he can refuse to let the African laborer's children go to school. "Education would just make hoodlums out of them," one farmer explained to a newspaperman. Such farmers, and their white overseers, are to a large extent the law and government to the 3,500,000 Africans who live on their farms.

The third slice is the only one that would count for much in a revolutionary situation — the urbanized, partly sophisticated 4,000,000 blacks who live in the cities, where they confront 3,500,000 whites who have control of the country's technology and weapons. Driven by hunger out of the barren countryside, or, more likely, drawn by the lure of moneymaking opportunities in the cities and the mines, nearly a third of the country's black population has moved into residential compounds built and tightly controlled by the whites, and now riddled by well-paid black police spies.

The urban Africans are ruled by a sprawling white bureaucracy that regulates every important phase of their lives. In the mining compounds, white company officials and mine overseers manage every detail, from diet to bedtime hours, of the lives of their 360,000 African employees. They are recruited on short-term work contracts and are often simple, uneducated tribesmen.

These are impressive machines of control the white man has developed to keep the odds even in the struggle for South Africa. But the most effective method of dividing the black majority has come from the Africans themselves. It is the tribe. There are hundreds of small tribal groupings within the four main linguistic groups of South Africa: Nguni (which includes Xhosa and Zulu), Sotho (the people of Lesotho and the Tswana of Botswana), Venda, and Tonga. Scattered and disrupted by the rise of the Zulu and Xhosa empires, the smaller tribes were segmented by settlers and the army. Long-standing tribal animosities sparked warfare between black and black, while the whites moved deeper into South Africa. The continuing inability of African tribes to live together is one of the main justifications white South Africans use today for continuing their rule. Without them as outside referees, the whites say, South Africa would become another Congo, or Nigeria, only much, much worse.

In the rural areas, it is easy for the government to seek to perpetuate these useful tribal identifications, which are strong there in any event. The Bantustans, the tribal states that the grand design of apartheid would create for each tribal nation in the rural areas of South Africa, would help deepen these divisions.

The African trek to the cities in this century, which has almost paralleled that of the Afrikaner at different stages, reduced these divisions in urban areas. With the help of British missionaries and educators willing to teach Africans and able to supply scholarship funds for them, the move to the cities and the integration of Africans into the modern cash economy produced a black elite of doctors, lawyers, and teachers. These were people not only eager but demonstrably able to adopt Western economic, religious, and social values. They even formed a political party, as the Afrikaner had done, to look after their own interests.

They were beginning to become a new black tribe. It was a tribe whose very existence would undermine the Afrikaner argument that he had built up the apartheid fortress to protect Western civilization, which God has chosen him alone to defend in Africa. It was a tribe whose growth could increase rapidly, since it depended on factors more mutable than birthrates. It was, in short, a tribe that had to be controlled more tightly even than the others.

The drive to control and eventually reverse the African move to the city is perhaps the strongest single force in the shaping of apartheid, both the theoretical and practical varieties. The Nationalists have spent two decades perfecting a vast bureaucratic and security apparatus that has three main aims, which are justified in various ways under the theory of apartheid: 1. Keep Africans from coming into urban areas. 2. Send back to the farms as many as possible of those not actually needed for labor. These are the unproductive Bantu, "the aged, unfit, widows, women with dependent children," in the words of a government memorandum. 3. Keep complete control over the lives of those who are allowed into the urban areas. While the growing need of the white economy for black labor has thwarted the first two aims, the third has been accomplished with an awesome mechanical exactitude.

THE LURE OF THE CITIES

The drift to the cities and the integration of Africans into a modern cash economy began at the end of the nineteenth century as they trekked to the gold and diamond mines. The sight of their cheap labor units walking away to the mines upset white Transvaal farmers so that they put a pass law into effect: the African in the Transvaal had to carry at all times a document signed by a white man showing he was gainfully employed, or face arrest.

At the turn of the century, there were 55,000 African men and 5000 women living in segregated townships around Johannesburg. These numbers doubled in a decade and continued to grow, with women gradually migrating in a more equal proportion as the Africans settled more conclusively in the towns.

They were being driven out of the homelands by hunger and poverty. The African's traditional shifting method of cultivation quickly exhausts the soil, and the perennial droughts that continue to assault South Africa were helping turn the tribal areas into giant dust bowls.

In 1913, the Parliament greatly spurred the African population shift with the Natives Land Act, which prohibited Africans from buying land outside the small government-approved tribal reserves, which then constituted 7 per cent of South Africa's land area. The effect was to turn the African into a wage seeker by reducing his land-owning and farming possibilities.

A rise in the price of gold in the nineteen thirties pulled more Africans to the cities, as new jobs in industry were spun from the gold profits and wages rose. On the eve of World War II, the African population of Johannesburg had grown to 244,000 — one fourth of it now women.

The war intensified the country's industrialization and urbanization. In six years, the black population of Johannesburg climbed from 244,000 to 400,000. Half of the total were women and children. A permanent black urban population was being born, in places called Sophiatown, Orlando, Pimville, and Alexandra.

No houses were being built with the war on, and shanty towns sprang up overnight. In 1944, tens of thousands of Africans poured out of the jammed slums and squatted on vacant municipal land, where they threw up cardboard, tin, and sackcloth shanties. Alan Paton's moving description of the birth of Shanty Town in *Cry, the Beloved Country* and Anthony Sampson's *Drum, A Venture into the New Africa* capture the strange mixture of squalor, despair, and joy that pervaded these townships in the decade after the end of the Great War in Europe.

White South Africa never recovered from the shock of seeing eleven African squatter camps spring up around its major city. Where artists like Paton and Sampson may have been able to uncover some redeeming graces, the white establishment saw only black depravity. "The rule of law was openly flouted," a 1969 government brochure on Bantu housing says somewhat stridently. "Gangster leaders imposed levies on the population, and imposed savage punishments . . . Disease was rife, and sanitary and other services were non-existent."

In 1948, the Nationalists, the party that campaigned against "the black peril," came to power. Seven years later, Sophiatown, four miles from the center of Johannesburg and established in 1905, was smashed on a February morning by government demolition squads.

The township's residents and their belongings were loaded onto trucks and removed to Meadowlands, a compound of brick, box-like houses owned and controlled by the city. Although Africans had been able to own their houses in Sophiatown, freehold was not allowed in Meadowlands. No thought was given to rebuilding homes for the Africans on the site of Sophiatown. They were moved fourteen miles southwest of the city into the area that became known as Soweto. It is not even an African name, but an alphabetical coupling of letters from the official name for the area — South Western Townships.

"Soweto had nothing to do with urban renewal as you Americans know it," insisted one white municipal government employee when I suggested that the pattern was not dissimilar to the case of the once black Southwest section of Washington, D.C., which is now almost all white. "You may have wanted to get poor blacks out of sight. We had to provide immediately quick and cheap housing. Then it became a method of control."

The process was the same throughout South Africa, with Johannesburg being the most dramatic example. Durban has Kwa Mashu as its black bedroom, Cape Town has Wynberg, and Pretoria has several compounds. The pattern of life in Soweto applies generally to them all.

BLACK TOWNSHIPS

Soweto is tucked away on the western slope of the heavily mined reef of gold that brought people to Johannesburg. More than 70,000 neat, almost identical four-room brick houses stretch toward the horizon in monotonous row after monotonous row. The April day that I saw Soweto, the houses had a grimy, sooty look. Smoke from the Johannesburg factories often slides into the valley Soweto occupies, one Soweto resident told me, and temperature inversions lock it close to the ground.

One quarter of Soweto's breadwinners work in the factories around and in Johannesburg. Thirty-three per cent work in commerce, most of them as messengers, chauffeurs, clerks, or perhaps stockboys. Seven per cent of the Soweto work force is employed by the municipal government. Some are social workers and researchers; most are gardeners or maids.

In many material ways, the residents of Soweto do, as the government claims, live much better than do the black slum dwellers elsewhere on this continent. The average factory worker living in Soweto earned in 1970 50 rand ($70) a month, more cash than a man in the homelands would see in a year and a considerable sum for a black worker on this continent, whose average per capita annual salary is probably in the range of $100 to $200. Rent in Soweto seemed to average about 5 rand for each house.

In its debates with foreign and domestic critics, however, the

South African government usually neglects to mention that this average industrial wage of 50 rand is 20 rand ($28) below the minimum monthly budget a Soweto family of five needs to meet the area's high cost of living. That is the figure calculated by the Associated Chambers of Commerce of South Africa, an employers' group. The average Soweto family has 5.5 members. The gap has to be filled by the wife's taking a job or selling illegal booze, the husband working on weekends and at nights, or their sinking more deeply into debt every month. Inflation seems to have eaten up much of the wage increases Africans have received in the past decade.

The white guide in the tourist bus usually also neglects to mention that only about 10,000 of Soweto's little houses have electricity, that there is little indoor plumbing, and that shops are few and ill spaced. The white administration deliberately encourages Africans to continue to shop in Johannesburg for everything but daily food and essentials. Recreation facilities are skimpy by any standards.

Despite these problems, life in Soweto remains much more materially rewarding than living on the eroded, overpopulated farms of the reserves. Both the government and the people who live in Soweto are acutely aware of this, and the government is able to manipulate with devastating effect the urban African's fear of losing his privileged position. He scrambles to keep that position by going along.

"The average man in Soweto is more worried about next month's payments on his radio set than about something called 'freedom,'" a white liberal told me ruefully. While his statement contained validity, it seemed to me that the truth was a great deal starker than that.

"They tie you down to one house, one job, one employer. If you lose any of those you go to jail, or back to the reserves, where you will starve to death. And the government bureaucracy has the power to take any one of them away from you at any time. It can forbid an employer to give you a job," an African legal clerk told me. His words echoed those of an African chauffeur, a much less educated man. "The white man decides everything for us — that we should live in Soweto, that no matter how many people there are in the family we should have a four-room house, that we are too ignorant for politics. He decides, not us, that we should be called Bantu. You are a Bantu, too. The word in our languages just means people. I have a name, but no white man ever bothers to learn it. I am James to them all, or just the Bantu." [2]

This was an extraordinary outburst from this quiet man. He is completely apolitical, and, I hasten to add for the South African authorities who may read this, a completely loyal South African. He is hardworking, earns perhaps 60 rand ($84) a month as a chauffeur, and spends much of that on school fees and expenses for his four young children. He has lived around Johannesburg for twenty years. He occasionally treats himself to a boxing match and a bottle of beer. He is proud to be more middle-class and temperate than most of his neighbors in Soweto.

Like the legal clerk, however, he knows that his whole existence can be overturned by one bureaucrat's order. Soweto residents all live in constant fear this will happen. Like Kafka's Joseph K. in *The Trial*, they are unsure just what act will provide the unseen forces that decide their fates.

Section 10 is *Catch-22* for South Africa's urban blacks. Even illiterate black laborers can recite Section 10 of the Bantu Urban Areas Consolidation Act and give its complete title. Section 10 requires an African to *prove* one of three things: that he was born in an urban area and has lived in that same place all his life, or that he has worked for one employer in that area for ten years, or that he has lived in one place fifteen years while being gainfully and continuously employed. If he cannot prove this, he is "endorsed

[2] The term Bantu is useful for historians and sociologists. It describes the tribes that belong to the larger subcontinental grouping called Bantu that migrated into Southern Africa, as opposed to the tribes such as the Hottentot who were already there. But the government's quasi-scientific base for adopting Bantu now has been largely erased by its repeated use as a political code word. Just as Strom Thurmond turned from a familiar racial epithet to NEE-gro, Piet Koornhof, a South African Thurmond, has turned to BAN-tu. The meaning for their white listeners has never changed, however, and calling an educated urban black South African "Bantu" in 1970 would get you about the same response as calling a young, black American college student "Negro."

out" — an endorsement is placed in his passbook ordering him to return to the homeland of his tribe. This all adds up to what Carl T. Rowan, the black American columnist who visited South Africa in 1970, termed "a delicate form of slavery."

Endorsing out is not just a question of a man and his family being deprived of the bright lights of Johannesburg. "The people fear they will starve in the homelands," which are already overcrowded and virtually without employment, the Reverend B. S. Rajuili, a black clergyman, said after he compiled a limited study of attitudes in Soweto for South Africa's Christian Institute. "If they strike or boycott they fear that their passes will be endorsed. The problem is more fear than apathy," he added, to explain the silence and acquiescence of Soweto residents.

The African is also required by law to carry a lodger's permit, showing that he has a place to live, and his tax receipts, including those for a poll tax that voteless Africans pay but which voting whites do not.

They all form part of the "passbook" — the central device of control for urban Africans. It had made a lot of progress since those Transvaal famers put it into effect 100 years ago.

"If you're unlucky, you're opening up the bloody book all day long," said G.T., an African laborer with whom I established contact through a friend of a friend. "Then other times you can go weeks without police checking it. They wait for you near the [train] stations. If you are slow getting the book out, they say you are cheeky and arrest you anyway." G.T. was called cheeky, which is the South African equivalent of uppity, when he once asked to see the policeman's credentials. "I was afraid he was going to run off with my passbook. The Dutchmen do that sometimes."

Every African over sixteen has to carry a passbook at all times. Since 1963 this has included women, who had previously been exempt from pass inspection. Helen Suzman's maid was arrested standing a few steps outside Mrs. Suzman's lovely house, in one of Johannesburg's most affluent suburbs one day. The policeman refused to let the maid go to the kitchen to get her passbook.

The passbook contains the African's photograph, tribe, an identity number, the signature of his employer, which has to be renewed each month to prove that he is employed, and his tax stamps.

G.T., who asked not to be identified by his full name, carried his passbook in a raveled and perspiration-soaked leather case, which also contained a photograph of his wife. She had lived in Soweto for almost a year as a fugitive before I met G.T. He met her when she came from her village forty miles away to visit Soweto two years before. They married and had a child a year later. They had lived with G.T.'s parents in Soweto, but when the child was born, he applied for their own house.

The authorities rejected his request. They said G.T. could keep the child in Johannesburg, under Section 10. But, having learned of his wife's existence, they endorsed her out, giving her seventy-two hours to leave. At first G.T. told me that she had left Soweto. After we had talked for an hour, he admitted that she was still there, living in fear of being discovered at any moment. They were not sure what they would do with the child, although they would probably leave it with G.T.'s parents. Otherwise, the child would lose its right ever to live in Soweto.

"I thought if you are married you will die together. But we got married and they said we couldn't stay together. My wife is not wanted here. It is because we have black skin." I asked him if he hated whites. "No, I no be angry for you if you do nothing to me. I be angry for you if you do something to me." He was twenty, had had five years of schooling, and earned 13 rand ($17) a week working in a factory.

In 1969, 693,000 Africans, almost 2000 a day, were arrested for "pass law" offenses of various sorts. Their cases are handled in the crowded, dirty, Bantu Commissioners Courts in Johannesburg, where assembly-line justice has been perfected by civil servants called magistrates, who devote an average of two minutes to each case before sentencing the defendants to as much as six months in jail for not carrying a tax receipt. The Episcopalian bishop of Washington, D.C., the Right Reverend William Creighton; the Dean of the Washington Cathedral, the Very Reverend Francis Sayre; and an American Negro judge, William Booth, dropped in on one of these courts in 1971 and wound up being questioned for twenty minutes by South African policemen about why they were so interested in the Bantu.

South Africa's daily prison population averages 90,555, about 71,000 of whom are Africans serving sentences of less than six months. In 1970, 164 African babies were born in prison, and 4308 other breast-fed infants were admitted with their mothers to serve out the same sentence.

Despite this concentration of law and order, Soweto residents say their main problem is crime. Official statistics seem to be lacking on this, but some unofficial ones I rounded up from colleagues make it appear that this fenced-in enclave of 700,000 people is one of the most violent spots in the world. It is certainly more violent than any urban area of Africa, with the possible exception of Lagos, Nigeria. There were at least 300 murders, 1600 rapes, 40,000 assaults, and 4000 violent robberies in Soweto in 1968. This would be a remarkable record, even for violence-ridden South Africa.

Soweto residents assert that most of the violent criminals who terrorize the township at night come from a floating population fostered by the pass system. It is generally accepted that there are at least 250,000 Africans in white areas illegally. They cannot "get regularized" with passes, so they cannot go into the white towns to work. Police rarely check passes inside Soweto or Kwa Mashu, and the passless ones roam the townships preying on those who do work.

Friday is payday, the day young thugs called *tsotsis* ride the trains. A man who has seen it happen often enough to start taking taxis home on Fridays described one mode of operation:

"Three tsotsis move through one of those crowded cars and stop in front of this man. They demand the pay envelope. If he won't give it up, two of them grab him and bend him forward. The other one takes out a short, sharpened bicycle spoke and inserts it precisely into the man's spinal cord and wiggles it. It's over.

Neat, not bloody. But the man will never walk again. The tsotsis move on, and nobody stops them."

Said another Soweto resident: "We aren't protected at all. There are no police out here, unless there is a robbery in Johannesburg. Then they bring the vans out here and just round people up. They couldn't give a damn about *us,* when there are three or four murders a night out here. People bleed to death in your front yard sometimes. But you don't dare go out there to help them." He does not have a telephone to call for help. The streets of Soweto are dimly lit, if they are lit at all.

Violence is the main bill of fare for the English-language newspapers directed at Africans. Some sample headlines I gleaned from page one during one week are "Nude Girl Found in Grave," "Hanged Nurse Tells Lover, 'Don't Weep Over Me,'" and "The Sunny Day That Turned Red with Blood," an account of multiple murder by a berserk man. (Whimsy sometimes creeps in, however. One of my favorites was this description of a Chinese man's failure to be classified by the government as white: "Wong Can't Make a White.")

THE BLACK PRESS

There were two strongly competing black-oriented English-language dailies in Johannesburg when I visited South Africa in 1970 — *Post* and the *World. Post*, by far the livelier of the two, died in 1972, apparently from financial problems, although the strong pressure the government had been putting on the paper to tone down its attacks on apartheid certainly did not help to keep it in business. The *World* continued publishing.

Both papers were owned and edited by whites, but they had a good sense of their African readership. Highly competent African journalists did most of their legwork. I dropped by to chat with some of them at one of the papers, and a white staffer set me up with "the man who can really tell you what is going on." A few weeks later when I dropped around again, a different white staffer was on duty. He asked to whom I had spoken on my first visit. When I mentioned the African staffer's name, the white said, "Oh, good. You've already seen our Special Branch [police spy] African. Now you can talk to some of those we think aren't with the police."

Post had three editions, daily sales of 250,000 throughout the country, and a much more pointed editorial outlook. Its bitter jibes at apartheid nettled the government enough in 1970 to produce pressure on the country's Press Council to bar it from membership. As long as a newspaper belongs to the Council, J. J. Kruger's censorship board cannot interfere with it. The more lenient Council is supposed to police its own members.

With an editorial staff of about sixty throughout the country, *Post* was owned by Jim Bailey, a white South African who has divided his time and family fortune between a large sheep ranch and building an African publication network that, for all its shortcomings, provided probably the best single barometer that existed in the nineteen-sixties to the aspirations and attitudes of the black South African urban population. Bailey, a man who avoids publicity as ardently as his reporters cast it onto others, owns *Drum*, a glossy and breezy twice-monthly *Life*-sized magazine for blacks. Three special editions of *Drum* are printed in London for the rest of Africa, where the magazine is very popular. Altogether, *Drum* was thought to have a circulation of about four million in 1970, although Bailey kept the totals confidential.

In South Africa, "If we want to perk up sales, all we have to do is put Cassius Clay or Sammy Davis, Jr., on the cover," one *Drum* staff member said. "Our customers will read everything we can print about them. But even when he was alive, if we put Martin Luther King on the cover, we couldn't get rid of the issue."

Clay and Davis "offer a little glamour for people who, God knows, have none in their own lives," a white psychologist who works with African patients told me. "They have made it. At the same time, a figure like Clay is especially popular, because he is still persecuted by whites and fights back. Dr. King was too forgiving, too much of a saint."

The most popular local hero with *Drum* readers then was easily Anthony Morodi, a hard-punching lightweight boxer who was featured four or five times a year in *Drum*'s pages. Sports figures are, in fact, virtually the only kind of heroes South African blacks have been able to develop inside the cocoon of apartheid.

Drum's reporters were locked in an internal debate in 1970. The magazine had splashed several issues with photographs and stories on models wearing Afro wigs and the growing acceptance of the "Black Is Beautiful" theme in South Africa. Some of the reporters ridiculed the idea. "In South Africa, Black Is Bitter," one said. Another pointed out that most South Africans are brown rather than ebony hued.

Africans elsewhere on the continent rarely think in "Black Is Beautiful" terms. Beautiful as opposed to what, many would ask. Except in areas like Zambia, and to a lesser extent Kenya where the white colonial presence has been high-profile, they have not formed the defensive reaction represented in America by "Black Is Beautiful." But here, where apartheid has forced everyone to think along the color line, and where there is an urban population bearing some similarities to the black Americans who live in northern ghettos, it could easily take root. Whether it does or not will be a key development for South African Blacks in the coming decade.

The black South African's access to ideas is even more tightly controlled than that of his white countrymen. Radio Bantu, the African broadcasting channel, is run by the government. Important African writers, from Frantz Fanon to Uganda's Ali Mazrui, are banned, as are black South African writers like Lewis Nkosi and Ezekiel Mphahlele. Even Martin Luther King's works have been censored here.

"He was a wily old bird," censor Kruger told me when I asked about Dr. King. "He sometimes preached insurrection subtly, and we had to control it." The Publications Control Board also snips away at and bans films, extending apartheid into the cinema projection booth. Films approved for whites are often banned for Africans. They are usually films "of violence, like these Italian westerns," Kruger said. "They would be dangerous to show to the Bantu." He didn't say dangerous to whom. An African workman told me: "Any time I see in the adverts that a film is limited to above age twelve for the whites, I know we won't get to see it. They treat us like children."

A BLACK BOURGEOISIE

There also seemed to be a concerted effort by the government to prevent a true black bourgeoisie from forming and to discourage expressions of individuality within Soweto. After crime in the streets, the greatest complaint I heard from Soweto residents was that they had no say in where they lived and what kind of school their children attended. The crime and residence problems are related. "I make one hundred rand a month," an African who held a job that would be classified as professional in the United States told me. "The man living on one side of me makes maybe forty-five rand, on the other a man who makes perhaps thirty-five. They both let out rooms to drifters to make ends meet. Now I know that I'm going to be robbed by one of those drifters one day. But what can I do? I have to walk in and out of the house."

Residences in Soweto are allocated on a tribal basis. Sotho live in one area, Xhosa in another. This may, as the government asserts, help keep peace between tribal groupings with long-standing animosities. It also helps to perpetuate those animosities and, more importantly, the tribal divisions around which apartheid is built. It justifies the government's practice of having the chiefs in the homeland appoint agents in Soweto. And, as a government pamphlet on Soweto happily notes, grouping "the various tribes according to their national units allows for their easy accessibility to schools teaching in the mother tongue."

That is, teachers in Soweto use tribal languages as the medium of instruction throughout primary school, rather than English or Afrikaans, the languages that might give them some kind of passport into white society. That is a major feature of Bantu education, which sets up a separate school system for all African children residing outside the homelands.

Education is not denied to African children. It is even encouraged up to a certain point. Hendrik Verwoerd, a man much franker than his successors seem to be, made it clear what that point was in 1953 when he introduced Bantu education. "Education must train and teach people in accordance with their opportunities in life, according to the sphere in which they live." Later he added that there was no place for the Bantu within the white community above the level of certain forms of labor.[3] In Soweto nearly two decades later, 4 per cent of the students who began school received the equivalent of an American eighth-grade education, according to statistics supplied me by the Johannesburg City Council. Education, free and compulsory for all white children, was neither for Africans. Black parents paid special taxes, helped pay the costs of school construction and maintenance, and supplemented teachers' salaries. They also paid the normal taxes that whites pay.

Despite this separate and unequal treatment, the white government was doing more for black education than it cared to take credit for inside South Africa. The government furnished a fixed contribution to African education each year from the general revenue fund. In 1970, the figure was 14.5 million rand. The Africans were supposed to pay for all expenditures above that with their special contributions, which in 1970 totaled 13 million rand. But the 1970 Bantu education expenditures were 45 million rand. The government put up the extra 17.5 million rand, just as it had advanced similar amounts in the two preceding years. The contributions had been previously labeled recoverable loans, apparently for the sake of white voters who do not like to see tax money spent on black children. But no one has any hopes the Africans will ever be able to pay this back, as the Minister of Finance seemed to concede in 1971 when he complained that a new arrangement would have to be worked out for financing Bantu education.

[3] Muriel Horrell, *Legislation and Race Relations: A Summary of the Main South African Laws Which Affect Race Relations.* South African Institute of Race Relations.

There is, as the government accurately points out, a great variety among the 700,000 people behind the gates of Soweto, "ranging from people still close to their tribal background, to people who have accepted much of Western life." Many of them are uneducated, undeveloped, and unprepared to blend gracefully into what is known as the Western way of life. But there is also that segment of them that knows nothing but the urban, Western way of life. Apartheid works cruelly against them, telling them they must belong to a decaying tribal culture they desperately want to escape. They can choose to return to it, or choose to remain as urban serfs, apartheid says. That is the only right they have.

Apartheid has created a small financial elite in Soweto, which the government can easily control: men like Richard Maponya, who profits from a large grocery store he runs in this government-created ghetto. One of five Soweto millionaires, Maponya has built a 45,000 rand ($63,000) house in Dube, the only township within Soweto where people are permitted to design their own houses. But Maponya will never be able to buy the land the house stands on. And it is government policy to encourage him to shut down the store and go "home."

He is a "professional Bantu," in the words of Central Circular No. 25, 1967, issued by the Secretary for Bantu Administration and Development, "doctors, attorneys, agents, traders, industrialists, etc. . . . who are not regarded as essential for the European labor market and as such they must also be settled in the homelands in so far as they are not essential for serving their compatriots in the European areas."

These are the people who are normally viewed as the black bourgeoisie. But, as the circular makes clear, they are marginal to white society. The white economy does not depend on African schoolteachers, journalists, store owners, or lawyers. These are in fact the people who emulate whites and who are therefore the most vulnerable to pressure and rewards. This is not the black economic class that will produce change in the coming decade. If such a class develops, it will spring from black skilled labor actually needed for the white economy — computer keyboard punch operators, switchboard operators, skilled construction workers. It is not clear that they will actually develop into an important force for change. But, as the government has realized, they bear watching.

In the meantime, the people in Soweto are likely to continue combining their need for status symbols with their need to drown their very real sorrows. Both are satisfied by the shebeen, the low-key African version of the speakeasy.

THE LAST RESORT

The government runs a dozen or so dull, sterile beer halls in Soweto. Women are not permitted in them, and a uniformed police guard greets customers at the gate. There are three scattered liquor lounges that close shortly after most of the workers get home from their long train ride from Johannesburg. Perhaps not surprisingly, the Bantu tend to ignore these conveniences and go instead to the illegal shebeens, open day and night. Drinks are more expensive and there is the chance of being arrested in a police raid, mounted from suspicion or spite, but the atmosphere seems to be a little more interesting.

I found there were four distinct types of shebeens, which are really houses converted into bars, reflecting the desire of Soweto residents for a little status in their lives.

"Shebeens are important for crushing down tribalism," a well-educated Soweto man told me. "They bring people of the same class together and let us talk about developing an urban African culture. Perhaps that is why the police don't like them."

The fourth layer is the tribal shebeen, which sells only homemade beer and the soupy, 3.2 per cent alcohol brew that the whites call Bantu beer and which the Africans call City Council beer because the government has a monopoly on brewing and marketing it. No women come here, only uneducated men who speak the same tribal language. The woman who runs it is unschooled; she cannot work as a maid. Her husband may make 10 rand a week as a menial laborer. "If the wife didn't sell beer, they would literally starve to death," an African told me.

All shebeens are run by women, who are called shebeen queens. Shebeens at the next level are typically run by divorced women, who have children. A typical one is a city girl, born in Johannesburg, and too proud to become a domestic. She operates on the premise that it will be six months before she will be closed down by the police. By then she will have made enough to pay her fine, or perhaps bribe the police into not arresting her and have enough left over to support the children. Her customers are young men, rough city boys who are likely to fight over the girls who come here to be picked up. Liquor, homemade and bottled, is on sale. Loud jazz records are the entertainment.

Clerks working for the City Council, schoolteachers — in short, people with white collar jobs go to their own special shebeens, where there is a strong mixture of Western and African customers. The woman who runs these is the wife of a salesman. She had a good job in a white store but quit. "I got tired of working for peanuts (40 rand a month). I was working harder than those white girls and getting less. And I had to say good morning to those girls who were younger than me, just because they were white. They should say good morning first to an older woman." She and her husband want to buy a car, so she has become a shebeen queen. She admits that after the car, the desire for new clothes or other consumer goods is likely to keep her in the business, unless the police raid her.

In the "deluxe" shebeen, in one of the few five-room houses in Soweto, gin, Scotch, brandy, and perhaps a European beer are served. Lawyers, doctors, school principals, and others gather to listen to the news on the radio and popular music on records. The women there tend to be married, but do not seem to be adverse to flirting.

On all four levels, the drinking is hard. "We know we drink this stuff too fast but what can we do," a man nipping down gin at a dollar a shot explained. "We know the police could come at any minute, and we don't want to be found with anything. So we try to drink it quick." Later, he said, "At least the shebeen is ours. We have little else. In the white schools, the children are taught what the flag is. To me it is just a piece of cloth. How can it be anything else . . . But then we are not really angry. When you have to struggle all day, every day, like we do, you don't have much time left for anger." He gulped another gin.

I visited Soweto several times, the last one illegally, at night, to see the shebeens. The most interesting trip was on Election Day 1970. While whites were choosing a government, I had a series of encounters with Africans who were outlawed from voting. The meetings seemed to me to illuminate much of Black South Africa's anguish.

My guide was an energetic young Afrikaner, André van Heerden, who worked for the Non-European Affairs Committee of the Johannesburg City Council, which managed Soweto. This is where you expect to see the bullwhips behind the door. Actually, van Heerden and his colleagues impress you as terribly sincere, well-meaning people. The United Party controls the City Council, and the City Council's members tend to take a very soft line on race. They are just doing a job. Van Heerden had voted early and didn't mind spending election day in Soweto. My driver, the mild-mannered man I mentioned earlier, didn't mind either, since he couldn't vote. So we set off.

The road from Johannesburg to Soweto curls past the towering, flat-topped mine dumps, along a racetrack, by "Uncle Charlie's Roadhouse" drive-in restaurant, through a decidedly working-class white neighborhood, along the side of Baragwanath Hospital's 150-acre complex (where, the young Afrikaner guide explained happily in the first of the set of statistics he was to toss at me during the day to quantify for me the Bantu's prosperity and happiness, there are 227 doctors, 2080 nurses, and 1200 operations a month on the Bantu), and finally into a wretched stinking slum.

"This is Old Pimville," van Heerden said. "This is what they were living in before. This is the last part of the slums, and we should clear it away shortly." I marveled that the government was going to throw away its instant museum for visiting firemen like me. We poked around the tin and cardboard shacks, our nostrils assailed by the white smoke of charcoal fires and the stench of open sewers. Then George emerged to stick out his hand. George was in his early twenties and obviously about half-drunk in the middle of the morning. He was well dressed, however, and talked about his car. He grasped very quickly that van Heerden was at a disadvantage with me along. Several times he said, "We have to be friends, don't we, André? We're together." When I asked him about the elections he said, "That isn't any of ours, is it?" a hard edge coming into his voice as he said the last two words. Later, he asked, "André, are you reliable?" When we climbed back into the car to drive across the highway and into the gates of Soweto, van Heerden said George was probably a petty criminal. It seemed probable. Anyway, he had shown George a lot more tolerance on this particular morning than he probably would have a white drunk.

Flags were flying in front of a lot of the little brick boxes that are houses (an average box covers 500 square feet, costs 350 rand to build, and rents for 2 to 5 rand a month, according to the guide). On Sundays, Africans assemble in the houses with the makeshift flags to worship in independent churches, that is, sects that have broken away from Christian churches. They often break away when they begin to see a gap between the love and brotherhood Christian churches preach on Sunday and the segregation that confronts them daily. There are an estimated 900 such independent churches in Soweto.

We stopped at a beer garden. A dozen men, apparently shift workers, sat inside, sipping plastic gallon bowls of the alcoholic malted milk called Bantu beer. An old man, dressed in a floppy patched overcoat, stood in the middle of the garden mooching drinks. He made for us. He said he was a university graduate, and perhaps he was. He spoke excellent English. He told us a sad story about how the government had dismissed him from a job and he was now destitute. Would we stand him a bucket of beer? Van Heerden did. I asked him about the elections. "I can't say, sir. We don't think about things like that." He wandered off, saying, "Good-bye, boss."

In the middle of the twenty-one separate townships that make up Soweto stands a great stone tower from which you look out over the monotonous collection of houses. This is the Oppenheimer tower. Sir Ernest Oppenheimer persuaded the mining houses to lend the City Council the money to put up the brick boxes. At the base of it is a quiet little tea room where the white tourists who have come to see black men practice their separate freedoms in their separate area can have a cup of tea. My driver, who lives in Soweto, had to wait outside. Van Heerden told me solemnly that the only reason we could drink here was that the Urban Bantu Council, which theoretically is a local governing body for Soweto, had given special permission for whites to use it.

Outside, an African employed by the City Council stood resting on his cane. He was a kindly, friendly man whom Van Heerden sees often on these trips. He is a gardener. I asked him about the elections. "I personally favor the present government," he said loudly. "It has done more for the Bantu than any other. Through the City Council it has raised the standard of living for us. I don't know about other people, but I favor separate development." I asked him if he was disappointed at not being able to register his approval of separate development at the polls on that day. He was puzzled and handled the question gingerly. "That is not for us to decide now. That is for the others."

A storekeeper, blind in one eye, leaned across his counter in one of the corner grocery stores we visited. "The educated ones talk about the elections. But it is all in English and very fast and I cannot understand. Most of us do not care. I am here, I want to make my money, that is all." Later, van Heerden said the storekeeper's attitude was probably the most representative one we had gathered from Soweto.

We stopped at another store, run by an African woman. Her husband was a doctor. She had taught school and now was managing this combination butcher shop and carry-out restaurant. It had taken them about $10,000 to start the enterprise. Apartheid, she said, "has helped the African businessmen by keeping competition out of Soweto. But I wouldn't say the people are in favor of it. My view of the government and the elections? I have my views, but I am not free to tell you." She eyed van Heerden throughout our conversation. "I think you understand." As we were leaving, she said pointedly to van Heerden: "There should be more contact between white and black at all levels so we can talk about our problems and work together to alleviate them. But you people never come out here."

Chapter Four

Not Quite White

"VORSTER. BURTON. De Klerk. Flandorp. Le Roux. See, nothing but good English and Afrikaner names." David Curry, a thirty-nine-year-old insurance salesman, thumbed through the large, bulging notebook and read out the names of his customers as we sat on a frayed couch in his living room. A pastel picture of Christ stood on the mantelpiece. A crucifix hung from the wall. Two gray cats were chasing around the small piano across the room.

Curry's distinctly middle-class home is located on the outskirts of Stellenbosch, the sleepy university town that is fitted into the rolling vineyards around Cape Town. A few miles away, the brightest children of Afrikanerdom were walking to classes on their green, quiet campus. It was midmorning. Curry glanced out the window. "See that road there? It's been unpaved for sixty years. If I were white I could get it paved, you know. But . . ." he shrugged his broad shoulders.

But David Curry and his customers are not white. Not quite. A tall man of lumpy form, Curry has a slight grayish-brown tinge to his complexion that outweighs his white name, his white religion, his white-middle-class habits and aspirations. The tinge, more than David Curry himself, decides where he lives, which cabs he rides in, what public toilets he uses, where he can look for a job, where he will someday be buried.

Curry and his customers with the English and Afrikaner names are part of South Africa's two million Coloreds, the large mulatto population that lives here in Cape Province. According to apartheid's central dictum — white and black are so different that they cannot be expected to mix peacefully and productively — David Curry and the others should not exist at all. But they do, and they form the most perplexing "racial" problem of all for South Africa.

Their very existence is a defiance of apartheid. The neat theoretical arguments that stress the lack of a common society, heritage, nationalism, etc., come to a dead end in the case of the Coloreds. Biology turns out to be common, and parentage even more so.

It is possible to argue from a moral standpoint that African tribes should live in their traditional homelands, speak their traditional languages, practice their traditional culture, and endure their traditional poverty out of the sight of the affluent white minority.

But not for the people who are branded as Colored, or Kleurling in Afrikaans, which is the language most of them speak. Their culture is the white man's, their religions are his, their languages, too. Their traditional homeland is on the white farms where they have been conceived and bred. Or more likely in the white cities, especially around Cape Town, where almost one-half million of them live. Cape Town is one of the loveliest cities in the world, and the government does not seem to be willing to part with it, even to prove the authenticity of apartheid.

The Coloreds form the one problem that Hendrik Verwoerd admitted that not even his cold, gray intellect could solve.

By refusing to absorb into their society the Colored elite, men like David Curry who are right on the racial borderline, the white rulers defy even the rational basis that apartheid supporters assert for the doctrine. It may be pragmatism, instead of racism, to argue that the numbers of the black majority would swamp the white man and his culture and therefore must be controlled, but this argument is not available to cloak the discrimination carried out against the Colored elite. Casting them out is an irrational act, an openly atavistic reaction to the stain of color that has crept into the nonwhite's "blood." Ultimately, it may be just as cruel, or immoral perhaps, to draw the color line farther down the spectrum, but it certainly is more logical. And neater.

An embarrassment to white supremacy and a dilemma of categories in apartheid's theoretical framework, the Coloreds have also become a potential force for change in South Africa's racial stalemate. They have felt the sting of apartheid as a personal insult perhaps more than any other ethnic group in South Africa over the past decade. Their essential status and rights have been more deeply affected by a generation of Nationalist rule than have those even of the black majority. Africans started out with almost nothing to lose. The Coloreds had voting rights, could live in central city areas, and had a chance to slip across the social color bar occasionally by "passing for white" at movie theaters and other places. All of that has been taken away, and little has been given to replace it. As this has happened, frustration and bitterness have replaced the once legendary lassitude of Coloreds.

The confluence of apartheid with the Coloreds' taking a greater share in the growing South African economy has succeeded in fashioning the Colored population not into a nation, as apartheid would have it, but into an economic interest group that is slowly developing cohesion as an emerging bourgeoisie.

But this has not completely resolved the ambiguous position of the mulatto in a polarized white-black society. There is still apprehension among Coloreds about their fate should the black majority come to power. The alliance that apartheid is forcing them into with the country's 15 million Africans is a tenuous and uneasy one. But it is growing more firm with each new apartheid measure that is passed.

The Colored elite denies bitterly that there is a Colored race, or nation, or even a group with special interests. When a white Cape Town newspaper tried in 1969 to produce a special daily section of Colored news in an effort to build up circulation, community leaders bitterly protested. They did not want anything to increase their visibility as a separate group, and thus their separation from white society. "We're not a race," one of the Coloreds told a white editor on the paper. "We are a shadow of you." The newspaper dropped the idea.

Definitions of what a Colored actually is vary. Perhaps the best came from the Colored leader who said: "A Colored person is one who is discriminated against in a particular sort of way."

If you ask a white government official charged with overseeing Colored affairs what the legal definition of a Colored is, he is apt to reply: "A person who is not white, and who is not Bantu." It may sound like a bad knock-knock joke, but it is a very precise summation of the Colored's legal and social existence. But like much of the official jargon South African bureaucrats use to discuss race, the answer helps avoid the real problem; Coloreds are in fact both white and black.

If you ask a Colored man when his "race" began, he is apt to reply: "Nine months after the first Dutch settler put ashore and saw a Hottentot woman." It is only a slightly exaggerated response.

Nearly 90 per cent of South Africa's two million Coloreds live in the Cape Province. There are also concentrations of them around Johannesburg and Pretoria and the Transvaal farmlands.

Their origins are complex. The first Coloreds resulted more from the seventeenth-century liaisons between whites and the slaves that the Dutch brought to the Cape from Malaya, India, Ceylon, and other parts of Africa than mixing between whites and indigenous tribes. Gradually, a mélange of ancestry developed as the Hottentots and Bushmen mixed with the half-caste offsprings who, while they were not subject to slavery, were not accepted by white society, either.

There were perhaps 10,000 mulattos living around Cape Town at the beginning of the 1830s, when slavery was abolished in South Africa by an act of the British Parliament. It was from this point that the Coloreds seemed to develop as a separate group, with whites tending to mix sexually with Coloreds rather than Africans — thus "breeding" the Cape Coloreds "whiter."

In private, Coloreds gleefully tell visitors of what they say was the role of their ancestors on the Great Trek of the Boers. "There was at least one Colored in every wagon," a Colored professional man told me. "That is why you have so many 'Black Afrikaners' today in the Transvaal." One does encounter a number of white supremacists with dark complexions in South Africa, but it is a touchy historical point with the Afrikaners and not the kind of subject a visiting correspondent, on a limited visa, digs into very deeply.

The Coloreds led a largely unfettered life in the Cape. Males were entitled to vote, just as were whites, if they had a good income and education. The Cape government raised the income levels when Coloreds and the Cape's few Africans began making more money, but it was done good-naturedly, and for all the races. The 1909 compromise on Union killed their theoretical right to sit in Parliament, but their right to vote was entrenched in the Constitution, meaning that a two-thirds majority of both House and Senate was needed to disenfranchise them.

In 1927, the first official sign that the existence of the Colored community was considered a danger, or an affront, to racial purity, appeared with the passage of the first Immorality Act. But it did not directly concern the Coloreds. It made extramarital relations between whites and Africans illegal. They, as the English were to do much later, felt it was the African's problem.

In World War II, the Coloreds were recruited and organized into separate units, handling transport. Before 1948, race relations in the Cape were easygoing and tolerant. Social custom dictated many restrictions on Coloreds, but there were few legal ones. They rode the same buses, lived in their own district in the middle of town, and could aspire to send the brightest of their children to the white, English-speaking University of Cape Town.

All of that was in another era, South Africa's B.A. era — Before Apartheid. Soon after taking power, the Afrikaners set out methodically to spin the web of segregation around the Coloreds and to cut them off from identifying with white South Africa.

The 1950 Immorality Act became one of the cornerstones of apartheid. There is little point, as several commentators have suggested, of making people sit on separate park benches if they have just left the same bed. Parliament forbade whites to copulate with nonwhites, including Coloreds. And there was no need to put in the "extramarital" proviso. Parliament had the year before made it a crime for a white man to marry a woman the state considered nonwhite, or vice versa.

(Breyten Breytenbach, perhaps the best poet ever to write in Afrikaans, made the mistake of falling in love with and marrying an Indonesian girl while living in Paris. In 1967 Breytenbach, a nonpolitical man, found that he could not go home again. The government refused to give his wife a visa.)

The National Party also established the Population Register in 1950. Every South African was to be officially categorized by race and was required to carry an identification document specifying his race: White, Colored, or Native. A major bureaucracy was created to decide who went on which side of what line, a problem particularly acute for Coloreds toward the whiter end of the spectrum and whites who might have had a strain of nonwhite ancestry that apartheid detectives could ferret out. The Afrikaner's concern with identification — his own and that of others — is reflected in the harsh application of apartheid to the mulatto population. The bureaucracy of apartheid handles personal relations on a day to day basis, down to the smallest detail, and frees the white South African from the wearying (and perhaps guilt-producing) process of making personal decisions about whom he will associate with, and on what grounds. This is the snare that has caught all "nonwhites," but especially the Coloreds.

THE COLORED NATION

The hardest part of the Nationalist campaign was breaking the constitutional guarantee of the Coloreds' right to vote for members of Parliament. In 1956, after packing the country's highest appellate court and enlarging the Senate with Nationalist appointees, the government managed to get the Coloreds off the common voters roll. Four seats in Parliament were set aside for whites elected by Coloreds. The Colored electorate consistently and overwhelmingly voted for vocal foes of apartheid. The Nationalists apparently wearied of this opposition and abolished the right of Coloreds to vote for Parliament in 1968.

Even with its passion for categorizing, the Afrikaner bureaucracy has had difficulties with its own creation, the Colored nation. Conceding the diversity of the group, the government set up seven subcategories, including Malays, Cape Colored, Griquas, Chinese, Indian, and a convenient "Other Colored" that is certainly a heresy against Verwoerd's rigorous racial compartments.

All of these groups now have one thing in common. The swarthy illiterate field hand and the light-skinned doctor virtually indistinguishable from a white except for his identity card are equally nonwhite in front of the law. Neither may go to the beaches that have been classified as white, or ride the buses reserved for white, or think about sending children to a white university. All of that, and more, has been wiped away by apartheid.

Apartheid has turned into an attempt to negate the white heritage of the mulattos, largely against the mulattos' will. They are defined in negative terms only — *non*whites. This being the case, the government must have a clear definition of what a white is before it can proceed to define the rest of the country's population. But it is exactly this task that the Coloreds so greatly complicate. The confusions that arise in South African life range from the comic to the grim, as the cases of Carol Busch's autographed thigh and Susan Kirk's loss of her identity card illustrate.

Percy Sledge, the American soul singer, had been touring the country while I was in South Africa and playing to packed houses of nonwhites. Sledge, as a foreign black, got white treatment, including the right to go to a private multiracial cocktail party in the swank hotel where he was staying in Cape Town. As he signed autographs, nineteen-year-old Carol Busch came up and asked Sledge to sign her thigh. "I put my foot forward, lifted my mini, and he did the rest," Miss Busch recalled later. "It was beautiful. I was in ecstasy."

The photographs of Sledge and the girl's light-skinned thigh that appeared in the press the next day did not bring much joy to Afrikanerdom. "This is what our country is coming to under the present regime," one right-wing Parliament member thundered. "In white hotels black men are writing on young white girls' thighs." An outcry from the Afrikaans press followed — until it was revealed that Miss Busch was classified as a Colored.

Once safely categorized as nonwhite, Miss Busch's attractive leg sank from view as an issue. The link between her and Sledge had not been altered, but the implications of it had, in the eye of the National Party. "Just leave my thigh out of the politics," Miss Busch asked the Nationalists.

Miss Kirk's case was reported in the admirably lean prose of the South African Institute of Race Relations Annual Survey of 1969:

Miss Susan Kirk is a blonde with blue eyes who lives in Brakpan. She and her parents and grandmother have always lived as whites, and have white identity cards. Miss Kirk mislaid her card, however, and applied for another. Meanwhile she married a white man. But the new identity card stated that she was Colored, and officials confirmed that she had been reclassified.

Her husband then applied successfully for their marriage to be annulled in accordance with the Mixed Marriages Act. Miss Kirk lost her job.

In 1970, a disabled World War II veteran was "downgraded" from white to Colored after a complaint and his meager pension cut in half.

"Coloreds more than anybody else in our society feel exposed," W. J. M. van Heerden, the Cape Afrikaner who was ostracized after taking up the Coloreds' cause in Parliament, told me. "The Africans became attuned a long time ago to the insult of segregation. And Africans have a stoical power. They can maintain their dignity despite everything, because of their knowledge of their long-term power potential, and their own culture and identity.

"But the Colored . . . well, each time he can't go to the beach he used to go to, or ride a bus, or is told he has to move, the insult is still fresh . . . It still stings."

Van Heerden, a round, affable little man, articulate and alert, probably knew the Colored community better than any other white man in the country. When I went to meet one of the Colored political leaders who had been under government pressure in recent years, he began the conversation by saying, "I wouldn't have given you the time of day except that van Heerden said you were all right. We just don't talk to white men anymore. Look where it has got us."

But van Heerden said that it was increasingly difficult even for him to judge the mood of the Coloreds.

"The tragedy is that they wanted to play ball with the whites. But they've got nothing for their good behavior. Apartheid is telling them that their attempt to move 'white' has failed. In time, they have to move toward the blacks. This bloody government is just increasing the odds against itself."

This ambivalence is part of a much greater uncertainty among the Coloreds about their identity and future in the racial riddle of South Africa. Their history indicates that they, like most mulatto people of the world, have identified "up" the social and economic scale, in this case with whites, rather than "down." There is little question that few of them see much advantage in changing the domination of a white group that outnumbers them two to one for that of a black group that outnumbers them seven to one, especially as many believe that the black majority tends to see them as part of the oppressing white society.

They have few points of contact with the black mass. Coloreds generally do not work in the mines or in industry in the Transvaal. In the Cape Town area there are only about 100,000 Africans. "Around here, African is largely a word," a Colored educator told me. "They come here only as garbage collectors, or farm hands, since the whites won't let them come to do anything else. It is a little difficult for us to identify with that."

Social values of the Colored community suggest a very definite white bias, with lighter-complexioned children being assumed to be the brightest. M. G. Whisson, a lecturer at the University of Cape Town, has said that fluency in English is also one of the highest status symbols for Coloreds. Most poor Coloreds speak Afrikaans, or an Afrikaans patois known as Gamtaal. Afrikaans is rejected by the Colored elite as the language of both the visible oppressor and the oppressed.

Whisson suggests that Coloreds may be more prepared to accept a society built on white supremacy than Africans. It would at least give them feelings of superiority to the black mass.

THE DORMANT VOLCANO?

The most bitter segment of the Colored community today is predictably those at the white end of the scale, who have seen the line they could easily drift across suddenly become a wall. These are the Coloreds that I talked to for the most part, and they still want badly to assimilate into white society. But apartheid's relentless destruction of their bridges into the white world may, in time to come, drastically alter their firm alliance with the white man, if it has not already begun to do so. Certainly, Colored leaders are now looking for alternatives for acceptance in the white fortress the National Party says it will build.

Some of them just give up on South Africa. Between 1965 and 1970, about 5000 Coloreds emigrated from the country. Many of them were teachers or other professionals who went to Canada or Australia, where they would not face officially condoned prejudice and large gaps between what they and white colleagues were paid. While they leave, the South African government encourages Europeans to come to South Africa in a bid to fill such jobs and to raise the white population. This perhaps more than anything else grates on the Coloreds. Here is one reaction from an upper-middle-class Colored man I met:

"They bring these goddamned Italians and Greeks here who can't begin to speak any of the languages of the country and treat them equal. I speak English, Afrikaans, Gamtaal, and a little Xhosa and have lived here all my life, and I'm not good enough to ride on the same bus with those bastards? Don't talk to me about apartheid being a way to preserve a culture or nationalism. It is a way of preserving the white man's ass. And a lot of us are beginning to think we ought to learn how to kick that ass all over the place."

NOT QUITE WHITE   III

I asked about thirty Coloreds, most of them considered community leaders, this question and promised them anonymity: If there were a black uprising, which side would Coloreds fight on?

A small majority answered, in the representative words of one, "We would go with the blacks. Either way, we lose, but at least we'd pay those white bastards back." Others, who asserted that theirs was a majority view of the population, guessed: "We would stay neutral. Coloreds will think again before fighting for the white man. We did it in the last war, and what did we get? Apartheid and lower pensions."

For a virtual nongroup, like the Coloreds, these kinds of predictions may be largely meaningless. It is still far from clear that John X. Merriman, Prime Minister of the Cape Colony, will eventually be proven correct in his 1910 prediction that denying rights to South Africa's Coloreds would "build a volcano, the suppressed force of which must some day burst forth in a destroying flood, as history warns it has always done."

But it is clear that there are new pressures building within the Colored community in South Africa that could seriously challenge the Nationalist government's apparent calculation that providing material gains and some protection to the Coloreds will neutralize the resentments over the social and political restrictions they face.

Apartheid's restrictions hit the Coloreds just as they were making rapid strides up the economic ladder and beginning to shake loose from a shiftless, no-good image whites in the Cape had fastened on them.

"Before they were a Cannery Row kind of people, always sitting around on doorsteps with bottles of wine in their hands," Harvey Tyson, assistant editor of the *Cape Argus* newspaper said. "Now they have taken off economically in an amazing way. They have shown that they really want to get ahead."

There are still plenty of wine bottles scattered across Colored doorsteps. In 1970, South Africans consumed forty-seven million gallons of wine. Almost 90 per cent of the consumption was of the cheap, fifty U.S. cents a liter bottle that is sold almost exclusively to Coloreds.

South Africans by any standards are hard-drinking people. But the suggestion that the Coloreds, 10 per cent of the population, may consume 90 per cent of the wine is a good indication of one of their principal social problems. E. J. Kahn of *The New Yorker*, noting the "truly heroic rate of alcoholism" the Coloreds have attained, quotes statistics showing a rate for Africans as four per thousand and for whites five per thousand. For Coloreds it is thirty-five per thousand.

Much of this stems from the "tot" system. White farmers have traditionally given their Colored laborers part of their wages in cheap wine, which the white farmer bottles or buys for next to nothing from his neighbors. "We start them at four-thirty in the morning and by the end of the day they are through two bottles of cheap wine," an Afrikaner farmer in the Cape told one of his relatives. Later the relative commented to me, "The Colored men on the farms are almost completely emasculated. They have nothing to protect them, and no way of protecting their women."

Disillusionment and despair also have been hallmarks of the males in the urban Colored population (now about 70 per cent of the total). In the 1950s, many of them tended to be unemployed drifters, and it was the women who held families and households together. They went to work as domestics and then garment-factory workers and within the last five years shop girls, cashiers, and telephone operators as white labor was pulled up into better positions by the rapidly expanding South African economy.

In the 1970s their daughters began to take even more of these jobs. More importantly perhaps, their husbands have also joined in the country's economic surge and Colored unemployment rates have dropped. Colored parents now, more than ever in the past, aspire for more education and better job opportunities for their sons.

THE ECONOMIC SURGE

Apartheid has allowed Coloreds to straddle the legal and customary color bars that reserve skilled and semiskilled jobs for white labor. Some "Colored jobs" are even protected by law from African competition, just as the "white jobs" are protected. Employers say it is easier to get an exemption from the government to hire, or promote, a Colored to a job for which no white worker is available than to try to put an African in that slot. Coloreds can belong to unions that have the right to bargain with management, but Africans cannot.

Wages also reflect this three-tier labor sandwich that has the Coloreds as its middle layer. A white editor in Johannesburg told me that the liberal publishing firm he worked for paid 340 rand ($476) a month to a Colored editor "who does the same job, only much better," as a white editor earning 470 rand ($658) a month. A ranking African colleague of theirs, with a different title but much the same responsibilities, received rand 130 ($196) monthly.

In Cape Town, firms routinely advertise for "slightly Colored girls" to work as receptionists. They will be accepted by the firm's clients as white, but they will get about half the salary a white woman would. Africans, of course, need not apply.

Part of the reason the Coloreds have been able to jump back and forth across the labor color bar is that they are employed primarily in industry, which developed later and along less racially rigid lines than the more traditional economic sections of mining and commerce. The most important occupations for Coloreds are, for women, in garment manufacturing factories, and for men, on the production lines of the country's automobile assembly plants.

The rising affluence of Coloreds has produced an interesting public relations bonus for the government. When South Africans argue, as they often do officially and privately, that "nonwhites in South Africa make better wages than workers in Mexico, or Greece" or some other area, and that "South African nonwhites own more automobiles than all the people in the Soviet Union," it is important to keep in mind that they are lumping the Coloreds together with the much poorer black majority.

The economic progress has also fostered an often unspoken but discernible ambivalence about apartheid among many Coloreds. Sometimes you come away from a discussion with the impression that for the Coloreds the main thing wrong with apartheid is that it is now being applied to them, too.

"If there hadn't been job reservation, a lot of us Colored people wouldn't be working right now. If there hadn't been influx control, we would have been swamped by the Bantu," says Tom Swartz, a pro-apartheid political figure in the Colored community.

Swartz's comment underlines a perhaps unintended accomplishment of apartheid. It has fashioned the Coloreds into a broad economic interest group by exempting them from many of the harshest economic restrictions while refusing to give them a completely fair economic deal. The general anguish and frustration that Coloreds have in the past expressed in the heavy drinking and indolence are now crystallizing around economic issues. A future white government may be creative enough to channel this discontent away from political or more violent expression. John Vorster's government has given no suggestion, however, that it can do so.

Apartheid, as practiced against the Coloreds, strikes most directly at the two areas most vital to a rising bourgeoisie —property and education. Just as a conversation with an Afrikaner invariably leads you, if you are an American, to the subject of race, the Coloreds will immediately tell you about District Six and how their children are being cheated in apartheid's schools.

The Group Areas Act, first passed in 1950 and broadened considerably since, has been used to drive Coloreds out of the cities and deprive them of property they have owned for years. The government simply zones an area as "white," takes it over, and settles the Coloreds in ghettos far from town. Compensation is sometimes fair, sometimes not.

This is what happened to District Six in Cape Town, and it has been the bitterest pill of all for Coloreds to swallow. Despite its slum characteristics, District Six occupied one of the city's choicest downtown sites, commanding a magnificent view of Table Bay, and including a number of good middle-class Colored homes. But Coloreds have been gradually transferred out to the bleak Cape Flats, twenty miles from town.

"What is the use of building anything anywhere?" said a Colored man who lives in Paarl, a large town between Stellenbosch and Cape Town. There were eighty-four Colored property owners in this area, and during the 1970 election they had been told they would have to move, that their school would have to go, that they would be relocated because the whites would come to live on the land they now occupied. "They can always move us again when they decide they want that land, too. What the hell is the use of anything in this country anymore?"

Port Elizabeth is one of South Africa's major industrial cities. Most of the large automobile assembly plants are located there. On March 7, 1971, perhaps 20,000 Coloreds gathered in Port Elizabeth's soccer stadium to protest a bus fare increase. Police arrested a Colored man for drinking (it was Sunday), and within minutes a stone-throwing mob of 2000 people had surrounded the local police station. The police, using pistols, dogs, sten guns, tear gas, and baton charges to break up the crowd, shot ten persons, none fatally. Twenty policemen were injured.

The Coloreds who had gathered to protest the bus fare increase were not accustomed to riding buses in the first place. They had been rezoned out of the city's industrial area and forced by the government to move to areas where they had to ride the government's buses and then asked to pay higher fares. "That was the last straw," a Colored clergyman said after the riot.

Many Coloreds are convinced that "their" university, established at Bellville, is far inferior to the white ones that they were eligible to attend before the Nationalists moved to establish racially pure universities. More important is the effect the last decade has had at lower levels, as the migration of teachers and government harassment of others who dissented openly from apartheid has drained from Colored schools many of its best instructors.

BROWN POWER

In 1968, the government banned multiracial political parties. In the same year, Colored representation in Parliament was abolished and the Coloreds given instead a partially elected Colored Persons Representative Council, which has limited advisory powers on Colored affairs. As with the other nonwhite groups, a white bureaucratic machine, the Department of Colored Affairs is the real governing power in Colored lives.

"The assumption was that the Coloreds wouldn't vote, since everybody could see the thing was a fraud," M. D. Arendse, a squat, fiftyish man said as we chatted in his cluttered office above a radio repair shop on one of the Cape Town's less distinguished streets.

"The people have always boycotted this kind of thing, because all we want is a multiracial society. But the government made a mistake this time. They gave us a legal party, legal meetings, a legal voice of dissent. And we decided to use it."

Arendse, who ran a variety of ill-defined enterprises out of the office and had the glibness of a wheeler-dealer, had been one of the main forces in building the Labour Party, which swept twenty-six of the forty elected seats in the Representative Council's first election, in 1969, on a strong anti-apartheid stand. But a few days before I saw him, in April 1970, Arendse had become one of the first casualties of the new rumblings of Brown Power in South Africa. He had been deposed by the party as its leader.

"These young people," Arendse explained, "they say, M. D. Arendse is a good chap, he knows his onions, but he is too slow. This younger element wants things done. They don't want to negotiate slowly for what's due to them now. I favor talking with Vorster. They don't. They are, well, more radical."

One of the "younger element" is the Stellenbosch insurance salesman, David Curry, who had been elected deputy leader of the party in 1970. He quickly emphasizes that the Labour Party leaders are not radical, or militant, as the terms are understood elsewhere. A prudent man, Curry seems aware that while Coloreds can speak more freely than Africans, they can still wind up in detention if they are too outspoken.

Saying several times that his group was "against violence in any form," Curry portrayed the Labour Party as "working to keep the anti-apartheid movement in the country alive, and to keep multi-racialism as an ideal in front of the people." The economy was the key, he said. By organizing labor and buying power, Coloreds will be able eventually to make political demands, and, if necessary, establish a political alliance with the black majority. "They [the whites] have put us in the same boat. We might as well row together."

Curry's ideas were at that point perhaps a bit nebulous, which may be a very good state for a nonwhite's ideas to be in when talking to a stranger about politics in South Africa. But the voice of the Labour Party was, in 1970, one of the few that South Africa's culture of the powerless could use to sound its frustrations from beneath the silenced surface. And the Coloreds-only political machinery was one of the few tools that could be used against apartheid, since it was itself a creature of apartheid. "The only thing nonwhites can do now is to call the white man's bluff," a Colored educator had said as we talked in his home. "We can show that apartheid is a sham, a fake, a fraud, by embarrassing the government." He referred to the Labour Party's victory in the Colored Persons Representative Council election in 1969. John Vorster had been forced to overturn the election results by using his appointments to pack the Council with pro-apartheid supporters like Tom Swartz, who had been defeated in his own constituency by a five to one margin, but who wound up as head of the Council.

"You say that is undemocratic, perhaps," Swartz replied when I asked about the composition of the Council. "I concede that it is undemocratic. But I didn't do it. Any questions about it will have to be directed to Mr. Vorster. Surely no one expects the government to put its enemies in power. They had to turn to reasonable men, and that is why we were appointed."

One of apartheid's greatest puzzles is this: Why has the National Party rejected the Colored elite, which they could have bought off easily? The Cape Afrikaners have been asking this since 1950 and have expressed open anguish on the treatment of the Coloreds. The Verligtes within the party generally favor counting at least part of the Coloreds as the white world instead of shoving them out. There are frequent wrangles within the party over the issue and contradictory statements from Cabinet members over the government's "solution" to the Colored problems.

It is a problem that is growing. The 1970 census showed that the Colored population increase was almost double that of the white. Two million coloreds produced as many babies as four million whites in the last ten years. Projections indicate that by the end of the century there will be as many Coloreds as whites in South Africa, six million each.

In Cape Town by the year 2000 the white population will have doubled to 633,000; the nonwhite population will have grown from its present 600,000 to 2,258,000.

The present government has no answer when asked where the Coloreds will find their "separate freedoms," as all racial groups are supposed to do when apartheid is in place. All John Vorster could tell his white Parliament, when pressed on it a few years ago, was that "our children after us will have to find a solution."

"Mr. Vorster may not think so," one Colored man told me as we strolled in District Six and watched afternoon fog spilling down from Table Mountain, "but my children, and millions of black children, will also decide the future of this country."

A COLORED FOOTNOTE

I have committed the same folly that the apartheid administrators commit in lumping Malays, Chinese, Indians, and others in with the Colored population in this chapter. Their differences with each other and with the mulattos is at least as great, and in fact probably greater, than their differences with the whites. It is even more meaningless to call them Colored than it is to apply the term to the mulattos, since they have identifiable cultures and ethnic backgrounds that they have retained rather than assimilated with other groups, even when this was permitted.

The most obviously perplexing group for the government are the Chinese. Their number is less than 10,000, so small that there are no separate housing areas for them, or other separate amenities. For the average South African they are virtually indistinguishable from the visiting Japanese businessmen, classified by the government as "honorary whites" because of the booming trade between Japan and South Africa. The government has tended not to apply apartheid rules to Chinese strictly unless a white complains. Then, out they go from the tennis match, restaurant, or even children's nursery, as in one case in 1970. I sat in an excellent Chinese restaurant in Johannesburg enjoying a meal until I suddenly realized that if I invited the pretty Chinese girl behind the cash register to sit down with me I would be breaking the law. My appetite disappeared.

The most important group within the Colored umbrella is composed of 600,000 Indians. They are descendants of indentured workers who were brought to Natal at the end of the nineteenth century for the sugar cane plantations because, as South African author Stuart Cloete has so adroitly written, "the local Bantu [Zulus] being found unreliable and heavy-handed workers."

As in East Africa, the Indians have established themselves as the small merchants and artisans of many areas of South Africa. The Indians have often been called the Jews of both areas.

The Verwoerd government's policy was to encourage them to repatriate, and free passage to India was offered. There were few takers, however. Apartheid supporters assert that this proved that apartheid is at least more desirable than the desperate poverty of India. Indians say it is because South Africa is now their home and India is a foreign land to them. The answer is probably a mixture, of uncertain proportions, of both.

The government is particularly quick to repress any political movements within the Indian community. Indian intellectuals played a leading role in organizing and financing some of the political parties that gained independence in East and Central Africa, although that role, for nationalistic reasons, has not yet been acknowledged. Indians have also long been politically active in South Africa. Mahatma Gandhi helped found the Natal Indian Congress Party in the eighteen nineties. The young lawyer had come to South Africa to fight a specific legal case, but he stayed twenty years and developed passive resistance tactics that would later help India win independence.

Despite the catastrophic race riots in Durban in 1949, when Zulu youths went on a rampage and killed 130 Indians in a week of looting and disorder, Indians continued to work in the passive resistance campaigns sponsored by the African National Congress in the early nineteen fifties.

As a group, they are perhaps the most affluent and sophisticated of South Africa's "nonwhites," although there is a great range of social and economic conditions within the Indian community. Since apartheid resembles a caste system, and since Indian communities have voluntarily segregated themselves from other ethnic groups in other countries in Africa, they are not as deeply affected by apartheid's social restrictions as are other groups. But the restrictions on education and being able to choose their own living areas (like the Coloreds in Cape Town, Indians are being chased out of the center of Durban) appears to them to be especially cruel, since they have money enough to establish good residential areas and children bright and well schooled enough to hold their own in white colleges and universities.

Chapter Five

Law and Order

AFRICAN NATIONALISM, the force that was supposed to end white minority rule in South Africa, folded under a hail of gunfire at Sharpeville in 1960. The black revolution was aborted; the white counterrevolution began. A decade later, the crushing of important open opposition to white supremacy was virtually complete.

Black political movements no longer exist above ground, although one of the continent's first and most sophisticated parties was founded here as long ago as 1912. Passive resistance and non-violent protest by nonwhites is forsaken, although Gandhi had originated both tactics in this country more than half a century before. White liberals in South Africa, who had been the most outspoken in all of Africa about the need for a multiracial society and integration, have been coerced into exile, into silence, or into ineffective, bitter shrillness. "They have reduced us to making snide gestures," one told me sadly.

Even gestures become the target of government reprisal. "Yes, it is legal to invite Africans to your house for dinner," one white English-speaker told me, "as long as you don't serve them any whiskey, and make sure they leave in time for the ten P.M. curfew. But I don't do it anymore. The last time I did, a policeman dropped around the next day to chat about my views on Communism. The Africans told me later they had been picked up for questioning. I don't want trouble, and I don't want to expose them, because they can get hurt so badly. It isn't worth keeping up my credentials as a liberal, which is all I was accomplishing anyway."

Enforcing the political code of apartheid has become one of the main tasks of the government's vast internal security network now that the immediate threat of a black takeover seems to have receded. But the heavy fist remains in operation as well. Black people continue to disappear in the middle of the night after police visits. The police, backed by a wide range of vaguely worded laws and the tacit assurance from Parliament that any others the police want will be passed, detain people indefinitely, incommunicado, without giving public notice of the arrest or charge.

White dissidents are usually treated more gently and with innovative techniques of "soft repression" that are likely to become models for future authoritarian states that want to preserve an image of orderliness. A white critic may be placed under house arrest. Another will be forbidden to make any public statements. In both cases, they become nonpersons for five years or longer.

Surprisingly for many outsiders, South Africa has not always been a police state and is not completely one now. Law and order exist in South Africa. The one has little to do with the other, however. Law is a courtroom nicety, reserved for white folks and those Africans whose cases come to public notice. Order is the urgent necessity, meted out by an unfettered police force to the black masses and those whites who sacrifice their protective coloration by becoming staunch integrationists.

Thus, in 1970, nineteen Africans charged with conspiring to commit sabotage were acquitted by an independent judge who said the government had not made its case. And thus they were immediately rearrested before they could leave the courtroom and placed in detention again under almost exactly the same charge by the same policemen who had been accused of torturing some of the nineteen. Brought to trial a second time, acquitted a second time, some of them were placed under house arrest. The Cabinet minister who ordered this said the house arrests did not conflict with the two acquittals. "Restriction is not imposed as a penalty for previous actions," said Justice Minister Petrus C. Pelser. "It is aimed at the prevention of subversive actions in the future." Secretly, at least one of the nineteen, a black news photographer, was rearrested and held for another six months before he was finally released.

This dichotomy is largely the result of the British-Boer division in white society. The courts are independent, at the higher levels at least.[1] They are English in temperament, if not in ethnic composition. At the same time, they are much weaker than the Afrikaner-controlled Parliament and the Afrikaner police force. Courts in South Africa cannot overturn or question laws passed by Parliament, including those that curb the judiciary's right to investigate allegations of police misconduct. The law remains partly intact, to be trotted out for visitors to prove that South Africa is not really a closed state. But the visitor should not think that law will prevent the government from jailing any person it thinks should be jailed.

All internal security forces are to some extent creatures of politics. The French police demonstrated this when they stopped bashing Algerians and their leftist supporters in the streets of Paris in 1961 and turned to setting up roadblocks to trap the rightists who were trying to topple de Gaulle. Americans learned it later when the Federal Bureau of Investigation, which had played a key role in reining in the Ku Klux Klan under the Kennedys, switched to infiltrating the Students for a Democratic Society under Nixon and Mitchell. Even so, the South African police force is remarkable in this respect. It has served the essentially unchanging viewpoint of the National Party for more than twenty-two years. More than 85 per cent of the country's 17,500 white police regulars[2] are

[1] Official attitudes on race may be a factor in sentencing, however. Of the eighty-nine people executed in South Africa in 1970, sixty-nine were Africans, twenty were Coloreds, and none was white. Between 1910 and 1970 there appear to have been only five cases in South Africa in which whites were executed for the murder of nonwhites, and no white seems to have been hanged for the rape of a nonwhite, although whites more often rape nonwhites than vice versa. Barend van Niekerk, the South African law professor who published these results of his research in 1970, was hauled into court on a charge of contempt, lectured by a judge who told him that "the judges go out of their way to interpret the law in such a way as to benefit the nonwhite," and then acquitted.
[2] There are about 17,000 white police reservists in South Africa trained to go on duty in emergencies. There are about 13,000 regular African policemen, including five who are commissioned lieutenants. They were told in 1970 that they would always be outranked by the lowliest white police recruit.

thought to be Afrikaners and come mostly from the lower economic and social classes that need little encouragement to identify with the government's white supremacy policies. How much of their extralegal work, such as visits to the houses of white liberals who entertain Africans, is spontaneous and how much is encouraged by the government is unclear. It is also immaterial. The goals, tactics, and political views of the Parliament and the police force are exactly the same. They are both part of the machine "created by Providence . . . to run the country," as Professor N. J. J. Olivier put it. No act done to protect the Afrikaner nation can be an abuse of power. And if justice is rough at times, that's the way it has always been on the frontier.

South African police shot and killed 54 people in 1970. According to government statistics, 149 white policemen were convicted by courts of assault in 1969; three were dismissed from the force. Of 165 African policemen similarly convicted, five were dismissed. Forty thousand prisoners were sentenced to whipping in 1969. South Africa's 89 hangings in 1970 accounted for about half the total known judicial executions in the world. (All of those executed had been convicted of violent crimes.)

The police are the cutting edge of the effort to break internal black opposition to the government. They are powerful and greatly feared by Africans, many of whom are convinced they will be tortured or perhaps killed by the police if they are arrested for political activities. Although the government denies that South African police mistreat prisoners, the record of the past few years indicates that Africans held under security laws develop unusual and often fatal habits, or perhaps even suicidal tendencies, while in the hands of the South African police. In 1969, for example, nine men being detained without trial in security cases died.

Solomon Modipane slipped on a piece of soap in a police shower, received "certain injuries," and died. Nicodiumus Kgoathe was arrested in the same case and met the same fate. He was given a shower break by his Security Police interrogators and also slipped, suffering a serious concussion. Before he died, he told a doctor that he had been assaulted by the police. The doctor, testifying at an inquest, said that the marks and lacerations he found on Kgoathe's body were more consistent with a beating. But the government-appointed magistrate conducting the inquest said he had no reason to suspect foul play and closed the case.

The death of Imam Abdullah Haron, a Moslem leader of the Cape Town Colored community and an outspoken critic of apartheid, was also certified to have been from natural causes. Detained under the Terrorism Act on May 28, he died on September 27. His widow, aided by two women members of Parliament, pressed for an inquest. The police testified that their clumsy prisoner fell down a flight of stairs just before he died. A pathologist testified that the twenty-six separate bruises that covered every part of the Imam's body could not have been caused by a single fall. Some of them were much older than others. Again, the magistrate absolved the police.[3]

Joel Carlson, a white Johannesburg attorney, told me that there had been at least eighteen deaths of persons being detained without trial under security laws between 1965 and 1970. One man jumped from a seventh-floor window of a room where he was being interrogated.

The death of another, James Lencoe, was a little more complicated. When he was dragged from his house in Soweto in the middle of the night, he left behind his only belt, his widow said later. A week passed, and police came to collect her husband's pass and the belt. The next day Lencoe hanged himself, with that belt, from the bars of his cell. Carlson, who handled several of these cases, arranged an autopsy that produced strong evidence that Lencoe received an electric shock on the day he died. Again, no investigation resulted.

Asked for details of such deaths, the government furnished in Parliament a partial list of those who had died in such a manner. It included this description of one of the cases: "An unknown

---

[3] The Imam's widow then took the only course of action left open to relatives of such clumsy prisoners and sued the Minister of Police for civil damages. In June, 1971, the Minister, rather than go to court, settled with the widow for 5000 rand ($7000). Asked about the settlement in Parliament, he denied that this was an admission of guilt.

man died on an unknown date of cause unknown." Joel Carlson commented to me, "Some day, some society will erect a monument to that unknown man."

In short, the breaking of African nationalism as an important force in the nineteen sixties was accomplished largely in the police cells of South Africa. That is where white power begins. It is understandable that many Africans, however, strongly as they may feel about majority rule, feel even more strongly about avoiding the white man's guns, jails, and stairways that they may fall down. The police are carrying out the powers, and the tacit mandate, they have been given by the Parliament, which in turn derives its strength from a white electorate that seems largely satisfied with justice South African style.

Even English-speakers defend their legal system by pointing out that the Afrikaner is by nature a very legalistically minded person. He wants specific authority on the book when he deprives others of their freedom.

For some Afrikaners, this penchant for the word is one of the gravest faults of their people, who have written out and codified their prejudices and disregard for human justice for the whole world to see. Most countries on this continent, and a number in Europe, such as Greece and Portugal, handle such matters as firmly but more discreetly, jailing arbitrarily while protesting their adherence to the rights of mankind. The Afrikaner is more direct than that. This, however, does not change the essential situation, which is that the Parliament has the power to write any law any way it sees fit. South Africa's traditional solution for all problems, the *Star* of Johannesburg noted editorially on June 2, 1971, is "to make a law and send somebody to jail." That is true, and sad enough, as far as it goes. But what happens in some cases is that the police send somebody to jail and then get Parliament to make a law.

The Terrorism Act, passed in 1967, is one example of retroactive legislation. It was made retroactive to 1962 so the state could use it to try thirty-seven Africans who had actually been arrested before the act became law. The thirty-seven, from the disputed territory of South West Africa, could have been tried for common law crimes, such as murder or arson. But the trials would have taken place in South West Africa and attracted more attention. The retroactive clause inserted in the Terrorism Act empowered the state to shift the trials to Pretoria.

The case of Robert Sobukwe, the most important black South African leader not currently in jail, is even more illustrative. Sobukwe, president of the Pan-African Congress and a leader of the antipass campaigns of 1960, was imprisoned that year for inciting others to protest against the law. He received a maximum three-year sentence and was sent to Robben Island, the prison fortress in Cape Town's beautiful Table Bay. Before his sentence expired on May 3, 1963, Parliament passed a law that gave the Minister of Justice the power to keep Sobukwe in prison for another year. The same law was passed every year for the next five years. Finally, in 1969, six years after a court had said he was to be freed, Sobukwe was released from prison, although not from the white security system's grasp.

How many other countries in the world would go through such elaborate and public procedures to keep a political prisoner it considered dangerous in jail? Was this an example of the Afrikaner's innate legalism? Or was it just to help shore up a façade of legal practice around an essentially totalitarian system? There is probably something of both in it. But beyond that, the handling of Sobukwe is just a continuation of the "salami slicing" tactics the government has consciously applied against political opponents over the past two decades. By renewing the extra detention each year, Parliament dangles hope before Sobukwe and his followers. If they are good for a short period things might get better. At the same time, the publicity surrounding the case reminds Africans that if they are not good, things could get very much worse for any of them.

Or it may just be another example of what the outsider comes to see after a period of time as a lack of logic, in the conventional Western sense, within Afrikaner bureaucracy. After his release from prison, Sobukwe was exiled from the Johannesburg area and restricted to a small suburb of Kimberley. He applied for an exit permit — a one-way visa that means he would never be able to re-enter South Africa — to accept a fellowship at the University of Wisconsin. The Minister of the Interior granted Sobukwe permission to leave the country. The Minister of Justice then refused Sobukwe permission to leave Kimberley. This refusal, upheld in South Africa's independent courts, meant that Sobukwe could not get to an airport or harbor. Tantalizing cruelty? Sincere disagreement within the bureaucracy? Or just part of a way of life that other white men will never quite understand?

The extensive restrictions placed on Sobukwe also forbid him to attend any public gathering, enter a school or printing plant, or publicize his opinions by speaking or helping in the preparation of any writing about himself (thus barring newsmen from interviewing him). Details of his lonely existence filter out through friends who visit him, one at a time and under the watchful eye of the policeman who lives next door. The friends tell you what their impressions are, not what Sobukwe says, for that might expose him.

A forty-six-year-old former university lecturer, national tennis singles champion, and the brother of an Anglican bishop, Sobukwe does not seem to have been maltreated physically while in prison. But he did suffer, as most prisoners do, from sensory deprivation during long periods of isolated or semi-isolated confinement. He seems to have feared that his release would make the African population think that he had been broken, that he had sold out and agreed to work with the whites. There is nothing he can do for the black movement now, but he does not think things will stay as quiet as they are.

Sobukwe had been a major figure in an African nationalist movement that had been alive for almost half a century in 1960. But, as it had at the other crucial periods in its troubled history, the movement split in that crisis. It could not present a unified front against white power. The results have been calamitous for the black majority.

Africans, like Coloreds, were given equal voting rights by the British when the Cape Colony was granted responsible government in 1853. The property and income qualifications (25 pounds sterling of property or 50 pounds annual salary) kept most Africans off the voters' roll. But it stirred an interest in politics. In 1910, an African, the Reverend Walter Rubusana, was elected to the Cape Provincial Council from a predominately African district. Four years later, he was defeated by a white candidate when another African, J. T. Javabu, entered the election and split the black vote. Thus did African legislative representation in South Africa come to a quick end.

Shocked by the British compromise on voting rights for non-whites at the Union conference, four African lawyers who had been educated by British missionaries and then trained in universities in England set in motion in 1912 the founding of the African National Congress "for the purpose of creating national unity and defending our rights and privileges." A.N.C., as it was popularly known, was primarily an organization of lawyers, doctors, and African intellectuals. An attempt by the group to lobby against the 1913 Land Act was futile. By 1919, the group had made inroads into the black mining compounds on the Rand and launched the first major passive resistance protest by Africans. More than seven hundred passbooks were burned. Many African miners went on strike. Mounted police charges on the protest crowds, and arrest of strikers, brought the campaign to an end. Soon the A.N.C. was competing with local chiefs, the newly formed Communist Party of South Africa, and a trade union, the Industrial and Commercial Workers Union (I.C.U.) for the allegiance of black South Africa. Throughout the next few decades, these forces fought each other as much as they fought white supremacy. In 1930, when the Communists mounted a pass-burning campaign, the I.C.U. urged Africans not to take part, and it flopped. The Congress opened its membership in 1935 to Indians and Coloreds, but the organization was badly divided in 1936 by the Hertzog government's successful drive to take African voters off the Cape voting rolls and establish an advisory Native Representative Council. Part of the Congress leadership took a moderate line, arguing they could accomplish more by working with the white government than fighting it. Others rejected this and predicted the Council would be ignored by the government. Time proved the uncompromising view to be correct. The eloquent words of the stirring debates in the Council, and its pleas for reform, fell on deaf ears.

The beginning of decolonization in Asia after World War II made the whites take African nationalism seriously. The success of Gandhi's passive resistance in India naturally had a tremendous impact in South Africa. Africans set out to emulate it, and the Afrikaner government set out to make sure that they would not.

Two key attitudes were evident in the clash. The leaders of the A.N.C. did not set out to establish complete black control over South Africa. They were working toward removing many of the restrictions that had been placed on the black majority and getting a share of the government. They may have envisioned eventual black domination, but as late as 1958, Chief A. J. Luthuli, by then leader of the A.N.C., spoke of the danger of seeking to bring to power "a racial majority masquerading as a democratic majority." This meant they were willing to depend heavily on white liberals for leadership and help, which, in the context of the times, may have been an error, one which in any event black leaders of South Africa would not be likely to repeat today.

For the Nationalist government, on the other hand, the maintenance and intensification of white domination, by whatever means necessary, was the only goal. The Nationalists set out to manipulate the law when possible, to bypass it when necessary. Gradually, over two decades, the government established its giant bureaucracy and gave it powers that most developed countries in the non-Communist world entrust only to the judiciary. As we have seen with the urban African population, bureaucrats can order people to change their places of residences, give up their jobs, or leave their families. Higher-ranking bureaucrats and politicians who deal with whites have the power to confine people to their houses for the rest of their lives. Perhaps the only other countries in the world that have trusted their bureaucrats with such powers are the Soviet Union and its allies. In this respect, South Africa resembles them more clearly than the West, or the rest of Africa, a comparison the conservative American allies of South Africa rarely seem to notice.[4]

The government fired the opening salvo in the battle by passing the Suppression of Communism Act in 1950. The act outlawed the Communist Party and gave the Minister of Justice the power to label anyone a Communist and then ban him from political activity. A Communist was defined in the act as anyone who worked to bring political, industrial, social, or economic change in South Africa by the promotion of disturbance or disorder or by unlawful acts or omissions. At the same time, the government set out to prove the supremacy of Parliament over the courts by breaking judicial resistance to removing Colored voters from the common voting roll in the Cape. Once that was accomplished, Parliament and the police were laws unto themselves.

In 1952, the three-hundredth anniversary of Jan van Riebeeck's arrival in South Africa, the A.N.C. launched what was to become the Defiance Campaign, a series of public protests against apartheid. Throughout the remainder of the year African men and women, often manifesting a religious fervor, sought arrest by sitting on park benches marked "Europeans Only." They paraded through train station entrances similarly marked and marched through the streets singing "Jan van Riebeeck has stolen our country" and shouting *"Mayibuye Afrika"* — Come back, Africa. In five months, more than 8000 Africans went to jail. Most of them served one to four weeks. Violence flared toward the end of the year when police and protesters clashed, but for the most part the campaign was peaceful.

The government struck back. It listed as Communists the A.N.C. leaders who had organized the campaign and banned

[4] Ranking police and government officials have said on several occasions that they are justified in using Communist methods to defeat the Communists they claim to be battling. One of the most recent instances was reflected in a June 3, 1971, editorial in the *Star* that twitted Police Minister S. L. Muller for saying that Communism must be fought with its own methods.

them from politics on threat of jail sentences. And it passed an inventive new law, which made it a serious crime to break any other law as an act of protest. Urging others to break a law in protest was also outlawed. Sitting on a park bench might be worth only two weeks in jail, but sitting on a park bench as a protest could mean five years in prison and ten lashes of the whip. The government added to its store of laws forbidding public demonstrations in the next year, and the campaign soon folded. "It is brave and honorable to spend two weeks in jail in protest," one white liberal who dropped out of the campaign in early 1953 told me. "It is something else to go to jail for three years, especially in this country."

The black nationalists and the government spent the next few years sparring. The government staged a series of treason trials against black leaders that produced no convictions, much harassment, and perhaps new stirrings of nationalism. In 1959, Sobukwe and a group of other young men who felt the A.N.C. was too dependent on white allies broke away to form the Pan-African Congress and aligned themselves with more socialistic policies. They voiced some nascent black power attitudes. In March 1960 Sobukwe hastily pre-empted A.N.C. plans for an antipass demonstration that year by calling his own nonviolent campaign beginning on March 21. A.N.C. leaders rejected his invitation to join the campaign. But about 50,000 Africans around the country did gather around police stations to invite arrests for having destroyed their passes. Sobukwe was arrested as the day began.

One of the places Africans gathered to demonstrate was in the African township of Vereeniging, in a Transvaal town called Sharpeville. What triggered the massacre that occurred there that day is a matter of some dispute. The most important facts are clear, however: "At 1:40 P.M. seventy-five members of the South African police force fired about 700 shots into the crowd, killing sixty-nine Africans and wounding 180. Most of them were shot in the back. At 4 P.M. a thundershower washed away the blood in the street outside the police station." [5]

[5] Mary Benson, *The African Patriots*, Encyclopaedia Britannica Press, New York, 1964.

The sparring was over; the grim battle had begun. The deaths themselves were quickly obscured by the reaction to them.

"I honestly thought this was it," a white South African told Cyril Dunn of the London *Observer* in 1970 as they both recalled Sharpeville. "I genuinely believed the revolution, the bloodbath, was about to begin. I laid in stocks of food. I bought gas cylinders for when the power supplies would be cut. Then we all stayed home and waited hourly for news. And nothing happened. Nothing whatever."

From that moment, Dunn's friend observed, the Nationalists realized that the Africans were never going to dislodge the whites from their advanced industrial base and massive resources. It occurred to them, this theory holds, that the "wind of change" had dislodged only those whites weakened by an inherent liberalism. And so they set out to obliterate black resistance and white liberalism.

As African resistance did not materialize, the government invoked emergency regulations and in five months detained more than 13,000 people without trial. One of those detained was Philip Kgosana, a Pan-Africanist official who dispersed a mob in Cape Town after he was promised a meeting with the Minister of Justice to discuss the crisis. When he showed up at the Ministry of Justice, he was arrested, according to historian Leo Marquard.

"Oddly enough, the Africans lost faith in the eloquence, and in the supposed sweet reason of the white man," after Sharpeville, says Professor Julius Lewin. Passive resistance and nonviolence had failed miserably and were abandoned. The younger African political leaders, and some of their quixotic white followers, turned to thoughts of guerrilla warfare and sabotage as, on the other side, the government stepped up its campaign of repression. "It is difficult to keep preaching nonviolence against a government which continually makes savage attacks on people," Nelson Mandela, now serving a life sentence in jail, said at the time. But, as Bernardine Dohrn of the Weathermen was to note in a similar context in America a decade later, it is also dangerous to preach violence against the power structure without possessing the means and knowledge needed to carry it out.

Most of the sabotage attempts were clumsy and ineffectual. One white man was arrested in Port Elizabeth after he had tested his homemade bombs by setting them off in his backyard on quiet Sunday afternoons. Enough were successful, however, to whip white hysteria to a fever pitch. The police, seemingly with reason, blamed a series of fifteen murders of white policemen and civilians, and an equal number of Africans, on an African terrorist organization known as POQO. On July 24, 1964, John Harris, a white schoolteacher who had been banned by the government, placed a bomb on the "whites only" concourse of Johannesburg's railway station. The explosion killed an elderly woman. Another eventual casualty of that blast was the Liberal Party, headed by writer Alan Paton and dedicated to multiracialism. Harris was a member of the small party and it never recovered from the embarrassment.

Parliament responded with increasingly stiffer laws. It moved from the Unlawful Organizations Act, under which African political parties were banned, to the 90-day detention clause, which was followed by the 180-day detention clause. Both have been effectively superseded by the Terrorism Act, with its unlimited detention clause. The Terrorism Act makes it a crime, punishable by death, to hamper any person in maintaining law and order with the intent of endangering the maintenance of law and order in the republic. In other words, it is a very vague law.

Interestingly, it is also permanent. There is nothing in it that indicates it was passed to cope with emergency situations; no time limit is fixed for its operation. South Africa seems to have gone beyond the point of thinking it is involved in a temporary struggle against its own people.

The government has consistently refused to disclose arrests made under the Terrorism Act, or even to disclose the total number of people who have been arrested under it. The figure may have been around 150 by the end of 1970, informed speculation in Johannesburg held, but no one could be sure. No one could be sure, therefore, how many people have been detained or convicted under the country's stringent security laws. Statistics published annually by the South African Institute of Race Relations suggest that as many as 5000 persons are likely to have been jailed under all security laws between 1965 and 1970. The government has acknowledged that the highest number of political prisoners held at one time during that period was 1825. On January 1, 1970, 809 persons were serving prison sentences for security convictions according to a statement made in Parliament by Justice Minister Pelser. Of these, 332 were Africans convicted of sabotage and 337 were Africans imprisoned for belonging to illegal organizations. One representative feature of recent South African law is that if your name is found on a membership list of an "illegal" organization during a police raid, you must then prove that you are not a member of that organization. Otherwise, you are liable to go to jail. Only fourteen whites were in the group, seven for sabotage and seven under the Suppression of Communism Act. The paltry number of white "politicals" and the neat symmetry must be considerable solace for the government.

The Nationalist regime avoids arresting white critics. White public opinion, essentially unconcerned about the lengthy detention of blacks without trial, feels uneasy about such detention of whites. Thus, arrests of whites usually has to be followed by trial. Increased trials of whites might provoke wider discussion and examination of the security laws, which in theory at least apply to the entire country, not just blacks. So the government prefers where possible to cow its white opponents rather than seek a direct confrontation in the courtroom. To do so, the Nationalists have developed a wide range of extrajudicial punitive measures that they apply with great discrimination. The heavy fist deals with open African nationalism, as we have seen. At the other end of the spectrum is what concerns us now — the "soft repression," seen in such devices as banning orders, the lifting of passports, the depriving teachers of the right to teach. These tactics, also used frequently against Africans, are especially dreaded by white liberals.

All of this enables the government to practice a distinct gradation of the stifling of dissent in South Africa. Africans are allowed only the most careful, guarded, and nonpolitical public criticism. Coloreds feel more free to criticize the government, but are hesitant to discuss even peaceful methods of changing it. Whites are free to criticize anything in the country — as long as they do so from an essentially white viewpoint. Mrs. Suzman and the Progressive Party, most editorial writers of the English-language press, and Anglican clergymen are free to argue that there is a saner, more moral, more rational method for whites to govern. They can say that continuing apartheid is folly because it presents a danger to the white community, because it will provoke a black explosion.[6] When whites stray across that line, however, they can expect trouble. If they identify their cause with that of the black majority, if they practice integration in a meaningful way, if they find ways to voice the frustration and anguish of the black majority or work for an organization that has or will produce black leadership, then they can expect to feel the harsh sting of the government. This, it seems to me, is the essence of the myth of freedom of speech in South Africa today.

Even private dissent has been greatly curbed by what many South Africans, black and white, liberal and conservative, see as the increasing intrusion into their lives of the state's security apparatus. By encouraging the belief that there is a vast network of paid informers and secret listening devices spread throughout the country, the Special Branch, or Security Police, ease their jobs considerably.

"You know what we do when we want a new car and need some money?" one African in an urban township asked with a cynical smile. "It's easy, man. We pick out two friends and sell them to the police. Everybody is an informer in this goddamned place." Actually, tips that don't pan out in a big way are worth only 10 rand ($14), another African told me.

"We have two informers in every organization in South Africa," a Security Police agent bragged recently to an English-speaking

---

[6] South African white liberals have a well-deserved reputation for courageously and effectively opposing the government. This discussion is an effort to put it into perspective.

businessman. "One is paid for his information. The other is a pa-
triot. And neither knows which is the other spy or what he is reporting." Some South Africans doubt such claims and think the
police tyranny is tempered considerably by their inefficiency.

I had been warned by South African liberals outside the country to expect to be watched during my visit and not to leave lists of
contacts in my hotel room or luggage. But I never had any experience that suggested any form of surveillance. Resident correspondents told me they assumed their telephones were tapped and
their mail opened. One told me that a few weeks after he had
moved into a new apartment on short notice, three telephone re-
pairmen knocked at his door. He assured them his telephone was
in good order and that he had not complained about service.
They assured him that it needed fixing and proceeded to do so.
"What was the point of arguing?" my colleague asked.

Security policemen routinely attend political party meetings.
"If we get a school principal at one of our meetings or a dance, the
security man is likely to call on him at his office the next day,"
said a leader of the Colored anti-apartheid Labour Party. "Then
we don't get the principal next time." Police also routinely raid
church and student organizations that are critical of apartheid and
cart away all their documents. Since a policeman can enter any
premise where he thinks someone may be in the process of breaking the law, and since there are so many laws to break, search war-
rants are passé in South Africa.

During the 1970 election campaign, Albert Hertzog, leader of
the Verkramptes and former Minister of Post and Telegraphs, accused the Vorster government of tapping the telephones not only
of liberals, but also good Afrikaners. Liberals gathered a sort of
grim satisfaction from all this, because they had always assumed
that Hertzog had been involved in tapping their telephones when
he was in the government. One Security Branch policeman, P. J.
Rudolph, joined Hertzog's party and said that he was quitting the
police force because "there were more investigations into people
on the right of the government than into Communists." The conflict went into limbo after the Verkramptes were trounced in the
election.

If it all seemed like a vintage Mack Sennett routine to outsiders, South Africans took it as deadly serious business. And it was. The Boss Act, as General Law Amendment Act No. 101 of 1969 came to be known, was perhaps the crowning achievement of a decade of legislation designed to eliminate virtually every judicial safeguard South Africans had once had. The Bureau of State Security was set up directly under Vorster's office to co-ordinate all intelligence and security matters, foreign and domestic. It became illegal for a newspaper to publish anything about the Bureau that the Bureau might view as prejudicial to police interests. It was made a crime for "any person who has in his possession or under his control *any* sketch, plan, model, article, note, document or information which relates to munitions of war or *any military or police matter*" to publish or "directly or indirectly communicate it to any person" (my italics). This law also gave Vorster or any of his ministers the power to prohibit a defendant in a security case from testifying at his own trial if that testimony would be likely to be prejudicial to the public interest.

Even the United Party, normally complacent on security matters, could not stomach the Boss Act and voted against it. Boss may turn out to represent the cresting of the government's demands for unbridled power. In 1971, Vorster denied that Boss was "a super police force" and announced that the government might consider some alterations to the act.

I met the head of Boss by accident one day (at least, I think it was by accident) when I called on another government official. General Hendrik J. van den Bergh is a tall, thin, bookish-looking man who appeared to be much more of an introvert than most Afrikaners I met. We chatted, he seeming almost as nervous as I was, and then he left, saying he had to get on with business. Recalling the Boss Act, I refrained from asking what the business was.

The humiliation and despair that the government can inflict on its opponents without sending them to jail have been so thoroughly chronicled in the past few years that it is not necessary to go into much detail here. The most popular government device is the banning order. The Minister of Justice uses it to restrict the movements, public utterances, and writings of anyone. Nothing a banned person says or writes may be quoted in any publication in South Africa. Two banned persons may not see or talk to each other. A banned person may not be in the company of more than one other person at any given time. What the Minister of Justice can ban a person from doing is limited only by his own ingenuity.

At the beginning of 1970, nearly 1000 persons had been served with banning orders since the Suppression of Communism Act became law in 1950. More than 80 per cent of them were Africans, many of whom were former political prisoners. They were served banning orders as they were released from prison. Some of the orders have been in effect more than ten years. At the beginning of 1971, it was estimated that nearly 300 Africans and 50 whites were then under banning orders. Another 45 to 50 persons were under house arrest for twelve hours each day. Ten of them were required to report daily to the police. If they failed to do so, or were tardy several times in reporting at the appointed hour, they were to be arrested.

One of the house prisoners was a gray-haired, sixty-six-year-old white widow named Helen Joseph. Mrs. Joseph had been a leading figure in the multiracialist Congress of Democrats, which helped with the Defiance Campaign. In 1956, she was arrested, charged with treason, and acquitted after a marathon trial four years later. In 1962, Vorster, then Minister of Justice, sentenced her to house arrest. She lived through the next eight years with a cat and a dog, forbidden to receive any visitors except a doctor and the police. She was effectively prohibited from continuing her work as a secretary by the terms of Vorster's banning order.

In the ninth year of what has been called "civil death" for Mrs. Joseph, the Rand *Daily Mail* printed an editorial asking the government to free Mrs. Joseph. "How old does she have to be before the State feels safe enough to stop persecuting her in the name of security?" the newspaper asked. The query was answered by the government in June: Helen Joseph had to be sixty-six, and gravely ill with cancer, before apartheid's grip would be relaxed.

That was when she entered the hospital for major surgery. The government gallantly lifted her house arrest temporarily so she could go into the hospital. While she was recovering, being careful to receive only one visitor at a time in her hospital room, the government "suspended until further notice" the house arrest and most of the other restrictions it had placed on her. Vorster apparently did not want to take the chance of Mrs. Joseph's becoming even more of a martyr.

The government's harassment and intimidation of whites who have become identified with the black cause has been thorough and effective. One of the things that struck me in the white liberals I met was a shrillness and dogmatism that equaled that of the most segregationist Nationalists. There is apparent a deep frustration within the white liberal community, a feeling of banging one's head against the apartheid wall and receiving only scorn from both the white and black communities for doing it. A few organizations (notably Black Sash, a women's social welfare group) and a few individuals do continue to speak out, but they are apparently being worn down as well. I mentioned this to a friend when we spoke of Joel Carlson, the lawyer who had defended Africans in most of the important political cases of the last few years, and who frequently helped African families fight the bureaucracy that was trying to split them up. I said that I had just had lunch with Carlson and he seemed very emotional about South Africa's problems. He was on the verge of tears at one point as he told me about the erosion of law in the country. "I expect Joel Carlson is emotional," my friend replied. "You might be also if your car had been shot up, a Molotov cocktail hurled into your house, and a bomb sent to you in the mail. To make it worse, the police officially make it clear that they are not going to do anything to find out who is behind all of this, and unofficially some of them indicate that they hope the next attempt succeeds. That is what Joel Carlson has been through in the last year. Yes, you might accurately describe him as being emotional about what he does."

When I saw him, Carlson had just been through what seemed to have been a turning point for him. He had defended the nineteen

Africans I mentioned earlier. Arrested in May 1969, held without charges until December, they were brought to trial under the Suppression of Communism Act. In February, after Carlson had obtained affidavits indicating the Africans had been beaten and tortured during interrogation, the prosecution suddenly dropped the charges and the nineteen were acquitted.

"Before we could leave the courtroom, they arrested the defendants again," Carlson told me. "The police have never been so openly arrogant and contemptuous of the law. They had police dogs right inside the Supreme Court. They were determined to demonstrate to everybody they were boss no matter what the Judge said. Before in South Africa, acquittal meant acquittal. Now, nobody knows what it means."

In a dispatch I wrote concerning the case, I used Carlson's words but did not identify him. That might have exposed him even more. I can quote him by name now. In April 1971 Carlson, who had started his career as a good bureaucrat in the Department of Native Affairs ("What I saw there scarred me for life," he says), fled South Africa, apparently in fear of his life. The government had refused to give him a passport. Because his father was born in Britain, Carlson was able to obtain a British passport. He renounced his citizenship and flew to London.

Ten years earlier, Julius Lewin, a friend of Carlson who now also lives in self-imposed exile in London, had written, "One by one, the lights are going out as South Africa enters its darkest age." The past decade has proven Lewin correct. Dissent has grown substantially weaker with each passing year, and multiracialism has been almost thoroughly discredited as a political ideal. The National Party has not been acting in just its name alone, but for the white population in general, which has agreed to give the government a free hand to combat what is perceived as a great danger. The United Party voted for the Terrorism Act in 1967. Only Helen Suzman opposed it in Parliament. At times, the white population seems even to be pushing for more draconian measures against those who disagree with not only white supremacy but also other prevailing moral and social beliefs.

The National Party, it seemed to me during my more pessimistic moments in South Africa, had reacted to a series of crises somewhat in the same way the Nixon administration might have if it had had a free hand to follow Middle American public opinion, enflamed by Watts, Newark, the hippies of San Francisco in 1967, and finally Chicago in 1968. The analogy is of course not exact, due in part to the respect Americans continue to have for the Supreme Court and the Constitution. John Mitchell could not have banned speeches or articles by Jerry Rubin or Dr. Spock, no matter how many votes that might have been worth in an election. It is certainly fanciful at this point in history to suggest any kind of comparison between the Westernized black mass of South Africa and the "youth" population of the United States, which to a large extent does not identify with the older "nation" that rules it. It is fanciful, too, to analogize the Chicago demonstration and Kent State with the antipass campaigns and Sharpeville.

But Americans might pause to reflect at the parallels in the flow of similar forces, viewed within their differing contexts: Unpopular, nonviolent demonstrations lead to turmoil, which seems to threaten those entrenched in affluence and power. Violent confrontations occur. The government hesitates, then senses that the public (i.e., white) opinion demands a hard line on dissent. Mass conspiracy trials of dissidents follow, "liberal" media and organizations come under government attack, and "liberal" solutions and nonviolent protest actions are discredited on both left and right as polarization rends the political middle. Ineffectual acts of sabotage bring increased retaliation from the government.

Whether or not this pattern can or will develop more fully in the United States is a matter of intense speculation at the moment of writing. In South Africa, it has been completed.

THE REDS AND THE BLACKS

One of the government's key tactics in mobilizing white opinion behind it was to link integration with Communism, and liberalism with both, in the public mind. This was relatively simple in South Africa, which is a very political country but not a very sophisticated political country. The search for an easy, all-embracing answer to political problems is perhaps characteristic of a rural-based society like Afrikanerdom. A few days after Kent State, I was talking to Mrs. J. M. de Wet, wife of the president of Fort Hare University, a great Germanic woman of bubbly disposition and enormous hospitality. She asked me why Americans had so much trouble with their students, and then, before I could answer, told me, "Oh, but it is all done by the Communists, isn't it? They cause all of this trouble. You Americans are too easy on your Communists." I thought for a moment she was going to say squishy soft, but she didn't.

Half a dozen English-speaking whites told me about the Afrikaner policeman who defined a Communist for them as "anyone who believes in white and black mixing" or "anyone who is against apartheid." The story sounds proverbial, but in some ways there is a grain of truth in it, and that grain tells us much about why liberalism faded so easily in front of the counterrevolution mounted by the National Party.

Much of the government's seemingly endless ranting about the danger internal Communism poses to it twenty years after the party was completely broken is a calculated effort to gain more support from the West, to seek capitalist allies who will excuse whatever failings apartheid may have since South Africa is a bulwark against godless international atheism. But some of it is for real. Communists have played a prominent if vain role in the drive for black majority rule in South Africa.

Just before he was sentenced to life imprisonment in the Rivonia Treason Trial in 1964, Nelson Mandela, then forty-six and South Africa's most popular and impressive black political leader, conceded to the judge that the A.N.C. and the Communist Party of South Africa had cooperated at times. Mandela insisted that he and other A.N.C. members were not Communists. Then he added: ". . . for decades, the Communists were the only political group in South Africa who were prepared to treat Africans as human beings and their equals; who were prepared to eat with us; talk with us, live with us, and work with us. They were the only political group which was prepared to work with the Africans for the attainment of political rights and a stake in society. Because of this, there are many Africans who today tend to equate freedom with Communism."

South Africa's Communist Party grew out of the local International Socialist League. The party was founded in 1921 by a group of men like S. P. Bunting, who were more English Socialists than Moscow Marxists. The party developed a trade union base on the mines, which is one reason it is despised so by the establishment here. But the Communists limited their early organizing to the white working class. They played a large role in the 1922 strike on the Rand, when striking miners carried banners reading, "Workers of the World Unite for a White South Africa." In 1924, the party supported the Hertzog–Labour Party coalition against Smuts, who was seen as the lackey of the capitalist mine owners. There was a major split within the Communist ranks that year over accepting Africans into the Youth Movement. When it was resolved to accept them, much of the white mining membership left the party.

Throughout the 1920s, however, the movement's character changed as the party came more and more under Moscow's control. In 1928 the order came from Moscow that South Africa was to be a Native Republic; black rule was to be the goal. "Vacillating elements" who had reservations about this were purged. The Communists continued to back universal suffrage until 1950 when the party dissolved itself, a few months before the National Party paid the small, intellectual-ridden Communist group the highest compliment in its lackluster history by banning it.

No other essentially white party has advocated democratic voting as consistently as did the Communists. Alan Paton's Liberal Party, when it was founded in 1935, advocated a qualified franchise, as the Progressive Party does today. The Liberals later came to advocate universal suffrage, but multiracial parties were already on the way out by then. The government formalized the trend in 1968 by outlawing integrated political parties.

Why has the ideal of multiracialism fallen so easily in front of the white counterrevolution? One possibility is that it had so little to offer either group by the time it came into vogue. The majority of whites became convinced that they did not have to give up power and therefore were under no compulsion to try multiracialism. Blacks saw liberals offering them restricted voting rights that would have ensured continued white domination, with more humane living conditions. That was hardly something they were willing to die for.

A final question: If the puny thrusts that black nationalism has made thus far have produced this kind of heavy-fisted treatment from the police and the army standing in the background, what would a really serious attempt at black rebellion bring? Many black South Africans think they know the answer to that and it is a key in the search for forces that act for change and those that preserve the status quo in South Africa.

Soweto, the sprawling housing compound of 700,000 Africans, is built on an open plain fifteen miles away from Johannesburg. On one side sits a South African air force base. Two other military installations are within minutes of Soweto. "People on the outside always ask why we don't revolt," David Curry, the Colored leader, had told me. "The white man has all the tanks, the jets, the guns. We don't have anything. In a revolt the blood that would be shed would be the blood of the nonwhites." Added Joel Carlson, before he left the country: "Power does not grow out of the barrel of a gun if you do not have a gun."

Chapter Six

The Uncommon Society

I HAD NOT GONE to South Africa to write about apartheid. So much had been written; it seemed so familiar; positions had been defined so long ago. I had gone to focus on the people of the country, its amazing economic performance, and its role in Africa in the future. And yet there was no way to write intelligently about South Africa without constantly referring to apartheid. It regulates South Africa's human relations and personal contact and is the matrix of the economy. And the first encounter with apartheid was not as predictable as I had expected it to be. No matter how well prepared the American visitor feels by the books, films, and articles that have described the country's distinctive racial practices, he is likely to feel a sharp jolt as he steps out of the impersonally efficient customs hall and into the cavernous, noise-filled waiting room at Jan Smuts airport.

They were building runways to take jumbo jets at the airport, but I felt a sudden push back two decades, back to the Southern United States of the early nineteen fifties — except not quite, for we in that South were never as mechanical, or perhaps thorough, or perhaps just efficient, about segregation as the Afrikaners are.

Discrimination is neither subtle, nor taken for granted, in South Africa. "Blanke" (white in Afrikaans) shouted big signs over the restaurants, rest rooms, and observation platforms. "Nie Blanke" muttered the small signs on the fewer, smaller, and dirtier counterparts. These signs cover South Africa's park benches, elevators, liquor stores, beaches, taxis. So this is apartheid, I said to myself.

Except it isn't. The signs are only a slice of apartheid. It is an important slice for the people who live in South Africa, even though they call it "petty" to distinguish this day-to-day segregation from "big" apartheid. Despite my original intentions, my quest across South Africa slowly turned into a search for a definition of "big" apartheid, a coming to terms with it, and an attempt to judge its sincerity or falseness, its efficiency or applicability. But it seemed at every turn to become more elusive, more of a will-o'-the-wisp, vanishing just as I thought I had seen its face in a remote corner of the Transkei or on a crowded street in downtown Durban. Like others, I was to find apartheid easier to argue about than to define.

Apartheid is a theory of human relations built around South Africa's peculiar clash of races and nationalisms. It is an economic system designed to feed cheap labor into factories and farms. It is a security system designed to control Africans. It is, say the men who have been entrusted with propagating it, a solution to a problem, a creative way of reducing racial friction and developing black nationalism. It is a method of dividing South Africa's land into two unequal parts and partitioning black and white. To outsiders, it is a hated symbol of white mastery over a nonwhite world.

Apartheid is in short many things to many people. It is just about whatever they want it to be, as evil or as altruistic as they desire. Despite an external image that it is rigid and unchanging, apartheid is remarkably flexible, and it shows signs of evolution. At least, the ideology as refined by Hendrik Verwoerd and applied by John Vorster seemed that way to me. Which is perhaps the way I wanted it to seem.

Apartheid is actually the ultimate refinement of a pattern of race relations that is deep-rooted in South Africa. It was designed to give the appearance of change to that pattern without significantly changing it. But I found that after a score and two years of life, apartheid seemed to have gathered a momentum of its own that was producing some change in South Africa's static race relations. Political careers had been staked on apartheid's performance and much money spent to further it. The lives of hundreds of thousands of people had been disrupted in its name, as one of the greatest peacetime movements of population for ideology's sake occurred since the Soviet Union's collectivization of peasants. And by 1970, it had become clear that apartheid's institutions were capable of being used by black and brown men in a way that the white supremacists who designed them may not have foreseen.

Even the language of apartheid had changed significantly. The stigma the world attached to the rigid, visible everyday segregation that apartheid first symbolized became so great that the government virtually abandoned the term. It gradually disappeared from official pronouncements to be replaced by "separate development," and more recently by "separate freedoms." The tendency was to dismiss this as a mere changing of labels that had no effect on the content of the package. But this semantic evolution seems to reflect a shift in the Nationalist government's approach to maintaining white domination in South Africa if not in its goal. The change in phraseology may even be helping to produce a shift, as ideologies are shaped by the words used to express them as well as the concepts they encase. This is especially true of apartheid, which has remained more theory than a program of action.

Racial separation in South Africa is as old as the country itself. But only recently has it been systematized and converted into an ideology.

Jan van Riebeeck's answer to the mixing of the races was to erect a bitter almond hedge around the settlement on the Cape. The hedge was to fence the Hottentots and Bushmen out and to keep his own men in. They had taken to pilfering goods and sneaking out to trade with the Africans. Understanding neither the whites who were to leave the settlement and become the Boers, nor the Hottentots, van Riebeeck failed, but his spirit lives on, as his descendants have now erected a giant metaphorical hedge around their settlement.

As van Riebeeck's heirs might say, the original contact between the Dutch and the Hottentots led to "friction." The original Africans attacked the Dutch in 1658 because, in the words of a wounded Hottentot questioned by van Riebeeck, the Dutch "kept in possession the best lands" and built up their houses and plantations as if they "intended never to leave again." Leo Marquard, who relates this encounter in *The Story of South Africa*, notes that the two men were speaking for Africa and Europe. "The white man had come to stay, and the black man was losing his land."

Territorial segregation, which would become the basis of apartheid, developed as the white expansion into the interior squeezed the Africans onto the less desirable land. After the Zulus were broken at Blood River in 1838 and the Xhosa decimated by the 1857 witch doctor prophecy, serious resistance to the white advance collapsed. Africans either went to work on white farms or remained sullenly on the land the whites did not want.

The Natives Land Act of 1913 passed by the all-white Parliament gave legal approval to this white-black division of the land. It became unlawful for Africans to buy land, except in a few very small areas that were historically still open to them. In return for prohibiting them from buying "white" land, the act reserved, or "scheduled," 7 per cent of the country's total area for tribal ownership. This was land that had long been secured to Africans by existing treaty rights and legislation. In 1936, another white Parliament decided that 7 per cent of the land was too little for the growing black population and passed the Native Trust and Land Act, which increased the area occupied by the reserves to 65,000 square miles — or 13.7 per cent of South Africa's total area. The rest was reserved for the whites.

These territorial laws were the midwives of apartheid, which is an Afrikaans word usually translated as "separate-ness" or "apartness." It was apparently coined by D. F. Malan as the slogan for his National Party's racial policies during the "black peril" campaign that won the 1948 election. Malan and his lieutenants offered apartheid as an alternative to the creeping integration they saw being fostered by the soft white-domination policies of the United Party. They promised apartheid would obliterate multiracialism.

J. G. Strydom, who later followed Malan as Prime Minister, spelled out what they meant in 1948: "Either you are the baas [boss], the equal, or the inferior, one of the three. If you are not baas, you must be a man's equal . . . If you say that you do not want to dominate the Native, it simply means that you stand for a policy of equality." Apartheid, he emphasized, was not such a policy.

In its first years, apartheid was directed at eliminating the most obvious examples of racial contact, which usually occurred in towns and cities. A Population Register was established, and all persons were required to carry identity cards (or, in the case of Africans, passbooks) that stated the racial group to which they belonged. This was aimed at ending "passing" by light-complexioned Coloreds. Mixed marriages and interracial sex were outlawed. After nonwhites won a series of court tests that established that separate facilities had to be equal, the Nationalist-controlled Parliament amended the law and made separate and unequal the order of the day throughout South Africa. Perhaps most importantly, the principle of land segregation was brought to the cities by the Group Areas Act of 1950, which gave the government the right to create racial ghettos and restrict interracial contact.

Under Malan, apartheid consisted largely of installing the color bar by law in places where it had existed in custom and ruling out any exceptions. It was a direct expression of white supremacy, without any pretenses attached to it. Afrikaners who continued to use the word apartheid in 1970 often seemed to do so defiantly, to show they did not care for the outside world's opinion of their racial attitudes or for the revisionism of apartheid's historical intent that recent Nationalist governments have undertaken.

Strydom, a former ostrich farmer, followed in Malan's path after he became Prime Minister in 1954. But in the same year, one of the most remarkable documents in the history of South Africa was published, and the history of apartheid was changed.

Known as the Tomlinson Commission Report, the meticulously detailed study was the product of a ten-man commission that had spent three years investigating the African reserves. They substantiated what everyone suspected: the land in the reserves was eroding and being exhausted at a fearful rate and the economies of the reserves were completely stagnant. The prospect of famine was a real one for Africa's richest country.

The Commission, headed by Professor F. R. Tomlinson, urged the government to invest $280,000,000 in a ten-year crash program that would stabilize the land and provide industrial growth. This would make the reserves self-supporting and make the Africans want to stay there instead of migrating to the cities. The Commission drew up a plan that called for seven African territories (which included the territory of the British protectorates that would become Botswana, Lesotho, and Swaziland), proposed that Africans be allowed to buy individual farms in them, and told the government that tribalism and rule by chiefs should be broken down so modern economies could be developed within the reserves. In most areas in the reserves, chiefs and headmen allocated the use of farmland to individuals.

The Commission's recommendations were largely rejected by the Nationalist government. It probably could not have politically survived advocating an enormous expenditure of money on Africans and was not going to sacrifice the valuable aid of tribalism. But Hendrik Verwoerd, the aloof, Holland-born professor of psychology who became Prime Minister in 1958, took the elements of the Tomlinson Commission report that suited his purposes, and wove them into the increasing discussion in the Dutch Reformed Church and Afrikaner intellectual circles of a "complete" territorial separation of South Africa's races. The result was the expansion of apartheid into an ideology, which Verwoerd popularized under the antiseptic, morally neutral phrase, separate development. This was the term that was most widely used in South Africa a decade after Sharpeville.

The reserves had long been considered the "national home" of the Africans. They had no rights outside the reserves. The Stallard Commission in 1922 merely stated what had long been in practice when it observed: "The Native should only be allowed to enter urban areas, which are essentially the white man's creation, when he is willing to enter and to minister to the needs of the white man, and should depart therefrom when he ceases to so minister." In the "white man's creation," the African was only a migrant worker. His only right was to barter his labor, and even that right was restricted. This is the underlying and irreducible principle of race relations in South Africa.

Verwoerd put a new gloss on this long-standing attitude by emphasizing the rights the Africans enjoyed in their own areas and constructing an elaborate justification for the disabilities that had to be imposed on blacks when they chose to leave the reserves. He devised "positive apartheid" — except that because the world had so poorly understood apartheid it would now be called separate development.

Verwoerd drew up a blueprint for eight separate Bantu tribal nations that would be created out of the territory of the reserves. Each Bantustan belonged to a tribal nation or an amalgam of related tribes. In these Bantustans the African could develop his own form of government, his own businesses and economic opportunities, his own culture and nationalism. He would have no reason to covet those of the white man. Under white guidance, each of the Bantustans would eventually attain economic viability and then political independence from white control. Depending on the division of the land for the large Xhosa tribe, there would be seven or eight black states and one white state, and they would form a South African commonwealth.

Every black South African belonged to one of the eight tribal nations the government had delineated — by heritage if in no other way. As a citizen of the Bantustan, the African could not be a citizen of the Republic of South Africa, which the two white tribes would continue to develop. The Bantu's rights resided in the homelands. When he chose to leave the homeland, he chose also to leave his rights and would have to accept the day-to-day pinpricks of segregation known as "petty apartheid," which were a hallowed part of the white man's traditional way of life.

The Bantustans were to provide visible institutions that embodied the reality that the Afrikaners understood, but which the outside world refused to consider at all: white and black South Africa did not share a common political or cultural heritage. In such an uncommon society, multiracialism was not possible. Either the blacks would eventually take power and because they were a majority crush the whites, or the whites would hold power and because they were a minority continue to discriminate harshly in an effort to protect themselves. The forces of race were too powerful in South Africa. Verwoerd maintained the answer was to interpose the forces of nationalism. Multinationalism in South Africa offered the races the chance to "live and let live — apart." There would continue to be contact and interchange between the white and black populations, but on a new basis of some kind of mutual respect for their separate nations. There would be vertical separation and co-existence.

It was a fascinating idea, one pregnant with important implications for all pluralistic societies, and it provided the chance for much invigorating debate over the relative strength of nationalism and race. The main problem was that the government of Verwoerd never gave any sign that it really took the idea seriously. For, having outlined his plan, Verwoerd turned his back on the only steps that would have given it a chance to work.

He refused to allocate any significant government funds to develop the Bantustans and prohibited private white capital from investing in the reserves. The reserves were in fact not large tracts of territories inhabited by separate tribes. They were composed of more than 250 separate pieces of land scattered across South Africa. Some of the "reserves" were nothing more than small African farms in white areas. Most were collections of tribal villages and farmlands. Only the Transkei and Ciskei areas, inhabited by the Xhosa and related tribes, existed as large territorial entities. The reserves could become potential states only if substantially more land than that called for by the 1936 act was added. This Verwoerd also refused to do. An attempt was begun to consolidate some of the smaller African holdings of land, known by the predictable bureaucratic term of "black spots," but the magic 87-13 division of the land was not to be altered. When they were pressed on the lack of viability of the reserves, government

officials held out the ludicrous possibility that some of the tribal
nations would come to "independence" as ethnic nations instead
of territorial ones.

Verwoerd's government also continued to reject the other key
recommendation of the Tomlinson Commission report. Apartheid would encourage tribalism rather than break it down. Tribalism had operated as a uniting force for the white minority, but a
dividing one for the black majority. It should be encouraged. Bureaucrats in Pretoria suddenly began trilling the praise of the
Noble Savage and the value of his customs, tribal languages, and
patterns of rule. They spoke of preserving the distinctive and "traditional ways of life" of both the white and black nations.

This was a remarkably accurate description of the real intent of
apartheid. The traditional way of life for the white man in South
Africa is as the affluent master; that of the black as the poor servant. The dividing up of South Africa (which must be a unique
exercise in the history of modern statesmanship: an offer to carve
up a country in the name of nationalism) reserved not only 87 per
cent of the land, but also all of the cities, all of the ports, almost all
of the good farmland, and most of the wealth of the country for
the whites, who had spoken much of the sacrifices they were willing to make for apartheid, but who had not made a single one —
unless you count reducing the number of maids and houseboys
they hired as a white sacrifice.

The whites did not apologize for the 87-13 division. It was, in
the words of Foreign Minister Hilgard Muller, "history's division
of the land," not the white man's. John Vorster defended it in
more pugnacious terms in an interview published in the November 14, 1966, issue of *U.S. News & World Report,* when he suggested that 13 per cent was a generous gift from the whites:

As far as the black peoples are concerned, we didn't take the land
away from them. Where they settled, we protected them. If the white
man — our forefathers, Afrikaans-speaking and English-speaking —
didn't protect them, they wouldn't have an inch of land today. The
white man, with his capital and his initiative, naturally would have had

all the land. But our forefathers took the view that, where the black man settled, the land was his, and they looked upon that as black land and they protected him in his ownership of that land.

In private, leading Afrikaners were prepared to concede that there might have to be an adjustment in the division if apartheid were going to be given a realistic test. But officially apartheid was repeatedly used to reinforce the white claim to the economic heartland. It ruled out realistic discussion of partition of the peoples of South Africa. "Apartheid keeps the whites from realizing that they are going to have to make some sacrifice," an Afrikaner graduate student at Stellenbosch University said.

As drawn up, the Bantustans could never become anything more than colonies of the white South African nation, even if local self-government were to be granted to these absolutely destitute territories. Instead of cocoa, or copper, or rubber the only export to the mother country would be human labor.

"Yes, the government is giving us separate freedom," said one African. "We have the freedom to stay in the white areas and eat, or go back to the homelands and starve. That is our freedom to choose."

The white economy could no more afford to do without black labor than the reserves could afford to do without the cash income the cities offer. Big apartheid would regularize the flow of black labor into the white man's creation and give a modern justification for an old and continuing system.

How far South Africa had come in presenting a sophisticated argument for its practices, while remaining true to the dictum expressed by the Stallard Commission, can be judged from this statement made by John Vorster in an interview published June 24, 1971, in France's *Le Monde* (weekly edition):

Those who come to work in the White areas will find themselves in the same situation as foreign laborers — Portuguese, Arab or Turkish — who come to offer their services in Europe but are not, on the strength of this, integrated politically. Every year Blacks by tens of thousands come voluntarily to the Republic to look for work.

The situation of black South Africans in Johannesburg and Turkish workers in West Germany is not quite the same, it would seem to me. People born in one place and spending their lives there are not migrant workers. The government also clearly treats some workers as more migrant than others. To bolster the white population, South Africa industriously recruits white Europeans to migrate to the country. The 35,933 Portuguese, Italians, Greeks, British, and other foreigners who came to live in South Africa in 1969 had an opportunity to obtain South African citizenship. But a black South African born in Soweto would never have the opportunity to become a South African citizen. He would always be "the foreign native."

THE NEW VISION

That Verwoerd would go to so much trouble to construct an elaborate justification for continuing South Africa's traditional ways of discrimination has surprised many outsiders. But separate development was designed not to make continued white supremacy in South Africa more palatable to the United Nations, nor to the black majority of South Africa; it was designed largely to make continued white supremacy more palatable to South Africans, as criticism from the outside and decolonization to the north began to be felt inside the laager.

For Verwoerd was launching South Africa on an unrealizable quest for the Great White Whale that is apartheid. Total separation of the races in South Africa is a dream, a myth, a wish. Verwoerd had abolished white supremacy in theory and limited it to practice. He had promised its destruction in the near future, so it could be left intact in the present.

With the same stroke, Verwoerd provided the Afrikaner with absolution and dispensation to continue what the world had recently come to regard as sinning. Creating a new theology called apartheid, he entrusted it to bureaucrats. They would replace Dutch Reformed ministers as the guardians of Afrikaner values in the cities. The Afrikaner, who would have a new mission in his increasingly urbanized and secularized environment, would reassert his morality in the face of a critical world by creating black nations, just as he had been chosen to create Africa's white nation.

Apartheid gained a marvelous new elastic quality from Verwoerd's elaboration of it as separate development and his failure to take steps to bring the theory closer to some sort of reality. The white electorate got a promise of a systematic return of all Africans to the reserves and a moral justification for the essentially immoral practices of petty apartheid.

There was even an innovation in the package for Afrikaner intellectuals and moralists. There was a channel for discontent, a safety valve for a little heresy in Afrikanerdom. The disillusioned could now criticize the government for its treatment of the blacks. By failing to live up to the grand design of apartheid, the government was depriving Africans of their rights. But the critics would remain safely within the Afrikaner nation, because they would not be advocating multiracialism but a more rapid advance to complete separation of the races. This led to the development of the Verligtes in the last years of the nineteen sixties. It was under their prodding that John Vorster began to adopt "separate freedoms" as a more modern description of the process that had begun with Malan in 1948.[1]

Perhaps the special genius of Verwoerd's contribution lay in his use of language to modernize the white man's vision of the African. Just as the Dutch Reformed ministers had portrayed the African as a hewer of wood and a drawer of water when the rural environment demanded that someone do these tasks, so did Verwoerd's apartheid bureaucrats portray the African in the mid-twentieth century as a "labor unit." Each of these units was "interchangeable," Verwoerd said. How can interchangeable labor units have rights?

In the language of apartheid, you would no longer hire a house-

[1] Vorster also allowed limited white investment, on an agency basis, in the homelands in a significant shift from Verwoerd's policy.

boy, but you would "requisition a Bantu" through the government influx control machinery. The Pretoria bureaucrat did not banish a jobless African widow from her home in the black housing compound of Soweto, he "resettled a nonproductive Bantu out of the white area." The bureaucratic description of Soweto as a white area contradicted all of the visible facts. There were 700,000 Africans living there, and even rabid apartheid believers admitted that there would always be a need for Africans to live there. It was even illegal for a white to enter Soweto without a special permit issued by the bureaucrats. And yet it was a white area. And, since it was a white area, Africans could not buy the land their houses stood on, or after 1968 even the bricks and mortar used to build the house. They had to rent it from the government, which could evict them at any moment. Since Soweto was a white area, the African did not have the unqualified right to open a filling station or a milk and bread store there. The government might allow him to do so, but he had to get the bureaucrats' permission.

On the farm, the Afrikaner had had direct contact with the African and chose individually to be kind or cruel, racist or paternalistic. The white and black move to the cities removed that element of choice and the directness of contact. Urbanization demanded a more efficient method of regulating and describing white-black relationships.

Apartheid's language was designed to obscure the reality of human relations in South Africa, rather than reflect it. What was wrong in practice could be fixed up in words, since the government thought it could control the content of the words. Whites would have no cause to fear the growing numbers of blacks near them because there was "influx control." Apartheid's language also helped speed the depersonalization of Africans. The white attitude that Africans existed only to work for them was deeply ingrained in South African society. What theoretical apartheid did was to make it proper again to voice that attitude.

For example, Johannes Pretorius, a thirty-four-year-old farmer in the northern Natal town of Glencoe, had had a little trouble with one of his labor units named Tryfina Kumalo, a twenty-seven-year-old African woman, while I happened to be in South Africa. Miss Kumalo had been sent to Pretorius' farm to work off a month's jail sentence for what was described only as "a minor offense," undoubtedly one involving her passbook. She apparently tried to leave the farm, was stopped by Pretorius and a local policeman, and was beaten with a hosepipe. She died as a result of the beating.

Brought to trial and convicted of assault after a murder charge was dropped, Pretorius and the policeman were each fined 300 rand ($420). "If I had not employed prisoners, I would not have had this murder charge hanging over my head," Pretorious said after the hearing. "I'll never use convict labor again." The policeman, a burly Afrikaner named Charles Marais, didn't have time to say anything. He was late for work at the station house, where he was to resume duties after the hearing.

In Pretoria a few months later, thirty white soldiers from a nearby military base attacked five African workers at a filling station after an exchange of words late one night. The Africans, one of them an elderly man, were beaten up rather badly. The white owner of the garage, Erasmus Koelman, said the next day: "My garage is open late at night as a public service, not for things like this to happen. It's difficult enough to get pump attendants these days. How am I supposed to keep them if there are to be incidents like this?" Police had broken up the fight. No arrests were made, not even of the Africans.

The Nationalist government's most transparent attempt to use big apartheid to obscure reality and preserve the status quo was in its "border industry" program. Tax incentives and coercive legislation that limited the number of black employees an industry could hire in designated white areas were used to encourage manufacturers to locate their new plants on the borders of the reserves. Black workers would then be able to live in the homelands, where they would enjoy their traditional rights. They would walk or ride a few miles each day to work and cross a "boundary" into white South Africa. In some cases, the distance involved would mean that workers would get home only on weekends and would live in dormitories at the factories during the week. They would remain an integral, actual part of the white economy; they would become a theoretical part of black freedom. By reclassifying black bedroom communities as part of the homelands, the government showed it intended to have its cake and eat it, too.

The tremendous gap between apartheid's promise and its practice was very clear by 1970. André Brink has noted that cultural separation had in almost every case meant cultural deprivation for the nonwhite groups involved: "In 1964, in one town in Natal the white library contained 4,890 reference books. The African branch of the library had two volumes."

But the census taken in 1970 gave the advocates of big apartheid their first significant claim to achieving a victory of sorts. The homelands had not been made economically viable, and the urban African population had increased in absolute terms, but the population in the reserves had climbed even more sharply between 1960 and 1970. The new census showed nearly seven million Africans living in the reserves, as opposed to four million ten years earlier. The percentage of South Africa's blacks living in the reserves had risen from about 38 per cent to 47. To express it another way, 62 out of every 100 Africans lived outside the reserves in 1960; in 1970, only 53 out of every 100 did.

Critics suggested that a great many Africans living illegally in urban areas had ducked the census or returned to the reserves temporarily. I was in South Africa on census day and had lunch in the home of a colleague. His wife apologized that their (illegal) live-in maid was away for a few days and could not be there to help. "Minnie's gone home to be counted," she explained. "We didn't know how much poking around they would do."

Also, three hundred thousand Africans had been shifted from the white areas to the homelands by the redrawing of the Bantustan boundaries to include black townships around the four white cities of Pretoria, Pietermaritzburg, Durban, and East London. And it was thought that the 1960 census had greatly underrecorded the number of Africans in the reserves in the first place.

Even with these reservations, however, the census indicated that the great efforts apartheid's keepers had undertaken to shift population was beginning to have an effect. Even though the expanding white economy continued to pull in 80,000 Africans a year, the stepping up of influx control was beginning to result in the endorsing out of 40,000 a year. And, as economists pointed out, without apartheid's efforts, the black flow into white areas would have been 90,000 a year or more.

Africans were also being squeezed out of the "black spots," the African-owned farms and villages completely surrounded by white territory. The government forced the Africans to sell the land and move into the reserves. By 1970, the government admitted to having moved a total of 90,000 people into the reserves from black spots, and critics in Parliament suggested that the total was probably much higher.

By far the greatest population shift had occurred under the Group Areas Act. Eric Winchester, a United Party Member of Parliament, made a detailed three-year study and concluded that up to September 1968 more than one million people had been removed from their homes under this act. The racial breakdown he provided of the enforced moves is a devastating comment on the practice of apartheid: 354,000 Coloreds were forced to move, 250,000 Indians, 472,000 Africans, 2624 whites. Winchester said his African estimate was a conservative one. "The number probably exceeds one million," he added.

How much of a victory the mushrooming of population in the homelands would come to represent was debatable. In 1960, the country's best economists had predicted that the government would have to create 23,000 new jobs each year just to keep pace with the natural population increase expected in the reserves. By 1970, only an average of 8000 new jobs had been created each year in the reserves, and almost all of those were attributable to the border industries that were actually a part of the white economy. The population explosion in the reserves made them even less economically viable than in 1960. Economic independence seemed to be receding instead of advancing.

"Of course," said an English-speaker. "The more apartheid fails, the more it succeeds. That is its beauty."

The growing perception of the economic failure of apartheid, as the reserves became more and more dependent on the export of labor and less self-reliant, produced the Verligte "revolt" within Afrikanerdom. The Verligtes asserted that they had been led to believe that apartheid was a sincere attempt to find a just solution to South Africa's racial problems. Young Afrikaners "have come to separate development out of the highest ideals. Now they want those ideals implemented," Leon Coetzee, an Afrikaner philosophy teacher, wrote in 1968 in *News/Check*, which was then South Africa's liveliest and best magazine, a slimmed-down, intellectualized version of *Time*.

The editor of *News/Check* also was a young Afrikaner, Otto Krause. His exuberance, hospitality, and determined air were remarkable even for an Afrikaner. After a party in Pretoria one night, we discussed apartheid over a gradually emptying bottle of Scotch, circling and looking at race from every angle until nearly dawn. Krause insisted that the Verligte approach was the only truly radical one in South Africa. It was so radical that the European-oriented minds with their outmoded guilt concepts would not be able to grasp it. The European fetish was for traditional answers that would fail. He argued that providing different homelands for entirely separate nationalities that have obviously conflicting interests would head off the kind of nationalistic wars Europe had experienced in its formation into nation-states. He accepted the comparison of the social disruption visited on blacks with that produced by Stalin in the Soviet Union, but maintained the results would justify it. It was a challenging evening, and as I wearily went to bed, I felt that I had begun to grasp apartheid. But the next morning, when I looked at the notes I had made of Krause's comments, I realized I had failed again. I scrawled beside those notes that morning: What is Krause's argument?

Piet Cillié put the Verligte case for apartheid in more pragmatic terms over a leisurely lunch: "Apartheid is just a way to get the white man to behave decently. You can be liberal only from a position of strength. We can only feel strong on the basis of separate freedoms exercised in separate areas. If I could believe in the one-nation concept, I could go around with a clear conscience like the liberals who live in rich villas in rich suburbs do. But it won't work here. We have to change the whole political understructure of South Africa." Apartheid's formula for transferring Africans to the homelands and leaving a number that the whites would not consider a threat "is our way of escaping from discrimination." Petty apartheid would fall away once fear had gone.

But a decade of big apartheid had been accompanied by an intensification of petty apartheid. And I had extreme difficulty in imagining South Africans being able to get the number of Africans needed for the economy down to a level that would make them feel secure enough to discard the valuable devices of petty apartheid. I asked Piet Koornhof, the Deputy Minister for Bantu Administration and Development, and a leading apartheid theorist, how many Africans would remain in white areas in the year 2000, when the African population is expected to have reached twenty-four million. He replied quickly and firmly: "Six million in South Africa, eighteen million in the Bantustans. Those are our optimum figures, and the range is somewhat flexible. But that is what we think it will be." There would be perhaps eight million whites in South Africa by then.

The absurdities and cruelties of petty apartheid have been amply described in a number of works and need no elaboration here. The large number of laws that govern human relations in South Africa range from the puzzling to the insulting to the ludicrous. The separate entrances that lead to the same train platform, the prohibition against a white man's giving a black man a drink of whiskey even in the privacy of his own home, the artificial distinction between Chinese as nonwhites and Japanese as "honorary whites" are only small if particularly well known examples of the entire system.

But the system is not designed just as an expression of racial hatred, or only to ensure white comfort in public facilities that would otherwise be swamped. Petty apartheid, like the grand design, is multifunctional. Not the least purpose it serves is the political mileage it provides the Nationalist Party.

"For most whites, keeping Africans off park benches *is* apartheid," one outspoken white government employee told me. "They don't have the foggiest notion what the big ideological plan is all about. But as long as they read in the paper that the government has passed a new law, and something is being done to the African, they think, 'Apartheid is being implemented.' "

Petty apartheid also is a visible expression of the continuing master-servant relationship that apartheid would maintain. It is difficult otherwise to explain such anomalies as those created by the scenes of white women contentedly eating food cooked and handed across a cafeteria counter by a Colored woman, while it is illegal for the white woman to stand behind the counter and serve food she prepared to a Colored woman. Or the contortions the government went through on banning whites riding in taxis driven by Coloreds in Cape Town. A white can ride in a taxi driven by a Colored if the taxi he rides in is owned by a white. Some Colored drivers who owned their cabs before this law was passed and who made their living hauling white passengers were economically forced to sell their cabs to white men and go to work for them on wages.

But perhaps most importantly, petty apartheid is used by the Afrikaners to perpetuate what one South African sociologist has suggested should be called the ethos of the conquerer and the conquered. It is a perpetual daily reminder to the Zulu, Xhosa, and others that they lost the wars and must now bear the consequences. This is an extremely valuable psychological aid for the whites and one they will not give up easily.

COUNTERAPARTHEID?

On balance it seemed that twenty-two years of apartheid had come close to accomplishing the task D. F. Malan set for it in 1948. It was not just that multiracial contact had been severely limited, it was also that the ideal of multiracialism had been largely suppressed, and destroyed, in South Africa. The institutions that advocated it, political groups like the Liberal Party, had been crushed. White and black leaders who had urged working together were separated, estranged, coerced into silence often. Multiracialism as a solution to South Africa's giant problem was not being seriously discussed in South Africa in 1970.

Separate development had created new institutions and given rise to new leaders in the brown and black communities of South Africa. They rose as brown or black leaders, not just as leaders. Driven from multiracial political parties by the law, David Curry of Stellenbosch and others had to form the Labour Party. When they won the majority of seats on the Colored Persons Representatives Council that had been created as an alternative to multiracial representation in Parliament, they forced the Vorster government into the embarrassment of having to pack the Council with appointments of apartheid stooges to keep control of it. The Urban Bantu Council of Soweto, a group of elected African businessmen with advisory powers, also embarrassed the white government with its growing complaints about its powerlessness and about the inequities of the practice of apartheid.

A black student union was formed, and suddenly black students who had previously taken secondary roles in the multiracial and white-dominated liberal National Union of South African Students were leaders in their group and speaking out, if in guarded terms, about Black Power in South Africa and how it was pointless to expect the white man to give them anything.

Past governments had also set up all-black advisory bodies to compensate for the refusal to give nonwhites any meaningful power in running their own affairs. There had been a Native Representative Council, which was supposed to function as an African forum for debate. This and other racially composed bodies came to be known as "toy telephones" by Africans and Coloreds, who quit participating in them because the whites refused to take them seriously.

Whether the new approaches are likely to fare much better in the long run is taken up in the final chapter of this book. But it is already clear that the new institutions had been formed in a different atmosphere, in the absence of any hope that multiracial approaches would gain anything in the near future. Some leaders decided to pick up the telephones offered them, since they had nothing to lose. Surprisingly, they found that they could reach an audience with them, both in their own communities and abroad. This was especially true of the Bantustans, where two contrasting tribal chiefs began to push the white government faster, and harder, than anyone would have predicted when Verwoerd unveiled the Bantustan concept.

Chapter Seven

A Place for Weeping

"THERE IS ONLY one thing worse than being black in White South Africa," an African journalist tells visitors to Johannesburg. "That is being black in Black South Africa."

The homelands where Africans are supposed to find their freedoms are desolate, remote patches of land. Precious little was done to develop them in the first decade of separate development, which was the second decade of apartheid. They were used in that time largely as dumping grounds for blacks not needed or wanted in the white economy and white areas — the widows, children, the elderly, farmers whose land was located in otherwise white territory. The promise of freedom that is supposed to exist there is far outweighed by the reality of the wretched poverty, disease, and isolation of these tribal reservations.

Seven million people inhabited South Africa's tribal reserves in 1970. Village life there resembled village life elsewhere on the continent and undoubtedly had much in common with village life in undeveloped areas in Asia and Latin America.

Most of the land is owned communally and is assigned by the chief, who also decides when crops are planted and harvested. Each family is entitled to the crops grown on its plot, although they may have to contribute part of their harvest to the chief's stores. South Africa's staple food is the thin, leathery maize grown on these small plots. Farming for sale to markets is negligible in the reserves.

Many tribes also raise small livestock and cattle, the chief status symbol in a number of tribal societies. A man's standing in his community is measured by the number of cattle he owns. A prospective bride's desirability is measured by the number of cattle a suitor is willing to give her parents in exchange for her hand (although cash has increasingly become an alternative for the bride price, with the growing involvement of Africans in the cash economy).

This stress on quantity has led to a lack of concern about the quality of livestock owned and has caused serious overgrazing of pastureland. It also inhibits the marketing of cattle. In the Transkei region, in 1968, there were 1,500,000 people and the same number of cattle. There were 3,000,000 sheep and goats.

Social and economic conditions in the reserves are as bad as they are in most of rural Africa and seem to be getting worse. The seven million population lives on lands that, from the estimates of the Tomlinson Commission, appear to be able to support adequately only two and one-half million people. The Commission estimated that the average per capita income of the reserves was $42 a year. John Sackur writing in *The Times* of London quoted an authoritative estimate placing the 1969 income per person at $36, a drop in real economic terms of 30 per cent in seventeen years. UNESCO studies have suggested that 60 per cent of African children in the reserves suffered from malnutrition. There were periodic reports of outbreaks of kwashiorkor, the dreaded starvation disease that produced the matchstick limbs and swollen bellies the world saw in photographs from Biafra. Tuberculosis is a major problem.

The pattern of education in the reserves resembles that of the urban areas, although the quality is thought to be even lower. Perhaps 85 per cent of African school-age children in the seven to fourteen years of age group are attending primary school. But only seven tenths of 1 per cent of them will make it through secondary school. White voluntary and church groups that had worked in education in the reserves were forbidden to do so after 1967.

The reserves form a broken arc around the industrialized center of the Transvaal. They swing north along the border with Botswana and Rhodesia, curve back toward Swaziland, and then run in a madcap checkerboard pattern inland from Natal's Indian Ocean coastline. White expansion and the military campaigns of the nineteenth century segmented the land on which Africans lived and dispersed the tribes. The homelands are scattered across more than two hundred separate patches of land, which are small and poor, with one exception. The Transkei is large and poor.

This was the unpromising material with which Verwoerd had to work in designing his Bantustan program. Under his 1959 Promotion of Bantu Self-Government Act, eight tribal nations were delineated. Under white guidance, each would develop its own governing apparatus. In addition to the country's two major tribes — the Xhosa and the Zulu, who each number about four million people today — they are the North Sotho, South Sotho, Tswana, Swazi, Tsonga (Shangaan), and Venda.

The governmental machinery set up by the white rulers consciously imitates the discarded colonial administration elsewhere in Africa. It depends greatly on indirect rule through chiefs, whom the Pretoria regime seems to view as natural allies. White commissioner generals were appointed to represent the government in Bantu areas, much as Imperial Britain had appointed governor generals to her colonies. The Minister of Bantu Administration and Development in Pretoria became a sort of colonial secretary and the effective power in the homelands. Atop this structure the white State President of South Africa remained "the Supreme Chief of all Africans." He retained the power to rule by decree in African areas.

Tribal governing bodies are built into the system at different levels. The Territorial Authority theoretically is the national governing body for all members of each tribal nation, in the reserves and in the white areas. The white government approves the nomination of chiefs and village headmen at all levels and pays the majority of them a salary. In cases where the chiefs refuse to cooperate, the government has installed its own candidates in chieftaincies, by force if necessary.

The power of chiefs had been declining in many areas in the re-

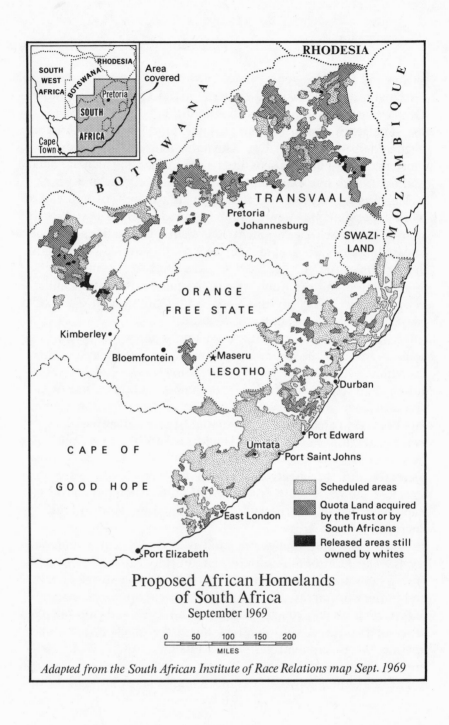

Proposed African Homelands
of South Africa
September 1969

Legend:

- Scheduled areas
- Quota Land acquired by the Trust or by South Africans
- Released areas still owned by whites

Scale: 0 50 100 150 200 MILES

Adapted from the South African Institute of Race Relations map Sept. 1969 serves, as it had elsewhere in Africa. But the separate development government has returned most powers over local matters to chiefs who maintain local jails and collect taxes to pay the large bodyguard forces they frequently need to protect them from their "followers."

Seven of the eight tribal nations have not advanced beyond the Tribal Authority level, and most are not likely to do so in the foreseeable future. The only functioning Bantustan is the Transkei, the Xhosa territory that is uninterrupted by significant white occupation and is therefore "vaguely viable" as a geographic unit, as one apartheid supporter explained it to me. Xhosa tribal authorities also proved to be more cooperative with the white government initially than did other groups.

The Transkei is a 16,000-square-mile territory in the southeastern corner of South Africa, between Natal and the Eastern Cape. One good national road spans it, twisting along ravine-pocked plains and sharply rising hills. Centuries of gusting winds and heavy rains have washed deep gullies across the face of the farmlands. An estimated three quarters of the Transkei is "very mountainous or very hilly," the Tomlinson Commission reported.

On the dry, temperate winter days when I drove across the Transkei, tall and lean Xhosa horsemen rode beside the road, dust swirling around them. They often smoked Dutch-style pipes and wore berets or wool caps. Around their shoulders the men draped blankets decorated with symbols that reminded me of those used by Indians in the Southwestern United States. According to Xhosa (the X represents the clicking sound on which their language is based) tradition, the tribe fought fourteen wars against the whites, and they claim to have won as many as they lost.

The Transkei was elevated from a reserve in 1963, when the white Parliament passed a Constitution that established a Legislative Assembly for the Xhosa. The Assembly, designed after consultations with Xhosa chiefs, was dominated by the chiefs — not surprisingly. It reserved sixty-four seats for them and provided for forty-five members to be elected by adult suffrage. African political parties, banned elsewhere, were permitted in the Transkei.

The chiefs formed the Transkei National Independence Party, which endorsed separate development and pledged to work with the white government. The Democratic Party, composed of more modern Xhosa leaders, opposed the establishment of the Bantustans and called separate development a sham. The Democratic Party won thirty-four of the forty-five elected seats in the first election in 1963. The chiefs ignored the popular verdict and elected their own men to the Cabinet that was to have limited executive power.

Kaiser Matanzima, a towering Tembu chief with ramrod posture and a cultivated air of regal aloofness, became the Transkei's Chief Minister. Because of his outspoken support for the white regime's apartheid policies, Matanzima was written off by many as little more than a government stooge. Critics pointed out that he was reaping a nice personal profit from separate development through participation in companies that were allowed to set up hotels and liquor stores.

But there were also recurring reports that this haughty man harbored a real if unspoken hatred of whites, and some of his actions clearly caught the white government by surprise. In 1964 he refused to drop English as an official language in the schools. He pointed out to the white officials who pressed him that Xhosa was hardly a world language that a sovereign state could use. And he appointed to his cabinet Curnick Ndamase, who had once been banned by the government for his biting criticism of apartheid.

In fact, Matanzima seemed to be trimming his sails enough to keep both sides guessing and to keep his options open. When I interviewed him in his office in Umtata, the trading post town that is the capital of the Transkei, for an hour he gave short, slow answers that were enclosed, offering little opportunity for probing or following up. He was dressed in a conservative dark business suit and a gray cardigan. It was a bleak day outside, but he had the blinds drawn in his office and sat in the somber shadows. As we began to talk, he called in an office messenger to send out for a pack of chewing gum. The youth was shaking as Matanzima gave him the money. In Africa, subordinates are often frightened of coming into contact with high-ranking officials, especially chiefs, who have in the past held the power of life and death over their servants.

"The Transkei cannot be an experiment," Matanzima said, taking exception to my having used that description in a question. "We have our own constitution as a state. Independence must come to us. I cannot tell you when, but we have our constitution, and we have the word of the government that this is to be our nation. This is a Xhosa state. We speak the same language, we have the same customs and traditions." He said it was not unreasonable to expect there to be a long period before independence would be granted. "We are like any other country just being formed. South Africa itself had to be financed from outside sources for quite a long time. Many African states have had the same experience. It is a long process. But it will come. Every people must have a way of self-expression. Every people aspire to run their own affairs . . . The African people have always wanted to take part in the making of law. Now we are doing so, here in our Assembly."

Verwoerd had promised that whites would exercise a "creative withdrawal" from the Transkei and gradually turn over or sell local businesses, government jobs, and white-owned farms to Africans. This would have seemed a painless enough exercise, since there were only 14,000 whites in the Transkei, most of them small farmers or traders living off commerce with Africans.

But seven years of much-advertised autonomy in the Transkei had brought little actual withdrawal and remarkably little transfer of important power to Matanzima's government. In the most visible administrative ways, apartheid's experiment (and despite Matanzima's sensitivities, that is the only word appropriate to what has been happening with the Transkei) in nation-building was lagging badly.

A half-dozen "white spots" had been carved out of the Transkei. These areas where white control would always remain included Port Saint Johns, a badly silted harbor but Umtata's natural port and a potentially sensitive security point. White farms and the main business district of Umtata made up the other white spots.

In towns like Tsolo and Qumbu, the white population suddenly realized that Africans would be able to elect representatives to the town management councils. The councils were abolished and white town commissioners appointed to perform those functions.

Matanzima's Cabinet had been given nominal control over finance, education, justice, agriculture, public works, and interior departments. But the Pretoria government still retained direct control over a wide variety of matters that included defense, police, foreign affairs, the post office, banking, and health. The white Parliament still could amend the Transkei Constitution, and laws passed by the Transkei Legislative Assembly had to be approved by South Africa's President. South Africa also controlled the Transkei's purse strings, since only $8,400,000 of the $33,600,000 budget in 1970 could be raised locally. The remainder had to come from central government contributions.

The commander of the Transkei police force was a white South African police colonel named A. C. Gerardy, who told me that none of his 111 African policemen could arrest a white in the Transkei. He had four white officers under him to supervise the force. There were another 500 regular South African policemen in the Transkei under a separate commander, enforcing a 1960 state of emergency declared by the white government and never rescinded. Of twenty-six district magistrates, twenty-three were whites.

The government agencies turned over to Matanzima's Cabinet were still being run for the most part by white civil servants on loan from the Pretoria government. In 1970, there were 330 white civil servants working for the Transkei government. At the head of them was J. H. T. Mills, whose title was Secretary to the Chief Minister. He was in fact the man who more than anyone else ran the Transkei.

Mills was a very optimistic, upbeat civil servant, who waved away my concern about the Transkei seeming to have so little to self-govern. "The Xhosa are an up-and-coming people. I'm amazed at how well the Bantu civil servants can take responsibility at such early ages and do the job. They are quite far advanced in government as far as the majority of things of interest to the ordinary citizen." I had asked Matanzima a question I had been asking many Africans — Was the "Black Is Beautiful" idea catching on in his area? — and had been told by the startled chief, "No. We don't have that here." I asked Mills the same question to see what he would say: "Yes. There is nothing antiwhite in it, just a more and more positive attitude." I decided he was a natural booster.

Perhaps the most immediately damaging blows to the white government's grandiose claims of creating freedom and justice for the Transkei came from the blatant discrimination that continued to be practiced in and around Umtata.

The mayor of the capital of the future black republic was white. Around the town hall were restaurants, toilets, post office entrances, and even parking places reserved for whites. For the first few years of its existence, the members of the Transkei's Legislative Assembly could come to Umtata to vote for their separate freedoms, but they couldn't spend the night there afterward. There was no hotel that would take Africans. (After a litany of criticism about this, a sparkling showpiece of a hotel was built for Africans.) In the town's only cinema, blacks could theoretically sit in the balcony on certain nights of the week, but few bothered, Matanzima told me. The number of African shop owners in Umtata had increased, but their shops were all confined to the shabby "black zone" of the town. Stores in the main street are owned and staffed by whites.

"Even here, all the amenities are reserved primarily for the whites," Knowledge Guzana, a lawyer who heads the opposition Democratic Party, told me. "You can see how much of a fiction apartheid is. This experiment is nothing but a sop for world opinion. The whites honestly believe they can silence criticism by setting up these fictitious states."

Mills waved me away again. "In South Africa, small discrimination is very much a way of life," he said, in effect counseling me to consider this trait as a South African stereotype, in the same way that tourists regard the French predilection for red wine or the Eskimo custom of rubbing noses. "The Bantu don't complain about this. They have complained about unequal facilities, but not about separate ones. Their legislature could change it tomorrow if they wanted to."

Matanzima had said that talking about such discrimination "is a waste of time. We cannot have a multiracial policy." His comment had originally come after the white Umtata town council refused to let Africans use the town hall for a beauty contest. He would not elaborate the comment for me.

The pace of economic change was also decidedly sluggish. There was progress in commerce, with the government's Xhosa Development Corporation providing Africans with 295 loans over five years to buy or build grocery stores, butcheries, liquor stores, and other small trade outlets. Matanzima's political opponents charged that the loans were based on support for his party and therefore for separate development.

But economic development fell well behind population growth in the Transkei, as it did in all of the reserves. In a decade, population in the reserves increased by 68.7 per cent (against a rise of 16.8 per cent for Africans in white areas), and population density swelled to 117.2 persons per square mile in the reserves (against 34.8 persons of all races per square mile in the rest of the country). Yet there was no appreciable increase in agricultural output, since farming methods and amount of land available remained the same. Nor was there any great increase in the number of jobs available. The number of industrial jobs created in all of the reserves between 1960 and 1970 did not exceed a total of 2000. The border area industries, sited in white areas adjacent to the reserves, created another 80,000 to 100,000 new work opportunities for a population that increased by about 3,000,000.

The economic record of the Transkei with "self-government" was not much better than any of the other reserves. With a population approaching two million, the region could supply only 42,401 wage-paying jobs for Africans in 1969. Nearly one third of that total was provided by the government; only 1280 people in the Transkei held jobs in manufacturing.

This lack of work continued to drive men from the Transkei into white areas. More than 90,000 Xhosa continued to work on the gold and coal mines, hundreds of miles away, and saw their families only periodically. Another 80,000 Transkei people had been recruited through the government to work in the white areas in 1969.

FREEDOM AND HUNGER

The essential economic fact of life for the Transkei and the other reserves is that the intensification of separate development has resulted in their becoming more dependent on the migrant labor system, which is the basis of economic apartheid. (The mechanics of this are explained elsewhere in this book.) This depleted, rather than strengthened, their economic base and their hopes for eventual freedom and kept the whites firmly in control. John Vorster noted in a 1971 interview that "for years to come, labor will be the only valuable export" from such areas. "They would be plunged into total chaos if they were prevented from exporting labor. South Africa will lead its Bantu homelands to independence. It is possible to be poor and independent." [1]

Whatever its intent, the thrust of apartheid has been to populate the homelands with the unproductive members of African society. The homelands are at the end of the line that begins with influx control and the endorsing out of "superfluous Bantu" from urban areas. The aim is to reverse the population profile of the white cities until it resembles again that of Johannesburg at the beginning of this century — almost entirely men, working on short-term contracts. They will visit their families in the reserves only periodically.

The Pretoria government has already cut back on the building

[1] *Le Monde* (weekly edition), February 10, 1971.

of secondary schools for Africans in the white areas and has stated it will build most such schools in the homelands in the future. The government has also indicated that it will stop building and allotting family housing for Africans in white areas.

"There will be no more Sowetos," the municipal guide had told me as we drove back into Johannesburg from our visit to Soweto. We were driving past a large brick building under construction. "That is all we will be building in the future." He explained it was a hostel for African male laborers. Women and children, he explained, would live in the reserves.

The places where many of these families wind up are perhaps the nastiest feature of the reserves. Called "closer settlement areas" in apartheid's jargon, they are resettlement camps for those endorsed out of urban areas and the tens of thousands of other Africans driven from "black spots" of land located in white areas. The Africans call these camps "tent towns" and have given them descriptive names like Stinkwater, Limehill, and Weenan, which means "a place for weeping."

The resettlement camps for South Africa's dispossessed blacks are in fact apartheid's artifacts, barren rural slums as bad as any on the continent. Their distinctive feature is that they have been created for ideological reasons, springing up as apartheid's compartmentalizing of races and land gains speed.

Large communities, numbering hundreds of families, have been packed into trucks, hauled away from areas they had occupied for decades, and deposited in the middle of open fields in the reserves. They have then been given tents they did not know how to erect and told to dig their own pit latrines.

This is the description given by Father Cosmas Desmond of an enforced move of 1200 people from the village of Meran in Natal province in 1968. Father Desmond, a thirty-four-year-old Franciscan priest, had done mission work at Meran and was present the day the families were moved to the camp called Limehill.

"The first arrivals sat in a bare field surrounded by their belongings, looking bewildered and utterly lost," Father Desmond recalled when I spoke with him in Johannesburg two years later.

"That night there was heavy rain and the tents they had been given were swamped."

That experience was the beginning of his yearlong study of the resettlement areas throughout the reserves. Clergymen are the only whites who are allowed to enter the areas without special permission.

Father Desmond reported that many of the camps he saw resembled the poorly prepared site at Limehill. In Weenan, he found 800 people living in makeshift shacks. An old man came up and asked him why the white man wanted to kill him and his children by sending them to "this place where we suffer."

Stinkwater was a different kind of misery. Families who had previously lived on the edge of Pretoria had been shifted to Stinkwater, forty miles further out of town. The men had to make lengthy bus trips to get to work, costing them $6 a week. Increasingly, they lived in dormitories in Pretoria during the week and saw their families only on weekends. There were no sanitation facilities in Stinkwater, and children attended school under a tree.

The result of Father Desmond's inquiry was a graphic and compelling book entitled *The Discarded People*, which was strongly critical of the government. He had hoped for an endorsement of the book from the Catholic Church of South Africa, but none was forthcoming. "This was something I felt the Church should be concerned about directly," he said. "It is the obvious application of the policy of apartheid, which should have been attacked in more vigorous terms from the beginning." He also found his colleagues working in the reserves to be of little help. They feared that his prying would get them in trouble with the white authorities. "Most clergymen in the reserves are little more than spiritual medicine men. They are frightened of becoming involved in this world, because they do not want to jeopardize the work they are doing for the next world."

He finally was able to persuade The Christian Institute of South Africa to publish *The Discarded People*. Expecting it to be banned immediately, he personally distributed the first thousand copies by driving 3000 miles in four days in a Volkswagen in March of 1970.

When I talked to him in May, the government had taken no action, however, and he was puzzled if somewhat relieved. But, as I had been told, the wheels of Afrikaner bureaucracy turn slowly. A year later, Father Desmond was served with a banning order that prohibited him from publishing anything in South Africa, from giving public speeches, or from talking to newsmen, as he had to me.

A NEW BLACK STYLE

There was, in short, much evidence to support those who suggested that the Bantustan idea had been conceived and carried out as a sham by the white authorities. Yet the homelands became an unlikely forum for the first important current of black leadership that was to surface in South African politics after the post-Sharpeville repression. By creating nations-in-waiting, the Nationalist government also created legitimate platforms from which Africans could speak to each other, and to the outside world.

Black leadership became more diffused (and therefore less vulnerable to the "head-chopping" tactics of the past) as apartheid's institutions proliferated. In the homelands, a new generation of tribal leaders, better educated and more in touch with the modern world, seemed to be coming to prominence at the beginning of the nineteen seventies.

The Bantustan experiment gives these leaders more bargaining power with the white rulers than any other blacks in South Africa now have. The power amounts to nothing more than the power to embarrass the whites by trying to hoist them on their own petard of repeated pledges of independence and justice for Africans. But it represents one of the few pressure points that South Africa's disenfranchised Africans possess. In 1970, what the American magazine *Africa Today* acutely labeled "The Buthelezi Factor" was having to be cranked into the calculation of apartheid.

This was a reference to Mangosuthu Gatsha Buthelezi, a hereditary chief in the Zulu tribe and a descendant of the legendary

Zulu warrior Cetewayo. Buthelezi had long been a focal point of opposition to apartheid and separate development among the Zulu. He was expelled in 1950 from Fort Hare, South Africa's leading black university, for leading demonstrations against the white government. He helped organize the Zulu opposition to becoming a part of the Bantustan system, which Matanzima and the Xhosa had accepted in 1963.

But in 1967, white officials told the Zulu leaders that they had no choice but to accept self-government. The Zulu reluctantly formed a Territorial Authority to work with the apartheid bureaucrats, and Buthelezi, finding himself with no other alternatives, turned to working within the system. In June 1970 he was installed as the chief executive officer of the newly formed Zulu Territorial Authority. The government was less than happy about Buthelezi's emergence as the national spokesmen for four million Zulu, but his personal popularity and tribal lineage was such that he was the obvious choice.

Buthelezi immediately began pressing the whites on a number of points. He asked for a timetable for the promised independence. "In my opinion, we should be given full independence within a maximum of ten years," he told the South African press in 1970. He called for a system of free education for African children as well as whites and criticized the tribal aspects of Bantu education.

He became the first tribal leader to establish strong contacts outside South Africa since Sharpeville. He had gone to school at Fort Hare with men who had become members of Jomo Kenyatta's Cabinet in Kenya and re-established links with them. He called for economic aid and investment in Zulu areas from Europe, international organizations, and the United States. He visited the United States in 1971 and made a series of speeches underlining his independent approach.

He brandished his ultimate weapon, that of embarrassment, in a speech at the University of Denver, where he asked for economic development assistance to be given directly to the Zulu. "Should the government interfere in this regard many people would consider its 'separate development' policy to be exposed as insincere," he said.

After Malawi's President Hastings Kamuzu Banda visited South Africa in 1971, and held a conference with the leaders of the proposed Bantustans, Buthelezi pointedly demanded that John Vorster meet the eight tribal nation heads in a conference of leaders on an equal basis to discuss South Africa's future. Vorster refused.

Buthelezi's verbal jabs at the white government created something of a sensation in South Africa, where cheeky Africans had long been absent in national political life. They also stirred Matanzima into a more aggressive posture. His political party issued a demand for an urgent approach to independence for the Transkei. Matanzima suddenly called for the immediate transfer of all departments still controlled by Pretoria to his government and asked increased financial support from the white Republic. He also asked for the transfer of Port Saint Johns to the Transkei.

The Nationalist government stood firm against these challenges, but the embarrassment they created for it was clear. A year before a Verligte Nationalist had mused to me in private: "What would happen if the Transkei demanded complete independence now? The government would say no, of course. But then it would have to face some of the realities about race that separate development obscures." In April 1971 the same question was being raised in debates in the Parliament.

Buthelezi and Matanzima did not, of course, have much of a chance in gaining any form of immediate independence. What they seemed to be doing was trying to obtain bargaining leverage on the two crucial issues confronting the reserves — better treatment for the migrant laborers in white areas and more land. They said that unless more than 13 per cent of the land was given to the reserves, separate development would be shown to be a fraud.

How much they will achieve is to be one of the key questions that will be decided in the nineteen seventies. Already they seem to have begun to foster a new mood in black South Africa that would be a refreshing change from the dispirited climate I found generally in 1970. As *Africa Today* editorialized in reporting the Buthelezi initiatives: ". . . the emerging picture of a new, black strategy is impressive. After years of enjoying a monopoly over all political initiative, the South African government has been challenged by those who are meant to be the docile creatures of its apartheid policies."

Chapter Eight

A Peculiar Economy

SOUTH AFRICA'S GOLD does not lie in riverbeds or near the earth's surface. It is locked deep inside rock, deep beneath the crust of the earth. An imaginative public relations man for the country's powerful Chamber of Mines describes it: "Imagine a solid mass of rock tilted, say, at forty-five degrees — like a fat, 1200-page dictionary lying at an angle. The gold-bearing reef would be thinner than a single page, and the amount of gold contained therein would hardly cover a couple of commas in the entire book. The 'page' has been twisted and torn by nature's forces, and pieces of it may have been thrust between other leaves of the book."

It requires an enormous amount of force and labor to free one-half ounce of South African gold from one ton of stubborn ore. The ore is dynamited, hauled to the surface, sorted, crushed, ground, and shot full of cyanide before it is melted. Only then does it begin to yield the yellow metal that the world's monetary system, South Africa's peculiar economy, and apartheid have been built around. The beloved country has been blessed with the world's largest supply of gold and saddled with the most difficult conditions for mining it man has ever known.

That may help explain why the gold fields of the Witwatersrand area brought only £10 to the man who is credited with having discovered them. George Harrison, an itinerant handyman and prospector, was poking around on the farm of a widow named Oosthuizen one day in 1886 and stumbled on the Main Reef, or gold-bearing vein, a few miles from where Johannesburg was to grow. Harrison sold his discoverer's claim cheaply and wandered off to the eastern Transvaal where, according to legend, he was eaten by lions.

He might not have fared much better if he had stayed on The Reef, as the seventy-five-mile belt of gold fields around Johannesburg came to be known. The small prospectors were soon devoured by the seven mining "houses" that were developed by men like Rhodes, Barney Barnato, and Sir Abe Bailey. The need to sink deep shafts and blast for the gold called for organization and concentrated application of capital, machinery, and labor rather than the pickax or the prospector's sluice and pan. The mining "house," which was an association of autonomous mining companies, could do this. The companies also joined together in the Chamber of Mines, which was given a monopoly to recruit the hundreds of thousands of African laborers who were eventually needed. The mines grew into one of the world's largest and richest industries as the yellow ore, buried in lands settled by the Afrikaners, was dug from the earth by the black labor of the Africans and marketed by the English. By 1970, fifty gold mines in South Africa were producing a total of 1000 tons of refined gold that brought more than $1 billion in sales to other countries.

But gold is a peculiar commodity in which to deal, and its peculiarities as well as its windfall benefits have done much to shape modern South Africa.

Gold is the only conditional, final means of payment of debts between nations. It is the yardstick by which the world measures the health of the international monetary system and foreign trade. There is always a market for it, and South Africa can sell as much as it produces. But gold is subject to the strictest form of international regulation. The price at which central banks of other countries buy it from South Africa ($35 an ounce until 1971, when it was raised to $38) is fixed and remains static over long periods of time — no matter how much costs rise for the producer or how much inflation increases other prices. Gold-mine owners are therefore even more cost-conscious than most businessmen, and more stingy with wage increases. If the official monetary price of gold remains constant for nearly forty years, as it did until the devaluation of the dollar in 1971, then the owners must seek ways to keep their costs at the same level they reached nearly forty years earlier, or see their profits reduced. In South Africa, the easiest way to do this has been to hold the wages of 80 per cent of the mining labor force, drawn from the disenfranchised powerless black majority, at an extremely low level. This has been done through a set of natural and contrived systems.

Gold is also a "wasting asset." It cannot be replenished, and South Africans have long worried that their golden goose would fail them some day. The economic histories of South Africa are littered with gloomy predictions that the shafts would shortly become unprofitable to mine because the gnomes in Zurich would not let the price of gold rise. The predictions seem no closer to coming true today than they did in the twenties or thirties; production of 1000 tons of gold a year represents to the mines what the four-minute mile once represented to athletics. South Africa has produced amounts close to that figure in every year since 1963, and profits and dividends have reached record levels.

But sensitive to the supposed ephemeral nature of the gold business, and aided by skillful government protection of local industry, the mining houses reinvested much of their profits in manufacturing and construction. After World War II, an industrial boom developed that produced a rising spiral of production of consumer goods, affluence, and consumption that resembled on a much smaller scale the rising prosperity the United States experienced at about the same time. Manufacturing output became more important in South Africa's economic structure, as this statistical trend indicates: In 1912, agriculture accounted for 21.6 per cent of South Africa's 307 million rand gross domestic product, mining held a 26.3 per cent share, and manufacturing 4.3 per cent. In 1967, the contribution of agriculture and mining had been halved. Of the nine billion rand GNP, agriculture accounted for 11.5 per cent, mining 12.2 per cent, and manufacturing 24.6 per cent. Commerce, the other large economic sector, remained fairly constant in that period.

In the space of three decades, South Africa developed into the greatest industrial power the African continent had ever known. Between 1947 and 1967, the gross national product increased more than 150 per cent in real economic terms, discounting inflation and population increases. The most spectacular part of that growth occurred in the past decade, with real growth averaging more than 7 per cent a year. Between 1960 and 1967, the national product rose from 5.2 billion rand to 9 billion rand. The standard of living for white South Africans has doubled and climbed significantly for Africans involved in the great industrial boom.

The remaking of South Africa from a poor and agricultural country into a boom-and-bust producer of valuable minerals, and then into an affluent and modern economic power, has transformed the structures of South Africa's race relations and the country's domestic political relationships. In the type of paradox that would paralyze the will of a lesser country, but on which South Africa seems to thrive, the greatest part of the industrialization has occurred during the time that apartheid and separate development were put forward to resolve South Africa's racial problems. Apartheid, crystallized from the rural and mining past of South Africa, is a centrifugal force, scattering the majority of the population outward along the edges of the white center; industrialization is a centripetal force, increasingly pulling people into the factory zones while the factories are expanding. They would appear to be in irreconcilable conflict. But appearances are often deceiving in South Africa.

That the economy has continued to grow while apartheid was intensified tells us a great deal about the relationship of the laws of economics to the laws of white supremacist politics in South Africa. Apartheid has proven in the past decade that it can bend the laws of economics to conform to its laws, while adjusting its own contours to economic changes. The interrelationship of politics, economics, and race in South Africa is so close and delicately attuned that one does not know whether to speak of the politics of a racial economy, or the economics of political racism. This is true to some extent in all countries with ethnic populations in conflict. But these three forces are intertwined and interact in extreme ways in South Africa, which has one of the world's most extreme racial situations, one of the most unorthodox economies, and a pronounced political tendency to extremism.

The surface conflict of a modern growing economy and apartheid's requirements has stirred an important debate in South Africa and among those outside who pay attention to what happens there. According to the optimistic view, fundamental change in South Africa's economic structures will force fundamental changes in its political structures; those who hope for black advancement should hope that the economy will continue to grow. The more industrialized and richer the country becomes, the better race relations will become. Economic growth will erode apartheid and become the most important force for change over the coming decade, this view holds.

This chapter attempts to examine the premises of that debate. It tends to deal with theory and statistics more than other parts of the book and more than I would like it to.[1] But without them one is not likely to understand the economic realities of South Africa, and without understanding the deep-rooted economic system of white privilege and black disability, one will not understand the heart of apartheid. For the economic components of apartheid have carved South Africa into two discernible principal nations: one white, affluent, and more protected by its government from economic competition than is any other group in the world; the other black and poor, whose contractual economic rights have been virtually destroyed by a government that boasts of its devotion to free enterprise.

Much of the system is older than the word apartheid, and it existed in custom and practice if not in law long before the Nationalists came to power. But the National Party has adopted almost all of the long-standing economic restrictions on Africans and made them part of its apartheid program. With the growing prosperity of the country, protection of white economic privilege has

[1] Even so, what follows is necessarily a rough sketch of the dynamics of South Africa's economy. The reader should consult the bibliography for more detailed works.

become perhaps the main product of apartheid and certainly the main political tool of the Nationalist government.

There is not a complete identity of economic interests within the white group, a crucial but often overlooked or misinterpreted factor in South Africa's racial-political economy. The white ethnic-coalition United Party government that lost power in 1948 tended to reflect more concerns of the English-speaking businessman, or mine owner, than does the victorious National Party, which pays special attention to protecting its two chief political patrons — the white farmer and the white worker, especially those who are organized into strong unions, like the mineworkers and the railway men. Both parties attempt, of course, to balance their approach and gain the most support possible from all these groups. But periods of great economic change, such as the decade from which South Africa has just emerged, intensify the differences.

The approach the Nationalists have adopted can be broken into four components. They are the pillars of what might be called economic apartheid. (The term "color bar" is often used in discussing economic restrictions in South Africa, but it is too imprecise to be of much use in any serious analysis. It will be avoided here.) They are:

1. The migratory labor system, which is designed to do away with a permanent black population in white areas while retaining the use of black labor for specified periods. The political appeal of this to all whites except factory owners and industrialists is obvious, given the present state of race relations in South Africa.

2. Job reservation. Through law and custom, most skilled and high-paying jobs are reserved for whites, and Africans are not allowed to supervise whites. White labor unions profit the most from this.

3. Restrictions on racial contact in places of employment. These bars are part of petty apartheid. Again, white workers see that their government is doing something to keep the kaffirs down.

4. Low wage policies. This is where the greatest number of white interests coincide and is therefore perhaps the most durable part of economic apartheid. White workers take a larger share of

salary cake since African wages are held down. Whites who own mines and factories, and foreign businessmen who invest in South Africa, see their profits rise.

The main controls on black wages include the government's refusal to allow Africans to form unions that can bargain for wages or to strike (this has a major political benefit as well as keeping Africans from organizing); monopoly hiring practices such as those used on the mines; a "civilized labor" policy, which establishes the idea of a minimum wage for whites that is not applied to nonwhites, even if they do the same work; and, of course, job reservation.

The nineteen sixties present a good illustration of the diversity of interests within the white group, which is no more of an economic monolith than it is a cultural or political one. A period of quick growth creates more jobs, skilled and unskilled. But it cannot create more whites to fill the jobs that are traditionally and legally occupied by whites only. Thus, a shortage of white labor develops, giving white unions and workers more bargaining power. They translate this into inflated wages, and the resulting abnormal rise in production costs brings them into conflict with the white industrialists and mine owners.

The industrialists complain to the government that their inability to use black labor efficiently (i.e., to reduce their total wage bills by using blacks instead of whites in some skilled jobs) is damaging economic growth. The government then has to balance the obvious political benefits of maintaining strict white supremacy against the economic benefits of relaxing job restrictions on nonwhites. In the last decade, the expanding economy required wholesale exemptions from the system of job reservations. But the Nationalist government was not prepared to pay the political cost of jettisoning the system, which white workers understood as a visible expression of economic security.

(When the economy contracts rapidly, the same sort of conflicts arise, but in a descending spiral. Because profits are dropping rapidly, the industrialists appeal to the government that they must have cheaper labor if they are to stay in business. As is the case with expansions, politics is at least as decisive in the government's response as economics.)

Those, in very broad lines, are some of the essential dynamics of South Africa's highly politicized economy. In a number of ways, economic laws and relationships are defied by South Africa's rulers with as much ease and satisfaction as are all those United Nations resolutions. The natural flow and competition of labor and capital is impeded by government action; so is the development of larger domestic markets and more consumption and increased personal savings by most of the population. In South Africa, race controls economic forces, not vice versa, although the Marxist, and the American businessman looking for a justification to continue investing in South Africa, are both likely to disagree, for very different reasons. The Marxist will argue perhaps that racism is a method of class control, with the whites constituting a privileged and exploitative class. But this, like most Marxist analysis, ignores the highly variable human factor in history. And there are few more powerful and universal human forces than racism.

WHITE PRIVILEGE: FARMER AND MINER

Agriculture has always been a tough proposition in the arid interior of South Africa. For the first two centuries of its white history, South Africa was an economic nonentity. Its only profitable export and source of wealth was wool. The Boer in the interior had little interest in farming for markets and in any event lacked the ability to do so on a profitable scale. He preferred to stake out a vast claim — 6000 to 8000 acres for a man and the other ten or twelve members of his family was long considered a minimum in some areas — and depend on Africans, who were also accustomed only to subsistence farming, to do almost all the work. This gulping of land quickly exhausted the great open stretches of South Africa. It also encouraged absentee ownership and land speculation, which lowered production drastically. By the middle of the nineteenth century, late-arriving whites found little land left to stake. Many became *bywoners;* they were allowed to live on un-used parts of the large Boer farms, but had no claim to land. They, too, depended on black labor.

The first test of economic competition was produced by the op-portunities for Africans to work in the mines at the end of the nineteenth century. The native, who was not supposed to under-stand Western ways, acquired a little capital and began to put it to use. Africans began to buy bits of land outside the reserves. They were willing to farm on a scale that Europeans rejected and will-ing to pay high prices for the land since they had few other living expenses and valued land and cattle above everything else. Dis-mayed at the thought of competition even on this modest scale, the outnumbered whites reached not for the gun, as they had in the past, but for a pen to write a law. They passed the Natives Land Act of 1913, and legalizing white economic privilege began to become a way of life in South Africa.

The mines played a key role in developing South African agri-culture as well as later laying the foundation for the industrial takeoff. A major share of the tax revenues coming in from the mines was diverted to aiding white farmers by extending credits, financing agricultural research, and subsidizing cheap transport and higher market prices. Production climbed and the export of fruits, quality wine from the Cape vineyards, maize, and other commodities joined wool to become important to the country's economy. Only a tiny fraction of the money spent on agriculture was related to African farms. Black farming remained at a sub-sistence level and contributed little to the national economy.

Despite all this help, however, white farmers have continued to be as much of a financial burden to the government as they are an asset. The Nationalist government continues to pay large subsi-dies, direct and indirect, to the white farmers, especially the small ones. And the farmers, 80 per cent of whom are Afrikaners, con-tinue to vote Nationalist.

South African agriculture has been unable to resolve its two major problems — an enormously wasteful use of manpower and uncertain weather.

Despite the drift to the cities, South Africa's farms continue to be overpopulated in relation to world standards and to the farmers' contribution to the national product. There are 93,000 white-owned farms, which have a statistical average of about 2100 acres each. They produce in an average year 10 to 12 per cent of the gross national product, yet they employ about 25 per cent of the country's economically active population, excluding the peasant African farmers in the reserves. (If they are included, the figure jumps to more than 40 per cent of the population producing 10 per cent of the national output.) In the United States, about 6 per cent of the population is employed in agriculture.

The main cause of this is the continuing inefficient use of cheap Colored and African labor on these farms. Nonwhite workers outnumber white farmers and workers on an average of 115 to one in some areas.

Chronic drought is the other major agricultural problem. Only along the coast and in parts of the Transvaal is there consistent rainfall. Most of the country averages less than fifteen inches of rain a year, and great stretches are arid, semidesert plains. From 1963 to 1970, one part of the country after another suffered from drought. The 1970 failure of rains was the most general and devastating. Farmers in some parts of the country boarded up their farmhouses and left their stock to perish because they could no longer afford to buy fodder for them. South Africa's thirty-eight million sheep, the world's eighth largest sheep population, were especially hard hit.

The entrenchment of white economic privilege in the mines was not as easy a task as it had been on the farm. It required a long and difficult struggle, which created the most serious rebellion that any South African government has ever faced. Surprisingly for a country in which a black explosion is expected, it was a revolt of white men.

The first generation of skilled white miners came from England, where they had gained experience in coal mines. But the Boers and the bywoners, driven from the farms, gradually took over the semiskilled and then the higher paying jobs on the mines. By the second decade of this century, a commission studying the mines was told that 75 per cent of the white miners were of Dutch origin.

The sensitivity of the white mine owners (who were English-speakers, not Afrikaners) to costs, and the growing evidence that African laborers could master many of the mining skills after they had worked several spells on the mines, became major concerns of the white mine workers' unions that were formed in the first decade of the century. Reacting to pressure from them, Parliament endorsed white supremacy with the Mines and Works Act of 1911. Regulations drawn up under the act prohibited the mines from issuing blasting certificates to Africans — thus cutting off their advancement to the technical rank of miner. Equally important, the regulations froze the white-black employee ratio, which meant that the mines could not fragment jobs and give them to blacks to save on wages. For every ten blacks hired, a new white foreman had to be hired, whether the mines thought he was needed or not. In 1911, there were 200,000 Africans working on the mines, and 25,000 whites.

The crisis came in 1922, as the price of gold dropped rapidly. South Africa's Supreme Court had ruled that the white supremacy regulations exceeded the scope of the Mines Act, and the mine owners, desperate to cut costs, proposed to the unions a "work-reorganization." It was in fact a plan to replace 2000 white workers with blacks, at lower salaries. Negotiations on the plan failed, and the white miners went out on strike in March.

They formed commando units and attacked black mine workers who refused to strike. They raided the mines and the offices of the mine owners and took over sections of Johannesburg. The strike took on a political air as the leaders, mostly Afrikaners, began to call for the declaration of a republic.

The Smuts government proclaimed martial law on the Rand and used cavalry, small artillery, and a few armored cars to end the closest brush South Africa has yet had with revolution. More than 240 persons had been killed, 600 wounded, and perhaps 4000 arrested, four of whom were executed for high treason.

Until the National Party victory at the polls in 1948, the Rand

Rebellion was the most important single event in twentieth-century South Africa. Smuts had broken the strike, but he had also broken his government. He was to be forced out of office two years later after a bitter campaign. The National Party of Hertzog and the English-speaking Labour Party campaigned on a single issue, neatly summarized by John Fisher: Was South Africa to be one huge black compound kept for the benefit of the capitalists or a prosperous white man's country? [2] The voters gave their answer in 1924 and the coalition Pact government, as it was called, came to power. In 1926, the color bar was written back into the law in such a way that the courts could not remove it, and the course of white-black economic relations for the next four decades was decisively determined. Politics and race had prevailed over economic forces. This was underlined by the rise in the mines' profits in 1923, when the color bar was partially suspended, and the subsequent fall when it came back into effect.

The attitude of the white miners, which persists today, was conditioned not only by fear of economic competition, but also by the need to reinforce the overall doctrine of white supremacy. As farm work had earlier, manual labor in the mines had become kaffir work. Allowing an African to become a miner would open white miners to ridicule in white society as doing kaffir work. Thus, levels of employment as well as specific jobs had to be protected. Also, it is difficult for the white race to be superior if members of it live in a way inferior to that of nonwhites.

A destitute white is a danger in the laager. He is a visible sign to the native that not all white men are superior, and he is a morale problem for his fellow whites. The white standard of living must be kept visibly above that of the nonwhites, as part of the ideology. This is one of the motivating factors in the government's insistence that white workers are to get a proportionately larger share of the economic benefits than they would if the society were run in a more economically rational manner. It is this desire to extend the ladder down to the lowest level of white society and

[2] *The Afrikaners*, p. 255.

drag it up to economic prosperity that invalidates a completely Marxist analysis of South Africa's political and economic linkage. Since 1948, the South African government has been run not to maximize profits for capitalists, but to maximize white domination and privilege.

This is also the base of the "civilized labor" policy, first enunciated by the National Party in 1924, reaffirmed as government policy in 1948 when the Nationalists came to power, and never disavowed. Under the policy, whites are to be paid enough to enable them to maintain "the standard recognized as tolerable from the usual European [i.e., white] standpoint," even for unskilled work. An African or Colored doing the same work will receive only a fraction of the amount paid to a white, since they do not have the usual European standard of living to maintain. This, of course, presents a great temptation to white employers to use black workers, a temptation that the legal reservation of jobs for whites helps them resist.

BLACK BARRIERS

Restricted from buying land and expanding their farms, blacks were forced to become wage earners to support their population growth. But the white polity has placed crippling restrictions on the Africans' ability to sell their labor. Apartheid ensures that they work on white terms, or not at all. The terms are perhaps roughest on workers in the mines.

I watched two mine workers begin the ritual 3500 feet down a mine shaft at Doornfontein, a gold field fifty miles west of Johannesburg. Willie, the white miner, crouched inside a four-foot-high pit, or stope as it is called by the miners. He had already marked the face of the rock wall for drilling. A black laborer, known to the company not by name but by an identity number, sat on the floor of the pit, his arms and legs wrapped around a jackhammer drill. As Willie dropped his hand as a signal, the black laborer started the drill. His body shook violently as the noise of the sharp, short bursts caromed around the stope. The damp dust and moisture dripping from the shaft's ceiling swirled through the passageway and choked the half dozen people in the tour group I had joined. At the end of the eight-hour shift, Willie would insert explosive charges into the 100 holes being drilled in the rock face, and the blasting apart of the gold and ore would begin.

Willie, an Afrikaner who spoke only rudimentary English, earned about 300 rand ($420) a month. The black laborer (technically miner is a rank that only whites can hold in South Africa) made 20 rand ($28) a month. The work they did is not all that different, the mining supervisor guiding our group conceded in response to a question. Then why the large gap in pay? "Because Willie's skin is white," the guide replied matter-of-factly. "It is the most valuable commodity you can have in South Africa. It is more valuable than this yellow stuff we blast out of the earth."

After we left Willie in the mine shaft, we were taken on a brief tour of the sprawling compound that housed the 9500 Africans employed on the Doornfontein mine. The African workers stared as intently and curiously at the white tourists as we stared at them. The regular guided tours the Chamber of Mines sponsors may be a kind of fringe benefit for the laborers. In the huge kitchen, where a lunch was being prepared for several thousand men, the powerful odor of great quantities of raw meat, waiting to be cooked, assailed us. On most parts of the continent, the company official showing us around noted accurately, Africans are lucky to have meat meals once or twice a week; here the workers get meat daily. He explained how the diets had been determined scientifically and, later, added that there had not been a fatality from heat stroke in the mines in over a year. His tone was like that of a Four-H award-winning farmer talking of well-kept and well-fed cattle. After assuring us that the Bantu were never happier than when they were in the compound, where they slept in crowded, small dormitories, the official added: "Well, at least they're not out running amuck, are they?"

Of the 9500 Africans working at Doornfontein, thirty-six had permission to have their families live with them. Most of these men were clerks assigned permanently to the mine. Most of the laborers would not see a woman for a year.

They could not leave the compound without the permission of white company officials. It would be a criminal offense for the Africans to break the six- to eighteen-month contracts they had signed and to try to go home. I had been told that an average of fifty Africans a week "desert" from the mines and usually wind up in jail. The Chamber's official spokesman, after a number of enquiries, assured me that the desertion rate was nowhere near fifty a week and "was in fact less than one per cent a year." That would be about seventy desertions a week.

South Africa's mines — gold, copper, coal, iron ore, chrome, platinum, uranium, and other minerals — employed 606,000 Africans in 1970. Like those at Doornfontein, all of them were on short-term contracts. During a year, an estimated 220,000 African workers, or about one third of the mines' labor force, would finish their contracts and have to be replaced. But they were not leaving the mines for good. Many of them were just going out of a continuously revolving door and would step back in six months or a year after spending time on their peasant farms in the reserves. Seventy per cent of those working their first tour on the mines would be back for a second stint according to Chamber of Mines statistics. Others would return for a third, or perhaps fourth, contract.

The revolving migrant labor system grew up for obvious reasons on the mines. It was not so much the physical hardships of mining that produced it, but the coinciding economic targets of the first generation of African mine workers and the mine owners. For the Africans, brief work periods on the mines offered a chance to accumulate cash, something they could never do on their subsistence farms. They could buy specific consumer goods they wanted, pay off debts to the white storekeepers who had begun to move into the reserves, buy more cattle or land, or, pay off the head tax the white government had enacted to make sure there was a steady stream of labor.

The mine owners in turn never had to worry about providing sick leave, vacations, pensions, or housing for families, or high wages. There was always another stream of Africans on the way. The massive turnover of black labor also kept Africans from developing the experience they needed to challenge whites for skilled positions and kept their families out of "white" areas.

The only major direct expenses of the system borne by the mine owners are recruiting and training new workers. As long as blacks are kept at the unskilled job level by the color bar, training is not a crucial problem. Recruiting for gold mines, which employ the bulk of African mine labor, is handled systematically and efficiently by a Chamber of Mines organization known as Winela, the Witwatersrand Native Labor Association. There are more than 200 mine labor "depots" located throughout Southern Africa. Illiterate young men who have no land to farm are first recruited by tribal chiefs, rural storekeepers, or special agents, who get a commission for each X on a contract, or the recruits may walk to the depots on their own. Then they are transported to Johannesburg, where they are screened and examined for health problems; if they pass, they are funneled out to the mines.

South Africa's Transkei region supplies about one fourth of the 360,000 Africans who work on the gold mines in a given year. The majority, however, come from outside South Africa's borders. About 90,000 Africans come from neighboring Portuguese Mozambique, the enclave nation of Lesotho sends 60,000, and 50,000 more come from another independent black-ruled and poverty-stricken country, Malawi. These "foreign natives," as they were called before Bantu came into vogue, are the basis for the oft-repeated South African claim that hundreds of thousands of Africans vote with their feet each year and show their approval of, or at least a lack of hostility to, apartheid by coming to South Africa to work. The point has been made by others that these workers do not go to South Africa. They go to the mining compounds. Mostly tribal Africans, they are kept in almost complete isolation there until they finish their contracts and are then forced to return to their own countries, which are without exception economically stagnant and offer the worker no alternative for earning cash other than a tour of the mines.

South Africa's white allies, the Portuguese, benefit from this arrangement. A portion of the workers' wages are remitted to the Portuguese government, in foreign exchange, to be returned to the laborer in the local Mozambique soft currency, minus taxes, when he returns home. In return for the guarantee of migrant laborers, the South Africans signed the Mozambique Conventions of 1928, which guarantees the Portuguese that a fixed percentage (currently 40) of all seaborne goods destined for the Transvaal will be imported through Mozambique ports and railways. The payments for this transit trade are a major source of foreign exchange for the Portuguese.

Portuguese officials were reluctant to discuss with me their ties to South Africa, so I asked a diplomat in Lourenço Marques, the Mozambique capital, about the labor recruiting. "It sounds on the surface like a tremendously exploitive thing," he replied. "When I started going out to the bush to talk to men who had worked on the mines, I was saying, 'Gee, that must have really been tough, huh?' But the men would say, 'No, actually it was kind of nice. I ate better than I ever do at home, I saved enough money to buy a new wife or some cattle, and I got a miner's helmet.' The hard hat is a real status symbol out in the bush. In some parts of Mozambique, you aren't considered a man unless you have worked on the mines in South Africa. That's partly because you aren't going to have the bride price otherwise."

He quickly added that he did not think the arrangement was entirely "wholesome," however. For one thing, it takes labor away from Mozambique and cuts farm production significantly. The same observation can be made for the other countries and the Transkei.

Perhaps the most significant fact about the foreign natives working in South Africa is that they are needed at all. There is no accurate count of African unemployment in South Africa, but published suggestions that there may be more than half a million functionally unemployed able-bodied African males in South Africa indicate that there is a problem. Why then should South Africa import massive quantities of unskilled labor?

One can only speculate. Part of the answer would seem to be political. It helps bolster the migrant labor policy and keep local Africans from becoming more organized as an economic force. Since independence, it has also become a method of retaining economic leverage against outside states. But perhaps the larger part of the answer is that it helps depress wages paid in mining to Africans. By widening the labor pool, the mines ensure they find men needy enough to accept the conditions and low pay on the mines. The indications are that the only reason an internal labor shortage exists in South Africa is that there are men in the reserves who can eke out a slightly better living, even under the harsh conditions they face there, than they can get from the mines.

If this surmise is correct, then it would not be in the government's interests (or perhaps more precisely, in the mine owners' interests) to improve to any great extent farming conditions in the reserves. This would lead to an even greater dependence on foreign recruited labor or to having to pay higher wages to local Africans. The disparity between what has been spent on help to white agriculture and to black agriculture may not be as clear-cut a case of simple racial neglect as it appears.[3]

The social impact of this vast migratory labor system that has been worked out for the mines is obviously detrimental to the African family. Professor D. Hobart Houghton, a South African economist and economic adviser to the Prime Minister, calls it "an evil canker at the heart of our whole society, wasteful of labor, destructive of ambition, a wrecker of homes and a symptom of our fundamental failure to create a coherent and progressive economic society." But there seems little hope that it will be reformed at any time in the foreseeable future. The drift of apartheid is in the other direction. When Harry Oppenheimer wanted to experiment with villages for married Africans at some of his mines, Verwoerd halted it with a reminder in Parliament that mar-

[3] Ralph Horwitz, in *The Political Economy of South Africa* (Praeger, 1967), p. 136, estimates that between 1910 and 1936, the government spent and loaned over £112,000,000 for white agriculture and around £613,000 for African farmers, mostly in the form of sheep and cattle dipping tanks and land purchases.

ried quarters would "become a channel" into the cities for children of the workers. It would also create a permanent black economic force on the mines, something the white mine workers and the government are not willing to allow.

The most important control over African wages is undoubtedly the legal prohibition against Africans bargaining collectively for wages. Only "employees" of "registered" unions can bargain with their employers as a group. The law excludes Africans from the category of "employee," and the government refuses to register unions that have Africans as members. It is something like the apocryphal tale of the Chinese newspaper Mississippi vote registrars are supposed to have used for their literacy tests for blacks. Africans can form unions, but the unions can have no purpose.

Most employers openly oppose giving Africans the right to form effective unions. The Chamber of Mines has issued statements saying that the African cannot understand the process of collective bargaining. The fact is that African trade unionism was at one time a strong force on the mines, and Clements Kadalie gained a world reputation as an African organizer there in the nineteen twenties. But the African unions splintered, and the leaders were either bought off by white industrialists or jailed by the white government. Anyone who raises his head today as a black union leader would be immediately slapped down by the government.

It is also illegal for Africans to strike for any reason. The only recourse African workers seeking higher pay have is to request the National Party bureaucrats in the government to look after their interests in a bargaining session with management.

In 1969, less than 15,000 Africans, or about three tenths of 1 per cent of the African labor force, belonged to unions. Thirty per cent of the white economically active population belonged to unions, which are politically powerful. Attempts to defy the system seemed doomed to failure. In April 1969, 2000 African dockworkers in Durban went out on strike for higher wages; the police were called in and the workers were told to return to work or be dismissed; 1500 of them refused to return, were fired on the spot, and given four hours to clear out of Durban. The company then easily hired another 1500 Africans who needed jobs to qualify to stay in Durban.

UNSCRAMBLING THE EGG

The rapid industrial growth South Africa has experienced under the Nationalist government has been something of a mixed blessing for the politicians who run the government. It has generated the sharp rise of the African population in the cities and made the task of separating the races into territorial compartments seem just about impossible. In 1970, 4,800,000 of the 7,000,000 workers in the "white" economy were black. Altogether, about 80 per cent of the labor force was nonwhite. Industrialization had effectively scrambled even more the egg that apartheid was invented to unscramble.

Looking wistfully at the situation, Hendrik Verwoerd once said: "If we had had here a white England and a white Holland, and if this white state could have developed to a self-supporting condition as those European states have developed by themselves, then we should certainly not have had the friction and the difficulties which we have today." Industrialization, however, had made his "ifs" impossible and his "then" a dream.

Like most politicians, the Nationalist leaders are not adverse to having things both ways when they think they can, so it is difficult to judge exactly how they intend to meet this challenge. They assure visitors that no one has ever suggested that all the blacks will be tucked away in their own separate nations when apartheid is in place. Then they hurry off to the campaign stump to suggest precisely that to the somewhat gullible white electorate. It seems clear that the intent of big apartheid is to reduce the number of Africans in white areas to the bare minimum needed for economic reasons and to exert stringent control over them.

To do this, the government appears to be now attempting to transfer to the industrial society the two major economic tools of control forged so long ago on the mines — job reservation and the migrant labor system. This is the major change that economic forces have brought for the shape of apartheid. The ongoing development of apartheid makes sense only in the light of current and near-future economic pressures in South Africa. Influx control and "endorsing out" may appear to be simple, mindless cruelties perpetuated by sadistic racists. They are in fact attempts (however misguided) to solve the conflict of the theoretical "push" of big apartheid and the actual "pull" of industrialization. The answer is the creation of a vast, floating population of black migrant workers who can be channeled to and from the white-owned mines and factories by bureaucrats, with the African laborers and the Hoggenheimer industrialists having little say about it.

Industry did not have a legal system of job reservations until 1956. Previously, what custom did not reserve for whites, pressure from the white unions and the Apprenticeship Act of 1922 did. The act reserved skilled work for those who had been apprenticed, and the unions saw to it that no Africans were apprenticed.

The growth of industry pulled Africans into semiskilled and skilled factory jobs vacated by whites moving up at the beginning of the nineteen fifties. White unemployment dropped to less than 1 per cent and skilled white labor became scarce. The government passed legislation enabling it to reserve any occupation on a racial basis. From 1956 through 1970, twenty-six "job reservation" orders were issued, usually in response to complaints by whites. Some of the orders cover small, specific areas and protect a handful of people. Others affect entire industries. The owners of automobile assembly plants, for example, were ordered not to replace a white worker with a nonwhite or a Colored with an African. Only whites can manufacture door and window metal surroundings in South Africa. In some areas, Africans can drive transport trucks weighing less than 10,000 pounds unloaded, but it is illegal for them to drive a truck heavier than that.

The government estimated that the twenty-six job reservation orders covered only 3 to 4 per cent of all occupations in South Africa. But the threat of job reservation hangs over all industry and hinders employers from promoting blacks.

Job reservation and traditional color bars increased the already fierce competition for white labor. White wages shot up out of all proportion to productivity in the final years of the sixties. There were just not enough whites to go around in South Africa. The government had to resort to granting wholesale exemptions to many of the job reservations it put on the book or to winking at industry's widespread disregard of the color bar. Firms hired African clerks and called them messengers. They fragmented one job once held by a white into three separate, simpler tasks and hired three Africans for less than it would have cost to have hired a new white (if they could have found a white to hire). In some factories, machines run by whites in the day were run by Africans at night, under another job title and at one-third the salary.

But the government refused to drop job reservation, despite the enormous confusion it created. "This crazy country has half its population employed issuing permits to the other half so they can go to work," Helen Suzman complained. "That is why nothing ever gets done." For the Nationalist, the advantages of the system outweighed the bureaucratic problems. It not only boosted the government's stock with the white workers, but also gave the bureaucrats another important pressure point against the businessmen. As long as the government held the power over granting or refusing the exemptions for badly needed labor, businessmen would be more reluctant to incur bureaucratic wrath.

Limiting the advancement of 80 per cent of the country's population and work force into skilled jobs has a number of serious effects on the economy. Three results stand out: inefficiency, inconvenience, and inflation. I met a number of extraordinarily hard-driving executives and workers in South Africa, but I also met some of the surliest, most inefficient cabdrivers, waitresses, and post office clerks on the African continent. These happened to be white. One has to think of Kinshasa or Dahomey's Cotonou to find places to compare with the depths of white South African service. There are people who desperately need apartheid's protection of their jobs.

More frustrating for the permanent resident is the inconvenience that is built into apartheid. Whites can only ride buses driven by whites. But the shortage of white bus drivers caused cities like Johannesburg to curtail white bus service by 20 per cent in past years. "Every winter morning that I stand at a bus stop and watch as half-filled buses driven by nonwhites roll by me, and jammed buses for whites refuse to stop because they are too crowded, I curse apartheid a little more·bitterly," said one white.

There were an estimated 65,000 vacant whites-only jobs in 1970. A total of 100,000 nonwhite workers were registered as unemployed, and many more were not registered.

Inflation and harm done to South Africa's balance of payments position are more serious consequences. Unrealistically high white wages make South African goods more expensive to produce and therefore more expensive to sell abroad. The cumulative effect of this pattern on the domestic scene became apparent in 1970 and 1971 as inflation reached 5 per cent a year. The government raised bank rates, taxes, and spurred price increases on selected commodities in an effort to curb consumer spending and produce a deflationary effect in mid-1971.

The migrant labor system to be developed for industry is still embryonic in comparison to that on the mines, but its mechanisms are already in place. Under a 1964 Act of Parliament, government labor offices have been established in each homeland. They are operated by white government employees. African work-seekers in the reserves must register with the office as they come of age and can leave the reserve only if they have obtained contracts of labor approved by the bureau. The government offices will be the entry point of Africans into the urban industrial areas in the future. The reserves will become occasional homes for the millions of migrant laborers who will go to work in the white area on contracts limited by law to twelve months. They will return home to visit the "unproductive Bantu," their wives and children, for a few months before signing up for a new contract in white South Africa. The hostel for male migrant workers that the guide pointed out to me in Johannesburg casts a chilling shadow across South Africa's future. Hiring will be done by the state. Private contractual rights between white and black, already at an extremely low level for a supposed free-enterprise state, will almost entirely disappear.

These migrants would form the bulk of unskilled labor needed in labor-intensive South Africa. Another black industrial population would be located in the border areas at the edge of the homelands and the white cities. The nucleus of black laborers needed for skilled jobs would be Africans who have lived in urban areas all their lives and have avoided trouble. They would number no more than 6,000,000. That at least is the outline of future labor apartheid that I constructed from available publications and interviews in South Africa.

THE SALARY GAP

The components of economic apartheid combine to create an enormous disparity between white and black earning power. The gap is greatest in mining. The average white miner earned 316 rand a month, seventeen times the average rate paid to black workers in 1969. Africans supplied 86 per cent of the labor for the mines, but received only 29 per cent of the 36.8 million rand annual payroll. African workers do receive free their meals and lodging, estimated to be worth an average of 20 rand a month; white miners, however, also receive fringe benefits that more than tip the balance back in their favor. Discounting rises in the cost of living, the 18 rand a month the average African miner received in 1969 represented less purchasing power than he would have received in 1911.

There are an almost equal number of Africans, around 600,000, employed in mining and in manufacturing. They made up 69 per cent of the manufacturing labor force, but drew only 23.5 per cent of the 124.4 million rand annual payroll in 1969. The average white wage was 278 rand a month against 48 rand for an African factory worker. Africans did well that year only in construction, which boomed in 1968 and 1969 as foreign capital fled the monetary crises afflicting Europe and poured into South Africa and created a monetary oversupply that sought quick investment. The 237,000 Africans represented 52.5 per cent of all construction workers; they received 34.4 per cent of the payroll. The white-black pay ratio was greater than 6 to 1.[3]

Perhaps the most remarkable and significant single statistic in South Africa is this: Africans, who make up 70 per cent of the population, control less than 20 per cent of the country's personal cash income. The 1970 per capita annual income of white South Africa's 3.8 million population was estimated at around $2700. Only Sweden, Switzerland, and Canada, which vie for second place to the $3500 per capita income of the United States, have figures equally high.

As noted, South African whites live extremely well. Although urbanization has increasingly created apartment-dwellers in Johannesburg, the white factory worker has a small house, a one- or two-year-old automobile, and either a small investment in the stock market or a savings account. Specific wage levels can be judged from some typical starting monthly salaries for whites in 1971, converted to dollars: $200 for a white high school graduate who has completed military service, $337 for a Bachelor of Arts graduate, $440 for an engineer graduating from college or for a lawyer just hanging out his shingle with a firm. In urban areas, prices for food tend to be slightly lower than in equivalent American cities, while prices for quality manufactured goods are somewhat higher.

Per capita income figures for any country are notoriously unreliable indicators; they cannot reflect what may be a great concentration of wealth at one end of the spectrum and general poverty at the other. They are especially ill-suited for black South Africa. The episodic employment of those who drift from reserves to mine to reserves and the vast numbers of permanent subsistence farm-

[3] The disparities are growing at a rapid rate. In 1971, the mining pay ratio had risen to 20 to 1, from 17.6 to 1 three years earlier. The construction and manufacturing wage gap had been 5.4 to 1 in 1963. For all industrial sectors combined, white monthly salaries rose an average of 48 rand between December 1966 and December 1969. African monthly wages rose 5 rand a month in the same period.

ers in the reserve who almost never see cash make average figures almost meaningless. In any event, South African government figures tend to be too optimistic, partially because of a calculated effort to bolster the government's frequent claim that blacks living under white rule in South Africa are more prosperous than blacks living under black rule in the rest of Africa. The government prefers to talk about the far more attractive per wage earner income for blacks and the total African cash income, which in 1970 was about $1.7 billion. More than two thirds of this figure is thought to have been earned by the urban quarter of the black population, meaning that many factory workers did have salaries in excess of $600 a year, a sum that is considerable for workers on the African continent.

But the growth in total cash income does not reflect the explosive African population increase that eroded much of the total wage increase, nor does it show the effect of the rising inflation on black purchasing power with these wages. In the reserves, in any event, subsistence farming has been calculated to equal an income of about $35 a year. Allowing for the great spread, a per capita income of $120 to $130 for South Africa's fifteen million blacks appears to me an accurate figure.

Comparing the general African economic position in South Africa with that position elsewhere on the continent is an almost impossible task. Statistics are even more unreliable in black Africa, and costs of living vary greatly from area to area. The statistics that are available, however, tend to discredit South Africa's propaganda points. The $130 per capita figure in 1970 would have ranked South African blacks below at least seven black African countries — Ghana, Gabon, Ivory Coast, Liberia, Senegal, Zambia, and Sierra Leone — and the four Arab North African states, according to per capita income statistics issued by the World Bank. (The gap within the African population of these countries is greater than in South Africa, of course, because there are no color bars on Africans.) But the great contrast between the undeveloped economies of all these countries and the industrialized might of South Africa blur this kind of comparison. Perhaps only one country can validly be compared to South Africa, and that is Zambia.

Harry Oppenheimer's Anglo-American Company is one of two companies that employ a total of 50,000 Africans on Zambia's copper mines. The International Labor Organization reported that African mine workers earned an average annual salary of $1820 in Zambia in 1968. In South Africa, black mine workers made $300. The average annual wage for the 6000 foreign white mine employees, most of whom were British, Canadian, American, or South African, was $10,640. Africans supply about the same percentage of mine labor (89 per cent) in both countries, but the Zambian miners take home about 60 per cent of the payroll and black South Africans, 29 per cent. South Africa's gold and coal mines are more labor intensive than are Zambia's copper mines. But the chief difference is the existence of effective black unions in Zambia and black political control, neither of which exists in South Africa. It is this sort of disparity that raises the fear in more sophisticated Afrikaners that the African may get the idea that the only way to economic power in South Africa is through political power.

SUCCESS AND FAILURE

There are two stories woven into the development of South Africa's peculiar economy. One is the undeniable success of that economy in a material sense; the other is its failure to have any meaningful liberalizing effect on South African race relations, as many had hoped. The past decade has seen economic expansion and the repression of black political and social rights proceed almost in tandem. This view was given me by one economist: "More economic progress means the government can buy more guns, bigger tanks, and pay its spies among the Africans a lot better."

The debate on the effect of economic growth on apartheid has been carried on in extremely imprecise terms. The difficulties the government has had in imposing job reservation and the migrant labor systems on an expanding industrial economy have been hailed as evidence of the imminent end of "apartheid." When white economic interests have come into conflict and white industrialists have criticized the government for not allowing them to hire more blacks in order to avoid high-priced white labor, the criticisms have been hailed as evidence of the imminent end of "apartheid." When the government, to keep the economy going at an unprecedented rate of growth, grants exemptions to the job reservations it has imposed in the first place, this too is hailed as the end of "apartheid."

What is demonstrated by such actions is not the end of apartheid, but the inappropriateness for a growing industrial society of two of the system's controls. There may well be an erosion of job reservation. But job reservation covers only 3 per cent of all jobs in South Africa, as the government notes when it is trying to convince outside critics that the system of job reservation is not very important.

As for the complaints of the industrialists, it is important to understand what is being said. After mildly complaining about labor restrictions in his presidential address to the Chamber of Mines in 1969, General Mining's T. F. Muller went on to set the record straight: "The industry has been criticized in extravagant terms for allegedly advancing Bantu to the detriment of the job security, safety and health of its white employees," Muller told his fellow mining magnates. "We are strongly opposed to any step that would undermine the security of the white or any other class of worker on the mines. This is not in any way proposed or threatened." (Muller's identification of whites as a class is an especially revealing point in his speech.) While American publications frequently have featured interviews with Harry Oppenheimer noting his criticism of apartheid and his prediction that "We will stagnate eventually unless there is a change," [4] rarely have they dug back into Oppenheimer's public statements for South African consumption. These include a qualification that he does not favor

[4] The New York Times, April 18, 1971.

black advancement at the expense of white interests.

In short, there was no important businessman in South Africa in 1971 challenging white domination of the economy — only the form the domination would take. "All the mines are asking for is the same kind of flexibility that industry has," Francis Wilson told me in his University of Cape Town office. Wilson is one of South Africa's most astute economists. "If they get it, the change will be heralded as the end of apartheid. It won't be, of course. It will just be shifting the color bar a little higher." Wilson, with a tinge of cynicism in his voice, noted that businessmen and mine owners "make a fuss about how unjust it is for a black man not to be able to work because of race restrictions. Hardly any of them ever say anything about the justice of making Africans live in Soweto, or not letting them have unions, or about voting." Wilson is white.

Big apartheid is tied to the theory of economic decentralization, the spreading of industries throughout the country in such a way that the black population will be dispersed and not concentrated in volatile masses at the edge of white cities. The decentralization did not occur in the nineteen sixties at anything approaching the rate the government had predicted. Economic expansion continued in the existing industrial regions of Witwatersrand, Pretoria, Port Elizabeth, Durban, and Cape Town. In this sense, economic growth has caused a mitigation or perhaps a retardation of big apartheid. The requirement for there to be permanent black residents in white South Africa to serve the labor needs of whites means that big apartheid can never be pure, in that black and white will not be completely separated geographically. In that sense, economic growth does undermine "apartheid." In some cases, the increasingly experienced urban Africans will work in close proximity with whites and move up in skilled employment. This, too, represents an undermining of job reservation and "apartheid."

But to believe that the Africans will be able to use that improved position to wrest political and social concessions from the white government is to indulge in wishful thinking and to make the kind of underestimation of the Afrikaners' ability and determination that his foes have characteristically made and which have been major factors in his success. "It would be nice to believe that economic forces will predominate," a man with a powerful voice in the National Party told me. He is disillusioned at the moment with the course apartheid is taking. "But they won't. The whites will say, 'The Africans must go. We want them out.' And they will go." A white man working for a liberal English-speaking company added later: "They could make an African general manager of this company, and he would still have to live in Soweto. It wouldn't change a damn thing but his salary, and that would still be lower than mine."

In the coming decade economic apartheid will be reshaped for industry and commerce. The important controls — civilized wages, refusal to recognize unions, conditioning jobs on the approval of apartheid's bureaucracy, and refusal to let a nonwhite ever supervise a white — will be continued as they are now. The government has already begun to probe for new ways to express its dedication to white supremacy in the economic sphere while relaxing its restrictions enough to allow Africans to take more skilled jobs. This was the substantive meaning of a thrust by Piet Koornhof, a National Party politician, during the 1970 parliamentary campaign. Koornhof, Deputy Minister of Bantu Administration and Development in Vorster's cabinet, issued a notice that he intended to bar Africans from white collar employment that brought them into contact with whites. "I am proud to announce the end of labor integration in South Africa," Koornhof was quoted in the South African press. The newspapers noted that thousands of African clerks, sales assistants, receptionists, and telephone switchboard operators would lose their jobs, even though there were no whites to replace them. Johannesburg employers were nearly as upset as the Africans.

After the election, Koornhof backed away from his threat, although he never disavowed it. I had a long discussion with him in his Pretoria office toward the end of a working day. Proudly displayed on his desk was an autographed picture of Chicago's Mayor Richard Daley, whom Koornhof said he made friends with during a tour of the United States, where he studied our racial problems.

Koornhof seemed to be an intellectual manqué, a man with a bright mind that has been dulled by the demands politics and race make on even simple truths. He was probably a good representative of a second-level Nationalist politician. He would have made Daley a good alderman.

Koornhof indicated that he had never intended to hamper economic growth by kicking Africans out of jobs. He claimed that the insidious English-language newspapers had misquoted him to stir up racial animosity in the country.

"We've got problems," Koornhof said after much preamble. "Europeans resent seeing the Bantu in these kinds of jobs. We've had friction. This is a new development. Now you get a Bantu female and a white female, working eight A.M. to six P.M. continuously, in one office, and you are going to have friction, let me tell you. We get a lot of complaints about it. Not only on the part of whites, mind you, but blacks, too. Some of them suffer because of this labor integration. So we must stop this. If European employers are trying to be difficult, we are going to tell them, 'Stop your bloody nonsense.' This is all new, it is not traditional, and we must adjust." Koornhof paused in what had developed into a monologue, and I asked him for some specific examples of the problems labor integration had created. He gave me four, three involving receptionists. In each of the four, the complaint had been made by a white offended at seeing an African doing such work. In each of the instances, the solution was to remove the black worker.

Koornhof and other Nationalist leaders have subsequently talked about the need to construct wooden partitions in factories and offices where Africans and whites work at close range. A Cape Town department store received government approval for its answer to "labor integration" problems: staffing one floor with Colored sales help and another with whites.

Such is the erosion of apartheid. Perhaps the most important economic change occurring in South Africa is not black advancement, but Afrikaner advancement, as I have suggested earlier. The creation of a class structure within Afrikanerdom is being accelerated by the fact that for the first time Afrikaner businessmen (Jan Marais, for example) have joined their English-speaking colleagues in publicly opposing the Afrikaner bureaucrats who manipulate the economic controls of apartheid (e.g., Koornhof). There is no significant black voice in the debate, and there is no point at which blacks can exert pressure themselves for their own economic advancement. It is all being decided for them by white men, who, whatever their momentary quarrels over dividing up the profits, have no essential conflict in the continuing white control of the society.

Industrialization did not reduce totalitarianism in the Soviet Union, nor did it in pre-World War II Germany — just the opposite. And it is not likely to do so in South Africa. The most that can be hoped for is that continuing prosperity will make Afrikaners view themselves as a more modern, economic- and class-oriented people, rather than as a tribe. This will undoubtedly lead to an elimination of some of the more blatant and cruel manifestations of the racism of South African society. But economic expansion alone will not transform essential race relations in South Africa. On the record of the past twenty years, anyone who expects the economy to erode white supremacy in South Africa is sadly mistaken, bluffing, or looking for an excuse not to seek any significant change at all.

PART II

OUTSIDE THE LAAGER

RISING IN THE HIGHLANDS of Central Africa, the Zambezi River plunges off the plateaus of Zambia and Angola onto the coastal plain of Mozambique to flow into the Indian Ocean. Along its 1650-mile course, the Zambezi carves deep gorges through the forests and stone mountains in its path. The river's valley forms Africa's great racial and political divide. It is the meeting ground of the struggle between black and white for the control of Southern Africa. At one end of the valley, Portuguese engineers are attempting to construct one of the world's great dams, the Cabora Bassa Hydro-electric scheme. At the east end, black guerrillas slip across the river on a sabotage mission to the south.

As Gamal Abdel Nasser did with Egypt, South Africa's rulers seem to view their powerful nation as the center of a series of circles of influence and responsibility. The first circle largely ends at the Zambezi. Inside the circle are Rhodesia, much of the inhabited areas of Portuguese Angola and Mozambique, the disputed territory of South West Africa, and three black-ruled states surrounded by the white powers — Botswana, Lesotho, and Swaziland. South Africa shares 2700 miles of border with these white allies and black satellites, which are militarily and economically vital to the survival of white rule in South Africa. In the past decade South Africa has established what amounts to a Monroe Doctrine for Southern Africa. In the coming decade, Pretoria is likely to try to group these seven potential colonies and the Bantustans, should they ever come to life, into a Southern African commonwealth dependent on South Africa.

North of the Zambezi lies South Africa's second circle of interest — black-ruled Africa. About thirty countries, with a total of 200 million inhabitants, came to independence in the last decade. Most of the new African countries immediately committed themselves to helping dislodge the white regimes of the southern subcontinent. Opposition to white rule was, in fact, one of the few issues around which these often weak and poverty-stricken countries could unite.

But guerrilla campaigns and calls for economic boycotts by the Organization of African Unity proved ineffective in the independence decade. A number of African leaders became disillusioned over their inability to affect events in the south. A few said so publicly; most remained silent. At the same time, the South Africans gingerly launched what came to be known as the "outward policy." They offered diplomatic relations, economic and technical aid, and investment to any African country that would agree to "nonintervention" in South African affairs. By 1971, the policy had produced concrete results: the black president of Malawi paid a visit to South Africa in search of more investment and loans, and other African leaders called for a "dialogue" with the white governments.

Having mastered African nationalism in every visible aspect inside the laager, John Vorster's government set out to challenge the assumption that black nationalism was a broad, powerful, and continentwide force. The outward policy is based on the belief that African nationalism is in fact narrow and inward looking and will lead black leaders to put their immediate national interests before the racial conflicts of Southern Africa. Apartheid's internal grand design is based on tribalism, but so is the functioning of a number of independent African countries. The outward policy became a direct appeal to African countries to perpetuate and develop (with South African help) the existing divisions of the continent, in the laudable name of national development.

Geographically, the Western world represents South Africa's third circle, but in many other respects, Europe and North America are at the heart of Pretoria's primary external concerns. The outward policy is calculated not only to stop African support for boycotts and guerrilla fighters, but, more importantly perhaps, to undercut Western support for such moves by enhancing South Africa's international image. Black Africa is in no position to harm South Africa. Britain, France, and the United States are. In the past decade, Western countries have repeatedly condemned apartheid. But they have taken few steps to bring actual change in Southern Africa. On balance, the actions have tended to strengthen the white governments. British and American businessmen continued to invest heavily in the flourishing economy of South Africa, and the French sold sophisticated weapons with a total value estimated to be more than $500 million to the South Africans and the Portuguese in less than ten years.

The white powers in Southern Africa sought to identify themselves with a worldwide campaign against Communism. They labeled anyone who supported majority rule as a Communist and therefore an enemy of the West. The shadow of Western military support projected by the large investment in South Africa and Portugal's membership in NATO has been a key factor in the unwillingness of the Russians and the Chinese to become directly involved in toppling the white-minority governments. Although nettled by continuing criticism of apartheid from the West, and especially from the United States, South Africa's leaders seemed to operate on the assumption that if "the crunch" came — if they appeared to be greatly endangered by a force the West perceived to be Communist — they could count on direct Western support. Nothing the Nixon, Heath, or Pompidou administrations did in their first years of existence gave any reason for that assumption to be doubted. On the contrary, each of these governments got on better with Vorster's regime than had its predecessor.

The nebulous force of world opinion, which was presumed to have been so important in removing white colonial rule from the Third World, seems to have had little impact in Southern Africa. The United Nations had proved to be totally ineffectual after more than a decade of resolution-passing. In 1970 Secretary-General U Thant labeled South Africa's continuing defiance of the

U.N. as the greatest danger that body confronted. It was causing many to lose faith in the organization's ability to do anything, Thant confessed in a speech to the Organization of African Unity.

South Africa's efforts to look beyond the laager were, however, largely in response to outside events and pressures. Pretoria extended its influence and responsibility reluctantly, and more than many Afrikaners would have liked. But the eruption of guerrilla warfare in the two neighboring Portuguese territories, Angola and Mozambique, and the attempt of much of the world to apply comprehensive economic sanctions to end the white settlers' rebellion in Rhodesia forged an alliance between the three white regimes. "Good friends do not need a pact," John Vorster said in 1967 in one of the first enunciations of the Monroe Doctrine for Southern Africa. "Good friends know what their duty is if a neighbor's house is on fire. I assure you that whatever becomes necessary will be done." Many analysts interpreted this assertion to cover all of the first circle, including the black enclaves. South Africa is, for example, providing most of the financing as well as guaranteeing a market not only for Cabora Bassa but also for the giant Cunene dam scheme in Angola.

The entente produced by the broadening of the white-black struggle to a regional level was an odd and at times uneasy one. Much more was involved than the personal conflicts between the Latin, Catholic Portuguese and the Teutonic, Calvinist Afrikaners, or between either of these groups and the English farmers who took over Rhodesia.

Lining up with the Portuguese and the Rhodesians, who clearly form the remnants of European colonialism on the African continent, does serious damage to the South African argument that they are an indigenous and in fact anticolonial people. The alliance suggests once again that race has overtaken nationalism as the driving force in Southern Africa, since there could hardly be two more antithetical interpretations of nationalism than those of the Portuguese and the South Africans.

For the Portuguese and, to a lesser extent, the Rhodesians, the association with apartheid is an unpalatable one. They endorse nonracialism, deny that they discriminate against black men, and at least indirectly criticize the South Africans for doing so. By rejecting apartheid, the Portuguese and Rhodesians provide virtual laboratories in Southern Africa for the testing of alternatives to that system. The great disparity in black-white ratios (twenty to one or more in Portuguese Africa and Rhodesia, nearly four to one in South Africa) makes any exact comparison impossible. But in some ways Rhodesia's approach to race demonstrates what South Africa might have been like if the softer apartheid advocated by the United Party had been applied to South Africa; Portugal's doctrine of equal rights for all civilized men of a certain class corresponds to the Progressive Party's program for South Africa. On balance, the Portuguese and Rhodesian approaches have produced little more real advance for the black majorities under their control than apartheid has in South Africa.

The immediate outlook then is that white power may prove to be as impermeable to outside pressures and influences as it has to internal ones. But there are a number of unpredictables. The most pressing short-term factor in South Africa's development is likely to be the staying power of its white allies. C. W. de Kiewiet has noted that South Africa has little to fear from the strength of its enemies, but much from the weakness of its friends. The Rhodesian regime appears especially brittle, and the Portuguese are being drained financially by the guerrilla wars. How South Africa reacts to changes in her neighboring territories could be the key to the survival of white power in Africa.

Chapter Nine

Rhodesia: Lotus Flowers and Scapegoats

WHITE POWER in South Africa is a problem of the present and the future. No sufficient precedents exist for the dismantling of an industrialized society controlled by such a sizable minority. The racial problems of South Africa will have to be resolved in conjunction with a number of other social and economic forces that are evolving throughout much of the world. The process of decolonization that ended direct white rule elsewhere on the continent has hardly affected South Africa, except for the backlash decolonization stirred among the country's whites and the false hopes it raised among Africans there.

White power in Rhodesia, however, is a problem of Africa's past. It is a worrisome anachronism, an unremitting hangover. While South Africa's political leaders subscribe, at least in theory, to promoting changes that will allow Africans some political self-expression, those of Rhodesia remain committed to a form of paternal white settler rule similar to that already discarded in Kenya or Algeria. Either of those countries should be able to provide a model for developments in Rhodesia. The Kenya solution involved a relatively controlled African uprising that led the British to encourage black political leaders willing to leave settler economic interests undisturbed. This kept the entire economy growing and provided a larger share of benefits for a Kenyan elite. Another approach would be Algeria's externally supported war of attrition, which led to a quickly negotiated settlement and a large white withdrawal.

Theoretical models count for little in Southern Africa these days, however. Neither Kenya nor Algeria borders on South Africa; Rhodesia does. Pretoria has a direct interest in events there and a great influence on them. The South Africans have demonstrated that they are prepared to intervene to preserve white power within their first circle of responsibility by providing security forces to fight African guerrillas in Rhodesia and by moving to thwart the economic sanctions the United Nations imposed against the white settler government.

The survival of that government into the nineteen seventies was a stunning defeat for world opinion, British authority, and African nationalism. Moreover, it underscored the failure of multiracialism in Southern Africa. If white and black could not come to some sort of arrangement for sharing power in the relatively uncomplicated society of Rhodesia, was it likely that they could do so in the complex South African society? If the 240,000 white settlers who controlled 4,800,000 Africans in Rhodesia could neither be persuaded nor forced to relax their grip, could the 4,000,000 whites in South Africa?

For the first sixty years of the twentieth century, Rhodesians had a comparatively low-key approach to racial matters, as these can be distinguished from problems related to differing stages of development. Those who went in for proclaiming the equality of the races did so without the fanfare of the Portuguese and without having to face the obstacles of Afrikaner-controlled South Africa. There were a few African students at the local university, a handful of educated black people on the voting rolls, and a sprinkling of blacks at the bars of Salisbury's hotels. Whites treated tribal Africans as something other than human, however.

After reaching power in 1964, the settler government of Ian Smith staged a steady retreat from the paternalistic approach of the past and inched the country toward apartheid. Separate development became an attractive phrase in the course of the 1970 parliamentary elections in Rhodesia, where men had previously claimed to follow the principle laid down by the country's founder, Cecil John Rhodes — "Equal rights for all civilized men." The shift from discreet but effective discrimination by class and economic power to open racial segregation seemed to support the Afrikaners' charges on the weakness of English-speaking commitment to racial equality.

To carry out this retreat, Ian Smith had to make his Unilateral Declaration of Independence from British control in 1965. U.D.I., much examined elsewhere for its international implications, was a symptom, not a cause, of the fundamental change occurring within Rhodesian white society, which was in rebellion against itself as much as it was against Britain. Moderate leadership was cast aside by white and black Rhodesians, and Smith's government became increasingly filled with petty and shortsighted men who welcomed the state of siege that the independence dispute thrust upon Rhodesia. The result was a shrill new racism in Rhodesian life that is likely to prove to have been a costly luxury for a white minority outnumbered twenty to one. Indeed, when the British and the white settlers decided late in 1971 to try to patch up their differences, black African resentment against the Smith government burst forth in peaceful and violent ways.

Internally, Rhodesia in the past decade has presented an important case study in race relations. It has great relevance not only for the rest of Southern Africa, but also for all pluralistic societies. Race is an issue that is particularly susceptible to the force of leadership. Racism is largely a product of conformity and is greatly influenced by the tone set by a society's leaders in their public pronouncements. The binding force of racism is the fear of being excluded from the group, of being ridiculed and laughed at, of being talked about, or of being discriminated against if one does not adhere to the racial code supposedly established as the community's norm. In social terms at least, a man's racism is not so much a fear of his opposites, but of his neighbors. If he is given moral protection from them, by community or national leaders, he often finds that race diminishes greatly as a concern for him. The surprisingly rapid forsaking of supposedly sacred racial barriers when enlightened leadership is forthrightly applied is evidence of this. A good example is the evident tempering of racial pressures in the Southern United States over the last decade. In Mississippi and Alabama, state leaders resisted integration of universities in the most vehement ways, and there was violence. In South Carolina, there was reasonably moderate leadership, and no violence. Elections throughout the South in 1970 showed a discernible trend to moderation that was a result of enlightened community leadership that had been largely absent in my own time there. To use South Carolina as an example again, the election of moderate John Carl West as governor demonstrated that electorates could be brought along.

There are enormous differences between the racial situations in the Southern United States and in Southern Africa. But it seemed to me that Ian Smith was proving in the same year that the electorate could also be shoved back, for the same ingredients that make race susceptible to influence from leadership also make it a ready mark for pandering. It is fairly easy to unleash racist stampedes by convincing the average man that all his neighbors are doing it, too.

MOVES TOWARD EQUALITY

The roots of white power are much shorter in Rhodesia than in South Africa or in the neighboring Portuguese colonies. The Portuguese originally claimed the territory, but they were unable to settle it. In 1890, Cecil Rhodes effectively added it to his personal empire within the British Empire. He equipped and dispatched from South Africa an armed force of two hundred settlers, called Pioneers. Drawn by the promise of fertile land and gold, and supported by five hundred policemen, the Pioneers marched into Rhodesia. They met little initial resistance and established Fort Salisbury. The land was fertile, but there was little gold worth mining and the settlement remained small. Rhodes ran the territory as a commercial venture under the control of his British South African Company. Before he died in 1902, he had pushed the railroad north into Rhodesia, where about 11,000 settlers then lived. Most were British, although Rhodes had encouraged a sprinkling of Afrikaners as well.

Company rule continued until 1923, when Rhodesia became a self-governing territory within the British Empire. Britain appointed a governor to the territory and retained powers of review over matters affecting the African population. But effective control of the country, including the local security forces, passed to the settlers, who formed their own legislature. There were then about 35,000 whites in Rhodesia and more than one-half million Africans.

Britain granted self-rule after the settlers rejected a proposal to unite Rhodesia with South Africa as a fifth province. In a vote of 8774 against to 5989 for, about sixty ballots were cast by Africans who met the financial and educational qualifications, which were similar to those that had been established in the Cape Colony by the English and which had been so bitterly opposed by the Afrikaners. The English faith in class structures seemed justified in Rhodesia by the outward evidence of the slow pace of civilizing. In 1948, less than 250 Africans voted in a legislative election in which 47,840 ballots were cast.

In World War II Rhodesia was used as a training station for British flyers. A number of those who came liked the country's pleasant climate, its open plains, and its easy way of life. Many came back to stay, and word of Rhodesia's attractions circulated through drab postwar England. The tide of white immigration rose. In 1951, the white population had grown to 130,000. Longtime settlers, who had come to form a sort of landed gentry, tended to look down on the newcomers. (Many still do, classing families socially by whether they arrived before or after World War II.) The new immigrants tended to set up in the cities or establish small farms. They were understandably ill at ease with the class lines the old guard had established.

The chain of events that led to the 1965 rebellion against Britain began in 1953, with a major alteration in the constitutional status of the territory, then known as Southern Rhodesia. Across the Zambezi lay Northern Rhodesia, a black colony directly under

British political control. The rich Copper Belt of Katanga continued into that butterfly-shaped colony and made it wealthy by African standards. Between the two Rhodesias and Lake Nyasa lay Nyasaland, a small, economically uninteresting colony also under direct British rule.

Rhodesia agreed in 1953 to join the two colonies and form the Central African Federation. In theory, the arrangement meant slightly more British involvement in Rhodesian affairs than had been the case in the thirty previous years. But there were considerable economic advantages for Rhodesia's infant industrial complex in establishing a protective tariff wall around the Northern Rhodesian market. Nyasaland would supply labor for the white-owned factories. The Federation added 4,500,000 Africans and only 50,000 whites. Each territory retained its own legislature, and it was assumed that the white politicians of Southern Rhodesia would run the Federation.

African nationalists in the two other territories, led by Kenneth Kaunda in Northern Rhodesia and Hastings Kamuzu Banda in Nyasaland, saw the Federation as a device to continue white control over them. Neither Kaunda nor Banda saw any point in trying to stay in the Federation and to seek a change in the attitudes of the whites in Southern Rhodesia. They wanted immediate independence for their own territories. Faced with pressure elsewhere in Africa, the British granted it to them in 1964, after allowing the two colonies to secede from the Federation. Northern Rhodesia became Zambia, and Nyasaland is today Malawi.

The British decision to allow the breakup of the Federation, which brought African governments to power on Rhodesia's borders, was viewed as a betrayal by many white Rhodesians. It was denounced in particularly bitter terms by Sir Roy Welensky, who had headed the Federation and who was viewed as a leader of the old guard gradualist forces. The breaking of the Federation destroyed Welensky politically. More importantly, it brought a new bitterness against Britain, and the strong identification white Rhodesians had felt with the worldwide culture of Britain began to fade. Much as English-speaking South Africans had after Pretoria's withdrawal from the Commonwealth, white Rhodesians sought a new, narrow sense of white nationalism. "Britain has lost the will to govern in Africa," Welensky said bitterly when the Federation was ended.

In Southern Rhodesia, internal politics had drifted back toward the right just before the dismantling of the Federation, after a period of relative liberalism. Southern Rhodesians had chosen Garfield Todd, a former missionary and an immigrant from New Zealand, as Prime Minister of the territory in 1953. Todd began a series of liberalizing trends in race relations. But he ran into strong opposition in his Cabinet on the issue of a wider franchise for Africans, and was forced to resign in 1958.[1] But his successor, Sir Edgar Whitehead, quickly came to agree with many of Todd's ideas and proposed a new constitution that formally endorsed multiracialism in Rhodesia. It gave Africans new voting rights and held out the promise of eventual majority rule. Whitehead argued that only an opening of the door to African aspirations would prevent a racial explosion and destruction of the white power structure. He also stressed the morality of the issue.

The Whitehead constitution introduced a new category, or roll, of voters who would elect fifteen members of Parliament. The qualifications for voting for these fifteen seats were much lower than those required to vote for the fifty seats on the "A" roll. This directly benefited the African electorate, since their registration on the A roll was not disturbed. Africans would in the distant future achieve a majority in the Parliament by continuing to increase their education and incomes.

Heeding Whitehead's arguments that Rhodesians were ready to move gradually toward a just multiracial society run by "civilized" men (i.e., by whites and Africans who accepted white values totally), the 90 per cent white electorate approved the constitution by a 41,848 to 21,846 vote. It was not that clear-cut a victory for racial gradualism, however. The new constitution also contained provisions that provided for greater direct local control over Rho-

[1] Cabinets in Rhodesia have traditionally exercised the power to unseat Prime Ministers.

desian affairs and was thus attractive to voters on those grounds. In any event, subsequent reactions to the Whitehead constitution indicated that the ideal of multiracialism was losing its appeal in Rhodesia.

Joshua Nkomo, the leading African political spokesman at the time, first favored the constitution, then rejected it. Younger men convinced him that independence was too near his reach in 1961 for Nkomo to accept the gradual multiracialism that might bring the first African government in fifty years. The nationalists had already rejected Whitehead's bid to work within a multiracial political party that would seek a gradual sharing of power. Instead, they demanded immediate majority rule, but the African movement split, largely along tribal lines. Later, when Nkomo and other leaders were placed in detention, black participation in Rhodesian politics was put on ice for the rest of the decade.

White reaction to the constitution was also sharp. Ian Smith, Whitehead's deputy whip, resigned from the ruling United Federal Party and pledged to work to reverse the move toward sharing power. He helped form the Rhodesian Front party, which criticized the constitution, charging that it would bring Africans to power before they were prepared to rule. A year after Whitehead's constitution was approved at the polls, he was voted out of office. The Rhodesian Front captured thirty-five parliamentary seats and a majority of the votes. Africans heeded appeals from the nationalist leaders to stay away from the polls. In several areas, African abstentions were on the order of 80 to 90 per cent and contributed significantly to Rhodesian Front victories.

The sudden turnabout was partly attributable, as Frank Clements suggests in *Rhodesia*, to the disorganization and petty quarreling between Welensky and Whitehead in the United Federal Party and the effective organizing of grassroots farming support by the Rhodesian Front.

But deeper changes in Rhodesian society were reflected by the turnabout. "The whites suddenly realized that we had asked them to share power with the Africans, and they said 'no,'" Welensky was to tell me nearly a decade later.

Welensky and Whitehead, who had accepted titles of English nobility, were representatives of the old rejected order. Winston Field, a farmer who became Prime Minister after the Rhodesian Front victory in 1962, was a transitional figure in what Welensky was to describe to me as "this Greek tragedy we've been caught up in." Field got along well with Africans personally, but he did not think they should be brought along too fast as a group. He had been educated in England.

Field argued that the ending of the Federation meant the ending of British supervision of Rhodesian affairs. He applied for a formal grant of sovereignty, but London refused. When Field, whose health was poor, appeared to be willing to take "no" for an answer, a Cabinet revolt forced him to resign in April 1964. The Cabinet, which demanded a harder line on both the British and the Africans, chose as the new Prime Minister Ian Smith, thus culminating the shift of power from Rhodesia's peculiar sort of aristocracy to a new white bourgeoisie that had been forming in Rhodesian society.

Attitudes and the actual composition of the white settler population had been changing in the late nineteen fifties and early sixties. Pre-independence rioting in Nyasaland and the intransigence of African nationalist leaders in Rhodesia, where there were also outbreaks of politically motivated violence in the African townships, frightened the whites. The chaos of the Congo in 1960 also had a traumatic effect on them. Many of the settlers who fled Katanga came through Ndola in Northern Rhodesia and some passed on through Salisbury, elaborating at each stop on the brutalities inflicted on whites by the Congolese.

Moreover, a new type of white immigrant had begun to arrive in Rhodesia. As independence from colonial rule came closer for Kenya, Zambia, Malawi, and other territories, settlers there packed up and headed south. Many were genuinely frightened by the Mau Mau revolt in Kenya. Others were just psychologically incapable of living under black political rule. Some of those coming to Rhodesia had originally fled to Kenya from India in 1948. Their versions of what happened when Africans took over a country were highly colored by their own insecurities and fears. It would be difficult for them to admit that whites had received fair treatment in Kenya and Malawi without also admitting that they had been wrong, that they had fled before a false threat. Their voices often seemed to have a slightly hysterical ring, as did that of a man who rose at a campaign meeting in 1970 to tell the crowd: "If we get fifty per cent Centre Party in the Parliament, we can all pack up and go across the Limpopo right now. There won't be nothing left." (The Centre Party, which was badly defeated in the election, favored a Whitehead-style gradualism.) The psychological impact of this immigration was greater than its statistical importance. This was also to be the case of the outflow of young white Rhodesians later in the sixties. A fearful brain drain developed as many whites out of sympathy with the increasing racialism in Rhodesian life decided to live abroad. Students decided not to return after finishing their studies in England.

Ian Douglas Smith had been born in Rhodesia, the son of a Scots immigrant who was a butcher and a farmer. Smith's family belonged to the older Rhodesian settler community. But he clearly saw his political role as representative of the new settlers, those who wanted Rhodesian society delineated on racial, not class grounds. (Just as Welensky, who had been born of a poor family and worked on the railway, played his political role as "Sir Roy," so Smith moved beyond his origins.) A determined athlete who was captain of the rugby, cricket, and tennis teams in secondary school, Smith was an indifferent student and went to university not in England but in South Africa. Like many of the immigrants who came after the war, Smith had been a pilot in the British forces. It fell to Smith to declare that Rhodesia, rather than accept British suggestions about bringing Africans gradually into Rhodesian political life, had taken its independence from Britain in defiance of claims of continuing sovereignty. The settlers issued a Declaration of Independence consciously modeled on the American one and were especially desirous of acceptance of their position by the American government and people.

REVERSING THE TIDE

My first visit to Rhodesia was in 1970 for an election that preceded South Africa's by a few weeks. Six years had elapsed since
Smith had come to power, and four since he had taken U.D.I.
Economic sanctions had been imposed, but had not brought
Smith down. He, on the other hand, had not achieved any international legitimacy. Not even the South Africans and the Portuguese would recognize Smith's noncountry while the dispute with
Britain continued; they did, however, play the major roles in
breaking sanctions.

Six years of isolation, and perhaps more importantly, of Smith's
leadership, had produced a mentality of siege in most white Rhodesians. On my first day in Salisbury, I stopped in a bank to get
some of the newly printed Rhodesian dollars that had replaced the
pound. (The clerk cheerfully ignored the "Not negotiable in Rhodesia" stamp put on my traveler's checks in Kenya.) I noticed on
the wall of the teller's cage a calendar that showed a smiling,
kindly-looking, middle-aged couple standing on their suburban
lawn, watching a pair of dogs frolic. "This is our country," the
legend beneath them read. A heavy line underscored "our." And
there was no suggestion that the legend should have read, "our
country, too."

The calendar captured some of the important vibrations I felt in
Rhodesian society. It was an aging country. The major contrast
between the crowds that I was to see turn out to hear Ian Smith
and those who would rally to John Vorster a few weeks later in
South Africa was that the Rhodesian groups contained few young
people or children. Also, like the couple, Rhodesia has a distinctly
suburban air. It is not an industrial settlement, like urban South
Africa, or a frontier one, like rural South Africa. Life has always
been relatively easy, relatively prosperous, relatively undemand-
ing. A large if varying percentage of Rhodesia's white population
has been composed of people who come to the territory for five to
ten years to make money and then return to England or travel
elsewhere to settle. Those who do settle permanently go into small

businesses or open small factories, and many retain a parochial view that is remarkable even by Southern African standards. "Salisbury is all right, but it's too far from town," an American visitor once observed. He referred not to the physical attributes of the bustling, attractively modern Rhodesian capital, but to its psychological makeup. A British journalist termed Rhodesia a "Surrey with a lunatic fringe on top."

About 70 per cent of the white population lived in Rhodesia's cities and towns before sanctions. It was a prosperous agricultural country, well known for its exports of quality tobacco. The major mining industries were coal and chrome, in which American business had about $50 million invested. For its size the country had a sophisticated financial and commercial infrastructure, with its own small stock market. But most white Rhodesians concentrated on the good life of golf clubs, swimming pools, and plenty of servants rather than making fortunes. They did not have to worry about the same kind of problems that industrialization and a major mining industry, with its huge demands for cheap labor, had brought to South Africa.

More to the point, most of Rhodesia's whites probably could not have handled such problems. Many of them were people who could not make it in South Africa, even with the help of apartheid to restrict competition. Although they are for the most part pleasant people, white Rhodesians deserve in many ways to be counted among the world's great mediocrities. That applies especially to the farmer-government that came to power under Smith. "Damn it, I don't mind being ruled by farmers," one sophisticated white Rhodesian businessman told me, "but I do mind being ruled by farmers who are failures. These chaps go into politics when they can't make good their crops."

Smith's Rhodesian Front, which expected to win a nearly unanimous vote in the election from the white population, seemed to encourage the siege mentality in these people. Smith and his lieutenants warned the electorate that to fail to help the Front keep every one of the fifty white seats in Parliament would be a victory for the strange coalition of the "hostile Afro-Asian bloc," the

United Nations, the Kremlin, and the West, which had inexplicably joined the campaign against Rhodesia's independence. This was, of course, an effective political ploy. But the neurotic ballot-badgering by Smith's party in the 1970 election seemed also to reveal a surprising insecurity. The three-week "campaign" was in fact little more than an emotional catharsis for the white settlers, an exercise in self-justification and in assuring the residents of the noncountry that they really did exist.

The other main point on which Smith apparently felt the white electorate needed reassurance was that the government was vigilantly moving against the Africans, Asians, and Coloreds that the old government had let get out of hand. The election underscored that six years of Smith rule had brought to the surface a strident white racialism that many white Rhodesians asserted had been absent, or at least rarely publicly voiced in the old days, when the Rhodesian self-image had been more patrician. Suddenly, Sir Roy Welensky noted in the middle of the campaign, "it has become not only respectable to be racist but almost compulsory." The black resentment that the campaign and Smith's segregationist laws created was to rebound on him in the violence that shook Rhodesia in early 1972, but Smith seemed oblivious to this possibility during the campaign.

The April 1970 election was the first in Rhodesian history to be legally segregated, with blacks allowed to vote only for blacks. This was required by the new 1969 constitution, which Smith had had drawn up and approved by national referendum. The constitution, which made Rhodesia a republic outside the Commonwealth, wiped out most of the gradualist provisions of the 1961 constitution. The Smith constitution said specifically that there could never be majority rule in Rhodesia.

African voters were segregated off the A roll, which continued to provide fifty seats in Parliament. Only African candidates could compete for the eight elected B roll seats. Eight more African representatives would be appointed by tribal chiefs or councils. As in South Africa, these were largely under the control of the white government.

African representation in Parliament was directly tied to the amount of income tax paid by Africans. In 1969, the African population paid less than 1 per cent of the total. African representation would rise as the income tax contribution rose.[2] But representation would be frozen at 50 per cent, a figure based on income tax contributions that were at least one hundred years away for the African population. The sixteen seats were, in fact, given to the Africans on credit, since their income tax payments entitled them to one seat in 1970. But even if at some future date the Africans should raise their income tax payments to 51 per cent of the total, they would not under the 1969 constitution get 51 per cent of the seats in Parliament. The 5 per cent white population would always have half of the seats. This was the principle of "parity," which Smith said he would never abandon.

Equally resented by Africans was the Land Tenure Act, which was entrenched in the constitution. The act, an expansion of old legislation, reserved for the 240,000 whites nearly half (44,000,000 acres) of Rhodesia's land. The 4,800,000 blacks received 45,200,000 acres. The whites got the cities, the Africans the reserves, which, as in South Africa, had the country's poorest farmland. Moreover, most African land had to be owned communally, which restricted African opportunities for qualifying under income and property qualifications for voting. The Land Tenure Act had been modeled to some extent on South Africa's ghetto-creating legislation, and the government was empowered to declare areas and facilities for whites only.

The failure of Smith to set a high tone in the government's public pronouncements was apparent in the electioneering. At meeting after meeting, Smith and his fellow politicians were asked about getting Africans out of theoretically integrated swimming pools and job categories and out of the actually integrated university and a few hotels. Demands were voiced for residential ghettos for the country's citizens of Indian origin and mulattos. In the

[2] Indirect tax contributions, such as the heavy sales tax in effect in Rhodesia, were not considered in determining representation.

flat, nasal Rhodesian accent that sometimes transposes vowel sounds, Smith would reply, "Yis, jist leave it to me, laydies and jintlemin."

At one rally African students and a handful of whites heckled Smith, and he retaliated by leading the crowd in singing an Afrikaans collegiate song entitled "Baboon Climbs the Mountain." Later, after he was criticized for this, Smith claimed that the song had been directed at both whites and blacks, an explanation that overlooks the special sting the slur carries for Africans. "I've sung this song one hundred times," Smith complained at a later meeting in Salisbury. "Why, when I sing it for the one hundred and first time, does it become a racial incident?" Then, to show his good will toward the African population, he pointed out again that there had been a handful of whites with the African students. "They were the brains behind this. The Africans were only the puppets, and the Europeans the puppeteers," he said, to reassure his audience that Africans would not be capable of mounting a protest themselves.

Smith's sensitivity to the nuances of race was also evidenced at this meeting when he attempted to deflect a question about a reduction in the government subsidy to mission schools, which were then teaching the great majority of African children attending class. Smith said he did not have the statistics he needed on hand to discuss it, but would reply to the questioner by mail. His questioner persistently suggested that Smith should answer on his final television campaign broadcast the following evening. But Smith dismissed this: Only "one or two per cent of the population of Rhodesia is interested in such a problem." In fact, the action threatened the schooling of several hundred thousand African children, since the churches contended they had to have the subsidy to continue operating classes. Smith's remark is entirely accurate, however, if one realizes that for him "the population of Rhodesia" means the white population.

"I am not a racialist," Smith protested at the meeting. "A racialist is one who is obsessed with the importance of and superiority of his own race, to the detriment of others . . . Others are diabolically racialist, because they insist that a black government is the only good government for Rhodesia . . . Our predecessors talked a lot about what they were doing for the indigenous people, but they did little." By being realistic and dividing the population into racial groups, the Rhodesian Front would prepare the blacks for economic advance. It was only the "voices from outside" that wanted to stir up racial discontent in the country. "You see the happiest African faces on the continent here." He also noted that the racial harmony under his government had led "to the lowest crime rate in the known civilized world."

At about the time he was saying this, a group of twenty African students who had been kept outside the packed meeting hall started an anti-Smith chant. White onlookers grabbed several of the Africans and began beating them. A half-dozen white Rhodesian policemen stood by watching. When the fight subsided, some of the Africans were arrested for disturbing the peace and taken away from the hall. The Salisbury morning newspaper carried a laconic account of the event the following morning, without mentioning the police having taken no action to stop the attack on the blacks. I asked a reporter on the paper why. "That's not news," he said, a bit sadly. "What is unusual is that the police did not join in." Later, I asked an African why the blacks had not fought back when attacked. "Would you have them commit suicide in that crowd?"

Smith's remarks about his happy Africans was only one example of a stubborn refusal by the Rhodesian whites to face reality. I encountered this on each of my three visits to the country. It is an especially grave fault in the matter of race relations, explained partially by the almost complete breakdown of communications between black and white that occurred in Rhodesia during Smith's first years of rule. But it is also evidenced in other ways, large and small, that have caused some of my colleagues to label Rhodesia as "Cocoonland."

I asked the government's chief press officer if an advance copy of Smith's major campaign speech, to be delivered in Salisbury, was available. The P.M., the man assured me, always spoke off the cuff and never used texts. Two nights later, I sat and listened as Smith, a poor public speaker, laboriously read word for word a prepared speech that he had used on almost every occasion in the campaign. The press officer's object undoubtedly was not to deceive me, but perhaps himself, with an image of what Smith should be.

Sanctions had cut the country's exports by at least 33 per cent and its foreign exchange reserves were falling. The tobacco industry was severely crippled, and prices and rents had begun to rise rapidly. Yet, repeatedly throughout the campaign, the Rhodesian Front told the electorate that "You never had it so good." Smith had just finished saying precisely this in those words and a dozen other different ways at a campaign meeting when a middle-aged woman stood up, glanced over at the score of local and foreign journalists covering the meeting, and asked the Prime Minister "to tell the press that we have never had it so good." Smith obliged. Having him say it over and over seemed to make it so. Later, he glared down at the local reporters and told them that Rhodesia was one of the few countries in the world that would put up with the seditious material their papers printed. In fact, the country had only recently lifted formal and tight censorship, and the Rhodesian press was still treading lightly in criticizing the government.

WHITE REVENGE

Election day came to Rhodesia twelve days before South Africans went to the polls. Smith's Rhodesian Front captured all fifty white seats. The Prime Minister, wearing a black suit and brown suede shoes, dropped by one polling station I visited. He awkwardly engaged in small talk with the poll watchers who were serving cakes and tea to the voters of the affluent northern suburb.

There were 87,020 voters on the A roll. Only 8326 Africans had registered on the B roll. In some districts, black candidates had to try to campaign in areas where there was one registered voter for every forty square miles.

"Unity, that's the important thing," Richard Hall, a white businessman and Rhodesian Front candidate said late in the day at the voting tent set up in Barrowdale. "We need unity to continue fighting the battle for Rhodesian existence."

John Staub, a twenty-one-year-old university senior and political science major at the university in Salisbury, had campaigned for Hall's more moderate opponent and was watching the polls for him that day. "There has been no ideological element in the campaign, just a question of different ethos," Staub said. "People here are interested in having a nice big house with a couple of slaves and they just want to be told that they can keep it. Smith is essentially tapping forces that were always there. He just tells the people, 'Stop hating yourselves. Stop trying to make things better just because the other governments said you should hate yourselves.' It has been very successful."

In his Salisbury office, Sir Roy Welensky, by this time the forgotten man of Rhodesian politics, advanced another theory to explain Smith's setting out on his racist course. It was partly to legitimize his taking of power from Field in 1964 and the drastic 1965 move of U.D.I., the Unilateral Declaration of Independence, Sir Roy argued persuasively.

U.D.I. came as a shock to many white Rhodesians, who had expected right up to the last minute a compromise, or at least a preservation of the status quo. It is inexact to describe U.D.I. as a "popular" move. Instead, it came to be viewed as a necessary one. Most whites certainly seemed to support Smith on it, especially after it became clear that he would get away with it. To legitimize its drastic actions, however, the Rhodesian Front had to escalate the black peril before the electorate, which in turn made the electorate demand more action from the government. The 1969 constitution and the 1970 campaign were used to lend the appearance of providing content to the pledges made in 1962 and afterward to reverse the tide in racial matters.

"The white man is getting his revenge for the Congo," Gaston Thomas Thornicroft told me as we stood in Salisbury's Market Square and watched heavy balloting. "But it is an overrevenge for a minority outnumbered twenty to one. We are beginning to learn to copy the politics of race. We don't like it, but we have to." Thornicroft was a portly, sixty-eight-year-old merchant. His mother had been African, and his father English. "The Europeans here are a frightened people," he said. The polling station was separated from the street by a low cement wall. Stretching along the wall was a long line of young African men, members of the race that the Rhodesian Front portrays as not being interested in politics. With a quiet intensity, the Africans watched as other men came and went, deposited their ballots, and returned to jobs. These young men had neither. They were for me one of two lasting images of Rhodesia, 1970.

There are outside Salisbury a series of huge boulders, precariously and mysteriously balanced on each other in unusual formations. Nature is apparently responsible for the balancing of the rocks, three or four high, on each other. On the side of them are ancient Bushman paintings, etched into the rock in iron oxide, depicting animals, hunters, and dancers. There are also obscure symbols, their meanings having disappeared with the Bushman. An African I had met, a man of middle-class education, income, and temperament, took me out to see these paintings on one of those glorious April Sunday afternoons when the sun slants softly across the beige hills and rolling green fields around Salisbury. My African acquaintance was intensely proud of this part of his heritage.

Afterward, he invited me to his modest house in one of the townships and introduced me to his wife, who spoke no English, and to his four children. Their school fees and other educational expenses, he told me, consumed 20 to 30 per cent of his small salary. As we sat in the shade outside the house, this man, who also belonged to the race that was supposedly not interested in politics, asked me surprisingly precise questions about the state of relations between Jomo Kenyatta and Oginga Odinga, Kenya's two main political leaders; about the Ibos in Nigeria; about Kenneth Kaunda's programs in Zambia; and about President Nixon's policy toward Africa.

Later, we went to a soccer match, where the crowd was generally and unobtrusively divided into white and black seating areas, but with a scattering of mixed seating that did not seem to perturb anyone.

How much longer, I wondered at the end of the day, would such an afternoon be possible in Cecil John Rhodes' domain? The combination of Smith's racialist policies and the earlier impatience of African nationalisms with white promises about gradualism have almost certainly destroyed the hope that there can be an equitable sharing of political and economic power between white and black in a unified system of government in Rhodesia.

There is not immediately evident in Rhodesia the open frustration and racial bitterness that strike the visitor who spends any time with black South Africans. There is in fact still a surprising display of obvious good will toward individual whites from Rhodesian Africans, many of whom are engagingly good-humored and polite, at least to white foreigners. But real communication between the races in Rhodesia has completely broken down in recent years, as the testing of African opinion on the November 1971 proposed settlement reached by Smith and Sir Alec Douglas-Home, British Foreign and Commonwealth Secretary, graphically demonstrated.

From the Rhodesian standpoint, economics pointed to resuming talks with Britain, despite the failure of three attempts at negotiations by Smith and Harold Wilson. Wilson's prediction that economic sanctions, imposed first by Britain unilaterally and then by the United Nations at Britain's request, would bring Smith down in a matter of weeks instead of months had been made to look foolish. There was a shortage of quality goods and petroleum rationing was maintained for several years, but French and Japanese cars, German machinery, American cosmetics, and many other foreign goods continued to be available in Salisbury throughout sanctions. Working through middlemen who received a healthy commission for forging certificates of origin and shipping through South African and Portuguese African ports, the Rhodesians were able to find markets for their base minerals and for much of their beef, tobacco, and other exports. The Portuguese and South Africans did little to hide their role in transshipping goods for Rhodesia.

But sanctions had visibly restrained Rhodesia's potentially expansive economy, and the pinch was increasingly felt in the beginning of the 1970s. Major new mineral finds of copper, asbestos, nickel, and other minerals were recorded, but there was a shortage of foreign capital needed to buy new machinery and the new equipment needed to modernize Rhodesia's railways, which were unable to absorb a large increase in cargo traffic. Sales of Rhodesia's distinctive tobacco, once a major foreign currency earner for the country, had been badly damaged by sanctions, and tobacco farmers survived only through a government subsidy system for stockpiling tobacco crops for sale when sanctions were lifted.

Politically, Edward Heath's decision to resume limited arms sales to South Africa, and his ability to make the decision stick with relatively little fuss from Black Africa, also encouraged Smith to go for a quick agreement with the Conservatives, who were at that moment eagerly moving toward membership in the Common Market. Heath apparently wanted to get the untidy problem of Rhodesia settled before England went into Europe, and he gave no indication that he was particularly concerned how it was settled. Although it was understandably denied in London, the clear image the Heath government projected for many sitting in Black Africa was that Heath was prepared to brazen out international criticism, as he had done on the South African arms issue. No one questioned that Smith would be able to control the opinion of Africans, who had been so quiet and docile since the outbreaks of the early 1960s.

The white Rhodesians had justification in asserting that Wilson, a man who seemed to believe that he could solve any problem if he personally became involved, had treated them with an arrogance that helped doom the earlier settlement attempts. But in the 1971 talks with Smith, the British arrogance was directed toward Rhodesia's Africans and those who were not willing to accept without question Sir Alec's view of what was best for the Rhodesian Africans. He talked to Africans, Asians, and mulattos in

Rhodesia in between his negotiating sessions with Smith. But virtually every delegation came away saying that Sir Alec had not come to consult them, but to tell them they would have to accept half a loaf, since he could not get them a full one.[3]

The arrogance toward outsiders was clearly reflected, for example, on the day the settlement was reached, by John Leahy, spokesman for Sir Alec's party. He told newsmen that the settlement was well within Britain's five principles and that everyone should agree when they had a chance to see it. Leahy apparently felt the newsmen were as pliable, or perhaps as ignorant, as Smith seemed to feel his African majority was. The weak agreement Sir Alec made with Smith bore scant resemblance to the five negotiating principles that Britain had insisted would bring unimpeded progress toward majority rule.

In return for the prospect of Britain's lifting sanctions and according full legal recognition of Rhodesia's independence, Smith agreed to a series of complicated provisions, filled with loopholes that he could manipulate. Even if the whites, who continued to control all the levers of power over African advancement, lived up to their part of the bargain to the letter — and no one who had had any dealings with Smith had any reason to expect him to do so — it would be well into the twenty-first century before Africans would have an opportunity to establish a parliamentary majority, which under Sir Alec's plan would always be a small one, despite the fact that they constituted 95 per cent of the population.

There were three principal advances over the 1969 constitution:

1. Voting, which would continue to be on segregated rolls until the distant date at which Africans reached parity in Parliament, would no longer be tied to income tax payments. The system would revert to the type of income, property, and educational qualifications previously used. A separate "Higher Voters Roll" for Africans would be established for those blacks who had the

---

[3] I interviewed most of those delegations. One exception was Joshua Nkomo, who was whisked back, after Sir Alec held a perfunctory meeting with him, to the lonely detention camp where Smith's regime has held him since 1964.

same income and education qualifications as whites, and special representation would be provided in Parliament on the basis of this roll. This was distinctly more racist than the 1961 arrangement, under which blacks and whites with similar incomes could vote on the same roll. But the British did not emphasize that point, while Smith did not have to.

2. Smith in effect agreed to drop his public political pledge that blacks would never achieve more than parity in Parliament. After the number of Africans on the Higher Voters Roll equaled the number of whites (a treadmill process since white immigration would certainly spurt after legal independence), and Parliament seats were equally divided, ten extra seats would be added to the 100 in Parliament and whites and blacks would vote on the same roll for candidates for those ten. They would hold the balance of power.

3. Smith would hold in abeyance the worse features of the Land Tenure Act, and he suggested that Rhodesia would be satisfied with the status quo in the racist laws it had passed. Sir Alec got nothing more than a weak promise from Smith to appoint a commission to review the Land Tenure Act and the other segregationist laws and not to pass any more such laws right away.

Britain also agreed to contribute up to 5 million pounds sterling a year for ten years to the Rhodesian government, which would match it and decide how the fund would be spent to advance African education and employment.

The proposed settlement, signed in Salisbury on November 24, 1971, was designed to resolve the constitutional dispute between Britain and the white settlers. Despite Sir Alec's overblown rhetoric in its defense, the agreement was only tangentially concerned with African aspirations and advancement toward majority rule. What the British, as a last resort, were asking the white settlers to do was to make some sort of return to controlling the black majority through class structures, and not to be so openly racialist.

The Pearce Commission, originally a sixteen-member body chosen by Sir Alec to test the opinion of "the Rhodesian people as a whole" on the acceptability of the settlement, arrived in Rhodesia in January 1972 for what many felt would be a fairly cut-and-dried test. Certainly Ian Smith thought that, for he had told newsmen that Rhodesian blacks were "the happiest Africans in the world," and said the majority of them supported his government.

The rioting in urban areas and the angry rejection of the settlement terms by rural Africans who the Commission greeted ripped the veil away from Rhodesia's troubled race relations. The Pearce Commission provided the first channel Africans had had in almost a decade to voice frustrations and resentments. Over and over again Africans said that no matter what kind of agreement Smith made, he could not be trusted to keep it. They complained that the qualifications for voting were too high and that the agreement would continue racism.

Smith expected the educated, urbanized Africans, less than 20 per cent of the black population, to oppose him strongly on anything. His main justification for his African policy was that only the rural, uneducated Africans in the reserves should be listened to. White Rhodesians modeled their idea of Africans on acquiescent tribal chiefs and their household servants. This is how J. H. Howman, Smith's Minister for Foreign Affairs, explained it:

I would like to cite the acute observation of an African member of Parliament who referred to the "Ideas of the Masses" when in actual fact they are the ideas of the detribalized young men in the urban areas who would like to spurn the chiefs in order to gain their own political ends. One thing that galvanized the chiefs into action was their almost intuitive appreciation — without the aid of statistics — that the system of "politicians" and "the vote" will turn the whole African structure based on age and seniority upside down and install literate youngsters in power, without experience or wisdom. Their view of "the vote" may be compared to the public reaction you would get if anyone suggested that leaders of teenage mobs should take over Government because of their noise and violence. And it is largely because of this that there exists the closest understanding between the Government and rural people . . . which has led to the harmony and good will that is so much a feature of our life in this country.

Howman said this to an audience of several hundred whites during the 1970 campaign. He went on to assure them that the vote "is a peculiar system developed in the United Kingdom. To take that system and plunk it down in the middle of Africa is absurd. Some people seem to think that the vote has some magical formula that means democracy . . . Well, I don't have to tell you, ladies and gentlemen, that that has not been the case in Africa."

But the proposed settlement met strong opposition in rural areas, despite the pressure the Smith government attempted to exert through the chiefs, whom it paid and could depose, and through the district commissioners, the white civil servants who were the overseers of the tribal areas. That Smith was so surprised by the rural opposition was a sign of the lack of feeling the white district commissioners had for the real sentiments of "their" Africans. That the chiefs were unable to deliver was a sign that the white government may have been beating a dying horse all along. Chiefs have become less important in Rhodesia just as they have elsewhere on the continent, as the role of education and communications increased in rural life.

There was at least temporary resurgence of African nationalist feeling in Rhodesia in the first two months of 1972. It seemed to herald the third significant rejection, within the space of a decade, of formulas that were designed at least in theory to lead to multiracial sharing of power in Rhodesia.

The first, and perhaps the only genuine rejection of political multiracialism since it may have been the only genuine opportunity to implement it, was by the Africans in 1961 and 1962. By rejecting the Whitehead constitution and boycotting the elections in which the Rhodesian Front came to power, Africans seriously undermined the white liberals and moderates and helped speed the repressive policies Smith was to adopt.

The second rejection of multiracialism was by the whites, first in the 1962 balloting for the Rhodesian Front and then in supporting Smith after Field was deposed. Factors in this have already been listed. It is important to recall that the shortcomings of white leadership have been major influences on the rising white supremacy movement in Rhodesia.

The 1972 rejection by Africans of what seemed to many of them to be a confidence trick engineered to get them to accord legitimacy to Smith's government sprang from a different set of circumstances than the 1961 movement, however. The warring factions of the old African political parties seemed to paper over their differences to fight together temporarily on the issue of the settlement, and the tribal divisions were not immediately noticeable. Moreover, noted one white scholar in Salisbury, who is uniquely well informed about African attitudes: "The movement of 1961 was a politically naive and optimistic one. The nationalists thought they could grab the whole loaf then and they attempted to impose their attitude on the peasants, who weren't really in sympathy with it." The 1972 demonstrations against Smith were "built on a profound distrust of the Smith government," he added. "The parents are agreeing with the younger and better educated Africans this time."

Smith had attempted to entrench white minority rule with British help and African acquiescence; the Africans had said no again. They were no more willing to be persuaded that they should cooperate with the whites after having seen the petty racialism displayed after U.D.I. than they had been ten years earlier. As is the case in South Africa, the political alternatives for Rhodesia's future have become clear: all-white rule or all-black rule. Trust has been destroyed on both sides, and multiracialism will become a dimly remembered moment of the past. "The whites will go on eating lotus flowers and finding scapegoats for their own failures until the end," Welensky had told me in 1970. Early in 1972, he said his judgment had not changed. "But I don't like to dwell on the thought of a confrontation," he said soberly.

IMPACT ON PRETORIA?

White power is vulnerable in Rhodesia. As in South Africa, the whites control the technology of armed might and will use it ruthlessly to maintain their positions of privilege. African nationalists can expect to continue to be harassed and jailed, and to see their parties banned, without being able to do much about it, probably for the rest of this decade. But even that is not certain.

The advent of the Smith regime and U.D.I. ended the embryonic attempts of white gradualists to create African political leaders to counterbalance Nkomo and the other nationalists. Some of the gradualists foresaw that Rhodesia would at some point need a black leader who could play the same role that Hastings Banda has been called on to play in Malawi — protecting white interests. With each passing year of rule by Smith (or the even farther-to-the-right politician who is likely to follow Smith soon), that solution becomes less possible. Disorder becomes more certain.

South Africa's reaction to change in Rhodesia will be crucial, not only for Rhodesia but also for South Africa itself. South Africa can help prolong white rule there, but it is not likely to risk its own existence on propping up the English-speaking farmers north of the Limpopo. As in most dealings beyond its borders, the response from Pretoria will be carefully measured and tailored to Afrikaner interests.

But what has already happened in Rhodesia in the last decade has major implications for South Africa today. Whitehead's 1961 constitution represented a sort of mixture of the United Party's soft apartheid plan and the Progressive Party's qualified franchise, which are currently the only alternatives to apartheid voiced by white political leaders in South Africa. The Whitehead approach represented a white paternalism that promised African advancement determined by whites, and which was admittedly motivated by the desire to head off a black revolution in the future. That is how it was sold to the white electorate, just as fear of revolution is the main selling point at the moment for the English-speaking Opposition's political views in South Africa.

There is not enough in such a program to hold the support of whites or blacks. In the Rhodesian context, Whitehead's proposals were bold. But an even bolder move was called for — a move that would have established a clear moral identification between sharing of power and Rhodesia's whites, while at the same time providing African political leaders with enough immediate gains to protect their positions from those who pushed for nothing less than immediate black rule. Such a program would have been an even bigger gamble than the one that led to Whitehead's defeat, and it might have failed even more spectacularly. But it also might have shifted the center of the debate on multiracialism far enough to the enlightened side of the spectrum to have influenced the course of events in the following decade.

Chapter Ten

Portugal: The Last Empire

THE PASTEL HUES of the villas, Catholic churches, and police stations that hug the green hillsides around Luanda's serene bay mark the city as part of Portuguese Africa. Their rose and pink shadings and red tile roofs, so familiar in Lisbon, seem incongruous this far south of the Equator, but Luanda in many ways forms a 3500-mile distant suburb of Lisbon, with palm trees, a tropical sun, and many of the people in the streets suddenly turned black. Luanda, the capital of Angola, is the overseas heart of the world's last colonial empire. White control is exercised in a different, more subtle manner here than in neighboring South Africa, or even than it was in other European colonies in Africa. A quick stroll through the streets of Luanda at midday is sufficient to suggest that to a visitor.

Noon is a drowsy, dead moment in Portuguese Africa. Businesses and offices close for two and one half hours. Workers retreat out of the glare of the tropical sun into the cool dark cafés in the center of Luanda. White and black waiters work side by side, placing small bottles of watery, frosted Portuguese beer before their customers, most of whom are white. A few, however, are Africans and mulattos.

In a small park nearby, four boys pitch pennies in the dust. Two are white. Two are black. All are shabbily dressed. A white drunk sleeps off a bad night at one end of a long stone bench. An African at the other end of the same bench snoozes in the shade and stillness. Posters taped to the small shop windows near the park show an African soldier standing beside a white one. A legend on the poster says they are fighting together for "a new Angola." Other government posters praise the population for building a racially mingled society. Interracial sex, a crime in South Africa and taboo in much of the rest of Africa, is something to boast of in Portuguese Africa. In contrast to the Coloreds of South Africa, the coffee-colored offspring of miscegenation are almost a favored elite in the Portuguese territory.

From these modest scenes the Portuguese conjure up a comforting vision of the world's most successful multiracial society.[1] It is a vision that has become one of their three principal justifications for continuing to stay in Africa after the other colonial powers have at least ostensibly departed. The Portuguese assert their continuing presence in Southern Africa puts them on a valuable and unique middle ground in the gathering racial struggle in the world. "We are not white Africa, or black Africa," Portugal's Foreign Minister, Rui Patricio, told me in Lisbon just before I began a two-month journey across Portuguese Africa. "Instead of criticizing us and giving weapons to murderers to use against our people, other countries should help us maintain our multiracial society." Patricio said that he was convinced that the Portuguese approach to race would have a moderating influence on South Africa.

The second pillar of Portugal's official rationale for continuing to cling to her African possessions in an era when that has become unfashionable is that Portugal's long history in Africa gives her much more substantial roots. "We have been in Africa five hundred years," a Portuguese National Assemblyman said in Lisbon. "The British and French were there less than one hundred and it took them ten years to get out. Why should not we Portuguese have five times as long?" Even this jesting timetable, however, is anathema to the more orthodox Portuguese officials who

[1] The Portuguese usage of "multiracial" — a term that occurs frequently in the government's English language publications and in discussions in English with Portuguese officials — differs slightly from the definition I have offered in the introduction to this book. As will be explained, the stress under Portuguese policy is on integration and assimilation to Portuguese values. There is also a positive pride in allowing Africans to adapt to Portuguese society.

insist that they are not leaving Africa — ever. To quote Patricio again:

"A country is formed by history, not geography. We are an old African country. We too suffered from the impact of nineteenth-century imperialism. Unlike other Europeans, we have never been a colonial power, because the Portuguese nation has been formed in Africa and in Europe."

From this comes the third, and principal, underpinning for Portugal's Africa policy: Portugal does not have any colonies. With the ostentatious courtliness they muster when trying to remind visitors that they consider themselves among the most polite and generous people in the world, Portuguese officials patiently correct anyone who refers to "colonies" and explain that the 850,000 square miles of territory under the red and green Portuguese flag form one nation, with equal rights for all of the 23.5 million inhabitants, who are all represented in the National Assembly in Lisbon. The overseas provinces, or states, are part of an independent country. Their people are bound to Portugal by an all-inclusive nationalism that the Portuguese have fostered in a process that seems diametrically opposed to apartheid's all-exclusive concept of white nationalism. The fourteen million Africans living under Portuguese rule are all Portuguese, and therefore Lisbon cannot abandon them any more than America could abandon its citizens in Alaska and Hawaii.

Embroidering these arguments is the theme of realpolitik. Portuguese presence stems the advance of Communism across Africa and helps protect the West. Portugal is a North Atlantic Treaty Organization member, and Communist nations are supplying weapons to the guerrilla organizations the Portuguese are fighting.

Has Portugal endured a decade of costly guerrilla warfare, diplomatic isolation in international forums, and growing but stifled anticolonial dissent at home to protect these "different" concepts of race, history, and nationalism? Probably not — there are other more compelling forces. But it is unlikely that there will be much significant peaceful change in Southern Africa in the next decade unless these doctrines are analyzed more closely in Portugal and seen for what they have come to be — largely excuses for blocking change. By denying that there are any racial or political problems in Portuguese Africa, Lisbon denies the need for drastic change. Myopia is the principal influence on Portugal's policy on Africa. "It is pointless to discuss change with the Portuguese government," an American diplomat in Lisbon told me. "The attitude is, 'We are splendid; how could we possibly become more splendid?' "

Many of those holding back change still dream of "Lusitania," an Iberian civilization extending across the globe to offer men the chance to worship Christ as good Catholics, to learn from a beautiful centuries-old culture that Africa can never duplicate on its own, and to profit from hard labor. That vision, as much as economic and strategic considerations, helps explain the refusal of Europe's poorest and most backward country to release her vast territories in Africa a decade after Britain and France did so. The empire is maintained at least partly to prove Portugal's cultural and political virility. "Without her overseas provinces, Portugal would cease to be a world power," a Portuguese official remarked gravely to a foreign friend in Lisbon. Echoing this idea, young army officers in the colonies say Portugal would become nothing more than the "western province of Spain" without her African possessions and would be swallowed up in the more materialistic, politically sophisticated societies of Europe. To these people — and they are the ones who seem to hold power in Portugal as this decade begins — Portugal is not fighting to save her African possessions but to save her very soul. If this may seem to be an antiquated idea to many, the Portuguese have never been embarrassed by seeming out of step with the rest of the world. Reverence for their history impales the Portuguese on a spike of stubborn romanticism and almost mystical conviction that they alone are right, that Portugal will succeed in the "civilizing mission" abandoned so hastily by the other European nations. Leon Trotsky's decades-old description of Portugal continues to apply; it is an underdeveloped nation — with a history.

Portugal's poverty and lack of political sophistication also tie her to Africa. Psychologically and materially, larger countries like Britain and France could afford to renounce overt political colonialism and bend with the winds of change. Insecure in world politics, Portugal seems unable to do that. In any event, one is constantly reminded, she does not want to.

Portugal has dealt from a position of weakness in her colonies since the seventeenth century. Britain wrested much of what was to become Rhodesia away from the Portuguese and came close to taking the southern ports of Mozambique. Other European powers nibbled at the Portuguese possessions at the Berlin Conference of 1885 that divided up Africa. Weakness has left Portugal suspicious of Western "allies" who urge her to give up her colonial possessions and frightened of what she sees as a Third World–Communist alliance against her. Trapped at the edge of the color and political lines that divide much of the world, Portugal fears that to move is to risk falling.

"We can't do what the British and French did," a young Lisbon industrialist who has businesses in Mozambique told me. His tone was unhappy, because he had spent a tour of duty fighting against guerrillas in one of the territories and had become disillusioned with the effort to hold the empire. "We don't have the capital, or the technological know-how, to hold the territories to us without the political structures. The Americans, or Russians, or South Africans would push us aside. We have to keep direct control or lose our territories."

Prime Minister Antonio de Oliveira Salazar's dictatorial rule did not allow the colonies to have local legislative bodies, which the English started and eventually built up as alternatives to direct colonial rule in their African possessions. The institutions and commercial links the British established were generally sturdy enough to ensure a period of rule friendly to British interests, at least in the first decade of independence. The Portuguese also refused, or were unable, to follow the French pattern of developing a local political elite that could be entrusted to watch over the economic interests of Paris while being popular enough to survive with a minimum amount of open security help from the French.

Partly by choice and partly because of their own poverty, the Portuguese have failed to provide a moderate alternative to colonialism.

Finally, there are important economic incentives to stay in Africa, at least for some of Portugal's most politically influential businessmen. A dozen or so large Portuguese companies reap major profits from the colonial arrangement, which they want undisturbed. Given the corporate nature of Portugal's fascist-styled political system, these companies and the families that run them have enormous influence on colonial policy. "In Portugal, you must have a check in the bank, or a regiment in the street, if you want to have influence," one of the country's most distinguished political leaders told me. (Like many Portuguese I talked to, he asked not to be quoted by name, since his politics differ from the government's.) Growing mineral wealth in the overseas territories also hardens Portuguese resolve and will provide the key calculation for Portugal's future in Africa.

THE EMPIRE: THE SETTING

As recently as the early years of Salazar's rule the Portuguese officially ranked themselves as "The Third Empire," behind Britain and France. But empire, like colony, is a word that has fallen into disrepute and is no longer used. With the gradual shrinking of the Portuguese world, it has also become less accurate. Many thought the empire had suffered a mortal blow when the Indian army pushed into Goa in 1961 and ended the dream of Portuguese India. It was a few months after the Angola uprising had begun. Ronald Segal, editor of the Penguin African Library, wrote in 1962 that the Portuguese "will be driven from Angola — and Mozambique and Guinea — as they were driven under different circumstances from Goa . . . Only the number of months left to them allows speculation, and the thoroughness of the break."

Nearly a decade later, this prediction by Segal and many others still had not come true. Mortified by the loss of Goa — which officially is still listed as a Portuguese territory "temporarily" under foreign control and which is represented in Portugal's National Assembly by three expatriate Goans — the Portuguese held on in Africa with an unexpected tenacity. The empire, or Portuguese nation, stood, composed of the Iberian homeland and the impoverished Atlantic islands of the Azores and Madeira; the tiny Asian enclaves of Timor and Macao, where Portuguese garrisons remain at the sufferance of Indonesia and Mainland China, respectively, which reap trade and commercial benefits from the Portuguese presence; and these possessions in Africa:

Angola, on Africa's southwest coast, was the notorious "Black Mother" of the slave trading era when perhaps three million Angolans were shipped off to plantations in Brazil and America. Today it is Portugal's most favored and strongest possession. Increasingly rich in oil, diamonds, and coffee production, it gets the best civil servants Lisbon can spare to run the local government, and investment is channeled to it. There is a vibrant, hopeful air in the local white community of 250,000 settlers that does not at all match the jitteriness and fatigue one might expect to find in a dying colonial outpost. The black population, still showing the lingering effects of the tribal wars and slave raiding that Portuguese settlement helped promote, stands at only 5.5 million. Formed by a coastal plain dotted with beautiful Portuguese-built harbors like Luanda, and soaring sparsely populated plateau country in the interior, Angola is fourteen times the size of Metropolitan Portugal.

Mozambique, strategically located on the eastern flank of Rhodesia and South Africa, along the Indian Ocean, resembles a faded Jezebel, retaining a certain sultry charm but living uncomfortably with South Africa, providing services but not being respected, liked, or really bothered about except for the services, and nervously watching for signs of change in the relationship. Mozambique's southern ports and railways are vital transport links to the Transvaal region of South Africa and to landlocked Rhodesia. A land of cotton, tea, and cashew plantations, Mozambique has been a financial drain on Portugal for the past few years. There are 7.5 million Africans and less than 200,000 white settlers.

Portuguese Guinea is a tiny swampland wedged into the West African coast between two former French colonies, Senegal and Guinea. The Cape Verde Islands are 250 miles offshore in the Atlantic. Once a great spot for exporting slaves, Portuguese Guinea (or Guinea-Bissau as it is called by the guerrilla movement that has handed the Portuguese their most severe military test) is now poor and uninteresting as a colonial possession. But the Portuguese have made it part of their domino theory for Africa and linked its fate to that of the two important Southern Africa territories. Portuguese military officers say they must remain in Guinea also to protect air and naval bases on Cape Verde from impending Communist takeover. Guinea has a population of around 600,000 Africans and less than 5000 Portuguese and Lebanese merchants and traders.

São Tomé and Principe are two flyspeck islands in the Gulf of Guinea. São Tomé's airport was used for food and weapon airlifts into Biafra during the Nigerian civil war, as the Portuguese lent open support to the Biafran rebels. São Tomé became a familiar dateline as bored correspondents waiting for a lift into the Biafran enclave passed time by writing descriptions of the picturesque, former volcanic island. With the sudden end of the Nigerian war, São Tomé receded into obscurity as a quiet plantation island and a much-feared penal colony for the Portuguese.

Colonies, or overseas states? Lisbon decreed in 1951 that the territories were no longer to be described as colonies. They would only continue to be treated that way. Two decades after the semantic change, white bureaucrats in Lisbon continued to rule the territories with a heavy hand and a tight administrative apparatus that strangled local initiative, whether it came from white or black. The half million white Portuguese settlers in Portuguese Africa lived almost as much under the thumb of Lisbon as did the fourteen million Africans in the territories, except the whites dominated top government and commercial opportunities made available to locals. Each territory was ruled by a governor-general appointed by Lisbon and responsible only to Lisbon's Overseas Ministry, although the governor went through the motions of obtaining advice from a local legislative council.

In the nineteen sixties, governors routinely served two- or three-year tours. Each new governor brought with him a complete new set of civil servants from Lisbon, who were often unfamiliar with Africa. They were empowered to make some low-level decisions without referring back to Lisbon. Mozambique's Provincial Secretary for Education in 1971 had been plucked from a high school in Portugal where he had been a principal to come to Africa. The Secretary for Finance and Economy had been an accountant for CUF (Companhia União Fabríl), a corporate giant with monopolies on many commercial activities in the colonies, and seemed to expect to go back to CUF after his tour in Mozambique.

In rural areas, white Portuguese administrators govern. Most of them have long experience in Africa, but their abilities and capacity for contact with the local people seem to be very uneven. Some district officers I met were really interested in rural development; others appeared to like the job primarily because they could kick around Africans. In guerrilla-troubled areas, it is the Portuguese army that governs.

This tightly controlled administrative structure, with its interlocking connections to the Lisbon companies that dominate the economies of the territories, stamps the present Portuguese system as a colonial one, despite the semantic change. It is the same system of government that was used by the English and French. It also sets Portuguese rule in Angola and Mozambique apart from the use of white power in Rhodesia and South Africa, where local whites were quickly given self-government and control over their own security forces. Concomitantly, white settlers' lack of influence on the governing of the territories is certainly one of the key factors in the development of multiracialism as the official theory of race relations in Portuguese Africa. The Portuguese government is not responsible to public opinion and least of all to opinion in the territories. The South African and Rhodesian governments are dependent on their white electorates. Thus, it is easy for the bureaucratic elite in Lisbon to design perfect policies on race, labor, citizenship, and other matters and sincerely proclaim them. They don't live in the territories. The distance also makes it easy for the policies to be ignored when they do not suit local conditions and when the Lisbon leadership does not follow up. This helps account for the great gap in policy and performance. "The policy on everything measures up to about here," a diplomat stationed in Angola told me, holding his hand above his head. "The practice is about here," he said, indicating his knees. "The attitude in Lisbon seems to be, 'We've passed a law, it's on the books, now we can forget about that problem.' Here, the attitude is, 'They've passed a law, it's on the books, now we can forget about that law.'"

With some important differences, Portugal's experience in Africa resembles that of the other colonial powers more than the Portuguese care to acknowledge. The Portuguese did develop harbors and layover stations along the African coastline long before other Europeans came to the continent. Like tiny teeth marks on the flank of Africa, their well-constructed sixteenth- and seventeenth-century coastal forts still stand; from Ghana's Elmina in West Africa to Fort Jesus in Mombasa, Kenya, African countries now independent have turned the forts into tourists attractions.

But the Portuguese rarely pushed beyond the coastal strip to settle in the unchartered interior. Only at the end of the nineteenth century, when Britain, France, Belgium, and Germany staged the "scramble" for African colonies, did an alarmed Portugal dispatch major exploratory missions to lay claim to the territory between the coastal forts. This attempt was partly thwarted at the 1885 Berlin Conference, where the basic boundaries of Portugal's colonies in Southern Africa were drawn — just as Africa's other colonial boundaries were for the most part.

Officially, the Portuguese appear to give little weight to the circumstance that the harbors and layover stations that form the basis for their 500 years of contact were developed primarily to promote the slave trade (or to provide temporary shelter for ships traveling to India). Although the territories' black citizens may not consider that particular type of contact an exercise in nation-building, the Portuguese do not appear to attach that much significance to it. "The Portuguese are not without sin in this matter," Alberto Franco Nogueira wrote several years ago when he was Portugal's Foreign Minister, "but we did not start the traffic nor did we gain the greatest profit from it."

The point is not that the Portuguese are unable to overcome this dark chapter of history. The point is that it is hardly realistic, or valid, to try to convert that history into a justification for continuing white rule in Africa.

When slave trading was finally reduced to an unprofitable minimum, the Portuguese colonies were allowed to sink back into their customary, unnoticed stupor. The interior of most of the territories was left uncontrolled, and a good number of tribes still refused allegiance to Portugal. What colonial interest there was in Portugal centered on Goa. Even after the scramble, the implanting of Portuguese presence in Africa was slow. In 1968, Don Manuel Vieira Pinto, the young Roman Catholic bishop of Nampula, told Stanley Meisler of the Los Angeles Times, that for all practical purposes the Church, usually in the vanguard of spreading colonial control, had worked in the interior of his northern Mozambique diocese for only twenty-five years. Where Afrikaners had insisted, "I was born here, my grandfather was born here, this is where I belong," the Portuguese in Angola and Mozambique would usually say: "My children were born here. This is my home."

As late as 1930, Angola and Mozambique had a combined white settler population of less than 75,000. South Africa's white population that year numbered 1,750,000. Development was nonexistent in Portuguese Africa, as the economy turned on crops like tea, cotton, and sisal, which seem to erode not only soil but the social conditions of the area in which they grow. Schools with African pupils were extremely rare, forced labor on plantations owned by Lisbon companies and noblemen very common. Africans were required by law to work. The Portuguese did offer those Africans and mulattos who fulfilled exacting educational and financial conditions the chance to become Portuguese citizens; they were called *assimilados* and had to carry cards to show their special status. In 1950, there were only 35,000 assimilados among the ten million Africans in Angola and Mozambique. The spread of civilization was shown in fact to be a tiny trickle. As more and more critics pointed to the number of assimilados as a rather accurate barometer of the success of Portugal's civilizing mission, Lisbon formally abolished the system.

The somnolence was shattered in the nineteen sixties as the guerrilla wars erupted, petroleum and iron ore were discovered and exploited in Angola, and South Africa began to look beyond the laager to offer Portugal help in fighting the African uprisings and potential competition for control of the Southern African territories. Moving to meet the threats posed by white and black power, the Portuguese spurred white migration to the colonies by offering Portuguese settlers free land and transportation. For its black population, pacification became the main object. Money for development poured in, working conditions for blacks improved, and social and economic barriers eased. This belated stress on development, the Portuguese apparently hoped, would substitute for political independence, despite the trend elsewhere in the last decade. "We should build a monument to the guerrillas when this whole thing is over," a young white journalist in Angola said. "Without the terrorism, nothing would have been done here for the next five hundred years, either." Slowly, a new argument for continuing Portugal's colonial role has evolved; the Portuguese assert that they can do more to develop the territories they neglected so long than could any independent black government. They may be right; that is not the point being disputed by the 25,000 black guerrillas who roam the forests of Portuguese Africa trying to dismember the Portuguese empire.

Neither is the argument primarily about racial prejudice and white supremacy, as it appears to be in South Africa. Most of the anti-Portuguese guerrilla forces acknowledge this, at least implicitly, by centering their propaganda attacks on political and social injustices created by the colonial system rather than racial prejudice. Perched on the western shoulder of Europe, the Iberians have been swept not only by the chilling winds from the north, but by Moorish invasions from the south. Moors from Africa mingled their blood with the Portuguese centuries ago. Perhaps as a result, the Portuguese generally do not display the ingrained aversion to and fear of black skin shown by Anglo-Saxon, Teutonic, and to a lesser extent Gallic colonialists in Africa.

The amount of racial integration in Portuguese Africa is in absolute terms by far the highest of any territory on the continent, whether it is white- or black-ruled. The sight of the white and black waiters in Luanda or of a white woman sitting beside a black man at a post office counter doing the same poorly paid job would be as unusual in Kenya, or Nigeria, as in South Africa (although hardly as dangerous for the black man). In the other European-ruled African territories, no large poor white class was ever formed to compete for such jobs. In South Africa the poor whites are protected from black competition. But the oligarchic Portuguese government refuses to extend that kind of protection to its poor whites. A predictable but crucial point about Southern Africa's differences in the exercise of minority power — and about the interrelationship of nationalism, class, and race — emerges here: The Portuguese, with one of the world's broadest concepts of nationalism and world culture, have one of the world's most highly structured class systems, which preserves entrenched interests. The narrow Afrikaner nationalism rejects class as a major factor within that nation and seeks another system of control. The English fall in the middle. The fact that the Afrikaners have chosen apartheid as their method to perpetuate minority control, and that the Portuguese have chosen class-structured integration, springs not only from the difference in numbers in the white minorities in these countries, not only from differing historical contacts with nonwhites, but also from their conflicting visions of themselves and their missions.

A veteran Portuguese air force pilot, born in Mozambique and now serving in Angola, one of those delightfully garrulous, out-spoken Portuguese, put it this way: "In Portuguese Africa, we have white niggers, too. We treat all niggers the same."

For the most part the Portuguese do not need strong color bars to keep the black majority down. An oppressively heavy class system accomplishes the job. Whites who wind up on the wrong side of the class line are left on their own for the most part. Driving through the poorer section of Lourenço Marques, the beautiful capital of Mozambique, a government official told me, almost with pride in his voice: "See those slums? White people live there, too. Beside the Africans." That apparently made the slums a virtue.

At the other end of the scale, the often stiff and awkward mingling of small white and black elites provides the other key ingredient in Portugal's proudly proclaimed multiracialism. Allowing a handful of educated, affluent, and cultured black men to sit in the same restaurants and theaters may indicate that the Portuguese do not yet feel really threatened by black power (as distinguishable from the danger of a social uprising). That the Portuguese expect their visitors to congratulate them on this is a devastatingly accurate measure of the quality of race relations in the rest of Southern Africa. The Afrikaner will not risk tokenism, even if it would ease world criticism. His society lacks the structures to contain it. It is too dangerous. The Portuguese use elitism as a justification for staying in Africa and are confident they can control its growth.

Again my friend the pilot had a way of saying it more concisely. With the growing military cooperation between the Portuguese and the South Africans, he has spent a lot of time in South Africa in recent years. He also once went to school there, as many Africa-educated Portuguese did before a university was established in the nineteen sixties in Mozambique. He admired the South Africans and, although he disliked some of its more blatant features, thought apartheid was the right answer for them. "The South Africans gave their natives too much education," he said. "If they let their natives have any rights now, why the blacks would take the place over." Did that mean, I asked, that if the Portuguese continue to give education to their natives, as they tell the world they are doing, that the natives will also take Angola over? "Maybe. But that won't happen tomorrow," he said with a smile and a wave of his hand. "Maybe in one hundred years, maybe. We have much time." (His point is a good one. It appears that even after a decade of hurried attempts to develop more opportunities for Africans, South Africa has more black university students than Portuguese Africa has African high school students. The "appears" is necessary, however, because one of the major differences on race between South Africa and Portugal is that South Africa keeps good statistics and Portugal does not. Like the assimilado system, statistics kept on a racial basis were abolished when they began to tell outsiders too much about the progress, or perhaps the lack of progress, of Africans. "You don't need those kind of statistics if no discrimination against colored people exists," Francisco Bonifácio de Miranda, press spokesman for Portugal's Foreign Ministry, told me in Lisbon. "In a general way, we know that more Africans are going to school." Then, in a comment that was to sum up a great deal of the attitude I was to find during my visit, he added: "The best thing is to forget the racial factor altogether when looking at Portuguese Africa.")

There are many other differences between Portugal's embrace of multiracialism and South Africa's denial of it. It is natural to view the two approaches to race as being antithetical. The Portuguese stress to visitors diplomatically but frequently how different their practices are and how much they personally dislike South African racial attitudes. "They treat us as honorary whites," one Portuguese businessman in Angola said of the South Africans. "What really bothers them is that they think we don't know how to handle blacks."

But in a very real sense, apartheid and Portugal's version of multiracialism are symbiotic, two unlikes feeding upon each other. Without the raw and open racism of apartheid next door, the black-white contact fostered by the Portuguese in Africa would seem even more paltry. And for the South African race ideologue, Portuguese Africa can serve as the awful example of a racially unbalanced society without apartheid. Portuguese Africa is the failure of integration in societies where a giant gap separates the people. Portuguese Africa has theoretical integration and equality; therefore it does not provide separate facilities and opportunities. The fact is, though, whites almost always dominate the supposedly equal competition in the system they have shaped.

These contrasts and similarities are not unlike those that have existed in recent years in the United States between the North and the South. As in the United States, the results of the superficially opposite systems seem to many blacks to produce about the same results in a distressing number of cases. And, as in the United States, it is possible to find blacks who prefer the harsh face of prejudice to the vague smile of multiracialism. "I knew where I stood with the South Africans, and they paid me for the work I did," a black welder told me in Lourenço Marques. He had lived for almost ten years in South Africa and learned his trade there. "Here, I can go into the bar of the Hotel Polana, in theory." The Polana is Mozambique's fanciest hotel. "But they charge twenty escudos [60 cents] for a glass of beer in there. I can't afford that on five thousand escudos [$170] a month. If they paid me eight thousand escudos a month, like they pay the white Portuguese welder who does exactly the same job, I could go to the Polana. But they won't."

South Africans never let a visitor forget that they have a crushing racial problem and the world misunderstands the solution they have chosen. The Portuguese never let a visitor forget that they do not have a racial problem, and therefore there is no need for the world to hunt for a solution to a problem that doesn't exist. "We may have made some mistakes in the past," they say in tones that suggest the qualified admission is a great concession. "But now we are working for the best interests of all our people, black and white."

Because of the somewhat amorphous Portuguese approach to race, attitudes of the white settlers seem to be less dogmatic than in South Africa. One is rarely hit with crude racism, and one does not find the shrill, emotional liberal white. This is partly because the Portuguese, still suffering from Salazar's authoritarianism, are not given to expressing themselves on any but the safest topics. It is also attributable, I think, to the inevitable bundling of contradictory racial attitudes into the liberal, i.e., multiracial approach, intensified in this case by the Portuguese feeling that whatever arguments exist about racial superiority, there is no question that Portuguese culture is superior to others and far superior to that of Africans.

THE SHAPING OF ATTITUDES

It was a few nights before Mardi Gras in Lobito, an Angolan port with graceful stands of sheltering palms, quiet sandy beaches, and elegant, warmly colored beach villas, and my candidate for Africa's only real tropical paradise. A Portuguese customs officer I had met in the hotel bar took me for a ride around his town. We stopped to watch two teams of high school girls playing basketball. The two African girls on the floor easily dominated the game. The customs officer was plainly proud of multiracialism in action. Then we drove up to an African township on a hill overlooking Lobito. In one street, the customs officer stopped as we drove by an African woman suckling her baby on a doorstep. He backed the car up and played the headlights on the woman, who held her hands in front of her eyes. "These niggers are something," he said, looking at the woman like a zoological freak. Then we drove on to a house where about twenty African youngsters were practicing dances they would perform in the streets on Mardi Gras evening. We strolled through the African township, alone, unarmed, well after midnight. There is none of the urban terrorism in Portugal's Southern African territories that helped break French resolve in Algeria. Portuguese officials credit this to good race relations and poor guerrilla organization and support in the towns. Some white settlers think it is more due to the guerrilla awareness that "What would happen to the Africans here would make what the French O.A.S. did to the Algerians look like a tea party. They dare not," one white told me.

Racial attitudes in Mozambique seem to be much harsher than in Angola. Despite Rui Patricio's contention that Portugal's multiracialism would have a moderating effect on apartheid, it appears that the Portuguese tend to adjust to South African racial attitudes more easily than vice versa. The cities of Mozambique are more South African and Rhodesian creations than Portuguese. "I don't like to go to Mozambique," a white secretary in Angola said. "The people aren't really Portuguese anymore. They even look down on us for mixing with the blacks." Lourenço Marques depends on weekend tourists from Johannesburg for much of its hotel and restaurant business; the result has been the establishment of virtual South African enclaves, like the posh Hotel Polana, where the management is always very careful to have white headwaiters looking over all African or mulatto waiters, unlike the better hotels in Angola, where the working staff is mixed. One of the main attractions Lourenço Marques holds for some South African male tourists is the number of mulatto and African prostitutes. They do not have to worry about the Immorality Act here. But even here the South Africans seem to have shaped the system more than Portuguese racial policies. In 1971, the going rates for prostitutes were graded racially — $10 for an African girl, $15 for a mulatto, $20 for a Portuguese white girl, and $25 for the few white South African prostitutes in town. When I asked a diplomat about this "civilized labor" policy and the demand for the more expensive South African girls, he answered: "I guess they're for the Dutch Reformed Church preachers who come over on the week; you know, the real apartheid purists."

As important to the nuances of racial attitudes in the two colonies as their relative proximity to South Africa is the diverging pattern of settlement from Metropolitan Portugal in recent years. Who are the Portuguese who choose Africa as home?

Mozambique, settled in the fifteenth and sixteenth centuries primarily to assist the lucrative trade with India, was governed from Goa until the middle of the eighteenth century. Some commercial centers flourished, but there was little interest in permanent settlement. Malaria, tsetse fly, and hostile tribes made Mozambique unattractive. A few soldiers, merchants, and adventurers who journeyed into the interior set up giant *prazos*, or plantations, which they ruled in a feudal manner. The plantation system, increasingly based on absentee landlordism and corporate ownership, has continued until today; it was only two decades ago that John Gunther called Mozambique "Shangri-la with a bullwhip behind the door." The plantations' low-profit, labor-intensive crops, the rail and harbor transit trade revenue, and the export of labor to South Africa's mines formed a shaky base for the Mozambique economy, which has bounced up and down over the years. The settlers who were drawn tended to be peasants so down on their luck that even Mozambique sounded good: administrators and technicians who were just passing through and commercial men who liked the sweet indolence of the tropics.

After a notorious start as a penal colony and one of the great contributors to the slave trade, Angola went into the same sort of decline as Mozambique. It was treated as an economic appendage of Brazil more often than of Metropolitan Portugal. But the diversity of its 481,351-square-mile territory and its more temperate climate gradually brought Angola an economic maturity that has always eluded Mozambique. A solid peasant community took root in the remote but fertile plateau land of southern Angola after a group of Boers inevitably had trekked across the vast Kalahari Desert into Angola. To check this South African expansionism, the Portuguese government hastily rounded up and dispatched Portuguese farmers to the area. Luanda, which had been Africa's greatest slave port, gradually recovered after a steep decline. It could offer work to those who came to farm and were disappointed. Both wages and prices were (and still are) somewhat higher than in Portugal. Many of those who first came to Angola thought they could get a little more out of Angola with a little less work than at home. They would put enough away to get back to Portugal eventually and retire on a small farm there. That is still the ambition of a surprising number of the 5000 government-assisted settlers who come from Portugal to Angola and Mozambique each year.

The past decade drew people who may be called "the new Angolans" into the colony. They see a big future for Angola, despite the simmering guerrilla war in the north and east, and want to get in on the ground floor. They have been lured by economic opportunities created by the growing exploitation of diamonds in the northeast and new discoveries elsewhere: iron ore in the south; a major petroleum find in Cabinda, an enclave of Angolan territory just north of the Congo River; and the rapid development of large coffee plantations in the north. Potentially, the new Angolans could form the base for a sizable middle class unknown in Mozambique (and most other countries in Africa, for that matter).

The evolving social structure of white settlement in Angola, and the influence this is likely to have on Southern Africa and the Portuguese empire, would be a major study in itself. A few thumbnail sketches of settlers I met and their surroundings may be the best way to describe some of the push for change and the obstacles to it.

Matala is a white settlers' colony in southern Angola. The Portuguese plan was to bring the peasant here from Portugal, give him land, and let him demonstrate to African farmers how he could grow cash crops. This would bolster the economy and increase the white population. The plan has not worked; it has been far too expensive in resettlement costs, and the white farmers have not served as an example to Africans, but have tended instead to hire local Africans to work the fields. By 1971, the Portuguese were quietly halting recruitment for Matala and other settlements and were moving instead to establish big cattle ranches and plantations, controlled by white Portuguese, German, South African, and perhaps American interests.

Antonio Leandro Marques had come to Matala only fifteen days before I met him, but he was already on his way to becoming obsolete. He had been an agricultural laborer in Madeira earning about $1 a day and came to Angola "to see if the life gets better." The government would give him about twelve acres of land outside Matala, and he can expect to clear $300 a year in cash if he works hard and hires enough Africans.

A Portuguese journalist who had been in Angola a few years

and lived in a stylish villa seemed confident about his future in
Angola. He, like others, said Angola could be another Brazil. In
theory, these people would want to create a hybrid country, in a
sense detached from Africa. Neither white nor black Africa wants
that to happen in this valuable territory; neither does Lisbon.

The career of José Mendoça probably tells us much more about
present-day Angola than any other case. José, in his late thirties,
was an army captain serving in Angola when the 1961 rebellion
began. He had already been attracted by Angola's relatively easy
life and was planning to stay on. His company was one of the first
units to move into the north after Holden Roberto's guerrilla organization, headquartered in the Congo, had launched the initial
major bloody assault.

"We played a little rough," José recalled one day in his smartly
furnished, fourteen-story office in Luanda, "sure we did. They
started it. We had to look at the babies and the women, split
open, hacked up, left to die. So we gave them a little of it back. I
remember nineteen sixty-one, and I still say these black bastards
should pay for that." His voice grew harder. "But everybody
knows I think we need to cut more heads off. That's one reason
I'm not still in the field with the army. They're softer these days."
José is now an executive in CADA (Companhia Angolana de Ag-
ricultura), which is said to be the largest coffee-producing company in the world. It possesses a score of plantations stretching
across several hundred thousand acres in northern Angola and
has come to represent perhaps the most important local Angolan
economic enterprise, obviously chafing at some of the economic
restrictions Lisbon's tight control of the colony entails. But José
was very guarded in discussing this, or Angola's future. He said
he personally saw no reason for a loosening of the ties to Lisbon.
For one thing, Angola's whites would need the Portuguese army
for a long time for protection.

In contrast to what is happening in apartheid South Africa
today, there are no visible developing black leaders in multiracial
Portuguese Africa. The driving underground or out of the country
of any potential black leadership has been even more complete
than in South Africa.

I asked José Ilharco, head of Angola's official government information service, for help in meeting "Africans prominent in the government or in commerce." Ilharco, a courtly, gracious man, thought for a moment and then said: "Unfortunately, he left last week." Angola's Provincial Secretary for Education, the only nonwhite in the local administration's top ranks, had just been promoted out of the territory to a job in Lisbon. Ilharco could suggest no one else out of Angola's 5.5 million Africans that I might find it useful to talk to. The same request directed to the government in Mozambique over a two-week period also produced not one suggestion, with the exception of a defected guerrilla organization official, then in Lisbon for a series of press conferences.

Why has 500 years of the civilizing mission, Portuguese style, been unable to produce a black elite of any size or strength? Why has multiracialism fared even worse than apartheid in many ways in giving economic opportunity to a black majority? These are not polite questions to put to one's amiable, courteous, and very likable hosts, the Portuguese, but they must be asked. To me it seemed the failure was rooted in a combination of conscious and unconscious attitudes and material conditions: the self-deluding beliefs that race relations really are good in Portuguese Africa, an overwhelming drive of cultural imperialism that equates "Portuguese" with developed and "African" with savage, and finally a crippling lack of resources that has defeated even those who really have wanted change. Complacency, exaggerated national pride, and poverty have wiped out most of the theoretical advantages blacks should enjoy under multiracialism.

Portuguese spokesmen stress the problem of poverty and deny, more or less, the other two. Arguing simultaneously that 500 years of contact with Africa proves how well the African and Iberian cultures mingle on the one hand and that, on the other, it is still too early to judge the excellent progress that Europe's poorest country is making in Africa after a somewhat tardy beginning, Foreign Ministry spokesman Bonifácio de Miranda told me: "Asking us why we haven't done more in Africa is like asking

America why it didn't go to the moon before now. We all have to wait until circumstances make these things possible."

For most Portuguese, the color of an African's skin does seem to be irrelevant. So is just about everything else about the African. "Development" has one purpose, Portuguese candidly admit: the creation of black Portuguese who will speak, think, and act like white Portuguese. It is a one-way process. The Portuguese as a group take less interest in the cultures of the Africans who live around them than any other whites I have met in Africa. I asked A. A. Marques de Almeida, Mozambique's Provincial Secretary for Education, why grade school history books in his territory contained little about Mozambique's history. "We do have Mozambique's history in the books," he said indignantly. "We begin with Vasco da Gama arriving here, and later the children study about how the British tried to take Mozambique away from the Portuguese." I asked a ranking official in the Overseas Ministry in Lisbon about Amilcar Cabral, the most outstanding guerrilla leader the Portuguese face. "He's brilliant, yes. But then, he has a Portuguese education, of course."

THE MIDDLE PEOPLE

The unshakable confidence of the Portuguese that their civilization will prevail over African culture is best seen in their handling of the large mulatto population of Portuguese Africa. The *mestiços,* or mulattos, provide a key component of Portugal's multiracial case in Africa. Long scorned by other Europeans for the readiness with which they hopped into bed with African women, the Portuguese now take a wry satisfaction in exploiting the tactical gains they see accruing from their willingness to mingle sexually. The assumption is that the mestiços will identify completely with Portuguese interests and help promote them. The rewards the mulattos receive in the way of jobs and social mobility in the process will show that color is not a bar in Portuguese society. Such theories have promoted miscegenation, once a matter of carnal convenience, into official policy, encouraged by the government and praised as patriotic. Officers have encouraged their soldiers to do their duty to Portugal by leaving at least six mestiço children behind when they finish their tours in Angola.

No one really knows how many mestiços there are in Portuguese Africa, since statistics are no longer kept on a racial basis. Census calculations are especially difficult in the case of mestiços, anyway. In the past many of them were counted as white, because they preferred it that way or because the government wanted to inflate the white population figures in the African possessions. Educated guesses suggest that there are 400,000 to 500,000; the figure should rise now with 140,000 Portuguese soldiers stationed in Africa.

Angola's estimated 100,000 mulattos appear to hold a larger number of the good jobs available in that territory's urban centers than do the 5.5 million Africans of the country. Visiting dignitaries are introduced in Angola to "Africans" holding key jobs. Many, if not most, are in fact mestiços, and some are not even Angolan. They may come from the Cape Verde Islands, where the greatest concentration of mestiços live. About 200,000 of the 250,000 population of the islands, which were used by the Portuguese as a slave-trading station, are of mixed parentage. They are also relatively highly assimilated and form a bureaucratic and commercial elite for the Portuguese. In Portuguese Guinea, members of the 10,000-strong Cape Verdian community occupy almost all of the government jobs and commercial opportunities open to nonwhites.

The mestiços form an insulating layer between the white elites that run the African territories and the powerless African masses below. The Portuguese accept the theory that mulattos will identify "up," toward that part of their ancestry that is economically and socially superior, if they are given a chance. The Portuguese see "miscegenation as a means of cementing Portuguese domination over the indigenous culture," Eduardo Mondlane, head of the Mozambique Liberation Front, wrote before his assassination in 1969.

There is truth in this. But equally important is the strong Portuguese sense of family that often seems to outweigh racial prejudice. Unlike South Africans, Portuguese men cheerfully, often proudly, acknowledge their brown offspring. They contribute money for their schooling and spend time with them. All of this is a tremendous advantage in the child's making his way through the Portuguese school system of the colonies. A dozen visits to schools in Angola and Mozambique produced this type of vignette a dozen times: A teacher, asked how many of his forty students at the high school level are Africans, replies, "Seven." How many of the seven are in fact mestiços? "Five."

One Saturday night in Lourenço Marques I sat in a gymnasium converted to a weekend dance hall and talked to a mulatto named José. He listened to pulsing African rhythms from the all-black band and sipped a beer. At thirty-two, more deeply complexioned than most mestiços, José was a skilled worker and earned a good salary by African standards. His father was Portuguese, a minor government administrator posted in a small Mozambique town. His father had cohabited with an African woman, but made no offer to marry her when José was born. He had always acknowledged José and given him money when the youth needed it. He had also helped José find a job when he got through school.

Like many mestiços, José is trapped on the middle ground of the white and black worlds in conflict around him. Most mestiços gladly accept the privileges their position offers, but they are uneasy. José could say in the same conversation: "Older people will tell you we are completely Portuguese and the white man has never done anything wrong in Africa. I am Portuguese, yes, in nationality, but I am African too." And: "We cannot have a black government. They are not prepared. We would be hurt. The whites are not doing what they should for us, but we mestiços get a better deal than we would from the blacks. They would treat us as sympathizers."

The mestiço elite may be providing a disproportionate number of the leaders for the guerrilla movements, although this is difficult to know. It would be a sign that the arrangement the Portuguese think they have with the mestiços may not be working out exactly as they think it should.

The Portuguese influence is an exceedingly powerful one on the minuscule black and brown elite that comes into intimate contact with it. Some of the best poetry written in Portuguese in recent years has come from Africans — several of whom are now leading the guerrilla movements. And these movements use Portuguese textbooks in the schools they have set up for the children of their followers. In part a wise tactical move, as they conceive of their struggle as a long-term one slowly expanding through the Portuguese-controlled territories, this is also something of an implicit tribute.

In Portuguese African society, education rather than money or nobility is the base of the colonial class structure. The educational system, conditioned by complacency, cultural imperialism, and poverty becomes the tool for keeping the white minority in the territories in complete control. By officially making no distinctions between the peoples of the empire, and rigidly basing entry to the mainstream of the society on Portuguese education, the Portuguese ensure that they will continue to dominate. Little effort is made to give special classes to Africans so that they can learn to speak and read Portuguese, or to offer scholarships, or to build boarding schools for Africans who do not have schools in their villages and who cannot afford to live in towns where there are schools.

Portuguese are deeply concerned about education, perhaps because in the past they have had so little of it. Anyone with a college degree can and usually does insist on being called "Dr." Visitors are almost compelled to visit schoolroom after monotonous schoolroom while the Portuguese beam with pride.

In Portugal, almost 40 per cent of the population is illiterate. In the colonies, an estimated 80 to 90 per cent of the black population is functionally illiterate, as are 20 to 30 per cent of the white settlers.

"If you can't get four years of primary school here, you can't get anything else either, from a job to a driver's license, whether you're white or black," said one resident of Luanda. "And it just happens that the odds against an African getting through four years of school seem to be around ten thousand to one." Unofficial figures suggest that for whites, the odds are twenty to one. This, however, cannot be verified because of the newly nonracial nature of Portuguese statistics — nor can the impressions, gained through interviews and visits to schools in the three territories, that a disproportionate share of education funds are spent on schools attended by whites.

There has been a dramatic upturn in the number of primary schools and students in all of the territories in the wake of the guerrilla uprisings. But it is not clear that the flurry of activity, much publicized by the Portuguese, will greatly increase the number of Africans with enough education to be able to test the Portuguese protestations that only ignorance keeps the black man down.

My visits to more than a dozen schools in the African territories suggest a pattern in which 80 to 90 per cent of the children in the first year of school are black, while 90 to 95 per cent in the last two years are white or mulatto. Few African families have enough money even for the nominal school fees, which rise progressively in most of the schools. And, for the most part, only Africans living in urban areas or where there are white settlements have any realistic hope of being able to get to a secondary school.

In Portuguese Guinea, the 26,172 students in "primary school" (the first four years) in 1970 represented a doubling of the total in 1960. In Pelundo I saw some of the students included in these statistics. They sat outside a two-room school playing games because there were no desks inside for them. Their teacher, who would conduct two hours of school a day for them, was a Portuguese soldier pulled off military duty.

In Angola, the number of primary school students has jumped from 100,000 in 1961 to 400,000 in 1970. In Mozambique, 1970's primary school enrollment of 592,000 represented a 40 per cent increase since 1965. But in the same period, the combined number of students in academic and vocational high schools had fallen slightly. The follow-through on the hurried primary school effort seems negligible.

Africans who hurdle the education barriers can generally find good employment. In Angola, the middle and lower ranks of the local civil service are filled largely by Africans. Private employment is much harder to find, partially because of the closely knit Portuguese family and the tendency toward small, family-owned businesses. There are only a few black faces behind tellers' windows in banks or at cash registers of shops. The number seems to be increasing, but slowly.

In some jobs, whites doing the same work get more money than Africans. One factory owner in Luanda explained that he pays his African workers a lower weekly rate because they are after "a target." That is, the worker comes to Luanda to earn enough to buy some land or a new wife and then returns to the bush. By keeping his wage down, the factory owner makes him work a reasonable time and gets increased production as the man becomes more experienced.

Augusto Bandeira, general manager of Angola's major railroad, explained why he has only one African among his 130 senior staff members: "They don't seem to be interested in this work. There is nothing against a colored man getting one of these jobs. But they don't do anything for themselves." Officials in Mozambique, where the 500 blacks among the 2000 employees on Beira's railroad are all at the bottom of the structure, echoed that attitude: "If they would just get the education, the black people would get the good jobs. But most of them don't want to learn."

Level of education and amount of income are also the qualifications for voting for the rubber-stamp local councils and the six or seven delegates to the National Assembly in Portugal each province has. Few Africans do qualify. It would make little difference if they did, given the present Portuguese political system and the minuscule influence public opinion has on it.

THE EMPIRE AND THE FUTURE

The growing wealth of Angola provides one of the important tests for the prospects of peaceful change in the Portuguese empire. The increasing revenues give Angola what the Portuguese assert they have lacked for 500 years — the resources to pay for the education and other welfare measures needed to develop a black elite large enough to share power under the equal rights that are supposedly available to all educated and civilized men. It is inconceivable that a decade hence the Portuguese will still be trying to say, "It is too early to judge . . ." or "We can't afford to go any faster in Angola . . ." Wealth will make such excuses totally lame and the face of tokenism the Portuguese have maintained over five centuries all the more flimsy and discredited. The Portuguese confront in Angola what to me is a dilemma. They will deliver on their promises to develop black as well as white society there (and, I feel, inevitably develop a stratum of African opinion that will agitate with increasing effectiveness for political independence) or they will renege on their promises and depend even more openly on the army to keep the Africans in line and see Angola be drawn more completely into the South African racial, political, and economic orbit.

At the same time, of course, Angola's flourishing economy gives Portugal more immediate incentive to maintain the status quo in Africa. Settlers in Angola speak only partly in jest about plans to declare the empire a federation and shift the capital from Lisbon to Luanda, where the real money is. By the best financial estimates I could get in early 1971 from economic experts in Lisbon, the wars in Africa and the social pacification programs they had sparked were still costing Portugal a little more in annual expenditure than the colonies were providing her in profit, despite the rapidly increasing Angola revenues. But a high percentage of Angola's exports earned foreign exchange, which was banked in Lisbon under a central banking system and which only slowly, if at all, trickled back to Angola. One of the essential problems the Portuguese seem to face is finding another way of balancing their foreign exchange accounts other than by relying so heavily on Angola's exports to do it for them. Until they come up with an alternative, they will not peacefully give up political control in Angola. That is my impression at any rate, although economists disagree on the true extent of Angola's contribution to Portugal's foreign reserve position.

The decisive pressures for change in the next decade, if change is to come, will be at home, in Lisbon, just as the decisive pressures to grant independence to Ghana and Senegal were in London and Paris, where it was shown that political control of the colonies had become unprofitable. In 1971, there was a whisper of change stirring along the halls of the rose and lavender palaces of the Lisbon administrators. Centrifugal forces were gently tugging at empire's fastenings.

Nobody talked about giving up the colonies; to do so would have bordered on treason. But there was a discernible casting about for a better way to run them. Defense appropriations, usually totaling around $300 million, consumed 40 per cent of Portugal's modest annual budget at a time when Portugal remained at the bottom of Western Europe's list in capital investment for growth, health services, education, and just about every other public expenditure except maintaining political police. Within the government of Marcelo Caetano, who followed Salazar, there was concern that these priorities might not be exactly correct.

As important as the drain on the budget was the changing pattern of trade for Portugal. Traditionally, the colonies take about 25 per cent of Portugal's exports and send raw materials that account for about 15 per cent of her imports. (In the true mercantilist colony system, many of the exports were processed versions of the raw materials originally sent from the colonies, which were restricted from producing the finished goods.) This favorable balance of trade was important to Portugal's economy.

Of growing importance to Portugal for trade are the European countries associated with her in the European Free Trade Association (EFTA) and those of the Common Market. EFTA countries, including Great Britain, took one third of Portugal's exports in

1970; the Common Market, more than 20 per cent; and the United States, around 10 per cent.

Prosperity in Europe's heartland has rippled out to Iberia. But the negotiations between the major EFTA countries, chiefly Britain, on entry into the Common Market presented the Portuguese with another dilemma, one that threatened to isolate them from Europe's upward climb. There would be almost insurmountable problems in associating Portugal's present colonial structure to the Common Market. This squeeze, not immediate but already evident, may be the key pressure in bringing change or cementing Portugal to defending the status quo.

The stronger pull of Europe against the empire is best seen in the patterns of migration from Portugal. Each year, an estimated 100,000 Portuguese risk arrest by walking hundreds of miles, jamming into crowded, unsafe trucks or taking boats to sneak across Portugal's frontiers to find jobs in France, West Germany, and elsewhere. At the same time, about 5000 accept government-paid trips to the African colonies. Much of the clandestine immigration to Europe results from young men seeking to avoid the draft for the colonial wars. But more important factors seem to be the better wages, and brighter lights, in Europe. The foreign currency the illegal immigrants remit to their families at home is so badly needed by the Portuguese to help with the balance of payments situation that the government cannot afford to crack down very harshly on the emigrants. This manpower drain is already restricting Portugal's growing internal economy. Channeling white settlers off to bolster the country's position in Africa is also becoming a debatable economic proposition.

In Portugal's corporate-state political system, these are the kinds of arguments that will carry or lose the day for the young technocrats identified as "Europeans" or for the "Africanistas," the business and professional army men with deep attachments to Africa. But public sentiment against the wars has become more noticeable, residents of Lisbon say. Students have begun to hold mild protest rallies, labor unions are less forthright in their support for the wars, and the number of army deserters and draft evaders have reached the point of being publicly mentioned by defense officials as a national shame. The most spectacular antiwar effort was a sabotage bombing of an airbase hangar, in which eleven aircraft were destroyed, as a protest in early 1971. Military personnel almost certainly helped stage the bombing.

But the public expressions of discontent are likely to remain for a long time less important than the economic arguments within the small elite that runs the empire. Many of them still seem to agree with former Foreign Minister Franco Nogueira that they have no obligation to investigate "the myth that decisions taken by the majority are always valid."

It is almost impossible to judge what the majority of Portugal's peasants feel about the struggle for the empire. In any event, their opinions don't matter much in Portugal, where until recent years only 20 per cent of the people have been eligible to vote. "Salazar left the people completely apolitical," one Portuguese intellectual told me. "It will take a decade before there will be such a thing as public opinion on anything in this country."

Chapter Eleven

The Guerrillas:
The Chairman's Shadow

THE ROLY-POLY SHADOW of Chairman Mao has fallen across Southern Africa in the past decade. The obvious failures of politics, economics, and morality to produce significant change have turned many to the only avenue that seems to remain open: externally supported guerrilla warfare. As America moved into the quagmire of Southeast Asia, Africans launched their "wars of national liberation" in the three Portuguese territories, staged sporadic raids into Rhodesia, and tried to organize for an eventual military strike against the South African redoubt. Operating from independent African states neighboring on the white-controlled countries, the guerrillas turned to Peking and Moscow for equipment and training and set out to emulate the Chinese and the Vietcong. Chairman Mao Tse-tung's works became required reading throughout Southern Africa, for white and black, as Lieutenant Colonel Augusto de Fonseca Lage reminded me late one afternoon in eastern Angola.

"The important thing in this war is winning the population," Lage, a trim, patrician, and tough soldier told me as we bounced down a muddy road outside Cangamba. "Our patrols go out and bring the population into the villages we build for them. Without the 'water,' the 'fish' will disappear. We know what Mao has said."

Lage slowed the careening jeep as we approached a bend in the muddy road and a stand of trees. A light rain was falling, and the sky was turning from a translucent icy blue to a storm-promising indigo. Clouds like elephants lumbered across the horizon, and a big, wet African wind was sweeping in off empty plains. It fluttered the coral scarf knotted around Lage's neck. "That is where the terrorists came in and hanged six villagers who were loyal to us. From those trees," Lage said in French, pointing. We were six miles outside Cangamba, the African town that was Lage's command post on the desolate, soaring plateau of eastern Angola. The Portuguese call this plateau "the land at the end of the earth." It runs hundreds of miles eastward into central Africa and has little vegetation or population. I had asked Lage about the claims of African guerrillas to control much of this area, and this jeep ride through the unguarded hills around Cangamba was part of his answer. He had ostentatiously left even his revolver behind, and we were alone.

"Down there, a few kilometers," the colonel said as we started along the darkening road again, "is where one of our cars hit a land mine six months ago. One of our men was killed." I glanced nervously around and Lage smiled. His words had achieved the effect he sought. "But that doesn't happen anymore. Our patrols have broken up the guerrillas. You will see for yourself tomorrow."

We crested a hill and stopped in front of a cement building that was surrounded by a dozen African huts and cornfields. Lage called into the mud-stained building, which was pocked with bulletholes. A humpbacked white man in his fifties shuffled out onto the porch and greeted Lage with a toothless grin. Three mulatto children, aged five to ten, stood behind the man, who fingered his wispy beard as Lage told me about him.

Lobo da Ferreira had come to eastern Angola thirty years before as a trader when the colonial administration opened up this area and had lived in this house since. "The terrorists have come and shot up the house," Lage said. "But they cannot drive Lobo da Ferreira away. He is Portuguese. The blacks living here help him, because they like the Portuguese." The man smiled again.

The struggle for Southern Africa had begun in Angola with a black uprising in 1961 that resulted in the butchering of thousands of blacks, by the guerrillas and the Portuguese alternately, and hundreds of whites. Separate but similar black revolts began in Portuguese Guinea in 1963 and in Mozambique in 1964. Before the violence erupted, Portugal had a few thousand white troops stationed in Africa. By 1971, it needed 140,000 soldiers as a shield for the three territories. The guerrilla wars were killing at least 400 Portuguese soldiers each year and six times that number of Africans. The warfare also consumed at least 27 per cent of Portugal's annual budget, and another 13 per cent went to related defense expenditures. Hundreds of thousands of Africans had been uprooted by the war and herded into the Portuguese version of the strategic hamlet the Americans had used in Vietnam. Insurgency had bred counterinsurgency.

Although not directly involved in the shooting war with black nationalism, South Africa and Rhodesia responded in the last decade by greatly building up their military machines, too. South Africa has more combat aircraft, and trained jet pilots, than the rest of sub-Sahara Africa combined. South Africa manufactures its own guided missiles. The 30,000-man army routinely stages large-scale counterinsurgency maneuvers. In 1968, asserting a doctrine of hot pursuit similar to that used later in Laos and Cambodia by the Americans and South Vietnamese, Prime Minister Vorster told African countries providing the guerrillas with sanctuary: "If you want violence, we will hit you so hard you will never forget it." Three years later, South African troops briefly crossed into Zambia in pursuit of guerrillas. Vorster at first proudly announced the incursion, then attempted to play it down when he realized the international implications of the South African action.

The military challenge from Africa has pushed the three white powers into a defensive alliance that has never been publicly stated, but exists in at least the tacit assumption that a military defeat for one of them is a defeat for the others as well. South Africa sent 300 special policemen to assist Rhodesia in fighting guerrillas and to get some experience that might be useful in the future, in September 1967. The units were still there four years later. The

South Africans have also extended offers of whatever military help is needed by the Portuguese in Angola and Mozambique. Officially, Portugal's leaders say they do not need any help, but rumors of South African units operating deep inside Angola and Mozambique are widely circulated. American intelligence sources reported to Washington in January 1971 that Rhodesian military units were dispatched into northern Mozambique as a result of a major guerrilla incursion on the south side of the Zambezi River valley two months earlier. The Rhodesians were reportedly pulled out after a month.

The three shooting wars are fought in the sparsely populated savanna plains and thick forests of the interior of Portuguese Africa. Most of the fighting is for small villages and the control of dirt roads in the African bush. These are areas that, for the most part, the Portuguese had never governed anyway and would have taken no interest in were it not for the guerrillas. Except for the southern part of Portuguese Guinea, the Portuguese were not physically ousted from areas; it was rather that the guerrillas moved in where there was a vacuum, and then the Portuguese sought to oust the guerrillas. A decade of guerrilla war is not at all reflected in the tranquil cities of Angola and Mozambique. Only in Portuguese Guinea's village-capital of Bissau do residents occasionally hear small arms fire in the distance. In mid-1971 guerrillas staged a long-range mortar attack on Bissau.

The African nationalists have achieved mixed military results in their drive to dislodge the Portuguese as a first step in taking Southern Africa. My 1971 travels through these territories convinced me that the guerrillas had effective control of about half the countryside of Portuguese Guinea and a great deal of popular support in the country; in Angola, the guerrillas could operate over 30 per cent of the vast territory and establish hospitals and schools deep in the bush; in Mozambique, however, they were bottled up in the northern forest. It was difficult to diagnose anything other than stalemate, for the present and the near-future, in a military sense.

This kind of judgment is hotly disputed by the Portuguese and by the guerrillas. Each claims to be winning the wars. Each churns out communiqués regularly with wildly conflicting statistics in efforts to quantify claims of progress and attract more help and sympathy. Portuguese papers print their army's communiqués as proof of imminent victory, and black Africa swears that the guerrillas are telling the truth and the Portuguese are about to buckle.

I had come to Cangamba, in Angola's Moxico district, to try to get a look at the people and realities that lay behind the communiqués. Moxico had been the scene of much of the heaviest guerrilla activity for two years. The Zambian border was less than 200 miles east of Cangamba, and the guerrillas from the Popular Movement for the Liberation of Angola were trying to establish the area as a staging point for a push into Angola's economic heartland. The Popular Movement, known by its initials in Portuguese, MPLA, was estimated by Portuguese intelligence to have a total of about 2500 guerrillas inside Angola and the same number in training in Zambia. They usually operate in groups of forty or less.

The Portuguese had about 60,000 soldiers in Angola in 1971. Colonel Lage, a battalion commander, had 450 combat soldiers to cover a 14,000-square-mile area larger than the state of Maryland. He also had several hundred black Angolan troops under his command. When I visited his group in February 1971, he and his men had been fighting the elusive guerrillas for fifteen months and yearned to be pulled back to a quieter assignment. But Lage was proud of his counterinsurgency record. "We have killed two hundred seventy-seven enemy, wounded ninety-four, taken one hundred six weapons, and captured three thousand eighty-nine civilian population," he told me as we sipped coffee on the verandah of the pink building that had once been a civilian district officer's headquarters and now belonged to the army. "We have captured more population than the other battalions in Angola combined. When the population realizes that the terrorists cannot defend them from our patrols, but that we can defend them from the terrorists, they will all come to our side. Fifteen months ago the snipers fired on this building at night. Now, there is no population to shield them and they cannot creep up here. Our patrols have disorganized the guerrillas."

Lage, a man of rugged good looks and a surprisingly soft-spoken manner, resembled many of the one hundred or so professional officers I met in my trips through Portuguese Africa. Many of them had served one tour of duty in each of the three territories, and they seemed completely dedicated to their struggle. Formed near or at the top of the aristocratic class system of Portugal, they struck me as good officers, disciplined and able to get the most out of their men.

They were only a tiny nucleus for the armed forces, however. Almost all of the lieutenants and noncoms were university students serving a compulsory four-year hitch. All the enlisted men were draftees. The conscripts seemed to me to be prepared to do what their country asked, but were not particularly keen on risking their lives to preserve Portugal's hold on Africa. I could see that morale, as Lage said, was the toughest part of his job. He did a good job, emphasizing the battalion's collective identity as "The Ace of Spades," an emblem that was everywhere at Cangamba. But at other posts I visited, conscripted officers frankly told me that the wars were not worth the cost and Portugal should get out. The better-educated young air force officers were especially cynical. I asked one about a socialist newspaper I saw him reading. "A friend in Sweden sends this," he said. "He couldn't get in the air force, so he left Portugal rather than serve in the army. I would have too if I hadn't got this easy job." Portugal's Defense Minister felt that desertion and draft dodging had reached the level of a national shame in 1970 and said so in a speech. But while it seemed to me that the seeds of a serious conflict in the Portuguese army were being nurtured and would probably burst forth before the end of the seventies, I found little during my trip that tallied with guerrilla propaganda claims that Portuguese morale was crumbling at that very moment.

ANGOLA MORNINGS

My trip with the 2635th Cavalry Company began as three large SA–330 helicopters whirred down onto Cangamba's muddy landing strip just after dawn one morning. Manufactured by France's Sud Aviation company, the three machines had just been delivered in Angola, a few weeks after French President Georges Pompidou had said in Dakar that France would no longer supply South Africa with arms that could be used for internal repression of black nationalism. Pompidou had not mentioned the Portuguese. This was to be the first combat run for the SA–330, which could transport twenty-five armed men instead of the four or five the Portuguese had been packing into the small Alouette helicopters France had sold them previously. The 330 would give the Portuguese an important increase in mobility, and two French mechanics flew on this mission to check for adaptions that should be made on future deliveries.

From Cangamba, we flew to Muie (pronounced Mu-yay), a small outpost deeper in the eastern zone, about 100 miles from the Zambian border. We touched down long enough to take on another company of soldiers stationed at Muie and then lifted into the drizzling skies again. I had specifically asked to go with a patrol from Muie, because the outpost had taken on a symbolic significance in 1970 after English author Basil Davidson, perhaps the leading expert on the anti-Portuguese guerrillas, had written a series of articles describing a trip into Angola with the MPLA. He asserted that he had crept to within 400 yards of the Portuguese garrison at Muie without being caught and then marched back into Zambia. "He probably did it," Lage had said with a shrug. "It is easy enough to sneak through those forests to look at a camp. We go into the forests to kill the enemy. That is the difference."

Forty miles south of Muie the helicopters dipped and hovered over a clear space. The wind from their blades like a giant unseen hand flattened the yellow-green swamp grass. The men of the 2635th Cavalry Company jumped clear of the flying machines, and I scrambled after them.

Their boots sinking into the marshy ground and forty-pound field packs digging into their shoulders, the soldiers sprinted desperately for a wooded rise that began a few hundred yards away. They had dropped into the same space six months before and had been ambushed by the guerrillas. This time it was quiet, and they collapsed into a heaving, exhausted circle once inside the cover of the trees.

The leader of this group was Second Lieutenant Luis Filipe Monteiro, a short, swarthy twenty-five-year-old accounting student drafted in Portugal two years before. Monteiro, who wore a three-day-old beard for luck, was from Coimbra, a university town in central Portugal; so were many of the forty other white soldiers in the group. Leading the white unit through the forest were two African soldiers borrowed for the mission from special African units the Portuguese have formed. The forty-fourth man was Second Lieutenant Francisco Magalhaes, a twenty-two-year-old architectural student, a mulatto with a Portuguese father and an African mother. Born in Angola, he had been studying in Portugal when drafted.

Another patrol group was being dropped fifteen miles farther south. This was an all-African unit that could march through the woods nearly twice as rapidly as the whites. "The natives heard the helicopter and ran from us," Monteiro explained as he led his men deeper into the woods. "They will come back to their villages after we go through. Then the other troops will catch them in the second wave. Capturing the population is the key to the war," he said, echoing his commander's catch phrase.

This was a "hunt and persecute" patrol, the more elegantly phrased Portuguese equivalent of Vietnam's search and destroy missions. Monteiro's men were to march through the wet scrub forest for three days, round up villagers suspected of giving help to the guerrillas, and, if they were lucky, encounter some of the phantomlike guerrillas and destroy them and their encampments.

Two miles from the drop point the soldiers found a settlement, a collection of half a dozen stick-and-thatch huts grouped in the middle of tall cornfields. The villagers seemed to have fled, but

Monteiro's African guides, moving in front of the unit, captured two emaciated, aged women out in the fields. They had apparently been left behind. They were "captured population" in the strange terminology of this strange war.

Sitting half-naked and shivering in the chilling downpour, one of the women watched in wonderment and fear as the young Portuguese infantrymen smashed down a field of ripe corn. The other woman was sent to collect her possessions, which barely filled the porcelain basin she balanced on her head, before the soldiers pulled down her hut. Some of the young soldiers, all draftees, giggled as they fitfully kicked into bits the hollow gourd calabashes used by villagers to store food and drink. Others conscientiously uprooted the corn. For a moment, the scene seemed to be a weird mingling of *Lord of the Flies* and *The Wild Bunch*, in Portuguese. After a cigarette break, the forty-four soldiers marched the two women prisoners into the Angolan forest. The women, each attempting to balance one of the forty-pound field packs on top of their heads, stumbled under the weight as the column advanced. "If we let these women go free, they would go and tell the terrorists where we are," Monteiro said. "Then we all would be ambushed and perhaps someone would be killed. These people must have been helping the turras. The turras wouldn't let them survive if they didn't." Turra, short for *turrista* (terrorist), is the soldier's slang for the guerrillas. The Africans call the white soldiers "tugas," a corruption of Portuguese.

The patrol fell silent as it moved into the bush. The only sounds were the slapping of branches against the wet ponchos and the automatic rifles of the soldiers, and an occasional low whistle to call a halt as the two African soldiers saw or heard something suspicious. The two women, marching in the middle of the column, slowed the pace, and by dusk the patrol had covered only eight miles.

Supper was cold canned tuna and corned beef and a can of fruit juice. Rations were shared with the women prisoners. The soldiers stretched their ponchos across branches to form small tents and dropped wearily onto the wet ground. The women only had wet blankets to huddle inside as protection against the still falling rain and the rapidly dropping temperatures of nightfall at an altitude of 4000 feet.

The camp's sentries slapped on the ponchos an hour before dawn, and the soldiers groggily arose. Thick grayish-white mists cloaked the forest floor ahead as the patrol split in two groups and moved out of the thicket. One of the women had told the soldiers of a large guerrilla camp near a village that was an hour's march away. Magalhaes, the mulatto lieutenant, took fifteen men to hunt the guerrillas while Monteiro and the others marched to the civilian village.

A faint thudding sound grew louder as the short column following Magalhaes twisted silently through the woods. The village flour mill's steady pounding was like a slow, monotonous drum beating. Leading the column was Chainda, one of the African soldiers. He was at least six feet four inches tall and an excellent jungle fighter. He found a well-beaten path in the woods south of where they figured the village was, and Magalhaes set the ambush there. Five minutes after the Portuguese had formed an arc along the side of the trail voices floated toward us. Two African men and a woman, carrying food and clothing bundles, were walking down the trail. Behind them came three guerrillas. They were not wearing uniforms; they did not need to: the automatic rifles they carried identified them for the Portuguese.

The Portuguese tensed as the seemingly easy prize moved toward them. As the first bearer approached, one of the white soldiers inexplicably lunged from hiding and tried to grab him as a prisoner. A startled, unbelieving silence hung in the forest for a second's fragment as the two groups of warriors realized what was to happen. Then the forest exploded. The bearer ducked past the white soldier and flung his load to the ground. The jangling of the tin pans he had carried broke the eerie silence. The Africans behind him dove into the thick woods along the trail just as the Portuguese rifles came up and fired simultaneously, erecting walls of lead that crashed through the bush. The guerrillas found the few holes between the walls of bullets and scrambled away. They fired a few rounds back, chipping bark from the tree behind which Magalhaes knelt. Then they were gone.

Cursing, Magalhaes rose and ordered the men to fall back fifty feet and prepare for a counterambush. "He's saying that white men don't know anything about fighting in the jungle," a Portuguese noncom who spoke French explained to me. "He's saying it very strongly."

The counterattack did not come. The unit marched away to rejoin Monteiro's group, which had rounded up five scrawny old women and a dignified-looking man dressed in tattered clothing at the village. They had also discovered two grenades, a bazooka shell with Chinese lettering, and MPLA propaganda booklets. Monteiro proudly pinned to his poncho an MPLA button that promised an Angola free of imperialism and colonialism. There were also bundles of MPLA correspondence that would be sent back to Cangamba and analyzed minutely by Colonel Lage's intelligence section. "You can see that the turras were here," Monteiro said. "They run and leave these old people. They come and tell these villagers that they will kick out the white man, and then the white man's cars and planes will belong to them. And so these simple people help the guerrillas. We will take them to a regrouping village. It is better for them. We don't mean these people harm."

The main guerrilla camp, deserted now, was half an hour away from the village. The ten small huts with open sides were completely covered by high, thickly foliated trees. Each hut covered a thin mat, and a wooden gun rest had been erected at the head of each mat. Several hundred yards away in another part of the woods was the kitchen, where the women lived and cooked for the thirty to forty men who regularly used the camp.

Portuguese intelligence officers had told me that there were hundreds of such small camps scattered throughout eastern and northern Angola. Each time the Portuguese discover one and destroy it, the guerrillas set up another one deeper in the woods. The Africans have also established some large camps in the east, where they operate rudimentary schools for children and bush health clinics. At one camp Monteiro's men helped destroy there was a beautiful garden, one soldier told me. The attempts of the guerrillas to keep these camps supplied is one measure of their determination. For a man carrying a heavy machine gun or a mortar and traveling mostly at night, it is a month's walk from the Zambian border to the camp we had found.

"We leave the camp alone this time, now that we know where it is," Monteiro said. "Maybe they will think it is safe and come back. And we will come back another day, too." In all three of their territories, the Portuguese seemed to have the power, as they claimed, to destroy any of the guerrilla camps they could find, with the exception of a few isolated strongholds near the borders. But the guerrillas have the ability to wait until the Portuguese leave, rebuild their camps, and seep back into the countryside. Control is a relative matter of who is where when. "The guerrillas are every place we aren't," a former officer in Portuguese Guinea told me in Lisbon. "We can go anywhere in the country, almost, if we use enough force. When we leave, the guerrillas come back." This seemed true for large stretches of eastern Angola and spots of northern Mozambique as well.

By nightfall of the second day, the patrol had found no other trace of the guerrillas. The march had quickened and covered twelve miles that day. The soldiers, beginning to drag, wearily dropped their packs and made their rough camp just before another nightlong rain began. A tall and friendly sergeant, a twenty-three-year-old former university student named Carlos, and I pitched our ponchos together so I could share the blanket he had brought. We shivered through the miserable night anyway.

"This last stretch is the most dangerous for us," Monteiro said the next morning. It was another ten miles to the rendezvous point, where trucks from Muie would be sent to haul the soldiers and their prisoners the last ten miles. The soldiers' soggy boots were now digging into a wet sand path leading through high fields of elephant grass. Each step seemed to add five pounds of sand to their shoes. "We have to follow this path through a lot of open country. The turras will have figured out our path by now." A few minutes later Chainda came to a halt at the front of the column. Across the path lay a thin wire, attached to the pin of a fragmentation grenade lying under a bush beside the path.

"A present for us," the African said as he nonchalantly handled the grenade and hurled it into the woods. It did not explode. Laughing, Chainda described Chinese workmanship in unflattering terms.

Two hundred yards further the other African scout found the guerrilla camp of the night before. He counted signs of twenty-nine men, all probably armed. The pace of the patrol quickened, despite the fatigue of the soldiers and the seven African captives, who remained as silent as they had been since they were captured. Humiliation flickered across the old man's face as the soldiers sent him with the women to fill their canteens with river water, but he remained quiet. Fetching water and carrying loads like the field packs is woman's work in Africa.

The terrain was marsh and river on the patrol's left flank, grassy open fields in front of them, and scrub-wooded hills on the right. The skies had been clear that morning for the first time on the patrol, and by noon a broiling sun had appeared. Gunfire sounded from the other side of the river, slightly in front of us. "The African units have already passed us," Monteiro said. "They can march." With six of the last ten miles gone in early afternoon, the soldiers came to their last danger point, a wooden footbridge across a small river. "They could ambush us from the other side, or mine the bridge," Monteiro had fretted earlier.

The seven African civilians were lined up to cross the bridge one at a time before the soldiers. The first four made it across. The fifth, a woman captured at the second village, deviated slightly from their path. She stepped on the mine.

The explosion spun her body into the air, lifting it in what seemed momentarily to be a strange, bloody movement of ballet. The pots she had been carrying on her head caromed off the bridge, and parts of her body splashed into the river. The screams of the other African women died quickly. The dignified old man remained mute, his eyes impassive. After a brief silence of horror and sickness had spread over the soldiers, the march resumed and finished uneventfully three hours later.

It had added one more statistic for the communiqués: one African woman, name unknown, age unknown, killed on February 21, 1971. The Portuguese recorded the woman as a civilian killed by the guerrillas, since it was an MPLA mine. The nationalists, if they learned of the death, undoubtedly categorized it as an African civilian killed by the Portuguese who sent her onto the bridge. In the end, the tragedy of the woman's death will have been reduced to a simple irony, a comment on the reliability of anybody's statistics in a war usually fought far out of the range of cameras and notebooks.

At Muie, the seven other African hostages were taken off to find lodging in the huts of the several thousand tribesmen the Portuguese had bunched around the post's perimeter. The young company commander, a captain, told me the three other groups in the operation had been more successful than ours. In all, three days of hunting and persecuting in the forests had netted five enemy dead, five rifles captured, and 147 civilians rounded up.

I had already seen at Cangamba what would happen to the captured Africans. Coughing and shivering, dressed in rags or almost naked, a group of 100 had stood in the muddy compound occupied by the Portuguese political police, who work closely with the army in disputed areas. It was late afternoon, and the chill wind was blowing along the plateau. These people had been captured a few days before. Most of them would be given food and a small plot of land to farm after they had been thoroughly interrogated, a burly, slovenly looking policeman said. Some of the younger men might be taken into the African military units if they seemed loyal.

These were a group of the people who, I had been told so often, were the key to the wars the Portuguese were fighting in Africa. Resettling them in secure villages would turn the tide against the guerrillas. The Africans stood silently as I guiltily and hurriedly snapped a few pictures, and I cursed myself for being a journalist and adding to their humiliation. Their eyes smoldered with resentment, and from some there came a look of clear intense hatred. The Portuguese did not seem to notice; I began to believe their theory that these people could become the key to the wars.

The tribesmen in the interior of the three Portuguese possessions had had little contact with whites before the beginning of the last decade, as the Portuguese stuck to their coastal settlements. The response to the guerrilla wars had changed this. The wars wrenched Portuguese Africans into at least a measure of contact with a world that had been largely unknown. Children in the most remote part of Portuguese Guinea are familiar with helicopters and jet fighters now. In Cangamba, I joined Lage and fifty of his soldiers one night to watch the weekly movie. It was Jane Fonda's *Sunday in New York*. A score of African children clustered close to the tiny screen, watching the images of Manhattan skyscrapers and listening uncomprehendingly to English. In some inexplicable way I felt that that evening would turn out to be one of Miss Fonda's more substantial contributions to black revolution.

The crucial factor, however, is the African reaction to the resettlement villages the Portuguese are forcing them into. In Angola and Portuguese Guinea, areas outside Portuguese control are declared "intervention zones," and villagers must choose to take their chances against bombing, artillery, and commando raids, or to come to the fortified villages around Portuguese posts. I asked a Portuguese major in Guinea what happened if the tribesmen did not want to move. "We encourage them by destroying their old villages," he replied. "But some of them want to move." Others come to the resettlement villages after their homes have been destroyed in the fighting between the Portuguese and the guerrillas, both of whom tend to use the same tactics in trying to persuade or coerce the unsophisticated villagers into supporting them.

If the Portuguese tactics are spreading the kind of resentment that pervaded the group I saw in Cangamba, they may find that they have done little more than purchase time at a high cost. If they fail to follow through on their promises of schools, hospitals, and economic development for the villagers they have uprooted, they will probably have created waves of embittered new recruits for the guerrillas. At the least, they will have formed a vast, hostile black population that will have to be guarded in concentration camp conditions. The success, or failure, of the resettlement villages will be the vital test for Portuguese counterinsurgency in the nineteen seventies.

RESETTLING THE WATER

Forewarned by the Angola and Guinea uprisings, the Portuguese moved quickly to establish the resettlement program in Mozambique as guerrilla war began to flicker there. They drew a line through the forests of the northern quarter of the narrow, elongated country. The land to the north, inhabited largely by the fierce Makonde tribe who had resisted all Portuguese pacification efforts, became an intervention zone; thousands of the Makonde fled to Tanzania to join the guerrillas. To the south, the Portuguese persuaded or coerced more peaceful tribes to move into new villages aligned in a belt across the country, a *cordon sanitaire* across Mozambique.

By 1971, there were 433,000 Africans living in resettlement villages in Mozambique, Portuguese intelligence officials told me. I visited a showcase, a town called Montepuez. Houses had been built for the Africans. They were European-style boxes arranged in neat rectangles along unpaved streets; Africans live in circular huts, in circles. Some health clinics had also been built. The Africans were probably earning more cash than they ever had when they were living in scattered villages. They had been given seeds and farming utensils, which they would pay for out of their profits, and assigned a plot of land to grow their food crops and cotton for marketing. In one representative African quarter around Montepuez, the government had established three three-year primary schools for 300 families. This was proof of Portuguese assertions that they were putting the Africans in the villages for their own good, said the civilian administrator who showed me around. He said they would add a fourth year to the schools the following year. If African children do get through the fourth year, they will then have the chance to try to get into an advanced primary school. The nearest one, I discovered, was 200 miles away, in a country with only the barest transportation system. Boarding school expenses were obviously beyond any of the parents living in that African quarter. The children would finish a few years of school, be entered on the charts that proclaim that resettlement villages have greatly increased the African school population, and then go back to the cotton fields.

Resettlement villages in Mozambique do seem to offer some prospects of increased economic development; in Angola and Portuguese Guinea, they have been hurriedly constructed for security reasons, as the authorities try to get the villagers out of areas in which the guerrillas are active. Apparently for security reasons, Portuguese officials in those two territories refused to tell me how many Africans they had placed in resettlement villages. My own estimate was not less than 50,000 in Portuguese Guinea and not less than 100,000 in Angola.

But the Portuguese counterinsurgency tactics were not in 1971 the obvious failures that the strategic hamlets had become in Vietnam. The smaller scale of the Portuguese wars and the low population density in the combat areas kept down destruction of non-military targets and consequent civilian resentment. Unlike the Americans, the Portuguese were not able to destroy most of what they wanted to destroy. The crucial difference in the struggles was the vast disparity between the fighting spirit and ability of the Vietcong and that of the African guerrillas the Portuguese opposed.

By Portuguese estimates, a total of around 25,000 guerrillas faced their 140,000 troops in the three territories. But tribal and ideological divisions have prevented the Africans from acting as a unified force. They have also been handicapped by the uneven support they receive from independent Africa.

The most united, and successful, black nationalist movement opposing the Portuguese is the African Party for Independence of Guinea and Cape Verde. Known by its initials in Portuguese,

PAIGC was founded by a brilliant agronomist and political thinker named Amilcar Cabral. Educated in Lisbon, Cabral spent two years traveling to every corner of his tiny country while taking an agricultural census for the Portuguese government. Then he went into exile. By 1971 Cabral's six to seven thousand effectives were considered by Western intelligence sources as well armed and well trained. The Portuguese traveled only in military convoy outside the main towns and their garrisons. They paid tacit tribute to PAIGC's striking capability by sending a small aircraft forty miles from Bissau to collect me and an escorting Portuguese officer to fly to another post ten miles away. A dirt road linked the two military posts, located in the northwest corridor of the country where the Portuguese hold was strongest. When I asked my escort why we didn't use the road, he smiled and changed the subject. The Portuguese had about 30,000 troops in Guinea.

PAIGC and the other guerrilla movements depended on ambush, mine laying, and mortar and bazooka attacks on exposed Portuguese positions. Large-scale encounters were rare, although PAIGC had on occasion massed 400 to 500 guerrillas and assaulted Portuguese bases.

In Angola, the guerrillas totaled around 10,000, but they were divided into three competing groups that sometimes fought each other rather than the Portuguese. In addition to MPLA's 5000 men in the eastern areas, there were perhaps 4500 irregulars operating in northern Angola under the banner of the United Populations of Angola (UPA). The third guerrilla group, UNITA, had fewer than 500 men. All of UNITA's guerrillas were inside Angola and had to depend to a large extent on the weapons and materials they could capture from the Portuguese and the other guerrilla movements.

The leaders of MPLA were Marxist-oriented. Their strong point was political indoctrination inside Angola, Portuguese officers told me. UPA, on the other hand, had failed to develop a clear political ideology other than black rule supplanting white. The Portuguese considered UPA as more of a tribal movement than a true nationalist group, and deepening ethnic splits weakened the organization in the late sixties. Holden Roberto, UPA's leader, was one of the few guerrilla chiefs who openly sought support from the West, and especially from the United States.

The Mozambique Liberation Front, known as Frelimo, had seven to eight thousand armed fighters, who were drawn largely from the Makonde refugees who fled into Tanzania. Frelimo was making steady, if unspectacular, progress against the Portuguese in the thick forests of the north, around the Makonde plateau, until the February 1969 assassination of Frelimo's able leader, Eduardo Mondlane. He was killed by a bomb in a package that had been mailed to his headquarters in Tanzania.

Two years later, the assassination remained unsolved. The death of Mondlane, who had been educated at Syracuse University and who was highly respected by American policy-makers on Africa, provoked a bitter power struggle that split the movement's leadership. The disorganization and an increased Portuguese war effort resulted in heavy setbacks for Frelimo in 1970. By mid-1971, under a young, little-known military leader named Samora Machel, Frelimo seemed to be regrouping with increased aid from Peking and stepped up guerrilla activity in the Tete district, around Cabora Bassa.

The guerrilla organizations — called "liberation movements" or "freedom fighters" by their supporters and "terrorists" by the whites of Southern Africa — provide a key test for the steady stream of rhetoric and threats that black Africa directs at the white minority regimes of the south. So far, much of the test has been flunked badly. Financial help from the north is small. Ghana's then Prime Minister, Kofi A. Busia, disclosed in December 1970 that only six of the forty-one members of the Organization of African Unity had paid up their assessments to the O.A.U.'s special fund to support the guerrillas. O.A.U. sources said that the fund was skimping along on contributions totaling $100,000 to $200,000 a year, while its budget called for $1,500,000. Many countries were refusing to pay up because of widespread reports that much of the money was being squandered by the bureaucratic committee the O.A.U. had set up to coordinate the liberation movements. Others were displeased with the committee's undisguised preference for leftist organizations.

Individually, the African states were of even less help militarily. The only significant military powers were the Arab countries in the continent's northern tier, and they are much too occupied with Israel to devote resources to a battle for Southern Africa. Algeria does, however, provide some training for guerrillas and sends advisers to work with PAIGC and MPLA.

The only competent and well-equipped black air force south of the Sahara was possessed by Ethiopia, which had American-trained pilots and half a hundred combat aircraft. Emperor Haile Selassie's verbal support for the liberation movements failed to obscure the reality that he was too concerned about the internal rebellion he had on his hands in Eritrea and too dependent on American support to become much of a revolutionary in Southern Africa.

There is also little chance of black Africa deploying large numbers of soldiers to help the guerrillas any time in the next decade. For one thing, most countries lack that kind of commitment to helping defeat the whites in Southern Africa. Only two countries on the continent — Algeria and, to a lesser extent, Kenya — fought for their own independence; the others gained it through political negotiation. And those countries that do feel strongly about helping the guerrillas with manpower recognize that it would probably be a mistake. "If the nationalists can't make it on their own, they'll never be able to rule the country anyway," a Kenyan leader told me.

African armies were not in any shape at the beginning of this decade to help anybody anyway. More than one third of them had seized power from civilian governments in the nineteen sixties and were trying to run their own countries, usually without much success. Almost all of the others were too weak and small, or too involved with putting down internal revolts, to be much of a threat.

The only sizable armies black Africa possessed in 1971 were in Nigeria (200,000), Ethiopia (40,000), and Congo-Kinshasa

(40,000).[1] The Nigerian force is an unruly, poorly officered army that swelled from 10,000 soldiers in 1966 to the 200,000 figure during the three-year civil war in Biafra. I traveled with the Nigerians a great deal during the closing stages of the war, and I doubt very seriously that the South Africans, or even the Portuguese, will have much to fear from it for some time to come. The Nigerians had to turn to Egyptian volunteers and British (and at least one Rhodesian) mercenaries to pilot the MIGs Nigeria purchased from the Soviet Union. According to colleagues who have spent time with the Congolese army during times of stress, it is one of the most undisciplined and ineffective military forces on the face of the globe. Even if Africa had soldiers to help the guerrillas, it would still lack the logistical capability to get them into battle on the southern tip of the continent. The Nigerians had major problems in moving troops a few hundred miles and keeping them supplied.

The major help African countries have given the guerrillas is to provide sanctuary and bases from which to operate. PAIGC had about twenty-five camps that ringed Portuguese Guinea in 1971. The larger ones were in the Republic of Guinea, which has been the most militant supporter of the fight against the Portuguese. PAIGC also mounted raids from smaller bases in Senegal.

UPA operates from bases in Congo (Kinshasa). The Congo's president, General Joseph Mobutu, who depends on American financing and advice, expelled MPLA from his country because of its Marxist-orientation and Communist support. Zambia, on the other hand, allows MPLA to set up bases but bans UPA. Frelimo's main bases are in Tanzania.

The poverty and weakness of Africa has forced the guerrillas to seek help farther afield; bilateral aid far outweighs donations through the O.A.U., guerrilla sources have confirmed to a number of newsmen. Competition between the West and the Communist world, and then between the Russians and the Chinese, for clients

[1] The former Belgian Congo changed its name from Congo-Kinshasa to the Republic of Zaire in 1971.

in Africa has enabled the guerrillas to obtain well-stocked arsenals.

The United States, militarily allied to Portugal and possessing major investments in South Africa, never really got into the game of backing insurgency in Africa. More than 85 per cent of the military equipment going to guerrilla groups came from Communist countries, Portuguese intelligence officials estimated in 1971. Holden Roberto's UPA was receiving American-, Belgian-, and Israeli-manufactured equipment from the Congo's Mobutu. Whether Mobutu was siphoning this equipment off from his own supplies, or whether he was acting only as a channel, the Portuguese would not hazard to guess.

A general decline in Soviet interest and activity in Africa toward the end of the sixties was reflected in what appeared to be the Russian attitude toward the guerrillas. Apparently losing confidence in the revolutionary zeal and staying power of the Angola and Mozambique rebels, the Russians reportedly cut back on supplies to Southern Africa. They focused their attention on PAIGC in Guinea and provided about 85 per cent of PAIGC's supplies — including long-range 122-millimeter heavy mortars and anti-aircraft guns.

The Chinese, on the other hand, have moved into the struggle for Southern Africa in a major way. They had become the chief source of military equipment for both Frelimo and MPLA by 1971 and were providing training in Peking for members of both groups. Perhaps more significantly, China was the only major power providing large-scale military training programs for guerrillas actually in Africa. (Cuba was the only other country that had large numbers of advisers on the continent.) There were an estimated 250 Chinese instructors in Tanzania in 1971. The Portuguese said that 100 of them were working at Nachingwea, the main Frelimo base in Tanzania. Another 500 Chinese instructors were located in the People's Republic of the Congo, but there were no reliable estimates as to how many of those were training MPLA cadre.

China crystallized its new long-term commitment by making

Southern Africa the site of its first big foreign aid project, the $400 million Tanzam Railroad, which will link Tanzania and Zambia. The two African countries turned to Peking for help after the West rejected requests to build and finance the 1100-mile railway, which was begun in 1970 and which is due to be completed in early 1975. Zambia then should be able to ship most if not all of its valuable copper exports through the harbor of Dar es Salaam, rather than through the Portuguese-controlled railways and harbors of Angola and Mozambique. Zambia's dependence on the Portuguese has inhibited its support for the guerrilla movements, and completion of the railway could free the Zambians to take a more active role against the Portuguese.

A number of South African officials have predicted that the railroad would be used to haul not only guerrillas but also hordes of Chinese troops into battle against the whites. The growing displacement of Soviet influence in Southern Africa by Chinese influence clearly alarmed the South Africans. Not only were they being opposed by Communists, but by nonwhite Communists. At the 1971 anniversary celebration of the declaring of the republic, Prime Minister Vorster told a public rally of more than 70,000 of his followers that the "Chinese bridgehead" in Tanzania was the greatest single threat that faced Africa.

Vorster did not elaborate, but it is not difficult to understand his apprehension about Peking. The Afrikaner recognizes the discipline and zeal Mao Tse-tung has imposed on the Chinese people, who once lived under white domination. The possibility that some of this may be transmitted somehow to Africans is what bothers Vorster, much more than the possibility of vast numbers of Chinese joining the guerrillas if race war should explode in Southern Africa. As the leading nonwhite military power in the world, China has a special stake in the destruction of apartheid, a stake that the United States and the Soviet Union do not have. And the Chinese model of trying to mobilize poor and uneducated masses may turn out to be the only foreign experience in recent history that will have much meaning for Africans trying to organize their own societies.

While the wind has been blowing from the East for the guerrillas, the white powers have turned to the West for help. The Portuguese manufacture most of the small arms and ammunition they need for their wars. Larger equipment has been purchased from NATO allies, although not directly through NATO. Helicopters from France, reconnaissance planes and G-91 jet fighters manufactured in West Germany, and even American jet airliners that are used to transport troops have all contributed to the war effort. The pious disclaimers of these countries that they are not aiding the Portuguese military effort range from open hypocrisy to skillful half-truths. The fact is that NATO-member countries individually, if not as an organization, give Portugal all the help she needs.

The South Africans supported their defense build-up in the nineteen sixties by developing an impressive arms industry geared for guerrilla and conventional warfare. They were able to manufacture their own jet trainers and small missiles. The French were active in supplying them Mirage jet fighter-bombers, large helicopters, and submarines. South Africa and Egypt were the only countries on the African continent with navies that had large warships and submarines. South Africa was scheduled to begin manufacturing its own Mirage jet-bomber in 1972, under license from the French.

Regular soldiers account for one third of South Africa's 30,000-man army. There are another 10,000 men in the air force and navy. Behind this front-line defense stand 20,000 policemen, many of whom are organized into highly mobile and well-armed units, and 300,000 trained white reservists. Military service is compulsory for all men.

The threat of conventional warfare with the rest of Africa is likely to decrease, rather than grow, over this decade. The South Africans, with one of the world's largest supplies of uranium deposits, will certainly by 1980 have the capability of manufacturing a nuclear weapon, although it may be another decade before they invest the tremendous amounts of money needed to manufacture one.

Guerrilla strikes against South Africa have been limited thus far to probing actions by small groups that infiltrate across Angola or the Caprivi strip. The guerrillas' most effective tactic has been planting mines in the strip. In Rhodesia, there have been periodic battles along the rough terrain of the Zambezi valley — usually around the time the O.A.U.'s Liberation Committee was meeting to decide how much support it should give to the Rhodesian guerrillas, who are even more deeply split and disorganized than the anti-Portuguese movements — but the guerrillas have not been able to launch any significant military action.

A DECADE OF INSURGENCY

Are there any lessons, or theories, to be drawn from nearly a decade of insurgency and counterinsurgency in Southern Africa? They would seem to be few, and perhaps conflicting ones.

The guerrilla wars in the Portuguese territories provided European colonialism with its first real military test south of the Sahara, and colonialism turned out to be a far hardier creature in the closing phase of this century than most would have imagined. Conditioned by the retreat of England and France from the continent, many observers expected Portugal to fade from the scene fairly soon after the Angola uprising began in 1961, but a decade later the Portuguese had not lost any significant amounts of territory to guerrillas in their two Southern Africa provinces. The Portuguese have provided a contrast to the English and French handling of their colonies and a significant comment on the immediate strength of African nationalism.

The object of the guerrilla struggles in Angola and Mozambique is obviously to bleed the Portuguese of enough men and money over this decade to make it unprofitable for them to stay. The failure of the resettlement villages will help the guerrillas, but the most they can hope for over the next ten years, it would seem to me, will be de facto control of largely unpopulated areas of northern Mozambique and eastern Angola. The Portuguese and, conceivably, the South Africans will continue to be willing and able to pay the price of holding onto the economic heartland and populated harbor areas of the two territories.

The future of Portuguese Guinea will be quite different. The Portuguese are likely to be out of that small, valueless territory by 1980. The only question left to be resolved is whether the Portuguese will be able to establish and maintain a friendly black government, in the manner of the French in most of their former colonies, or whether they will look for a face-saving way to turn Guinea over to PAIGC while they draw back to the Cape Verde Islands, which Portugal will not relinquish. Portuguese officials seem to consider PAIGC to be the only guerrilla movement they face in Africa that has genuine nationalist support inside the country and they may be willing to negotiate with Cabral.

Portuguese withdrawal from Guinea will have an impact on Angola and Mozambique. Portugal's application of the domino theory to Africa has always been one of its main justifications for staying in Guinea. But the elasticity that theory allows its propagators has already been shown in Vietnam.

Some observers, most notably Professor Dennis Austin of Manchester University, have suggested that the overextending of white power may lead to its military downfall; that is, South Africa's sending troops and equipment into the neighboring white-ruled territories as the guerrilla threat grows there would leave South Africa itself vulnerable to a combined internal revolt and external guerrilla strike, or, at the least, greatly tax and damage the country's economy. It is true that South Africa is short of ground troops for any major military effort inside its own borders without seeking to try to police an area of two million square miles containing thirty-five million Africans and five million whites. But the Austin theory seems to me to be predicated on a South African reaction to a threat that won't exist at any time in the foreseeable future. From where will come the military danger that will lead South Africa to extend significantly its defense perimeter in the next decade?

I put this question to one of America's diplomats best informed on the guerrilla struggles. "I don't know," he replied. "And any-body who says that he knows is just guessing, whether it is the people who say the guerrillas are winning or those that say the whites are going to remain impregnable. The only evidence we have to go on is what has happened. Five years ago, we didn't give PAIGC much of a chance. But Cabral has shown that a good leader, a blank check for arms, and intensive training by foreign instructors can create a strong guerrilla force. I wonder if anyone is training Angolan or Rhodesian refugees for that kind of effort five years from now. I don't see any signs, but then if they are doing it as effectively as they should, I wouldn't."

The chances of military force bringing change in Southern Africa in 1971 were, in fact, so bleak that more and more African countries were looking for alternatives to the guerrilla wars. "I sometimes think that all we are doing is sending brave young men off to their deaths," one Africa foreign minister told that year's O.A.U. conference. From such despair arose Africa's newest hope for influencing the white regimes of the South: the proposal for dialogue.

Chapter Twelve

Black Satellites

THE SHARP SENSE of irony that history has displayed in weaving the crazy quilt of Southern Africa's peoples and lands has presented South Africa with three proto-Bantustans, despite Pretoria's efforts to prevent this development. They are the independent enclave-nations of Botswana, Lesotho, and Swaziland. Their African leaders bristle when anyone suggests their countries resemble Bantustans. In the context of pan-African politics, the comparison is admittedly unkind and somewhat inexact. In the context of South Africa's plan to redesign the crazy quilt into a protective commonwealth of weak black nations that it can manipulate, the comparison is a valid one. Economically dependent on South Africa, the B-L-S countries, as they are called in American diplomatic jargon, are politically independent to choose any course of action — as long as they choose courses of action that white South Africa does not consider inimical to its interests.

In varying degrees of enthusiasm and utility, these countries provide bridges between white-ruled and black-ruled Africa, that is, between South Africa's first and second circles of concern. Their leaders sit in the councils of the O.A.U. in Addis Ababa and have respectable contact with the rest of independent Africa. They visit Pretoria, which then has the chance to entertain them decently and show the world that apartheid is not really the product of pure racism, but the result of special internal conditions that should not affect South Africa's relations with any other country.

South Africa's main bridge to the north, however, in history's perverseness, has turned out to be Malawi. Less dependent in many ways on South Africa than the B-L-S countries, Malawi was led to independence in 1964 by Dr. Hastings Kamuzu Banda, then one of the continent's great symbols of African nationalism. In 1971, Banda traveled to South Africa for a warm greeting from the country's white rulers, and his metamorphosis into what many Africans saw as the world's greatest Uncle Tom seemed complete. If Botswana, Lesotho, and Swaziland are, as some onlookers have described them, hostages of South Africa, then Malawi is its client.

These four black satellites of South Africa came to independence in the last decade. So did twenty-six other black-ruled countries to the north, joining the handful of African states already free from colonial control. With at least the outward appearance of European rule removed elsewhere in Africa, the South African whites suddenly found themselves forming an island not just within a black majority in the country, but on a black continent. Technology, which had served the white man so well in controlling the black majority inside South Africa, now served to underline his isolation. Africans in Kenya and Ghana (or at least the elites that ran those countries) had daily access to information on the plight of black South Africans. Impressed (perhaps overly) by the march of independence in the Third World, the Western media and government institutions devoted much attention (perhaps too much) to the rhetoric of African leaders and their verbal battles with apartheid in the first half of the nineteen sixties.

The South African white elite faced simultaneously a confrontation and a vacuum with its regional neighbors. Contacts with the rest of Africa had always been through white colonial bureaucracies and their officials. As a member of the Commonwealth, white-ruled South Africa had no problems from essentially white-ruled Ghana or Tanganyika. Pretoria's withdrawal from the Commonwealth and the end of colonialism broke those ties. As the nineteen sixties began, South Africa had to devise new diplomatic strategies to deal with its neighbors. At first the answer was to sulk, rattle an occasional saber at the north, and reinforce the laager against the outside wind of change.

But internal changes helped force a dramatic shift in this posture before the decade ended. The apartheid economy, with laws forbidding 70 per cent of the country's population to bargain for wages, effectively stunted the growth of the internal consumer market needed by South Africa's rapidly expanding industries. Export markets were also limited. The distance from Europe and America and the inefficient and costly use of skilled labor made most South African goods uncompetitive in world markets. The entry into the Common Market by Britain, South Africa's main trading partner, seemed to imperil that lucrative outlet for South African agricultural products. New markets would be urgently needed in the future. Some South African industrialists, led by Anton Rupert, the Afrikaner cigarette king, argued that the only logical place to find them was in unindustrialized tropical Africa, which depended on other continents for most of its manufactured goods and much of its food.

The result of these political and economic pressures was the "outward policy." As it took shape after 1967, the policy offered South African diplomatic and economic links, including monetary aid, to black African nations on a basis of "mutual respect" and nonintervention in "internal affairs." South Africa, which possessed a great potential for mischief-making in shaky black-ruled countries to the north, held out the promise of peaceful coexistence to those who would stop backing the guerrilla movements and keep criticism of apartheid down to a polite level. Prime Minister Vorster made this explicit by offering in 1970, and again in 1971, to negotiate "nonaggression pacts" with African countries. Beginning gingerly, Vorster entertained Chief Leabua Jonathan, Lesotho's Prime Minister, in January 1967, and took him to lunch in Cape Town. By 1971, he had progressed to dinner with Malawi's Banda in Johannesburg. Lesotho and Malawi were receiving significant financial and technical aid from South Africa and were backing South Africa's drive to increase its hegemony on the continent.

Banda was for several years "Africa's lone wolf" as he himself frequently put it. Gradually, however, South Africa pierced the wall of silence and isolation the militant African leaders had tried to build along the Zambezi River. Surreptitious trade was established and expanded with at least half a dozen important officially hostile black-ruled countries. The South Africans said that the number trading with them was in fact much higher. In 1970 Ivory Coast President Félix Houphouet-Boigny, perhaps the single most influential politician in French-speaking Africa, called for a "dialogue" with South Africa to replace the ineffective policy of isolation and support of the guerrilla movements. He received public support from eight to ten other African countries. African unity dissolved on the issue that above all should have logically held it together — white minority rule in the south. Pan-Africanism, in political retreat since the euphoric days of Kwame Nkrumah's stirring pronouncements and the founding of the O.A.U., suffered what some observers saw as perhaps a fatal setback as Africa divided over isolation and dialogue, over according the continent's industrial and economic giant a role in continental development and supporting guerrillas to destroy that giant. Suddenly African nationalism on a continental scale faced the same danger of fragmentation that apartheid posed for black unity in South Africa.

Although the Afrikaner overseers of the outward policy probably have never formulated it in this manner, the policy seems to seek to convince the Europeanized black elites who run tropical Africa that they have more to gain in identifying with the white elite who run South Africa than they have in identifying with the black masses living under apartheid. African leaders, with three or four exceptions, have identified with the white colonial elite in gaining their present positions. The South Africans and their dialogue partners, Banda and Houphouet-Boigny, stress independently the benefits of the development of the capitalist system in Africa and the danger that Communism and revolution present to "stability." This tends to underline their common spheres of interest. It is an oversimplification in a number of ways, but to better understand the "outward-dialogue" syndrome and its relevance to the entire continent, imagine that South Africa's minority is saying to Africa's tiny black elite, "We will help you entrench yourself in your position against a black mass from which you, too, are separated by culture, education, and affluence, if you will lend us a little support in dealing with our black mass." The warm response French-speaking African leaders have given the dialogue proposals are significant in this light. In general, they are more completely separated from indigenous African culture than are their English-speaking African counterparts.

Perhaps equally telling is the rancor of the Afrikaner Verkramptes in the 1970 elections and afterward. The outward policy brings together their fears of a sellout on race and the development of class instincts within Afrikanerdom. John Vorster lunches only with foreign Africans of certain standing. The Verkramptes present an exaggerated view, but it does have a logical consistency that Vorster's approach lacks. Apartheid barriers have not been removed for the Malawi mine workers in South Africa although they are foreigners, too. Dr. Banda of Malawi possesses rights in South Africa that no black South African possesses. The Verkramptes have had a field day with the disorienting effect of John Vorster's split vision of Africans. But a number of those who theorize about South Africa see dialogue as the last great hope for the bringing of peaceful change. Banda cloaked himself in this argument as he trundled off to Johannesburg asserting that African leaders visiting South Africa would make the white government see the absurd dichotomy between apartheid and the outward policy. His premise that the Afrikaners would then give up apartheid instead of the outward policy was an interesting one.

SURVIVAL OF THE WEAKEST

The Verkrampte-Verligte debate over contacts with black Africa is perhaps only the second great foreign policy issue in South Africa's history.[1] The other had been South Africa's relationship

[1] South West Africa might be considered a third in view of United Nations and World Court involvement and the security implications. But within South Africa, it has not been much of an issue, since there is near unanimity behind the government's policy.

to Great Britain, as Afrikaner and English-speaker quarreled over participation in the two world wars and remaining in the Commonwealth. As in most countries, the movement of South Africa's foreign policy paralleled the flow of domestic pressures and conflicts. As the two white groups de-emphasized their separate nationalisms in favor of a racial coalition against the black majority, Pretoria turned to the foreign policy aspects of race. After a clumsy start, the diplomat-bureaucrats who sit in the elegant Union Buildings and gaze out over Pretoria from one of South Africa's most beautiful hills could claim to have done fairly well.

Credit should also be given, however, to that historic foe of the Afrikaner, the British Colonial Office. The British steadfastly rejected South Africa's claims over the territories now known as Botswana, Lesotho, and Swaziland. These nations were carved out of South Africa by the competing expansionism of the four great powers that have contested for the southernmost corner of Africa — the empires of the Zulu, British, and Germans and the republics of the Boers. They escaped white rule through the skillful diplomacy of their chiefs, the greed of Cecil Rhodes, and the caprice of history.

The Mfecane, the early nineteenth-century wars and raids that accompanied the rise of Shaka's Zulu empire, scattered tribes across Southern Africa and disrupted the social organization of many of them. The weaker ones retreated to the more easily defended mountains and plateaus of the interior, where gradually the strongest tribes among them conquered and assimilated the others.

In the green and fertile hills of the eastern lowveld lying between the Transvaal and the sea, the Ngwane tribe established its dominancy and gradually absorbed other tribes into what became the Swazi nation. The Boers, coveting the fertile Swazi areas for winter grazing, moved into the area in the middle of the nineteenth century. Through venality, ignorance of the European interpretation of land contracts, or fear, the Swazi chiefs' heirs increasingly ceded territories to the whites.

The Boers wanted to build a railroad to Kosi Bay to end their dependence on the Cape. The Swazi territory lay in the Boer path, however. The Swazis, preferring the rule of a queen located far away overseas to that of the Pretoria burghers, appealed for British protection against Boer annexation. The British, noting the predominant influence the Boers had already established, at first declined, but after the Boer War, the British established a protectorate over Swaziland, taking responsibility for the 7000-square-mile kingdom, in which two thirds of the territory was owned by whites.

The history of the Sotho, the people who inhabit the mountainous kingdom now known as Lesotho, is less peaceful than that of the Swazis. A young warrior named Moshesh established strong defensive positions in the mountainous territory west of the towering Drakensberg range in Natal and gradually gained control over nearby grazing lands. Moshesh appears to have been one of the most far-sighted diplomats Africa has ever produced. As early as 1842, he feared Boer settlement. The whites had reached the Caledon valley, one of the richest corn-growing areas in Southern Africa. Moshesh appealed for protection from the British, who were attracted by the idea of a buffer state between Natal and the Boers inland. The decision a decade later to curtail the area of British responsibility in South Africa caused the agreement to be abandoned, however, and in 1858 the Boer commandos struck and with superior weapons and fighting tactics eventually conquered and occupied one half of the Sotho kingdom. The Sotho were driven from most of the fertile land they had occupied back into the harsh, unproductive mountains.

The British, worried about the continuing push of the Boers into the Sotho land, finally agreed in 1868 to extend their protection once again to Moshesh's territories, then reduced to 12,000 square miles. The arrangement was made formal in 1884, fourteen years after Moshesh had died and more than forty after he had warned the British that they must make common cause with Africans against the Dutch.

Bechuanaland, as Botswana was called before it became independent, was partly shaped by a renegade warrior named Mzilikazi, who led his men northwest across the Transvaal after deserting from Shaka's army. They settled at the edge of the vast tableland and desert that stretched to the Zambezi River and launched a decade-long series of raids that depleted and fragmented the tribes living there, leaving them in eight weak groups. In 1829, Mzilikazi met Robert Moffat, who had established a mission station at Kuruman. Later another London Missionary Society envoy, David Livingstone, would set out from the station on one of the most famous journeys in Africa's history. Livingstone was Moffat's son-in-law.

Defeated in a clash with the Boers who were moving north in 1837, Mzilikazi withdrew across the Limpopo River to establish a new kingdom — Matabeleland, in what would become Rhodesia. Jutting north like "the neck of the bottle," Bechuanaland seemed to have little value in itself, but a great deal of value as a transportation link. The Boers of the Orange Free State eventually pressed a claim for the territory, but were staunchly opposed by Livingstone, who asked the British to halt the spread of Boer racialism into the area. Then Cecil Rhodes, dreaming of a Cape to Cairo railroad and seeing Bechuanaland as his "Suez Canal to the north," intervened to argue against the Boers. But it was the shock of German occupation of South West Africa in 1883 that pushed the English into action. The Bechuanaland territory of 238,000 square miles (about the size of Texas) was made a protectorate. Rhodes got a strip of land and built his railway to Rhodesia (still the only one linking the two white-ruled countries). And the Boers fumed once again about British imperialism, which kept taking territories they wanted.

History thus produced three states that could not stand on their own feet. All were landlocked and had to depend on white-ruled South Africa and Mozambique for their commercial activity. Much of their most valuable territory had been appropriated by whites. With the formation of the Union of South Africa, Pretoria asked Britain to administer the coup de grâce to the three struggling territories and give them to South Africa. The British hesitated and said the territories would become part of the Union at a later, unspecified time. As concern about South Africa's racial policies grew, however, the British hedged on the 1909 promise.

At the same time, there is no evidence that the British ever seriously considered the three as anything but appendages that would be absorbed into South Africa when the nastier aspects of racialism had been toned down. The three territories were ruled by Britain's high commissioner (ambassador) to Pretoria and thus became known as the High Commission Territories. The South Africans viewed them as Native Reserves temporarily under administrative control of the British. Their migrant workers were encouraged to continue to seek employment in South Africa. White South Africans — including plainclothes policemen — moved freely in the territories and acted more or less as if they were at home.

The push for territorial apartheid made the acquisition of the three territories all the more vital for the South African government. For one thing, the inclusion of the vast, unproductive territory of Botswana in South Africa would erase the 87-13 division of land that was becoming embarrassing even to the South Africans. Include that land, the mountains of Lesotho, and the 7000 acres of mostly arable land the Swazis had held on to, and the blacks would have almost half of South Africa's land reserved for them. The attraction this has for apartheid theorists still burns bright, even after these three countries have taken seats in the United Nations. Official government statements have pointed out that the three territories should be regarded as part of the white-black land division in South Africa, which gives some indication of how South Africa really regards the sovereignty of these states.

Sharpeville and withdrawal of South Africa from the Commonwealth under mounting African criticism made it impossible for Britain to surrender two million more Africans to the political control of the Pretoria government. Declaring Lesotho, a territory half the size of the state of Maryland and a great deal poorer, to be an independent nation may have had all the economic effect of declaring Central Park independent of Manhattan, as a diplomat told me, but the alternative would in the eyes of most of the world

have had the moral effect of handing over a supply of young vir-
gins to the Marquis de Sade.

Flanked by integrationist Portuguese and confronted by kaffir-
run states in the north, the South Africans now had to contend
with black-ruled countries advocating multiracial policies in their
very midst. Nothing seemed to be going right for South African
whites. In fact, the timing of independence for the three B-L-S
countries coincided roughly with the passing of power from Verwoerd to Vorster and undoubtedly accelerated the development of
the outward policy and of the Bantustans as geographical units.

Botswana, Lesotho, and Swaziland could be used to show that
the Bantustans would work, that South Africa could fashion black
elites beholden not only economically, as the B-L-S countries
were, but also politically to the white government. Pretoria would
give the Bantustans "independence," and they too would behave
in a cautious, obedient manner "in order to preserve their economic lifeline — rather as the French-speaking African states are
doing [with Paris], only more so," as Allister Sparks, the perceptive foreign editor of the Rand *Daily Mail*, said caustically in 1967,
imagining a visionary apartheid theorist viewing the three ex-protectorates.

These countries gave South Africa the chance to test its ability
to create black colonies inside its borders and to get in step with
the rest of the white world by passing to the stage of neocolonial-
ism (a much misused word, but appropriate here, I think) that Europe had already adopted. If the leaders of the ex-protectorates
proved tractable, so would those of the Bantustans, especially as
many of the Bantustan "citizens" would be walking into white
South Africa to work each day and back to their "nations" at
night. By demonstrating that "foreign" African leaders were well
treated on visits to South Africa, the government would also encourage black South Africans to want to become "foreign." This,
at least, must have been the thinking of the more imaginative Nationalists who sought, and achieved, a soft approach to the three
black enclave-nations.

BOTSWANA: THE UNCERTAIN SATELLITE

Botswana became independent on September 30, 1966, under the leadership of Sir Seretse Khama, then forty-five years old. The son of a feudal tribal chief, Khama was sent to universities in South Africa and then to Oxford to gain an education that would suit him for modern African politics. In England, he also acquired a wife — a former secretary who would become Lady Khama and one of the most charming and effective first ladies of Africa. But in 1948, marriage to a white woman created embarrassment for Khama's tribe, for the white supremacist government across the border in South Africa and for the British. Khama was exiled for six years. He eventually renounced for himself and his children all rights to the chieftainship that he was due and was allowed by his tribe to return. He devoted himself to building the Bechuanaland Democratic Party, which swept the pre-independence elections in 1965, and he became President of Botswana at independence.

Botswana is less dependent on white power for its survival than the other two ex-protectorates, and Khama has skillfully sought to exploit his options while taking care not to give the South Africans an opportunity to intervene in his affairs. Botswana cannot allow guerrilla movements to use its territory, nor can it allow exiled black South Africans to be politically active, Khama has said a number of times. But he uses international forums to attack apartheid and to oppose South African policy. In the tons of rhetoric delivered at the Nonaligned Summit Conference in Lusaka, Zambia, in September 1970, Khama's short, reasoned speech stood out like a tiny jewel. Terming Southern Africa a "critical long-term problem for peace and security . . . for the world as a whole," Khama defined Botswana's position: "If we appear reluctant to play an active and prominent role in the struggle for the establishment of majority rule throughout Southern Africa it is not because we are unconcerned about the plight of our oppressed brothers in the white-ruled states of our region. Rather, it is because we are concerned about our peculiarly exposed position and the severe limitations it imposes on us. We want to see majority rule established not only throughout Southern Africa but throughout our Continent. And we are determined to contribute toward the achievement of this noble goal. We are aware, however, that there is a limit beyond which our contribution cannot go without endangering our very Independence."

While Lesotho and Malawi supported Britain's plans to resume limited arms sales to South Africa, and Swaziland remained silent, Khama used the Nonaligned forum to urge Britain to reconsider. "An arms race in Southern Africa and the Indian Ocean and the accompanying dangers of Cold War involvement would present a real and growing threat to the stability of the area. Increased Western involvement in the minority regimes of Southern Africa makes such an arms race more likely." Khama wondered sadly how Britain could assert that its security "depends on military cooperation with a Government which denies freedom and dignity on grounds of race and color."

Khama's commitment to multiracialism was represented in the flag chosen for Botswana at independence. On a field of blue, two small white stripes flank a large black bar. In its 1971 estimated population of 600,000 Botswana counted only about 4000 whites. Most of them lived in the ranching areas of the east, near the South African and Rhodesian borders. Throughout the early years of independence, Khama's government issued a number of warnings to the whites to change their segregationist habits. Shops in some towns continued to serve whites before blacks, social organizations still refused black members, and businesses discriminated in hiring. The fact that the warnings were repeated at regular intervals indicated Botswana's lack of success in influencing white racial attitudes.

Botswana is far from being a free agent. About 45,000 Tswana (as Khama's countrymen are known) work in South Africa, and Botswana's currency is the rand. Its only railroad is run by Rhodesian Railways. But Khama has sought to reduce the white grip on his country. He has rejected South African financial and technical aid and kept his close ties to the British, who agreed to subsidize the Botswana budget deficit after independence. British civil servants who agree with Khama's liberal views have been kept in positions of influence.

A major mineral find in 1969 in Botswana raised the country's hopes of adding economic independence to its new political status. Diamonds were found by the South African De Beers group, and a discovery of nickel and copper deposits promised even more important development. The World Bank expressed interest in providing a major loan for the infrastructure Botswana would need to build to allow for the exploitation of these resources.

With prospects of a stronger base, Khama announced in 1970 his intention to establish diplomatic relations with the Soviet Union. This sparked an uproar in the South African press and drew veiled threats of retaliation from Nationalist Party politicians, although Khama specified that no resident diplomats would be exchanged. (The relations involved the accrediting of the Soviet ambassador resident in Zambia to cover Botswana as well.) Undeterred, Khama signed a trade pact with Zambia and announced that a highway and ferry system would be built across the Zambezi River to link Botswana and Zambia. The two have no common land border, but they claimed that under international law their borders extended and met in the middle of the river. The South Africans disputed this interpretation in a stiffly worded note they sent to Khama. But, after being reassured that the United States would contribute the $6 million in aid it had offered for the road, Khama announced the plan would proceed.

In five years of independence, Sir Seretse Khama had hardly broken the hold the white powers exerted on Botswana. He was still very much at their mercy, and he realized it. But he had demonstrated that a black government in Southern Africa could withhold support for the Pretoria government and survive, could in fact sharply criticize apartheid and gain the respect of the rest of the continent, could seek to diversify its dependence on outside governments and find support from Britain, the United States, and elsewhere.

LESOTHO: AN EMBARRASSING COUP

Lesotho, also independent for five years in 1971, had taken a very different course. The country possessed none of the advantages that had enabled Botswana to look north — not geography, not size, not minerals, and not an imaginative political leader. Established in October 1966 as a constitutional monarchy, Lesotho was ruled by a paramount chief, Moshoeshoe II, as king. But the country's Prime Minister, Chief Leabua Jonathan, gradually gathered more and more power to his office. Jonathan, a large, burly man of little formal education but quick wit, accepted South African offers of help. Soon the country's small judiciary was run by South African civil servants up to the Supreme Court level. Other government agencies were soon filled with South African officials who were technically on loan to Lesotho, but whose salaries were being paid by Pretoria. The South Africans advanced a grant in aid estimated to have been worth $560,000 for Lesotho's police, over which they possessed considerable influence. Jonathan's dependence on the South Africans became an issue in Lesotho's 1970 general elections, the first since independence. When it appeared that Jonathan's party had lost, he declared an emergency, canceled the elections, and imposed a virtual coup d'état. The king, who was thought to have given support to Jonathan's more radical opponent, was exiled to Holland (to be allowed to return a year later), and Jonathan's opponents were jailed.

The incident was an embarrassing one for Vorster's government. Abroad, it was thought that the South Africans had supported the coup to keep an ally in power. For South Africans, it showed that political instability was endemic in African states, even those over which South Africa had direct influence. What hope could there be for the Bantustans? Despite the embarrassment, however, the South Africans must have been relieved that Jonathan, and not the strident anti-apartheid group that opposed him, was in charge of Lesotho.[2]

[2] The real extent of South African participation in the coup and the fighting that followed have never been adequately assessed. The main fighting for Jonathan seems to have been

Lesotho's 1971 population was about 1,000,000 people. Four fifths of the enclave consisted of high mountains and steep hills. Its only economic resource is manpower, which is exported to South Africa's mines and factories. Lesotho can supply only about 20,000 salaried jobs, and the overgrazed and badly eroded farmlands do not offer even subsistence-level farming opportunities for many. The country is vitally dependent on the $10 to $11 million the 120,000 Sotho working in South Africa send back each year. Lesotho's national budget is smaller than that of most American universities — $12 million in 1970. Yet, the country possesses one of the highest literacy rates on the continent — more than 80 per cent of its citizens can read and write. These conditions make for a volatile situation that is likely to test South Africa's abilities to shape events in Lesotho even more severely within this decade.

SWAZILAND: THE ENTREPÔT

Swaziland, on the other hand, came to independence in a burst of tranquillity. The British handed over the government in 1968 to Chief Sobhuza II, who became the most unabashedly tribal head of state in Africa. The septuagenarian king conducted affairs of state from a cattle village where he and his scores of wives lived. Swaziland had a 1971 population of about 400,000. Although some land had been regained by the Swazis, nearly half of the country was owned by the 8000 whites who lived there.

Swaziland has tried to remain friends with white and black Africa and has managed surprisingly well. South African investment was encouraged in Swaziland and it helped establish a multiracial gambling resort, where more avant-garde Afrikaners could be seen on weekends, but technical aid was kept to low-visibility

---

done by his British-supervised police. An estimated 500 Sotho were killed in fighting, and Jonathan declared that Lesotho would be given "a holiday from politics for five years." Thirty people were also given two-and-one-half-year holidays in jail for opposing the coup. See *Africa* magazine, Number 3, 1971.

areas. Depending on the circumstances, Swazi officials were prepared to give quite subtle, but essentially conflicting, views on apartheid. This helped make the country an increasingly important commercial go-between for South Africa and tropical Africa. Countries that would have been embarrassed to import South African goods imported South African oranges and sold them as "Swaziland oranges." The jest that Swaziland's main industry had become stamping "Made in Swaziland" on and repackaging of South African goods is only partly a jest. As well as developing into a major entrepôt through which South African exports and imports flowed, Swaziland also flourished as a discreet spot for diplomatic contacts that might have raised eyebrows in the Third World if they had taken place elsewhere.

The most important formal pact the South Africans have with the B-L-S countries is a customs union agreement that has existed in different forms since 1910. There are no internal customs barriers among the four. Most of the enclaves' exports and imports were routed to or through South Africa, and they agreed that South Africa would set joint customs and excise duties and collect them. Pretoria dispersed shares to the three territories on a formula arrived at through periodic negotiation. As in most economically stagnant African countries that must import a major part of the goods that are sold, customs duties are a vitally important part of the economy. Lesotho's share of the duties usually provides 50 per cent of that country's normal revenue. In 1970, when the agreement was renegotiated, the three newly independent countries were able to obtain much better terms from the South Africans than they had ever been able to get as British protectorates.

Five years after independence first came to the former High Commission Territories, South Africa's hopes that they would show the way for the development of model Bantustans seemed only partly justified. The economic relationships had remained unaltered and had shifted in fact to slightly better terms for the African-ruled countries. Politically, only Swaziland had provided no problems.

LOOKING NORTH

Vorster's best political bridge to the north turned out to be tiny, poverty-stricken Malawi, which had gained independence from Britain in 1964 under the fiery leadership of a frail, puritanical African physician, Hastings Kamuzu Banda. Malawi is a sliver of a country, stretching about 400 miles down the western shore of Lake Malawi, the third largest lake in Africa. Slightly smaller in area than the state of Virginia, Malawi has 4.5 million people, 95 per cent of whom are poor farmers. In 1970, there were an estimated 140,000 wage-paying jobs in the entire country. Known as Nyasaland before independence, Malawi had been treated in the words of one British statesman as "an imperial slum." It was used as a labor reservoir for Rhodesia (to which it was attached in the Central African Federation) and for South Africa. There were in 1970 more Malawians employed outside Malawi than inside. Government officials estimated that there were about 200,000 Malawians in Rhodesia and perhaps 110,000 in South Africa (with at least 50,000 of those working on the mines). White employers in these countries told me that they preferred Malawian laborers because they were more industrious, and more docile, than local labor. They also worked for lower wages.

Malawi's migrant workers have been remitting to their families about $10 million annually, a major sum for a country whose total annual budget is only about $70 million. Retaliation from South Africa or Rhodesia against Malawi would present it with a major economic crisis. Malawi's dependence on Portugal is even more dramatic. Mozambique half surrounds the southern part of Malawi, where most of the population lives and where most of its agricultural production is. Imports and exports are handled almost exclusively through the Mozambique ports of Beira and Nacala. Extending like a long finger into the middle of Mozambique, Malawi would have been a good base for Frelimo. But Banda's government refused to allow guerrillas to operate from its territory and exchanged intelligence with the Portuguese. There was also evidence that South Africa supplied Banda with arms to help him against Malawi exile forces.

Instead of seeking alternatives, as Khama was doing in Botswana, Banda moved decisively to strengthen the ties that bound
him to the white-minority regimes. His metamorphosis provided
one of the most fascinating stories of Africa's independence decade. The South African foreign policy planners hoped it would
also turn out to be one of the most significant.

Born in 1906, Banda walked, barefoot, 1000 miles to South Africa when he was thirteen years old to look for work. Employed
as a clerk on the gold mines, Banda saved enough money to go to
the United States. He attended Wilberforce Institute in Ohio, the
University of Chicago, the University of Indiana, and Meharry
College in Nashville, where he received an M.D.

In 1937, he traveled to Britain, where he practiced medicine for
sixteen years, mostly in white working-class areas. His office in
suburban London became a gathering point for African students
and exiles, including Kenya's Jomo Kenyatta and Ghana's
Kwame Nkrumah. Banda was in touch by mail with the younger
Africans in Malawi who were beginning to feel the stir of African
nationalism and talk of self-determination. When the British imposed the white-settler-dominated Central African Federation on
Malawi and Northern and Southern Rhodesia in 1953, Banda quit
London and went to Ghana.

Little has come to light about Banda's actual relationship with
leaders such as Kenyatta and Nkrumah during those years outside
Malawi. But his early association with these men, and his ringing
denunciations of "the stupid Federation" projected an image of a
fiery African nationalist. When he returned home in 1958 after
forty years abroad, thousands of Africans gathered at the airport
to cheer a man who had taken on mythical proportions in his absence. Within six months serious rioting had erupted among his
followers and the colonial police jailed Banda and hundreds of
others. He was released after a year and headed the political campaigns that led to negotiations, the breaking of the Federation,
and independence in 1964.

The Organization of African Unity held its second summit conference that year, in Cairo, and the conference was delayed until

Malawi became independent so Banda could attend as head of state. He warmly embraced Gamal Abdel Nasser and renewed his friendship with Nkrumah. Within a few years, however, Banda had quit attending inter-African parleys, where his name had come to assume the same connotations that Quisling's did in Europe during World War II.

When Banda culminated his rapprochement with the white governments by visiting South Africa in August 1971, he stressed that he was merely following the policies he had advocated all along. The record, however, suggests that there was a significant shift of emphasis in Banda's approach to the South.

"The independence of Malawi will be meaningless as long as there is an inch of African soil under colonialism and imperialism," Banda said in his formal speech to the 1964 OAU conference. Banda seemed clearly to bracket Portugal and South Africa by the use of those terms.

Then, after noting Malawi's dependence on the Portuguese territories, Banda said: "I am quite certain that it is not the will or wish of anyone in this assembly that in order to help his brothers and sisters still under colonialism and imperialism a man must cut his own throat. . . . The geographical position of Malawi makes it impossible for me and my country to sever all ties, diplomatic, economic, and cultural with a certain power now still controlling great portions of our continent." This, Banda continued, was "not because I do not want to help my brothers and sisters now still under colonial rule in that territory, but simply because it would be impossible for me and my country to carry out such a resolution without economic strangulation of Malawi, and with economic strangulation would come political strangulation. The government would fall and there would be chaos . . ." His remarks at that stage bore a striking resemblance to those of Seretse Khama six years later.

Later in 1964, the authoritarian Banda clashed with six of his Cabinet ministers who wanted more of a say in the running of the country. They favored a more "nonaligned" stance in international politics than Banda's decidedly pro-Western, anti-Communist position. The ministers were dismissed or resigned and went into hiding or exile to mount efforts to topple Banda. They failed and Banda established a benevolent but iron grip over Malawi. He surrounded himself mostly with yes men and brooked no public or private disagreement with his ideas. Increasingly, those ideas dealt almost exclusively with his relations with the South Africans and Portuguese, who were ardently wooing him.

On March 29, 1967, he explained to Parliament why he had sent Goodwill Missions to South Africa and Portugal and why he had renewed lapsing trade and transit agreements with those countries. He echoed the necessity theme he had used exclusively at the 1964 OAU meeting: "Even a child knows we are a land-locked country . . . we have no choice, we have no alternative, but to negotiate new treaties, new agreements, and new conventions with the Republic of South Africa and with Portugal."

But Banda also unveiled a new framework for his stronger links with the Vorster and Salazar governments. He derided those African countries that were criticizing him and ridiculed their leaders for their impotence against the white powers. Echoing points made by many foreign critics of Africa, Banda said the pressing problems were of "economc inviability or dependence, political instability . . . and disunity . . ."

Then Banda stressed for perhaps the first time the word that a few years later would split the continent on the issue of the South. "The African states . . . have to learn to live with the Republic of South Africa. Because the Republic of South Africa is here to stay. The Republic of South Africa has to learn to live with the African states. Because the African states are here to stay.

"In my view, the policy of boycotts and shouts has failed. The politics and diplomacy of bluff and bluster have failed." He asserted that "behind all this policy of apartheid . . . are fear and ignorance. This fear and ignorance will . . . be removed and can be removed only by contact . . . Somehow, somewhere, someday, sometime there must be a *dialogue*" between black and white in Southern Africa and between white leaders and black leaders from the rest of the continent.

Banda's speech was made a few months after Chief Jonathan of Lesotho had visited South Africa and lunched with Vorster. The twin seeds of the outward policy and dialogue sprouted quickly. Malawi and South Africa exchanged diplomatic missions at the legation level. The Malawi mission in Pretoria, headed by a British civil servant, included a black Malawian as first secretary. As a foreign African, the Malawian lived in an exclusive mixed "diplomatic suburb" near Pretoria, and the government did what it could to shield him from apartheid.

South Africa lent Malawi $26.6 million in 1968 to begin building a new capital city and to complete a new rail line to the Portuguese harbor of Nacala in Mozambique. The South Africans sent a half-dozen civil servants to Malawi as technical advisers. They also promised to encourage private investment for Malawi, but by 1971, there had been little visible South African investment. The Portuguese were in fact more active. They opened up a new bank, which was expected to become the country's bank of issue. Portuguese interests controlled 60 per cent of the bank and 70 per cent of the monopoly company that distributed petroleum products in Malawi. A holding company completely controlled by Banda, who said he felt he had to set a good example of capitalism for his people to follow, was a partner in these enterprises.

Vorster paid an official visit to Malawi (his first abroad) in May 1970 and was entertained by Banda at an official dinner that was conspicuously integrated. Black and white sat side by side. By that time, Banda had largely ceased arguing that he was forced to have contact with the South Africans and was instead portraying dialogue as the only hope black Africa had to promote change.

Calling Vorster and himself "pioneers of inter-African relations," Banda told the South African: "Let's face it. One of the problems between us — your people and mine — is that we have been brought up under different kinds of life. To the majority of Europeans, or white men, in the Republic — Rhodesia too — a civilized man is synonymous to a white man . . . It is only contact of this kind that can reveal to your people that there are civilized people other than white . . ." Banda's thesis was that by demonstrating that blacks can establish stable and conservative governments that will not harm white interests, he could ease white fears and help pave the way for eventual cooperation and harmony between white and black. He often pointed to the Arabs in the north of Africa as a people who had for centuries enslaved and discriminated against black Africans, but who were now considered as brothers of the African people. Some day, perhaps in a century, Banda said at different times, the white South Africans might be looked upon that way.

(In his reply to Banda's speech, Vorster may have inadvertently given his own interpretation of the effectiveness of Banda's theme that dialogue and contact would change the white South African mentality. Complimenting Banda by saying, "You can go to worse countries than Malawi for your first visit," Vorster listed three things about Malawi that had impressed him: First was that Banda had been able to establish a stable government. Second was the good service he had received in his visit. Third was the country's beauty. "You will get good service in Malawi and that is important too in these days, very important," Vorster promised to tell potential white South African tourists.)

This meeting, and a similar one in Johannesburg during Banda's visit to South Africa, brought together the threads that had been running through the outward and dialogue initiatives. Three main sets of questions have to be considered:

1. Is there a broader significance to the transformation of Banda from a symbol of African nationalism into one of servility? Does it in fact spring from Malawi's special economic problems and Banda's highly egocentric temperament? Or is Banda correct in saying in effect that he is a prophet of an inevitable change, or at least redefinition, in the force of African nationalism itself?

This involves Banda's image as much as his real views. "Looking back on what he was saying in nineteen fifty-eight, you now recognize that what he was in fact saying wasn't that radical at all," one scholar who had studied Banda's career closely told me. "His condemnations of the British and the Federation were that they had failed to do anything to develop the country. But any black man who became involved in politics at that time tended to be viewed as a radical or an Nkrumah-style socialist. The world took its image of Africa from Nkrumah and a few others. Banda and a lot of other black leaders were misinterpreted. Their essential conservatism wasn't seen."

In varying degree, his comment could have applied not only to Banda but also to others, including Jomo Kenyatta, the "leader to darkness and death," as the British called him during the Mau Mau Emergency, who went on to rule Kenya in a conservative manner that largely protected the rights, property, and interests of those whites who stayed. In Ghana, Nkrumah had been deposed by Anglophile army officers who paved the way for the election of Kofi A. Busia, a quiet-spoken Oxford sociologist, as Prime Minister.[3] Military regimes, which tended to devote little time to the Southern African question, had come to power over 100 million, or about half, of tropical Africa's population. In general, Africa took on a more conservative air.

In his usual blunt, colorful style, Banda once described the basis of his challenge to the popular conception of a broad Pan-Africanism that united all Africans in a common struggle against the white rulers in the South:

"Now this country is supposed to be poor, no mines, no gold, but people are far better off here than they are in many African countries. They are not starving, whereas in other African countries people are starving. Why? Difference in leadership. Other leaders are . . . busy shouting against South Africa whites . . . busy serving the poor Africans in South Africa, when their own people right at home are starving, are going about naked. To me, charity begins at home."

Home for Banda is Malawi, not a geographical region known as Africa. He articulates his primary duty as developing Malawi (within the capitalist system), even if that means accepting help from South Africa in return for lending support to the white regime. This view dovetails neatly with the South African con-

---

[3] When Busia was toppled early in 1972, it was again by Western-trained army officers.

ception of black Africa, which to a large extent is derived from
their view of their own black population. The white presence is
seen as a pacifying dividing force between tribes that would not
accept domination by Africans as readily as they accept it from
whites. One of the most instructive instances of this attitude was
South Africa's support for the Biafran rebellion during the 1967–
1970 Nigerian Civil War. The extent of that support is a matter of
conjecture. There was unquestionably strong moral support from
the South Africans, and persistent rumors indicated that there
were financial and arms support as well. South Africa's sympathies for Biafra were generally seen as an example of Pretoria's attempting to stir chaos in a black country. But the bid by Nigeria's
Ibo tribe to set up an essentially tribal state was an ideological
windfall for the South Africans, who had constructed the grand
design of apartheid around tribal states. Biafra would have fit
perfectly into their theory. So did the perception that many independent African governments were being manipulated for the
benefit of tribes rather than to build a sense of nationhood.

A most significant case was Kenya, the only black African
country that successfully fought for independence. The Mau Mau
uprising was not a national war of liberation against colonialism.
It was a largely tribal struggle, fought almost entirely by Kenyatta's Kikuyu on the issue of land. After independence, the Kikuyu
made it increasingly clear that they would run Kenya primarily
for their benefit and privately justified this on the grounds that
they had done the fighting. Colonialism in Kenya had been toppled by strong tribal nationalism, not African nationalism. In
general, African leaders who evidenced in the first decade of independence a strong commitment to eradicating tribalism and building a broad nationalism within their countries also showed a
strong commitment to helping to bring an end to white rule in
Southern Africa. Julius Nyerere of Tanzania, Kenneth Kaunda of
Zambia, and Kwame Nkrumah of Ghana were the best examples;
perhaps Sékou Touré of Guinea could also have been included at
one time, but the turmoil Guinea lived in after 1968 effectively
ended Sékou's role as an important African leader. The Kikuyu

Über Alles philosophy that guided Kenyatta's government after independence was comforting reassurance to the South Africans that they had diagnosed African political instincts much more accurately than the liberal American and British sociologists and political scientists who saw Pan-Africanism as an inevitable force that would overcome white power. By controlling the reality of tribal nationalism at home and seeking to perpetuate it abroad, the white South Africans seemed to feel that they would not have to worry about a concept called Pan-Africanism.

2. Is there a role for South Africa, the industrial and economic giant and political leper of sub-Sahara Africa, to play in the continent's badly needed economic development, as the South Africans claim? Could South Africa provide much of the financial and technical assistance African countries have to seek from other continents?

Many variables are involved. Given present economic and political trends in Africa, my guess would be that South Africa's role in Africa will be a small one outside the first circle of Southern Africa. South Africa does not appear to have that much technology or public capital available for export. Investment in Africa is likely to be limited to areas that will not produce industrial competition for South Africa's own factories. Tourism is a prime example of areas private South African capital will flow into. So is mineral extraction.

Trade with Africa is the key economic relationship to be fostered by the outward policy. The growing markets of Africa —especially those countries like Kenya and the Ivory Coast where an affluent white community remain — have become increasingly attractive to the South African businesses squeezed at home by slowly growing markets and abroad by the changing pattern of trade. As British entry to the Common Market drew nearer, for example, South Africa's fruit growers and processors estimated that they might lose $100 million a year in sales.

Africa has been the only continent with which South Africa has had a favorable balance of trade in recent years. To avoid embarrassing those African countries that defied the O.A.U. ban on financial dealings with South Africa, and to cloak the amount of trade it has with the rebel government in Rhodesia, South Africa lumps all its trade statistics for the continent together in one sum, which has been running at about $500 million a year — and growing.

An official of a South African import-export firm showed me documents that controlled large shipments of timber imported from the former French colonies of the Ivory Coast, Gabon, and, surprisingly, Congo (Brazzaville), which is far left politically but has an economy still controlled by France. The usually reliable Johannesburg *Star* published a report that in 1968 South Africa imported 4.5 million tons of goods from the Ivory Coast. Planeloads of Rhodesian and South African beef and mutton were flown twice a week to Gabon in 1971. What one Ghanaian politician called "the apples of apartheid" were on sale in Ghana, Congo (Kinshasa), and other countries I visited that year. Kenya sold soda ash to Swaziland, which then exported it to South Africa. Western petroleum countries shipped surplus petroleum refined at Mombasa, Kenya, to South Africa.

3. Finally, what are the chances that Banda might be right after all? Can dialogue change white South Africa?

The visits of black leaders have certainly produced a disorienting effect on white politics in South Africa, and Banda's 1971 visit was a tour de force in which he was joyfully welcomed by thousands of Africans in Soweto, where he criticized apartheid. These visits were a major factor in the Verkrampte-Verligte split in the National Party, which still has not been completely resolved.

At this writing, the question remains, dialogue with whom and about what? Fourteen Central and East African countries offered in 1969 to talk with the white minority regimes. The offer came in the Lusaka Manifesto, a document that took its name from the city in which representatives of the fourteen countries met.

"We would prefer to negotiate rather than destroy, to talk rather than kill. We do not advocate violence; we advocate an end to the violence against human dignity which is now being perpetrated by the oppressors of Africa," the Manifesto stated. "We are not hostile to the administrations in these states because they are manned and controlled by white people. We are hostile to them because they are systems of minority control . . ." The Manifesto pledged that a black majority's coming to power should not involve "a reversal of the existing racial domination," but a rejection of racialism against white or black. The structure of the Manifesto, which included stinging criticism of apartheid and Portuguese colonialism, made it clear that the object of the dialogue that these countries, led by Tanzania's Julius Nyerere and Zambia's Kenneth Kaunda, had in mind was the dismantling of both those systems and the movement to majority rule. But the Manifesto did not demand rigid preconditions to talks. The South Africans officially said parts of the Manifesto were of value, but they never moved publicly to start talks on the basis of the Manifesto. When a senior American diplomat visiting South Africa two years later tactfully suggested to Vorster in a private conversation that the Manifesto was probably the most moderate document that would emerge on Southern Africa from responsible African countries, Vorster did not even respond.

When he announced in 1971 that he would discuss apartheid with visiting African leaders, Vorster made it clear that he expected to do the talking and the Africans to do the listening. He would then explain apartheid to them. "More nonsense has been written and spoken about the policy of separate development than any other subject I know of," he told an all-white press conference in Cape Town. Vorster repeatedly assured his white electorate that nothing visiting African leaders said or did would have any effect on the implementation of apartheid. Again, I tend by and large to take the Afrikaner at his word on the subject of maintaining white supremacy. Dialogue will help ameliorate the lot of black South Africans, perhaps, by pointing up some of the more apparent absurdities and crudities of apartheid. But South Africa has already produced many of the most literate and cultured black men on this continent. Contact with a few more from outside is not likely to change much any time soon.

Chapter Thirteen

The Dollar's Shadow

IN THE SIX MONTHS that followed Sharpeville, foreign capital fled from South Africa at the rate of $17,000,000 a month. British and American investors who had come to South Africa looking for quick and big profits had seen instead the specter of racial holocaust and economic disruption projected by Sharpeville. South Africans themselves sent money abroad to hedge against a black uprising. By the end of 1960, $207,000,000 had left the country. South Africa's foreign reserves, which had totaled $425,000,000 in December 1959, had been cut to $240,000,000. The flight continued into 1961, and by June, reserves were down to $215,000,000. Government officials publicly expressed their deep concern about the damage done to the economy by the loss of "investor confidence."

A decade later, foreign reserves had risen to a record level of $864,000,000. American and British investors were competing to find new industries in which to invest in South Africa, and the annual net inflow of capital had risen to an average of more than $343,000,000, six times the level of the pre-Sharpeville figure. Three American automotive companies alone — Chrysler, Ford, and General Motors — had invested more than $75,000,000 in South Africa between 1960 and 1970 and were reaping handsome profits. Six out of every ten cars and trucks sold in South Africa were made by American companies. Half of the gasoline and oil that kept them on the road was refined by American companies. America's trade with South Africa had risen by 79 per cent, Britain's by 88, and Japan's by 379 per cent since 1960.

This dramatic turnabout, partially induced by strong economic controls the government put into effect in mid-1961, showed South Africa's financial experts to be skillful in managing a resilient modern economy. But the point made was a much broader one. Foreign investment, which is particularly important to South Africa's peculiar economy and strategic position, began to return to the country only after the bite of the harsh repression that followed Sharpeville began to be felt. Money returned to the country when it became apparent that the white minority was not only determined, but also able, to remain in power by enforcing segregation more harshly than ever.

Stability, as the investors saw it, was the important point, not the form it took or the morality of it. Doing business continued to be the business of business, and the government's cheap-wage policies coincided with the desire for greater stockholder profits, which meant larger executive salaries. Morality was not involved. It was only immoral, it seemed, to trade with countries that disagreed on the philosophy of profits, not those that strayed slightly on race.

The rapid growth of investment and trade links with the outside world also helped South Africa repair much of the diplomatic damage done by Sharpeville, and by 1970, there was a distinct warming of official relations between South Africa and those Western (i.e., white) countries it saw as its natural allies. These relations were extraordinarily important for a small white nation marooned at the tip of a black continent, 5000 miles away from other important white societies.

South Africans had particularly begun to look to America, instead of Britain or Holland, for psychological kinship. Both were frontier countries and had records of being unsophisticated in approaching perils such as the black race and Communism. But the year of Sharpeville was also the year of John F. Kennedy's election. A deep chill developed between Pretoria and Washington, at least diplomatically. The return of Richard Nixon and his enunciation of a doctrine based on limiting American involvement abroad cheered the South Africans as the decade ended. So did the coming to power of Edward Heath's newly "pragmatic" Conservatives in London. The threat of the West tolerating an international campaign of sanctions or force against South Africa seemed to recede.

Contacts eased not only in the West and some parts of Africa, but in areas within the Third World as well. Trade with Latin America, Iran, Madagascar, and especially Japan provided South Africa with new diplomatic opportunities that it sought to exploit.

At the beginning of the nineteen seventies, South Africa was farther out of isolation, symbolized by the laager, than at any time in its history. Paradoxically, at about the same time, American and British liberals began to mount what is likely to become the most concerted effort yet made to isolate the Pretoria government and demand changes in apartheid. Attacks were made on fronts ranging from investment and trade, sports and culture, to diplomacy. Africanists who had been saying that South Africa could become the next important foreign policy controversy in America after Vietnam began to gain some credence.

In sum, the impact of a generation of apartheid was as divided in the international sphere as it was at home. International business profited from apartheid, since it underscored the existence of power sufficient to ensure a vast and disciplined pool of cheap labor. At the diplomatic level, apartheid had not proved to be an insurmountable barrier to relations with the states South Africa counted as important.

But apartheid increasingly became a public issue abroad, as other societies that had once practiced the same type of political and social discrimination at least made efforts to move away from officially endorsed prejudice as South Africa intensified it. The conflict of the currents is likely to grow rather than diminish over the coming decade as the world and South Africa face a growing debate: Will a decrease in the international pressure on and isolation of South Africa produce liberalizing trends in the country's race relations, or will it merely decrease the reasons why South Africa would feel it necessary to change?

THE INVESTORS

More than 275 American firms were doing business in South Africa directly or through subsidiaries in 1970, according to the United States Department of Commerce. The book value of their investments was $750,000,000. Unofficially, American consular personnel estimated that there were well over 300 American firms in the country, and from detailed studies of stated book values of several operations, these officials felt that the true level of investment was easily above $1 billion at current values, and probably closer to $1.5 billion. American business had at least a 15 per cent share of all foreign investment in South Africa.

This investment was widely scattered across mining and manufacturing. Twelve of America's twenty largest firms had investments in South Africa. A measure of the involvement of American business in South Africa today is how completely at home an American visitor will feel in any South African city. South Africa's whites are as avid consumers of goods as are Americans, and they openly have set out to emulate the world's highest standard of living. "From barbecues to supermarkets, we're American all the way," Jan Marais, who introduced super-American banking methods to South Africa, had said. His tone suggested: "Nothing is too good for us."

South African business executives rent their Chrysler Valiant (the best-selling car in South Africa) from Avis or Hertz, drink Carling's Black Label beer with lunch, and pay the bills with American Express or Diners Club. At home, their wives iron with Westinghouse, keep food in Frigidaires, vacuum with Hoover, and make up with Max Factor.

The discovery of gold and diamonds had brought foreign investment as well as people to South Africa. The capital needed to organize mining companies came largely from Britain. The British established a predominance in investing in the lucrative South African economy that they still maintain. In 1966, the United Kingdom held a 57 per cent share of the $5.3 billion book value of the foreign investment in South Africa. By 1970, that total was thought to have grown by another billion dollars and the British share to have declined slightly to 55 per cent.

American investment also came into South Africa relatively early and provided an important boost to South Africa by supplying capital and a transfer of some technology into the infant manufacturing sector. By 1926, Ford and General Motors had established car-assembly plants at Port Elizabeth. All parts were imported and then the cars were put together in South Africa.

After World War II, American capital moved decisively into mining and helped free local capital for manufacturing investment. Charles Englehard, who had inherited a family industrial empire that developed into the world's largest refiner and fabricator of precious metals, became especially active in South African mining through his Englehard Hanovia firm. He set up the American–South African Investment Corporation in 1958. The list of other American firms involved in mining is a blue-chip register: U.S. Steel, Union Carbide, American Metals Climax, and Newmont Mining Corporation are a few.

Banking and finance have been largely dominated by British firms, especially the Standard Bank and Barclays. In 1958, the First National City Bank entered South Africa, and Chase Manhattan opened offices there a year later. They and nine other American banks made available to the South African government a $40,000,000 revolving credit, which expired in 1969.

The financial crisis sparked by Sharpeville retarded American business expansion into South Africa, as investors nervously watched the unfolding events all across the continent. In Leopoldville as well as Langa, in Blantyre as well as Bloemfontein, the white man's stake in Africa did not seem to be that good a bet. Within five months of Sharpeville, the white South Africans felt they had established themselves as complete masters of the situation and waited for foreign capital to resume its inflow. As noted, it did not.

In June 1961 the government moved to halt the continuing flight of money. Tight exchange controls were imposed, and the transfer of capital abroad was greatly restricted. Securities could no longer be freely transferred between the Johannesburg and London Stock Exchanges. These restrictions, which are the kind that foreign investors scream about when they are imposed by Latin American or tropical African countries,[1] were coupled with indirect market-guarantees for industries set up in South Africa. A system of automobile import permits was established that virtually eliminated imports of cars, for example.

The government also was helped through the crisis by financial credit from abroad. A $30,000,000 loan arranged by Harry Oppenheimer and Charles Engelhard from American sources was especially vital to the mining sector.

It was 1963 before the tide turned and a major net capital influx was recorded by South Africa, but once the trickle of new investment had begun, it quickly turned into a flood. The 15 to 20 per cent a year pre-tax return on initial investment that was being recorded by many firms was too lucrative to pass up. An investment could be recovered in five to six years, and the white government certainly seemed to be entrenched for that long. As it became more apparent that the whites would probably be around a lot longer, American investment, like Topsy, just grew and grew.

(Foreign capital of all kinds poured into South Africa in the last three years of the nineteen sixties as the world's monetary system underwent a series of crises and financiers sought the safety of gold. South Africa is one of the few countries that can usually count on profiting from disaster striking others in the free world's money markets. The inflow of capital was so great, however, that the South Africans soon faced an inflationary spiral that they had to take drastic actions to curb.)

Robert S. Smith, Deputy Assistant Secretary of State for African Affairs, estimated in a speech that in 1969 U.S. manufacturing investment received an average 14 per cent return. A 1971 State Department memorandum on U.S. firms in South Africa places American investment at approximately 1 per cent of all U.S. direct

[1] The ease with which American business accepts certain kinds of controls from European countries and South Africa may indicate that for many it is all right for a white man to be an economic nationalist, but slightly indecent for black and brown men to be so.

private investment abroad and noted that the South African share collected 1.6 per cent of the total worldwide profits generated by American investment overseas. Other estimates put the return at 2 per cent. Total sales of U.S. firms operating in South Africa in 1969 were about $826,000,000. In trade, the United States sold $518,000,000 worth of goods to South Africa and bought only $151,000,000, gaining an important trade surplus.

South Africa represented, in short, an extraordinarily profitable and simple proposition for American businessmen. It is reasonable to assume that Americans made at least $100 million in profits from South African investment in 1970.

Foreign investment also represented a desirable arrangement for the South Africans, who have long-term balance of payments problems. Gold is South Africa's key export, financing as much as 40 per cent of all imports in the nineteen sixties. But gold had remained at the same official price level for nearly forty years, while prices of imports continued to rise. And the nature of mining, and the industrial boom of the nineteen sixties, required large imports of costly capital goods and machinery. South Africa annually records a tremendous deficit in trade, if gold sales are excluded. Foreign investment helps redress the imbalance.

Perhaps more important has been the transfer of technology that foreign and particularly American investment has facilitated. The Americans often went into areas where the British and other investors were too cautious to tread. Automobile assembly is by far the best example and presents perhaps the clearest case of the South Africans skillfully using foreign investment for their own purposes.

The Sharpeville crisis identified areas of vulnerability, and government leaders resolved to correct them. Exploration for petroleum, the one vital natural resource South Africa lacked, was stepped up, with American firms playing the major role. For the automotive industry, the advantages that had been established under the import controls in 1961 depended on the firms systematically increasing local manufacture of component parts. In 1960, as much as 87.5 per cent by weight of all materials used in automobile assembly plants was imported. The government set a target of 65 per cent by weight of domestically manufactured parts by 1975. In 1970, spokesmen for General Motors South African proudly said that the firm was ahead of that schedule. GM's Ranger, a model designed for South Africa, was advertised in 1970 as the first all South African car.

As The Council on Economic Priorities, a reform-minded American group, pointed out in a report published in October 1970, the local content program not only helped reduce imports into South Africa and thereby improved the balance of payments, but it also increased South Africa's control over an industry that would be essential in the event of a major conflict. The report quotes *Financial Gazette*, a National Party newspaper, as noting in June 1966 that ". . . in times of emergency or war, each plant could be turned over rapidly to the production of weapons and other strategic requirements for the defense of Southern Africa." Tom Muller, the head of General Mining, had said to me, "We are increasingly independent of foreign investment. Twenty to thirty years ago it was an important source of capital for us, but not as much now. What we need from abroad is specialized equipment and technology."

The Economic Priorities report is a detailed, dispassionate study of labor practices, wage rates, and the attitudes toward apartheid of executives of Ford, General Motors, and Chrysler in South Africa. The scrutiny the report focused on these three firms in 1970 was one of a number of signs that operating in South Africa might turn out to be a major headache for American business after all.

THE NEW ACTIVISTS

Opposition to American involvement in South Africa had previously come only from the small, fragmented liberal Africanist lobby in the United States, and especially from the American Committee on Africa, a New York-based group whose executive director was the Reverend George Houser, a Methodist minister. The ACOA urged American business to "disengage" from South Africa, Rhodesia, and the Portuguese territories, as a tactic to force concessions from the white minority regimes. This approach was opposed by a number of other Americans (like the ACOA, almost entirely white) some of whom also viewed themselves as liberals on Africa. Many of them had economic ties to South Africa. They argued that isolation would only worsen the lot of Africans in South Africa, increase the rigidity of the Afrikaners, and be fruitless since other foreign investors would move into the gap left by the U.S. American business could do more to help change apartheid by staying in South Africa, David Rockefeller, head of the Chase Manhattan Bank, hinted in a March 1967 speech. "We are convinced that over a period of time, the . . . Bank can exert a constructive influence on racial conditions in South Africa." He also noted that Chase was only following the American government's lead. "If the government maintains friendly diplomatic relations with a country, as it does with South Africa, then we ordinarily do business with that country."

Most American business leaders did not even bother to respond to the ACOA and others, however. The strident tones of the liberal Africanists, the almost complete focusing of attention on Vietnam and America's urban disasters, and a general disillusionment about the course of events in black Africa contributed to a lack of public attention for most of the nineteen sixties.

How and why a foreign policy issue captures even a small piece of the fad-conscious American imagination is always difficult to determine, especially when the issue, as involvement in South Africa is at the time of this writing, is still building. But it became apparent in 1969, as extreme weariness with Vietnam set in, that South Africa was claiming more attention, especially among American college students.

In March 1969 Princeton University's Board of Trustees rejected a recommendation from the faculty that the university sell $127,000,000 worth of securities in thirty-nine major corporations that did business in South Africa. A week later, seventy-five

Princeton students occupied an administration building to protest the decision. Students picketed the Chase Manhattan and Chemical Trust banks in New York. In October 1970 the University of Michigan Placement Service decided to refuse to participate in recruiting done by companies operating in South Africa unless the companies could prove they did not practice discrimination there.

But more important perhaps was the linking of American involvement in South Africa with the broader question of American corporate responsibility, and responsiveness, an issue that had grown from Ralph Nader's early crusades to a major national concern. A new type of activist became involved in the South African question, and the voices calling for change became more diffused. A number of them came from within the companies, or even from within the board rooms, and their impact was surprisingly sharp.

A good example of the new interest group was the Council on Economic Priorities, a nonprofit, Washington-based information body established to publicize corporate practices in the general areas of minority employment, effect on environment, defense production, and foreign investment.

Much of the research for its report on Chrysler, Ford, and General Motors was done by three young Americans: Tim Smith, Reed Kramer, and Tami Hultman. Smith, staff member of the United Church of Christ's Council for Christian Social Action, had also been active in a church campaign to spark a boycott against Gulf Oil Corporation, which had invested $170,000,000 in discovering and exploiting oil in Angola. Kramer and Miss Hultman were political science graduates from Duke University and went to South Africa in December 1969, sponsored by church groups but also to work for a year on their own research projects. Since they had access to both American executives and a large number of black South African citizens, their research on the implications of American investment is perhaps the most comprehensive yet done.

Their conclusions, drawn from interviews with the highest ranking executives of about twenty American firms, resembled those that I had formed from interviewing a smaller number of executives and diplomats in South Africa. The principal conclusions were that American business could point to almost nothing to support the argument that its presence had had a tempering influence on apartheid; that companies tended to send conservative executives to South Africa, whose personal opinions were often not incompatible with apartheid; that many American companies seemed to be ignorant of which apartheid practices were legally prescribed and which ones were only custom; and finally, that blacks felt encouraged when outside firms or governments put pressure on the white government, but did not necessarily view total withdrawal as an effective force for positive change.

". . . U.S. subsidiaries and affiliates have not been conspicuously different from other firms in South Africa," a 1971 State Department draft position paper observed. An American diplomat in South Africa had described U.S. investment to me as "a neutral factor, at best." Fred van Wyck, head of the nonpartisan and prestigious South African Institute of Race Relations, agreed with that assessment: "Any effect American companies are having on apartheid is negligible, and seemingly incidental to their money-making interests." Van Wyck cited several instances of American-owned factories having far worse conditions in salaries, working conditions, and even racial attitudes than the South African norm.

Almost all of the American firms declined to contribute money to the Institute of Race Relations for its valuable research projects, van Wyck said. The Institute scrupulously avoided becoming involved in party politics, but its detailed publications necessarily raised profound questions about apartheid. The government was known to frown upon the Institute's work, and American firms avoided contact with it on the grounds of "politics." At the same time, Union Carbide, General Motors, Caltex, and many other large American firms contributed generously to the South Africa Foundation, a public relations outfit designed to project a pleasant image of South Africa abroad, and one which the Nationalist government smiled on. This apparently was not considered "politics" by the American firms.

In Johannesburg, I visited Stephen Pryke, a Chase Manhattan vice president, who received me pleasantly but was reluctant to speak for publication until I pointed out that David Rockefeller's assertion about being able to exert influence in South Africa was on the public record. "There is no way you can point to something concrete and say that our presence is having a positive effect on the racial problem," Pryke said at last. "Like all American companies here we have to operate within the requirements of the law, which restricts how much we can do. But I do think international investment has helped speed economic growth in the country, and that has meant a better standard of living for both whites and blacks."

Although there are no legal limits on salaries, there is no evidence that American firms have paid wages much if any higher to Africans or Coloreds than South African firms — wages that were often below what these workers reasonably required for subsistence. Chrysler was reportedly paying an average monthly wage of $81, which would be $3 below the government's poverty line for a family of five, to African workers in 1970. A year and a half before, Chrysler had been paying African workers only $43 a month. Many American companies also adopted the "civilized wages" policy and paid whites higher wages than nonwhites for doing essentially the same jobs. Citing Chrysler again as an example, Tim Smith noted the firm had a comprehensive medical scheme for its white workers, but nothing for nonwhites. White artisans at Chrysler's facilities are represented by the strong Iron and Steel Workers Union, but Chrysler strenuously opposed a move by its Colored workers to form a union, which is legal under South Africa's labor laws, Smith reported.[2]

Many American firms had segregated facilities, such as elevators, which are not required by law. They have evolved from custom. More importantly, Reed Kramer found that hiring and promotion patterns were defended on grounds of apartheid re-

[2] American firms did begin to increase wages and provide some benefits for nonwhites after the Polaroid case publicized the issue.

strictions that did not exist. "Custom, not law, dictates many of the most blatant inequities," Kramer said when I talked to him in Nairobi after he had been deported from the country in a South African crackdown on foreign church workers in February 1971. "The pressures from white unions against changes would be great, and the government might pass laws if American firms did try to make changes. But presently, American firms have a much greater flexibility than most take advantage of."

"Individually, American businessmen generally support the racial policies of the South African government or a slightly modified form and work contentedly within the white South African context of labor relations," Tim Smith wrote. He, Kramer, and Miss Hultman provided detailed quotes from American executives working for Ford, Union Carbide, International Harvester, and others to support that conclusion.

These findings are interesting, but as Kramer conceded after he left South Africa, not at the center of the question of American involvement in South Africa. Firms headed by executives with strong segregationist sympathies varied little in their practices from one headed by a Eugene McCarthy-supporting Democrat. Guidance from the home office, local pressures, and more importantly the possibilities for profit were the key factors in determining what American firms did and did not do in South Africa.

Nor is Smith's conclusion that American business involvement in South Africa has done little more for Africans than help produce "a nation of slightly better fed and clothed political and economic serfs" likely to cause investors to rethink their participation in South Africa. Enough research materials have become available by now for any reasonably objective person to conclude that American investment has not had a liberalizing effect on race relations in South Africa[3] and in fact has probably helped strengthen the apartheid government's logistical and financial position. American firms have been insisting otherwise to justify a presence they intend to maintain in any event.

[3] Unless one accepts the theory that anything done to further industrialization erodes apartheid, a theory that as I have explained I view as untenable.

South Africans also looked upon the engagement debate as an interesting intellectual exercise. Rejecting both the notions that American investment helped erode apartheid, and that withdrawal would bring changes from the Afrikaners, Piet Cillié had said, "The idea is laughable. Those who want to influence us from abroad will have to send in a few army corps to do it." Helen Suzman added later: "People outside are bluffing themselves if they think they have any effect on this country through investment." Tom Muller at General Mining smiled about the possibility of disengagement and said, "We would be happy to pick up most of their mining investments. They are quite profitable, you know, and we generate enough capital here to do it easily." David Curry, the Colored political leader, also rejected both poles of the engagement-disengagement debate. "My people need economic growth to get ahead. I can't talk about politics to them if they don't have bread in their stomachs. General Motors shouldn't pull out. But it sure as hell should give us better jobs, and better pay. It hasn't done anything better than the South African firms." His attitude resembled that of Gatsha Buthelezi, the chief of Zululand.

By 1970, however, Nader and environment had gained importance in America and the debate was joined more effectively. And in England, a prominent businessman, Neal Wates, refused to invest in South Africa after having made a tour of the country. "The idea of doing business in South Africa is totally unacceptable to me," Wates said in a remarkable public statement he issued for his company, Wates, Ltd., one of Britain's biggest building and construction concerns. The company would make enormous profits from exploitation of black labor "and ultimately end up with a vested interest in its maintenance," Wates stated. In relatively unemotional tones, he compared apartheid to Nazism.

In America the United Church of Christ's campaign against Gulf's Angola operation so nettled Gulf president B. R. Dorsey that he threatened to bring legal action against the Church for what he termed defamatory remarks about Gulf. Although Church spokesmen said they would welcome a suit and the chance to subpoena Gulf's documents on their African operations, no action had been initiated at the time of writing.

In February 1971 the Episcopal Church in the United States, which owned 12,574 shares of the 285,500,000 shares of General Motors stock then outstanding, urged General Motors to get out of South Africa. The Reverend Leon Sullivan, a black American minister who had been appointed to the twenty-three-member board of directors partly as a result of previous criticism of GM's domestic racial policies, announced that he backed the Episcopal stand. This created what the *New York Times* called "the first public disagreement within memory" on the board. The call for disengagement also gained the support of Campaign GM, a corporate responsibility group. At the annual stockholder meeting in Detroit in May 1971, the withdrawal proposal received only 1.3 per cent of the 229,473,228 shares voted. But the bid received much attention in the American press.

POLAROID: PROGRESS OR P.R.?

The largest public impact was to come from an American firm that had one of the smallest financial stakes in South Africa — Polaroid Corporation, which had no investment in South Africa, and whose sales there through an independent distributor amounted to roughly $1.5 million annually, or one half of 1 per cent of its total revenues. The firm also apparently had given orders years before that its film would not be sold directly to the South African government for passbooks or identity cards.

A very small group of black American Polaroid employees formed the Polaroid Revolutionary Workers' Movement in the fall of 1970. (Polaroid would say later that only three employees had publicly identified themselves as members of the Movement.) They distributed leaflets around the company's Cambridge, Massachusetts, headquarters and demanded that Polaroid end all sales in South Africa and contribute the profits earned there to African liberation movements.

Polaroid checked with its South African distributor, Frank & Hirsch, and found that about 10 per cent of the film used in the South African identity book system was Polaroid. Senior vice president Arthur Barnes issued a memorandum on October 21, 1970, stating that Polaroid was "discontinuing sale of any Polaroid products including film, directly or indirectly, which might be used in this identification program." Because photographs "have such symbolic importance, we are convinced of the correctness of our program of denying use of any of our products for discriminatory identification," the memo said. The final sentence of the memo, which was addressed to all members of the company, read: "We oppose the policy of apartheid in any manifestation either in South Africa or any place else in the world."

Dissatisfied, the Movement repeated its call for an end to all sales in South Africa and called for a worldwide boycott to pressure Polaroid. The demand received coverage in the Boston *Globe*, and soon demonstrators picketed the Polaroid headquarters. Again, Polaroid responded. A fourteen-member committee of employees, white and black, was appointed to study Polaroid's involvement in South Africa. Four men from the committee, two whites and two blacks, were sent to South Africa for an eleven-day fact-finding tour. The committee recommendations were published in a full-page ad Polaroid took in a dozen major American daily newspapers on January 18, 1971, and in twenty black weeklies.

"We decided whatever our course should be it should oppose the course of apartheid," said the advertisement, which was headed, "An Experiment in South Africa." The prime purpose of the four committee members' going to South Africa "was to ask Africans what they thought American business should do in their country. We decided the answer that is best for the black people of South Africa would be the best answer for us." The advertisement then laid out what it said would be a one-year experiment.

Polaroid would continue business relationships in South Africa but "on a new basis which Blacks there with whom we talked see as supportive to their hopes and plans for the future." Polaroid would oblige its distributor "to improve dramatically the salaries and benefits of their non-white employees." Business associates in South Africa "will also be obliged (as a condition of maintaining their relationship with Polaroid) to initiate a well-defined program to train non-white employees for important jobs within their companies."

"We believe," the advertisement continued, "education for the Blacks, in combination with the opportunities now being afforded by the expanding economy, is a key to change in South Africa. We will commit a portion of our profits earned there to encourage black education."

The company said it intended not to take on investments in South Africa but would consider creating a black-managed company in one of the Bantustans.

"How can we presume to concern ourselves with the problems of another country?" Polaroid asked in a final paragraph that perhaps unintentionally, but quite deftly, struck at the heart of American business's fallback position of not becoming involved in internal affairs of a foreign country. "Whatever the practices are elsewhere, South Africa alone articulates a policy contrary to everything we feel our company stands for. We cannot participate passively in such a political system. Nor can we ignore it. That is why we have undertaken this experimental program."

In practical terms, the company's program had little immediate impact. Frank & Hirsch had a few Colored and Indian employees and 155 Africans. It had a handful of African supervisors, some of whom received a $14- to $28-a-month raise after the Polaroid announcement. This pushed their salaries to the level of between $210 and $280 a month. "This is similar to the range of salaries F&H, like other Johannesburg firms, pays its junior white typists," the *Financial Mail* noted in an article entitled "Progress or propaganda?" (January 22, 1971). Noting that the government had made it quite clear that Africans would not be allowed to supervise whites, the article suggested that the promises of upgrading blacks would be difficult to meet.

Promises to underwrite educational expenses for about 500

black students at various levels of study and to help support and upgrade black teaching were viewed as more realistic and generally praised by South African liberals.

The Revolutionary Movement continued to reject this approach. Caroline Hunter, a twenty-four-year-old chemist, and Kenneth Williams, forty-one, a design photographer, became the first persons to testify against a private American business before the sixteen-nation Apartheid Committee of the United Nations in February 1971. Calling Polaroid's suggestions a trick and an insult, Miss Hunter and Williams said they planned to step up their plans for a boycott.

Miss Hunter and Williams are black Americans. They had organized the original campaign against Polaroid. Williams resigned from the company after it began, and Miss Hunter said she was dismissed from her job a few days after her appearance at the United Nations. The company declined to comment to newspapers on the reason for her dismissal.

The implications of Polaroid's actions were far greater than their practical effect. An American company operating in South Africa had broken away from the camp. If an American company took the position that a moral issue was involved in the sale of film to the South African government, what can be said of the sale of Bell helicopters, Leer executive jets, and General Motors trucks to South Africa? Or IBM computers that could be used in the same identity-security system Polaroid rejected? And what could be said of the American government licensing the sale of such items (denied to Mainland China as potential military items)? Polaroid had publicly thrown over the shibboleth that American investors could not afford to criticize internal politics. "We cannot participate passively in such a political system," Polaroid had said. This was an at least implicit criticism of those who remained silent on apartheid.

In Washington, the South African Ambassador, H. L. T. Taswell, used one of his favorite denunciations (he had earlier applied it to Robert Kennedy after the 1966 visit) by asserting that Polaroid was displaying a "holier-than-thou" attitude. Which it was. Happily, considering the "thou" involved.

American and British business response to the Polaroid and Wates decisions was slow to form publicly. In general, the companies seemed to look on the campaign against involvement in South Africa as a problem in public relations, not human relations. Most chose to stand pat, repeating when pressed that their being in South Africa helped blacks economically. The few that moved seemed to be more concerned with sprucing up their images back home than changing conditions in South Africa. Barclays and Standard Bank (now partly owned by Chase Manhattan) announced with much fanfare that they would abandon the "civilized wages" policy (although for understandable reasons they did not identify their previous practices with those words) and give nonwhites equal pay for equal work. This affected about 300 people, most of them Colored. Other American businesses finally took notice of the Institute of Race Relations and began to look for education funds to which they could ostentatiously contribute. The American Embassy in South Africa began advising American businessmen on how to meet the public relations difficulties they faced. Suggestions focused on wages and fringe benefits for nonwhite workers and contained warnings against actions that would upset the South Africans "and engender harmful reactions."

The Polaroid experience was also important in that it buoyed black hopes, Reed Kramer reported. "Africans we talked to were glad that someone outside was putting pressure on the government, apparently in their behalf." Their reaction suggested that while there might not be much support inside for total disengagement, a campaign of selective pressures against American business and thus against the white government would win support from Africans, although it would necessarily be covert.

In terms of the future of campaigns against American business in South Africa, four principal points can be seen in the Polaroid case:

1. The smallness of Polaroid's stake in South African business gave it more room to maneuver than companies with multimillion-dollar investments there. Polaroid could afford to risk losing its

entire business there, if necessary, and could probably have recouped it elsewhere from the favorable publicity that would have followed, had the Nationalist government reacted sharply against its denouncement of apartheid.

2. Their programs cost them relatively little. With a nonwhite payroll of perhaps 170 in South Africa, they could easily afford raises for nonwhites, just as could the banks. This is a different proposition for General Motors, or Chrysler, with nonwhite payrolls ten to twenty times as large as that of Polaroid's distributor.

For American business, this is the crucial point in its involvement in South Africa. It is hard to imagine that General Motors is very concerned one way or another as to whether South Africa keeps apartheid as a political system or whether Bantustans succeed or fail. Apartheid matters to Detroit and Wall Street only to the extent to which it produces and ensures disciplined, productive labor. What matters most directly to General Motors and other American companies is the Nationalist government's cheap wages policy and the government's determination to keep Africans from organizing unions with the right to bargain collectively and strike.

If somehow John Vorster were to remain Prime Minister, but those two wages and unions policies reversed so sharply that profits were eliminated, then General Motors would consider getting out of South Africa. If Robert Sobukwe were to become Prime Minister but cheap wages and anti-union restrictions were to continue, I suspect General Motors would continue doing business in South Africa. (This is a pleasant little fantasy, of course, since the conditions that would keep the Nationalists in power will also maintain the exploitation of black labor.) That, at least, is the experience of independence in black Africa in the last decade.

"It is impossible to pretend that this above-average rate [of profit] does not come to a large extent from the very low wages paid in South Africa," *The Economist*, the conservative-leaning English journal, said of British investment in South Africa in an editorial on June 5, 1971. The same is true for American and all other foreign business.

The Polaroid case shows that the first response of a company coming under strong pressure will probably be to raise wages of nonwhite employees. They are so derisively low that this will not be hard. But a strongly mounted campaign urging companies as large as General Motors to give equal pay for equal work would present much more difficult choices than the total disengagement campaign. (There should be no doubt, however, as to what the outcome of the choices would be. There would be slight economic improvement for the nonwhites and no social or political improvement at all.) As long as there are no effective African unions, every concession made by American companies will be paternalistic, almost solely with an eye to minimizing profit losses in the domestic American market as a result of bad publicity.

3. Polaroid is a company that had already established a reputation for concern with minority hiring and other civil rights problems in the United States. Its management was likely to be more responsive than many other firms.

4. Caroline Hunter and Kenneth Williams established a strong credibility for the Polaroid protest that many previous actions against American companies had lacked. They could show direct personal concern. They were Polaroid employees. And they were black. Polaroid effectively muted the racial implications of the protest by appointing a multiracial committee and sending two black Americans on the trip to South Africa. But I think an important point for the future had been made.

One of the weaknesses of the anti-apartheid movement in Britain and in the United States has been that whites have played most of the leadership roles.

In most cases, the criticism that white American or English liberals are working out guilt complexes about their country's own situations by becoming deeply involved in fighting the battle for South Africa's blacks may be an overstatement. But it contains enough appearance of truth, it seems to me, to damage their credibility on the issue, especially when the target is the profits-eager businessman looking for reasons to ignore a challenge. "Another bleeding heart" is pretty easy to shake off along Wall Street, but a black American starts with an automatic credibility. If he develops this through acquaintance with the realities of the South African situation and a reasoned approach, he makes a much more formidable adversary. My own feeling is that if the anti-apartheid movement really is to get anywhere in the United States, it must rapidly develop truly concerned, articulate, and informed black leadership. White liberals must take a secondary role. Whether the black community, deeply involved in its own struggle in American society, will be able also to provide this kind of leadership on African affairs is perhaps the critical factor in a larger question: Can America have any positive effect on South Africa in the near future?

For, just as there is no inevitability that white domination will be ended in South Africa, there is no inevitability that corporate involvement in South Africa will grow as an issue in America or that pressure exerted from America will produce any significant beneficial changes in South Africa. It is still very much a media issue, and companies in America are reacting to the fear of bad publicity more than any moral concern. Another sustained foreign policy crisis such as Vietnam or a broad Middle East conflict could snuff out American attention to South Africa and let the businessmen go back to the simple operation of making profits.

THE VIEW FROM FOGGY BOTTOM

Official American policy toward South Africa is largely shaped by five often conflicting currents, which have different sources and constituencies within the policy-making machinery of Washington.

Investment, as has been suggested, is an important one. This is not so much because of its size (only 1 per cent of all American investment abroad) or even the valuable help it provides with the balance of payments deficit. It is the type of investment in South Africa that is important. It is diversified and spread among many companies, a number of which are major contributors to campaign funds of both parties. These companies are also major American taxpayers. The White House and the Departments of Commerce and the Treasury are especially attentive to their views.

South Africa's role as a major supplier of minerals, especially gold, platinum, and uranium, is also important. The United States obviously would not want this supply endangered.

The third factor is related to the first two — that of military importance. Investment and mineral wealth project a shadow of military protection from the United States against a Communist or Communist-supported invasion. The South Africans have also done a fairly good job of selling to more conservative Americans the idea that shoring up the white government is our only insurance in the Cold War. (Anybody who is that much against black people must really be against Communists, too, is the way the argument seems to go at times.) A South Atlantic Treaty Organization, to resemble NATO and including the South Africans, has always been one of Pretoria's dreams. How importantly Washington views South Africa's military role in the anti-Communist crusade today is difficult to determine. But it would be surprising if there is not in the Pentagon considerable support for the white regime as solid anti-Communists.

Fourthly, there is the question of America's relations with the rest of Africa. The importance of black Africa in American thinking waxes and wanes with the continent's own problems and promises and with the changes of administration in the United States. Africa's most important constituency is the Bureau of African Affairs in the State Department. The Bureau's diplomats and desk officers are more consistently sympathetic to black Africa's views than is any other government agency. The general mood at Foggy Bottom, as the State Department area is known, has been generally anti-apartheid, pro-majority rule brought about in an orderly fashion. This would please the largest number of State's clients as well as vindicate a long-standing opposition to apartheid by the Africanists.

America's own racial situation has been the fifth and least important factor in Washington's policy on South Africa. In the nineteen sixties, Africa in general and South Africa in particular were not issues on which black Americans attempted to exert influence, although this may not continue to be true in the nineteen seventies.

The emphasis on policy toward South Africa has shifted along a fairly well defined spectrum as these currents become more or less prominent in the decision-making process, as a result of a number of internal and external influences, and according to the relative strengths of the bureaucracies within a given administration, although this is often overlooked.

The Kennedy, Johnson, and Nixon administrations followed the same general lines on Southern Africa by rejecting the broad alternatives. None of them was sufficiently convinced of the immediate wisdom of bringing about an alternative government in South Africa to take any action that substantively affected the balance of power there. They were not prepared to break diplomatic relations, or to take steps to bring a reduction of American investment. But neither did they feel they could publicly offer the white government comfort and aid with its problems, or forgo an occasional criticism of apartheid. American policy on South Africa seemed to be to "strike, but not to wound," *News/Check* magazine said.

Until 1958, the posture was not even to strike. Official statements on Africa hedged bets. Lip service was paid to the force of African nationalism while America's European allies were reassured that we did not favor "premature independence." South Africa was not the subject of a major policy statement. The United States abstained from United Nations resolutions condemning South Africa's racial policy. Only in 1958 did the American delegation at the United Nations endorse a resolution expressing "regret and concern" on the racial policy of South Africa.

Sharpeville — coming in an American presidential election year in which the incumbent administration seemed well behind in the contest for the ethnic minority vote — forced a dramatic change. On March 22, 1960, the State Department issued an extraordinary statement commenting on internal events in another country, events in which American interests were not involved. Regret was voiced at "the tragic loss of life resulting from the measures taken against the demonstrators."

This established a new pattern of .the United States' joining other countries in purely verbal condemnations of South Africa, but stopping well short of endorsing any resolution that seemed to imply that the use of force was required, or even justified, in bringing about changes in Southern Africa. Thus, the Americans opposed mandatory sanctions against South Africa — which would undoubtedly require force to implement. The United States has also consistently voted against resolutions calling for the diplomatic and economic isolation of South Africa. This has been the essential American position in the United Nations toward the problem of South Africa.

The election of John F. Kennedy raised great hopes among liberal Africanists, who had been impressed by Kennedy's 1957 speech attacking Eisenhower's supplying of arms to the French for use in Algeria. American policy on Algeria was "a retreat from the principles of independence and anti-colonialism," Kennedy had said. In the 1960 campaign, he scored America's record of neglecting Africa. Kennedy also indicated that he favored a strong State Department, which would increase the relative influence of those policy-makers opposed to cooperation with the white regimes of Southern Africa.

But most of those hopes had been left unfulfilled on November 22, 1963. Kennedy had never really been able to get around to Africa. Cuba, the Soviet Union, and the beginnings of Laos and Vietnam had pressed for his attention. His administration did establish a moral tone on the domestic racial issue, which carried over into the debate on Southern Africa. This infuriated the South Africans and the Portuguese and won America some points in black Africa.

But the administration's actions on Southern Africa were confusing and often contradictory. Kennedy apparently was unable to resolve on African issues what Roger Hilsman calls the conflicting "pulling and hauling" of government bureaucracies struggling to get their viewpoints reflected in national policy. The Kennedy administration took into account the Africanists' view much more than any other had, but when major decisions were pronounced, there was always something in them for the European desks in the State Department, which continued to have major influence on our actions toward Africa, and for the conservatives or those with business interests in Southern Africa.

The confusion was clear even in the voluntary arms embargoes the United States imposed against Portugal and South Africa, the only two substantive steps the United States has yet taken to back its rhetorical condemnation of white minority rule.

According to official State Department statements, since 1961 the United States has prohibited the export of arms from private as well as public U.S. sources to or for use in the Portuguese African territories. The $2,000,000 worth of American military supplies given and sold each year to Portugal in the last half of the nineteen sixties was for use only within the North Atlantic area. Soon after adopting this partial embargo, the United States abstained in the United Nations on a resolution asking member states to refrain from the sale or supply of arms and military equipment to Portugal for use in the Portuguese overseas territories. "The United States thus put itself in the curious position of refusing to vote for a resolution asking all the members of the United Nations to do what the United States, according to its own statement, had already put into effect," Waldemar A. Nielsen writes in *The Great Powers & Africa*. The logic, or perhaps illogic, behind this has never been adequately explained and can only be the subject of speculation at this point.

(In any event, evidence presented by African guerrilla movements and observations I made during my trips through Portuguese Africa leads me to believe that the intent of this embargo has not been completely enforced. I saw what appeared to be post-1961 American-manufactured large-caliber ammunition and bazookas in use in Portuguese Guinea and Angola. There was no way of determining whether they came from private or public sources. The Portuguese were also using napalm and American-manufactured herbicides in their wars. American military attachés stationed in Lisbon frequently visit the African territories. "Your attachés are always coming in and telling us how great we're doing against the Commie bastards and how much they'd love to get a crack at them," a young Portuguese officer who had served in Portuguese Guinea told me. In the other territories, I heard nothing but praise for our attachés, who had made visits in the company of South African military attachés on some occasions. An American military attaché stationed in South Africa was so taken with its way of life that he told colleagues in 1971 that he was going to retire there.)

The embargo against all arms shipments to South Africa was made by Adlai Stevenson at the United Nations in August 1963 — just before the U.N. was to vote on a resolution calling for such an embargo by all member states. This would seem to have facilitated the continuing shipment of American arms already sold on contract, and of spare parts, to South Africa, as Nielsen suggests. But it may have also been that by instituting an arms embargo on its own initiative, the United States felt more free to relax that embargo if the need arose in the future.

Dallas ended the hope, and Vietnam ended the possibility of strong American action in Southern Africa. The Johnson administration continued the strong moral tone on Southern Africa, but could devote few resources and little time to that question. The African reaction to the Stanleyville airlift and Nigeria's plunge to civil war soured Americans on African problems in general. Rhodesia, the Johnson administration said, was a British problem, and the Tanzam railway was not an economic proposition.

But the low level of political interest by the Johnson White House in Southern African affairs coincided with the greatest period of economic growth of American investment in South Africa and the Portuguese territories. On his accession to power, Richard Nixon found America with a bigger than ever economic stake in "stability" in South Africa. Executive agencies more attentive to economic and security clients, such as the Commerce and Treasury Departments and the National Security Council, began to eclipse the State Department on decision-making on Southern Africa, although the policy statements continued to criticize white minority rule. The Nixon administration neatly symbolized the change by dropping liberal academics who strongly opposed apartheid from the government's African Advisory Committee and appointing American businessmen with important interests throughout Africa, especially South Africa. Academics who favored a conciliatory approach to the white governments were also included.

In part, this eclipse of the State Department Africa specialists on decision-making was only one facet of a more general shift of power within the Executive Branch. The shift had begun under Kennedy, as his White House foreign policy staff became the focal point of decision-making, a trend accelerated under Johnson and perhaps peaking with Nixon's almost complete reliance upon Henry Kissinger, whose global view of realpolitik had little place for Africa. The State Department had previously tied together the often conflicting foreign policy recommendations within the Executive Branch and presented the package to the President for a decision. Now, it has become another of the agencies competing for attention when the package is put together at the White House, and under Nixon it does not seem to have done as well on Southern Africa as Commerce or Treasury.

That is perhaps the clearest explanation of the erosion of American policy on Southern Africa that occurred in the first few years of the Nixon administration. Here are some of the important examples: Union Carbide was allowed to import 115,000 tons of chrome ore from Rhodesia despite vigorous State Department dissent. Helicopters and executive jet aircraft — which South African newspapers noted could be easily converted for security use — were licensed for sale to the South African government, in a departure of philosophy, if not policy, from previous administrations. Boeing 707 jet airliners were licensed for sale directly to the Portuguese government, another departure from past practices. At a time when the wars in Africa were putting a considerable economic pressure on Portugal, Nixon renewed the American lease on the Azores, which the United States had been using without formal arrangement since 1962, when the lease formally elapsed. In return the United States agreed to authorize Export-Import Bank loans to Portugal up to $400 million. Premier Caetano effusively praised Nixon as a true ally and termed the new agreement a "treaty" between Portugal and the United States. The United States used a veto in the United Nations Security Council for the first time in history to reject a resolution that called for the use of force by Britain to settle the Rhodesian question. A conservative Texas oil millionaire fond of hunting replaced the American career diplomat who had been ambassador in South Africa and gave what was reported to be the only large, official segregated social function that the American embassy had staged in South Africa since Sharpeville.

To balance against this, it should be noted that the Nixon administration also took these actions: The consulate in Salisbury was closed, after Britain had sent a stiffly worded note to the United States on the status of the rebel colony and after Secretary of State Rogers urged the President to close the consulate. The administration imposed a technical curb on American investment in South West Africa. Like the Polaroid action, the curb had little practical effect, but represented an important precedent. A hard line on South West Africa was continued, with the United States voting for U.N. resolutions calling for South Africa to get out of the disputed territory. Nixon met with representatives from the Organization of African Unity in 1971.

It was obvious by the end of 1971, however, that the Nixon administration had consciously opted to have more contact and to be more friendly toward the white governments of Southern Africa. This appeared to be a policy decision made at the presidential level in January 1970, after a broad review conducted within the administration on American policy toward Southern Africa. Kissinger's National Security Council staff argued for increased communication and "selective involvement" with the white governments, a line opposed by the State Department. The National Security Council victory soon became apparent. In a move that dovetailed nicely with South Africa's call for dialogue and American business's desire to remain "engaged" in South Africa, the State Department's top staff officials in 1971 began to stress two subjects almost exclusively in public pronouncements on Africa: the need for more "communication" by the outside world with South Africa and the role American business could play by staying in South Africa.

"We do not discourage U.S. firms from investing because we believe U.S. firms can exercise an influence for good, even within the system," Deputy Assistant Secretary of State for African Affairs Robert S. Smith told the American Society of International Law in April 1971. "General withdrawal would have moral value, but it would probably harden the resolve of the South African government to maintain its present system, reduce opportunities for the communication for change . . . and probably not upset the economy of South Africa."

This approach also fitted into the enunciation of the Nixon Doctrine and the general acceptance in America of the limits of American power to change things abroad, as illustrated by the debacle in Vietnam. The South Africans began to stop worrying about the United States leading a naval blockade against them (a possibility the more paranoid of them seemed to have considered very real in the Kennedy era), and South African officials said they received more understanding from the Nixon administration than they had past governments. Radio South Africa commended Assistant Secretary of State David D. Newsom for voicing the new American approach in an appearance in Nairobi in April 1972.

There seemed to be little chance of the Nixon administration's accepting recommendations that the government act to reduce private American investment or official American presence in South Africa, which is much higher than is generally realized. The tide was in fact running the other way. And Congress was in an even more conservative mood. In the Senate, traditionally the legislative branch's more liberal arm, a bill to cut South Africa's sugar quota was defeated. Both houses passed an amendment attached to a military procurement bill by Senator Harry F. Byrd,

Jr., that authorized the United States to break economic sanctions against Rhodesia by resuming the import of chrome ore. The Nixon administration presented only nominal opposition to the bill, through the Africa Bureau of the State Department. Despite the fact that there were several alternatives to the administration's resuming the imports, the Treasury Department issued import licenses in January 1972 not only for chrome ore but a number of other Rhodesian minerals as well. The Treasury chose to take this action just as African protest against the Smith regime had reached its peak during the early testing of the Pearce Commission and at a time when the white settlers of Rhodesia were badly in need of all the support they could get. This placed the United States in the company of South Africa and Portugal in openly defying United Nations sanctions.

Official American policy toward South Africa is most concisely stated in a reference aid called the Gist, which is circulated to American embassies abroad as a guideline to our diplomats in answering queries or accusations about controversial aspects of our foreign policy. In the 1971 Gist, four options are listed for American approaches to South Africa. The first three are rejected. The United States could not: 1. Accept the situation as it is, since that would "violate our own fundamental beliefs in human rights" and lose support in nonwhite nations. 2. Actively support liberation movements, since violence would be ineffective and "lead to extreme reactions which would be enormously costly to the people of South Africa." 3. Break diplomatic relations, end investment and trade, and seek to isolate South Africa, since that would "make the white community turn in on itself" and harden present beliefs and practices.

Communication, the chosen course of action, was defined as maintaining "formal, if not cordial, relations while making clear our abhorrence of South Africa's racial policies." The United States would maintain its present contacts and attempt to persuade South Africa "to modify its racial policies," would not actively promote American private investment, and would not provide grant and loan assistance to South Africa.

In practice, however, the American presence has in recent years been a high one and has tended to promote more investment than racial change. In 1970, in addition to about twenty-five State Department diplomatic personnel and fifty other "official Americans" engaged in various governmental capacities in South Africa, the United States maintained a Commerce Department attaché who was usually boosting American investment in South Africa. That was, after all, his job. The Commerce Department's counterpart to the Gist is a pamphlet called *Economic Trends.* The one being circulated while I was in South Africa differed markedly from the State Department's published moral censures. "South Africa is a growing and dynamic market," the Commerce pamphlet noted, and the only South African government policy it mentioned was the one "aimed at achieving a satisfactory rate of growth." [4]

The National Aeronautics and Space Administration maintained a tracking station, which employed 250 South Africans. As Dan Greenberg reported in *Science* magazine on July 10, 1970, NASA was helping train South African engineers in valuable advance technology. The U.S. Atomic Energy Commission has provided training for scores of South African scientists at Oak Ridge and financed what Greenberg described as a "high-energy neutrino detector experiment" in South Africa. South Africa's lone atomic reactor was purchased through Allis-Chalmers. And the United States was purchasing at above the world market prices 60,000 tons of sugar from South Africa under an officially sanctioned quota arrangement. This sent $4,500,000 a year to South Africa.

Both the idea of "disengagement" and that of "communication" are based on an assumption that outsiders, and especially Americans, can have an influence over attitudes and events in South Africa. Before analyzing the potential of these two specific and conflicting options, a general picture should be given of the South African sensitivity to outside influences. It is perhaps one question

[4] *Economic Trends,* ET 69–61.

tion that a foreign correspondent — whose job it is to portray South Africans to the outside world — is in a good position to try to answer.

THE OUTSIDER FACTOR

The Polaroid case and the growing debate on engagement received much more attention in South Africa's English-language press than in the American press. Even the Afrikaans press noted it. Few peoples of the world are quite as concerned with what is said by outsiders about them and their country as are South Africans. This is especially true of English-speaking South Africans who, having retained much of their estrangement from their Boer compatriots, often feel they must look abroad for friendship and understanding. The need is not as intense among the Afrikaners, who very consciously nonetheless seek the approval of other white men. (This is why they react so sharply when they are rejected.) The distance, the deep loneliness that pervades the vast South African landscape and the country's human relations, and in recent years the diplomatic opprobrium heaped on the country have produced a fierce sense of isolation.

It is so fierce that hardly a week goes by without an important National Party politician defensively reassuring his countrymen: "We are not isolated!" John Vorster probably says just that publicly on an average of once every two to three weeks. Doth the South African protest too much? How often does the leader of Luxembourg, Uruguay, or, for that matter, Tanzania reassure his people that they need not feel isolated, because the government has diplomatic contacts with three-score countries?

As Richard West has noted in *The White Tribes of Africa*, South Africans frequently protest that they do not care what outsiders think about them, but in fact they care deeply. A judgment from a foreigner, no matter how hastily conceived and how shallow, is immediately adopted by the South Africans, West asserts, provided it is favorable. It is only the critical ones, no matter how well documented, that are rejected as "unwarranted interference in internal affairs," to use the beloved phrase of the National Party politicians, who are continually looking for outside demons on which to blame their country's troubles.

This attitude recurs through much of the discussion of their country by South Africans. A favorable opinion by an outsider is quoted and requoted as proof or justification. Jan Marais explained apartheid to me in terms of a comment made by an American visitor, "a man who had been an adviser to your Presidents Kennedy and Johnson." This important unnamed man had not understood apartheid at first, but a few days after he arrived in South Africa Marais took him to his beach, "which is quiet and well kept, and then we went over to the Colored beach. And after he saw those crowds of people washing their faces with watermelon, he said he understood. Apartheid helps me keep my beach uncrowded."

A foreign journalist is put on trial almost immediately upon his arrival in the country. At the beginning of most discussions, no matter if he has been in the country less than a day, he will be asked, "Well, what do you think of our country?" If the answer is equivocal, the next questions become more precise, as his attitudes toward race are explored. This is one of the reasons that it seems to a visiting journalist that white South Africans continually talk about race. I deliberately refrained from bringing the subject up in many discussions, but I did not have to worry about not getting my host's view on the subject. Race is, after all, the yardstick of South African society, and once you have discovered where a man stands on that you have discovered everything about him, as far as most white South Africans are concerned. If you cannot discover where he stands, then he is to be treated with extreme suspicion.

If the constant measuring and testing that goes on in South Africa uncovers in the visitor an unusual interest in the condition of Africans or the views of white liberals, then a distinct chill develops. Douglas Brown, an English journalist who lived in South Africa from 1951 to 1956, succinctly described the foreign journalist's task in South Africa in his book *Against the World: Attitudes of White South Africa*: "Where Nasser's Egypt, say, may treat one as a potential spy, white South Africa tends to treat one as an actual traitor, protected from retribution only by the laws of hospitality." For a journalist to try to acquaint himself with the views of the nonwhite majority "is to place himself in the position of a guest in a fine house who spends part of his time in the servants' hall. This is seen not only as bad manners but as an act of treachery."

My own analogy to the reaction of white South Africans to many of my questions about apartheid was similar. It was as if I were interviewing a beautiful matron dressed in a rich and splendid evening gown and I kept bringing up the subject of the dirty slip and underwear sticking out from under her dress and the crow's-feet around her eyes. When there was so much to marvel at, why did I have to focus on such details?

South Africa's concern with its post-Sharpeville image abroad, and the effect that image had on foreign investment in and military support for South Africa, was reflected in the forming of the South Africa Foundation in November 1960 to combat "the international vendetta against South Africa" in the words of its literature. Lavishly financed by the South African and foreign business communities, the Foundation maintains an office in the United States and distributes publications "to promote international understanding of South Africa."

By any standards, but especially by South African ones, the Foundation's approach is sophisticated and soft sell. It seems to reflect more the conservative English-speakers' views and attitudes than that of Afrikaners. English-speaking businessmen like Harry Oppenheimer have put up much of the Foundation's money. The facts in its publications are accurate, and it maintains a nonpartisan approach.

But the Foundation's vision can be said to be a limited one, devoted to presenting only unqualifiedly positive aspects of South Africa. The country is portrayed in two manners: as a solid economic success where investment is well treated and as a vital link in the West's defense system in the battle against Godless Communism.

What is considered to be important about South Africa will vary greatly from individual to individual, or from organization to organization. But by any standards, the Foundation's choices seem a little unusual. In its 1970 *Information Digest*, a small seventy-eight-page pamphlet, for example, the Foundation listed under "Milestones in South Africa's History": 1962, removal of restrictions on sale of liquor to nonwhites. But the *Digest* did not note the 1948 election (or any other elections). The Closure of the Suez Canal was listed for 1967, with the note "Cape Route regains international importance." Under 1960, South Africa's worst mine disaster, at Clydesdale Colliery, was there. Sharpeville was not. Not a "milestone"?

Not only was the word apartheid not mentioned in the *Digest*, I couldn't even find a reference to separate development. Nonwhite housing was described in technical terms, and there was no mention of residential restrictions. Border industries were explained this way: "Border development is another name for decentralization of industry." Its only other aim was to stimulate the economic growth of the Bantu who live in the homelands: "The emphasis in South Africa is on *attracting* development to Border areas rather than forcing it there, and the inducements are considerable" (italics in original), the *Digest* said, which is an interesting statement in view of the Physical Planning Act of 1967. The Foundation, like its liberal opponents, seems to spend most of its time preaching to the converted, supplying reinforcing information to those who want to know good things about South Africa.

Sports, one of South Africa's most important self-image builders, was the only area in which outside activists showed that they had helped wear away, if not break down, apartheid in the nineteen sixties. As explained, South Africans are sports-crazy. They are excellent athletes, having produced world champions in a number of categories, and are extremely proud of their international victories. "What else do South Africans, and especially Afrikaners, have to be proud of?" an English-speaking professor asked me. "We have no literature of world standards, no music, no cinema, no art. Only our gold, and our sportsmen, attract notice in the outside world. We produce excellent cricket teams, rugby teams, and world champion swimmers. If the world won't let us compete, then we become almost complete outcasts in everything." Added Progressive Party Leader Colin Eglin, a sports fanatic himself: "South Africans love to be able to say, 'You can vote against us at the U.N., boy, but Gary Player still brings home the check from Augusta [the site of the Masters golf tournament]!' "

England's cancellation of the Springbok cricket tour and the expulsion of South Africa from the International Olympics Committee in the spring of 1970 came as a stinging blow to South African morale. It followed the barring of South Africa from the Olympic Games of 1964 and 1968 because of South Africa's discrimination in sports at home. South Africans were also barred from international championship competition in boxing, basketball, soccer, fencing, volleyball, judo, weightlifting, and Ping-Pong.

These pressures produced a series of concessions on sport from the government and a significant outcry at home for more lifting of apartheid's restrictions on the playing field. It is pointless to list here the zigzag changes the government has gone through on sport in recent years; not only are they too vague, but they will assuredly be changed before this is in print. What it seemed to boil down to in 1971 — and not even South Africans could be sure because of the nebulous government approach — was that nonwhite athletes from abroad would be allowed to compete in South Africa against white South Africans (just as nonwhite foreign presidents could have lunch with John Vorster) in international competition. South Africa would send multiracial teams abroad, but the trials would be separate. The irreducible commitment of the government seemed to be that white South Africans and black South Africans would not compete against each other in South Africa. In a vague statement in May 1971, Vorster hinted that even that might be bent if there were signs that it would significantly affect the Olympics Committee's decisions on South Africa. Subsequently, government officials held out the ludicrous possibility that interracial trials might be approved if no spectators were allowed.

The move to enforce a sports boycott against the South Africans was effective in producing at least a suggestion of concession in apartheid not only because South Africans are sports-conscious, but also because they are generally "good sports." People who do not give a second thought to depriving blacks of jobs do feel guilty about depriving the nonwhite of a chance to compete in sports and to have the use of good sports facilities. Moreover, sport is a nonessential area. A country that says it wants nothing to do with South Africa in sports is not threatening South Africa's survival. Although South African spokesmen portray decisions of the International Olympics Committee as having been put over by the Afro-Asian and Communist blocs, this sounds even more risible than their other fantasies about the international campaign against South Africa. It is not, in short, an issue around which the government can circle the ox wagons and get everyone to jump inside the laager.

There have also been attempts at cultural and intellectual boycotts of South Africa by artists who have refused to have their works performed, distributed, or displayed in South Africa, or who have refused to go there to perform. The decision to refuse to perform in front of a segregated audience (especially an audience consisting of the segregator, rather than the segregatee) is a highly personal one, and probably a correct one. But in other respects, the cultural boycott is the only type of pressure on South Africa that is clearly counterproductive. For a playwright to refuse to have his works performed in South Africa is not going to hurt the Afrikaner policeman or apartheid bureaucrat in the slightest. It does make life a little harder on the already isolated white liberal. And it does keep new ideas out of circulation in a society that desperately needs new ideas. There is little point in outsiders doing the censor's work for him.

DISENGAGE OR COMMUNICATE?

A complete withdrawal of American investment in South Africa and the breaking of diplomatic contact would not produce a voluntary relinquishing of power by the white government to the nonwhite majority. My judgment is that there is no course of action, short of armed intervention, available to outsiders that could produce this fundamental change. Thus there seem to me to be only three premises upon which one can rest an argument for the breaking of all American contact with South Africa.

The most tenable of these is a moral argument based on the impact of disengagement on America instead of South Africa. The case is that the system in South Africa is so evil that the United States should not be contaminated by having any dealings with it. The involvement exacerbates our own racial tensions, and disengagement would be a clear statement to our black population of America's private and official commitment to ending racial discrimination.

There is also a cynical premise. Rarely stated, it should nonetheless be recognized. It is simply that American disengagement would create economic disruption in South Africa. Since nonwhites are the most economically vulnerable part of the working force, this would add greatly to their frustrations and increase the pressures on them to revolt. This is not an argument that can be made very convincingly by one outside the country who will not be in South Africa to accept the consequences of that revolt.

Perhaps the most pragmatic use of the argument for total disengagement is as an ultimate pressure, which actually aims at producing changes and improvements within the existing system. Just as the Black Panthers made the NAACP more acceptable to the white American Establishment, demands for total withdrawal may make "moderate" proposals more acceptable. This argument only works, however, if disengagement carries some credibility of its own. The present attitude and actions of American business and more importantly the American government in South Africa greatly reduces such credibility.

It is important to recognize that South Africans have shown themselves to be highly sensitive to selective pressures that do not threaten the existing power structure. Sports is the best example of this. Another revealing reaction is South Africa's continuing testiness about the American government's refusal in 1967 to allow an aircraft carrier to call at a South African port after Pretoria made it clear that black American sailors aboard these ships would be discriminated against. This subject is often brought up by South Africans when they meet visiting Americans and reportedly was a major concern of Information Minister Mulder when he visited Washington in 1971.

A campaign of selective economic pressures is likely to be more effective than general calls for withdrawal. Companies like Polaroid, which have room to maneuver in their business dealings with South Africa, are more likely to respond to boycott campaigns. Against the larger companies, which are not going to withdraw anyway, campaigns organized on specific themes, such as equal pay for equal work, recognition of African unions, and shared facilities where these are not specifically outlawed, have a greater potential for embarrassing and thus getting concessions than demands for complete withdrawal.

The greatest unused potential for American pressure currently lies within the labor movement. Although the racial aspects of the South African situation cannot be expected to attract a great amount of support within the generally conservative American labor movement, the crushing restrictions of South African law on collective bargaining might — especially in view of American business involvement there. This is an area activists in the United States must increasingly focus on if they are to be effective in exerting pressures.

"Communication" is in itself not a bad policy, but it is currently being used by the American government to reinforce, not change, the existing system in South Africa. The results of communication over the past two years, in terms of strengthening white attitudes and confidence in the ability of the whites to dominate the black majority, have been worse than the results of breaking off all contact would have been, in my view. Our government hardly communicates its concern about majority rule by bending its arms embargo to allow the sale of aircraft that will clearly be used against the black population in the event of an uprising or by giving all-white official receptions. Current American policy toward South Africa as it is practiced is at best naive, at worst cynical.

What can America do about South Africa? Even if a new administration, more sympathetic to African aspirations than the Nixon regime, were to come to power in the United States in the near future, it would have a difficult time in implementing policies that would bring fundamental political advancement for the black majorities of Southern Africa. The post-Vietnam period is not likely to be one in which the United States will be prepared to embark on physical intervention in South Africa. (Indeed, such direct intervention would probably prove to be unwise from all viewpoints. With whatever material support they can gather from whatever sources willing to supply it, the Africans of Portuguese Africa, Rhodesia, and South Africa must accomplish their own liberation if it is to have any value.)

Short of an invasion, a selective mixture of communication and disengagement is perhaps the most effective policy. Americans in official and private life should establish and maintain communication with those South Africans who clearly show that their ideals are at least vaguely compatible with America's commitment to ending racial hatred and discrimination. The State Department's arrangement of a tour for Chief Buthelezi is one of the few positive actions taken by the Nixon administration on Southern Africa and should be repeated for those Africans willing to speak out. There are a number of South African clergymen, academics, journalists, opposition politicians, and others whose dissent should be encouraged from outside.

Potential steps in a limited disengagement policy have been listed by a number of persons and organizations and are well known to policy-makers within the Nixon administration, who do not seem disposed toward them. They include ending the sugar quota, extending the technical investment curbs enacted against South West Africa to South Africa, and the assigning of black Americans as Foreign Service officers to South Africa and black scientists or administrators to the NASA tracking station. (South African officials have publicly stated that American blacks will not be allowed to work at the tracking station. As a number of persons have pointed out, either this insult to America's own stated policy on racism should be removed, or the tracking station should be.) The United States should stop training South African scientists. As long as we are dealing in what should be instead of what is likely to be, the idea of a special tax on American profits made in South Africa to fund projects to help minority groups in the United States (with a special point of including Indians) should be mentioned.

The most important task confronting official policy-makers is to make a much clearer analysis of the forces at work in Southern Africa today. That analysis must be more honest than anything that has yet been produced in the executive branch of the American government. The real choice that remains in Southern Africa is white power or black power, as I have already stated. To opt for the fiction of eventual multiracialism, and to base a policy on that, as the State Department says we should, is to choose to have no policy at all and very little influence on what is going to happen in Southern Africa. Having a nonpolicy does strengthen white power, since the whites are the stronger force and benefit the most from nonintervention by outside powers. But it does so in a way that gains the U.S. little influence with those we are actually backing and helps perpetuate the present situation, which we so eloquently abhor.

A coherent American policy toward South Africa can flow from the decision that white power will survive in South Africa over the next half-century at least and that American interests lie in saying so. An open statement of this premise would have more advantages than merely supplying a refreshing contrast in candor to the present hypocritical stance of trying to deny that we are not involved in South Africa on the side of the whites. It would also make it clear that the best the United States or any other country can hope to help achieve is a coexistence of the races based on what the whites feel they must give up. This implies backing the grand design of apartheid and the creation of independent institutions that may help compensate Africans for their inability to exert influence through a central, unified government. To be more specific, and to use Buthelezi as the example again, the Zulu chief's suggestion in early 1972 that he wanted foreign aid should have been immediately and publicly noted by the American government, without waiting for Pretoria to say whether it was all right for the Bantustans to ask for foreign aid. Buthelezi is badly in need of reinforcing pressure, and America's role under a white-power-indefinitely analysis should be to supply it where it will help separate the races. This policy also necessarily implies that America will seek ways to exert pressure on the land question, for peaceful coexistence will be possible only if there is something approaching equity in the division of land and resources and the Bantustans are given a chance to work economically. The question of conferring "foreign" citizenship on South Africa's Bantu, and the new rights that should evolve from this, is another area in which America should seek to press the whites.

Would such a policy constitute unwarranted interference in the internal affairs of South Africa? Perhaps. But the United States is already interfering massively in South Africa. I am suggesting that we change our stated goals and choose methods more suited to bring those goals about. Only those comfortable with hypocrisy can really support continuing our present policies. Beyond that, if the peaceful actions I have suggested do interfere with South Africa, I do not think them unwarranted. Are we to reject being a "pitiful helpless giant" in other parts of the world and to accept it in Southern Africa? Is the question of trying to prevent a racial war that could seriously worsen race relations in America and endanger $1 billion worth of American investment really one we want to ignore? Finally, do we believe that men are in fact created equal and that we have some obligation to act on that belief? Admittedly, there are a number of places in the world where men are not treated equally, according to different political, religious, economic, and social criteria. The most obvious instance of inequality enforced by law happens today to be in South Africa. If we are not to begin there, it is clear that we will never become involved in any real attempt in any part of the world to foster significant social change based on the equality of man. We will be saying that this must be done by others, if it is to be done at all. The implications of that view on America's role in world affairs in the future should be sobering enough to make it easy to answer whether what happens in South Africa matters to our interests.

A key to the success of this policy would be convincing the Soviet Union that its interests also lie in identifying with this view, as the Russians become increasingly conservative and a white power. A more unified approach toward Southern Africa by the United States and the Soviet Union should be one of the first aims of American policy-makers in attempts to arrange a lasting détente. Southern Africa is an area where Soviet and American foreign policy aims have not in the past been in great conflict; if a more unified approach toward seeking peaceful concessions from the white minority there cannot be agreed upon, is there any real hope that American and Soviet aims can be reconciled in any part of the world?

The policy analysis that African nationalism will regain its strength and complete the move to self-determination on the African continent provides easier policy choices. Simply, we should then support the guerrilla movements in Southern Africa, and in Portuguese Guinea, at least to the extent that they do represent genuine nationalist aspirations within their own countries. Certainly PAIGC already qualifies on that criterion, and MPLA and Frelimo are capable of doing so. The Rhodesian and South African situations are more complex, and at the moment the real voices of African nationalism, at least as they can be heard by outsiders, are inside the country, still working in essentially peaceful ways for change or already locked up in prison. For the time being at least, the United States could attempt to strengthen financially organizations that might provide bases for African national sentiment. In Rhodesia, African trade unions would be an ideal channel. They should also be encouraged in South Africa. Two points are important, however. The help will probably have to be provided covertly, in view of the likely reaction of the white governments; we should have the ability to do this. Secondly, it would be self-defeating to attempt to do this for the purpose of co-opting the groups. This mistake has already been made elsewhere in Africa, largely by C.I.A. outlets. In any event, we should begin preparing for the time when effective nationalist groups do develop in Southern Africa. The fact that this will be a lengthy process should not be viewed with despair. As white South Africans say repeatedly, the African majority is not yet unified enough to run the complex South African country. A protracted struggle would help solve that problem. We could begin our support immediately, however, by dropping the present policy assertion that violence will not solve the problems of Southern Africa. Why should Southern Africa be different from the rest of the world? If violence does not solve problems, there should have been no American Revolution, no point in going to war against Hitler, no birth of Bangladesh. And why are we in Vietnam? Violence in each of these cases did solve problems. They also created new ones, as an uprising in South Africa would do.

I am not suggesting that it should be American policy to encourage such uprisings; they will undoubtedly be costly to the Africans and only they can decide if the price in blood they will have to pay is to be worth the likely outcome. I am suggesting that we immediately abandon the presumptuous stance of advising blacks that the price cannot be worth it. Where and when the genuine frustrations and aspirations of the people have brought into being organizations that do represent the desire for change, we support them with money, weapons, and military training — if, to repeat, it is the American analysis that black power is the probable outcome in Southern Africa. Again, establishing an understanding with the Soviet Union would be essential, so that the ideological competition between nationalist groups can be minimized. Identifying with the nonwhite groups on this issue could also open up the possibility of seeking cooperation with China in Southern Africa. It is, in fact, the only course of action in Africa that would further the opportunities for a triangular superpower détente.

Since this book is essentially descriptive instead of prescriptive, I will not argue which of the two alternatives should be chosen, but will only argue the necessity for the choice's being made now. The reader who has surmised that intellectually I see the white-power option as the only realistic one for South Africa, while emotionally feeling that we should do whatever we can to help bring about a chance for the black majority to gain control over itself — by violence if that is the only way in which that objective can be achieved — is correct. It is an agonizing ambivalence for which I do not apologize.

Conclusion

After the Fall

THERE IS NO SATISFACTORY WAY to conclude a book on Southern Africa, for there are no apparent and truly satisfactory conclusions for the immense and tragic problems of the region. The violence, injustice, and deprivation of the past and present seem certain to continue into the future, whether it is whites or blacks who are in control of the southern part of the continent. Like the characters of Sartre's *No Exit*, the different tribes and nations of Southern Africa seem condemned to torture each other without hope of cessation. Only the positions of perpetrator and victim are mutable. Those of us who would make judgments about the future of South Africa can do little more than state a preference for the group we wish to see harmed, and for whose profit.

This account has attempted to catalogue and assess the failures of the past decade that have made such a conclusion, however unpalatable, inescapable. The failures are those of English liberalism transferred to the Southern Hemisphere, African nationalism, Portuguese multiracialism, economic forces, and others. They have not substantially affected the successful white counterrevolution of the 1960s that continues today. Although there may be dramatic change in Rhodesia and Portuguese Africa, I do not see much hope that in the coming decade there will be a change in the fundamental condition of South Africa, which remains the key to the region. That condition is accurately described as white tyranny — complete white control, exercised as harshly as the whites feel is necessary to maintain their economic advantage and their false notion of racial superiority.

The two alternative courses of development that are most frequently proposed are the hope that multiracialism will be resurrected from the ashes of apartheid or that black revolution will succeed. As the reader will have gathered by now, I do not see either as a likely prospect for South Africa in the 1970s, and perhaps not in this century.

Multiracialism, a cooperative sharing of political power and economic benefits among races in a single polity, was stillborn in South Africa. The whites never wanted it, and the blacks no longer do, if they ever did. Chief A. J. Luthuli's 1958 assertion that Africans aspire to "a truly multiracial country" where "democracy should by the nature of things be colorblind" is an echo from the past. The voice of the future comes from Africans like Steven Biko, a young medical student. As leader of the South African Students Organization, an all-black student group that had been recently set up, Biko delivered a remarkable speech to an educational workshop arranged by the Abe Bailey Institute in Cape Town in January 1971. His cool and analytical view of young black South Africa's response to the various forms of white domination is worth considering in some detail for its implications on the coming two decades:

"The major mistake the Black world ever made was to assume that whoever opposed apartheid was an ally. For a long time the Black world has only been looking at the governing party and not so much at the whole power structure as the object of their rage.

". . . It never occurred to the liberals that the integration they insisted upon as an effective way of opposing apartheid was impossible to achieve in South Africa . . . The myth of integration as propounded under the banner of the liberal ideology must be cracked and killed because it makes people believe that something is being done when in actual fact the artificial integrated circles are a soporific on the Blacks and provide a satisfaction for the guilt stricken Whites . . . who possess the natural passport to the exclusive pool of White privileges . . ."

Speaking of whites in general, Biko added: "Not only did they kick the Native but they also told him how to respond to the kick.

For a long time the Native has been listening with patience to the advice he has been receiving on how best to respond to the kick. With painful slowness he is now beginning to show signs that it is his right and duty to respond to the· kick *in the way he sees fit*." [Biko's emphasis]

". . . Over the years we have attained moral superiority over the White man; we shall watch as Time destroys his paper castles and know that all these little pranks were but the frantic attempts of frightened little people to convince each other that they can control the minds and bodies of indigenous peoples of Africa indefinitely."

White liberals in the National Union of South African Students (NUSAS), the multiracial group from which the Africans had split, reacted much as the white liberals did in the United States at the beginning of the black power movement. They were hurt, but they were unable to offer any convincing alternative. As Biko and others insisted, the growing black "awareness" and determination to go it alone did not represent a victory for apartheid. It reflected more the failure of liberal white attitudes, based largely on the assumption that class differences would continue to protect white privilege (except for the unfortunate poor whites, who would have to be sacrificed in the name of multiracialism). With some notable exceptions, the non-Communist "left" in South Africa has not advocated the elimination of white privilege, but merely a change in its form and a reduction of its worst excesses. The English-speakers of South Africa and Rhodesia, and the Portuguese, have stood for a permissive multiracialism. Blacks who can emerge from tribal society should be left unfettered. But in societies where the gap between the advanced minority and the majority are as great as they are in Southern Africa, that again constitutes having no policy. It is a wish, an idea, a good intention that has no substantial effect. Without courageous national leadership, it falls easily before the force of organized prejudice, for liberal attitudes are more concerned with the preservation of class structures than with race. For many self-described liberals, the racial issue is a blind, one on which they will make concessions, while to the others it is a real and decisive human issue. This has been shown to be the case not only in South Africa, but also in the Northern United States in recent years.

The stirrings of black awareness, and the skillful use of apartheid's institutions by Buthelezi and others, should not be taken as heralding the long-delayed black revolution, however. All available evidence indicates that the threat of revolution is not a realistic prospect, for lack of method, not for lack of cause. There will probably be outbreaks of mass racial violence over the next decade in South Africa, but they will resemble America's Watts and Newark in scale and result — stacks of black bodies in a charred ghetto inhabited by blacks, white policemen blowing smoke from their gun barrels, and a few token dead whites. It is reasonable to assume that without major outside intervention, which would probably have to come in the course of a general war between the superpowers, the whites will continue their control of the country's technology and armaments and will increase that control at least in proportion to the population increases that are supposed to spell doom for the whites by the end of the century. More hungry Africans may give increased reason to riot, but will not necessarily increase their effectiveness in fighting the whites.[1]

Despite this, African violence to come should not be unquestioningly viewed as "counterproductive," to use the American bureaucratic cover word for the argument for maintaining the status quo. Violent manifestations of frustration and despair will probably be necessary to force any significant concessions out of the white rulers, who now operate on the assumption of African apathy and acquiescence. Only if there is credibility to the threat that they run the risk of losing everything will the poor whites be convinced to yield anything.

This is not a call to the barricades. Only a moral coward would sit outside and urge the Africans to get themselves killed in a battle that they can win only if they are committed to fight to the last

---

[1] See *Politics and Law in South Africa*, by Julius Lewin (Monthly Review Press, 1963) for an application to South Africa of Crane Brinton's theory on prerevolutionary conditions, as outlined in Brinton's *The Anatomy of Revolution*. The application seems to me to be valid.

man. That is a decision they have to make. But if it is made, only a charlatan will deplore it. Violence has been under way some time in South Africa. It is the white government that is currently perpetrating it. The government's policies make counterviolence justifiable *if it is the only way to alter the status quo.* The uncertainty of the consequences of such counterviolence is a terrible consideration, but the continuation of what is happening in South Africa today cannot be justified on that basis.

Violent upheaval can possibly still be avoided, if white South African leaders will grasp the opportunity. To suggest that the opportunity exists does not mean that I assume they will.

There have always been a great number of solutions for South Africa. Nearly everyone seems to have one. What is impossible to get people to agree on is a definition of The Problem. For the Afrikaner, it is preserving his identity, his sense of mission, his grasp on power and his institutions. He does not want to be done unto as he has done. For the English-speaker, The Problem is more one of preserving material welfare and the establishing of guarantees that black advancement will not be at his expense. For Coloreds, The Problem is simply how to be treated fairly by either whites or blacks, since they will always be an in-between group. For the blacks, The Problem is a three-tiered one: first, to break the present cruelties and humiliation inflicted upon them; second, to achieve majority political control; third, to adopt a unified approach on the exercise of political control once it has been achieved.

The failures of the two grand theoretical solutions — multiracialism and apartheid — have caused many thinking white and black South Africans to begin to examine the prospects for some form of racial coexistence, achieved through a restructuring of South African society that would take into consideration a compromise of all these goals. Compromise will undoubtedly mean a continuation of much of the worst injustice in the present system, but in the absence of the means of revolution, it may be necessary for the black majority. The search for compromise will be a difficult one, and the following discussion of some seminal ideas is intended more to indicate particularly troublesome areas rather than to draw a blueprint that will resolve the problems of Southern Africa, problems that can be resolved only by the peoples of Southern Africa, white, brown, and black.[2]

If it were turned into a sincere program for change, grand apartheid could offer some impetus for such a compromise by allowing the creation of independent black governmental bodies that could then seek greater international involvement in the problems of the region. It would also unfreeze the present situation by promoting the redrawing of boundaries in the region (and perhaps even in other areas of sub-Sahara Africa, which are also bedeviled by the colonial juxtaposition of hostile nations and tribes inside artificial borders). As a theoretical exercise, at least, the idea of a federation of South African states, in which there would be a system of checks and balances operating to guarantee rights for each of the ethnic groups in the different federated states, has a certain validity.

There should be no more than four or five governmental bodies formed on the basis of ethnic identification. The four million whites would constitute one, the four million Zulu another, the Xhosa a third, other African tribes one or two, and the Coloreds one. Each would have its own political parties and would elect leaders to deal from a position of equality with the white leaders. Treatment of Africans and Coloreds by white employers and other whites would be regulated by agreements between the units, judicable in federal courts.

For this arrangement to be a starting point in the search for a more equitable compromise, however, there must be present two elements that are currently absent in the formulation of apartheid. As long as they continue to be absent, the world can be certain there will be no meaningful peaceful change in South Africa.

The first is that the arrangement of South Africans into tribal

[2] The tribal system seems to be inimical to the process of reaching compromise outside of small, well-defined groups. This is seen not only in South Africa, where Afrikaner and Zulu have never been able to compromise with other groups, but also across the rest of the continent. It is one of Africa's gravest difficulties.

and racial groups must be acknowledged to be a transitional phase, to be followed by a regrouping of the African population into larger governing units not based on tribalism. The white government must acknowledge that tribalism is a dying political force in Africa. It must concentrate the help it has promised the black states to achieve the eradication of tribalism. It must stop trying to turn the clock back for its own advantage and must begin moving with the currents of history. Such a change in the public position of the South African government in this decade would be a key indication that there is still some hope of avoiding violent confrontation. Without it, apartheid remains a transparent confidence trick.

Secondly, the black South African federation units have to be able to bargain with the whites on the shape of what will follow the racial and tribal federation. The only bargaining power they can have is their labor, which they must be able to withhold and yet survive. In the transitional phase, the black states will in fact resemble large labor unions. For this, the units will have to be economically self-sufficient in the sense that they will not have to depend on white South African industry and commerce to survive.

The South African government can contribute to this. It should implement the recommendations made on agricultural development by the Tomlinson Commission a generation ago. The 87-13 division of the land must be altered. Until it is, the concept of Africans being given "their" rights outside a central political unit will remain a hoax. The land must be divided on a basis other than the distorted and deceitful version of the ownership of land used by the present government. Finally, the white South Africans should let the Free Enterprise system they so warmly endorse function in their country. They should test the myth that Africans are in fact so different, so inferior, that they cannot do white man's work. If this is so, there is no need for apartheid's economic restrictions. If it is not so, there is no possible justification for them. In coordination with this, the government should expand its social welfare plans for whites who will be affected, to reduce the backlash this will cause, and make more equal educational opportunities for all races.

Equally important would be the role of foreign governments. Providing enough economic aid to the federation's black states to make sure they would be in a position to bargain should be an area of joint effort by the United States and the Soviet Union. It should be a priority program for both, and for Europe, especially if, as I assume, the South African white government continues to refuse to take seriously the prospect of dividing up South Africa.

These actions would help end the dangerous practice of the Vorster government of keeping a double set of books. While assuring the white electorate with a big wink that the promises of change and "freedoms" for Africans mean nothing, the government also tries to convince trade and investment partners that it can be shown to be working for justice, if it is just given a little time. Vorster is lying to one or the other, or perhaps both simultaneously. If he is interested in partitioning South Africa into viable units, then he should go at it in a serious manner, not as a game. And he should be prepared for major international involvement in working out an agreement between black and white that would be a compromise. Perhaps the only way majority rule could ever be achieved peacefully in a unified South Africa would be through an arrangement guaranteed by the major powers, including the Soviet Union, who would be bound to intervene to protect carefully drawn and equitable guarantees for the white minority that would come into effect after majority political rule.

In the present context of regional and world politics, these suggestions sound utopian, although they fall far short of complete justice. I would be the first to admit that. It is easy to draw up political structures and alternatives in a vacuum, difficult to make them work when they collide with the human realities. The most glaring weakness in the ideas that I have been setting down is the simple fact that they have little if anything to offer the white working class, which will be required to make most of the sacrifices. Unless this class becomes convinced that sacrifices will enable it to head off a potentially successful uprising or an invasion, there is no reason at all for it to support such changes. Only moral pressure from strong leadership could prod the whites into changes. There are men capable of doing this in South Africa, but it is inconceivable to me that any of them can rise through the stultifying machine that now runs the country.

Those expecting grand turning points in South Africa in the next decade, then, are likely to be disappointed. Change will be incremental and will not mean any fundamental alteration of harsh white domination. Of the trends discussed in this book, four are likely to bring some amelioration in the condition of the nonwhite majority. They are the growth of class structure in the Afrikaner society, the Verligtes' moral arguments against petty apartheid and their discomfort at the plight of the Coloreds, the rejection by young, urban Afrikaners of the most extreme expressions of racism, as indicated by the 1970 campaign, and the increasing use of the institutions of apartheid by blacks and Coloreds for their own ends. But none of these forces is likely to bring more than marginal change to the racist status quo.

Nor is the movement of young whites out of South Africa's colleges onto the beginning rungs of the ladder of the establishment. There does not seem to be any significant generation gap in white South Africa today. Several days spent on the campus of Stellenbosch University indicated to me that the laager mentality has not been significantly weakened in young Afrikaners. Afrikanerdom's brightest and more liberal young people attend Stellenbosch, located in the Cape Province. "No, we know that we cannot afford to be irresponsible," a pretty young coed told me when I asked if there was any chance of student unrest in South Africa. "If we want to continue to survive, we must have discipline and authority." She said it was pointless to fight English-speakers now, but indicated she did not trust them. "They are part of the permissive society." Another Afrikaner graduate student, in a representative comment, said; "Nobody has been able to formulate a realistic alternative that would protect us from black domination. We have grown up while Africa to the north was in chaos, and we don't want it here."

The English-speakers' feeling of powerlessness in the country was mirrored at Witwatersrand University in Johannesburg. "Yes, I'm leaving the country," Ken Costa, president of the student council in 1970, told me. "They [the Afrikaners] wear you down. There is no point in staying anymore." Lee Hayden, a journalism major, spoke of the two worlds she was trapped between: "I talk to Afrikaners and they say they want to get rid of all the black men, however they have to do it. And I talk to the few Africans I know as friends, and they say they've given up, all they want to do is cut the white man's head off and throw it back into the ocean. God, do I feel trapped."

Perhaps the best hope for change in the attitude and values among the young whites lies in the still uncertain impact of science and technology on South Africa in the coming decade. The often unforeseen social and political side effects of technical improvements in transportation, communications, medicine, and other areas can be enormous, as many nations have begun to realize. Automobiles in America shift political power from city to suburb, television makes new demands on political candidates, and I think it will soon be widely accepted that the birth-control pill has reshaped political as well as social attitudes in America and Europe within the last decade, especially among the young. The even more fundamental (and less fortunate) changes the computer will make in our political and social choices are still not clear. The possibilities, of course, are enormous.

South Africa lags at least five to ten years behind America and Europe in widespread acceptance of many of these technological changes. It is still conceivable that the country will not prove to be immune from the apparently deep and sudden shifts in the attitudes of the young seen elsewhere in the past ten years. But the South African government does better than most in controlling such influences. The Vorster regime was ridiculed for dragging its feet on establishing a national television network, but I think it is one of the few governments in the world that has given the effect of television its due. But it must be remembered that the increase in technology that brings the possibility of these changes in the white population also adds to its store of repressive strength. Like most forces at work in South Africa, this is a double-edged one.

My presentiment that white tyranny will continue unabated in the foreseeable future is a frustrating one, representing in some ways a surrender to the notion that life is, after all, absurd. I would feel much easier if I could report that there are signs in South Africa that history has an inevitable morality, that there will be justice in a society that almost completely lacks it today, that man is a rational and moral being, or, at the very least, that there will be retribution for his not being so. Those ideas are refuted daily in South Africa, as well as elsewhere.

For all of its mighty flaws, however, South Africa retains mighty potential for proving prophets of doom wrong. It is a magnificent land that is worth the unending struggle to master it. There is a vibrancy of life, and therefore a demand for hope, for a coming to terms with the absurdity of existence. The result is a strange, attractive mixture of exuberance and melancholy in the people who live in this Elysian setting, where beauty and betrayal set off each other in dazzling contrast. South Africa is Eden after the fall but before the expulsion. As man came to know the terrible joys of his own humanity, the full limits and determinate nature of earthly existence only through the fall, perhaps South Africa can come to know its full human potential only by passing through the dark night that currently envelops it. Like Camus, we must leave Sisyphus at the bottom of the mountain, where hope seems most futile but also most necessary. Perhaps in watching the South Africans shoulder their heavy burden of racial conflict we will all learn something. If not, that burden will surely crush first them, and then us.

Selected Bibliography

Index

Selected Bibliography

THIS LIST is intended to serve as a guide to readers interested in more detail on Southern Africa and to indicate some of my principal sources.

Except where otherwise indicated in the text and below, statistics largely come from these sources: South African government publications and those of the South Africa Foundation; *A Survey of Race Relations in South Africa,* 1968, 1969, and 1970, published by the South African Institute of Race Relations and compiled by the indefatigable Muriel Horrell; and the *State of South Africa Year Book,* 1968 and 1969.

Two books helped shape major portions of my work. They are C. W. de Kiewiet's *A History of South Africa, Social and Economic* (Oxford University Press, London, 1957) and *Politics and Law in South Africa,* by Julius Lewin (Monthly Review Press, New York, 1963).

The reader will also want to consult two excellent books by historian Leo Marquard, *The Story of South Africa* (Faber and Faber, London, 1966) and *The Peoples and Policies of South Africa* (Oxford University Press, London, 1969, Fourth Edition). South Africa in the early part of the 1960s is nimbly depicted in E. J. Kahn Jr.'s *The Separated People* (Norton & Company, New York, 1968). Allen Drury tackles the same period in a different style in *A Very Strange Society* (Trident, New York, 1967).

One of the most informative and well-written accounts of early African history in the region is *The Zulu Aftermath: A Nineteenth-Century Revolution in Bantu Africa* by J. D. Omer-Cooper (Northwestern University Press, Evanston, 1966).

Two independent organizations in Johannesburg have in recent years produced a wealth of probing, knowledgeable publications and research papers that are of great value to anyone interested in observing how the South African society actually works. The South African Institute of

Race Relations has long been established as an objective and reliable source of detailed information. Especially noteworthy is Muriel Horrell's *Legislation and Race Relations: A Summary of the Main South African Laws Which Affect Race Relationships,* and a number of other works by Miss Horrell.

More recently, the Christian Institute and the South African Council of Churches have sponsored the Study Project on Christianity in Apartheid Society (SPRO-CAS), directed by Peter Randall. The project gathered a number of useful research papers from a cross section of notable South Africans and at the time of this writing is publishing collections of them as Occasional Publications. The first of these was *Anatomy of Apartheid* (1970) and the series had reached Number 5, *Education beyond Apartheid,* by mid-1971.

Chapter 1

The Afrikaners, by John Fisher (International Publications Service, New York, 1971) is a sympathetic historical account of the forming of the Afrikaner nation. The Voortrekker Monument guide is published by The Board of Control of the Voortrekker Monument, Pretoria. My debt to the inventive research of Professor J. L. Sadie on the economic rise of the Afrikaner is clearly indicated in the text. I also found useful "The Urban Trek: Some Comparisons of Mobility in American and South African History," a research paper prepared for the African Studies Association of New York City by Richard B. Ford, Assistant Professor of History at Clark University; and Joseph Lelyveld's article, "The Afrikaner Feels Lonely . . . ," February 6, 1966, the *New York Times Magazine. Afrikaner and African Nationalism,* by Edwin S. Munger (Oxford University Press, London, 1967), presents an analytical approach.

Chapter 2

Popular historical accounts on Britain in Africa include Anthony Nutting's *Scramble for Africa* (Dutton, New York, 1971) and *The African Dream* by Brian Gardner (G. P. Putnam's Sons, New York, 1970). *The Churches and Race Relations in South Africa,* by Lesley Cawood (South African Institute of Race Relations, Johannesburg, 1964) was consulted for some statistics.

Chapter 3

Statistics on urban Africans can be obtained from the Johannesburg City Council and Institute of Race Relations publications. The flavor of life as it was in African townships before Soweto comes best from *Drum, the Newspaper That Won the Heart of Africa* by Anthony Sampson (Houghton Mifflin, Boston, 1957) and of course from Alan Paton's *Cry the Beloved Country* (Scribners, New York, 1948). For the modern flavor, see *Sounds of a Cowhide Drum,* by Oswald Joseph Mtshali (The Third Press, New York, 1971). *Black Anger,* by Wulf Sachs (Grove Press, New York, 1969) is a powerful work, full of insight.

Chapter 4

Little research has been published on the Coloreds as a group. Fatima Meer's *Portrait of South African Indians* (Lawrence Verry, Mystic, Conn., 1969) deserves special note.

Chapter 5

Mary Benson, *The African Patriots* (Encyclopaedia Britannica, Inc., Chicago, 1964) provides valuable detail on the origins of African political parties. *Time Longer Than Rope,* by Edward Roux (University of Wisconsin Press, Madison, 1964) is also good on African political parties and the history of the South African Communist Party.

Chapter 6

For differing views on apartheid, see *Why Apartheid?*, a speech by Hilgard Muller published by the Department of Information, Pretoria; and *The Price of Apartheid,* published by the South African Institute of Race Relations.

Chapter 7

The African Reserves of South Africa by Muriel Horrell (South African Institute of Race Relations, Johannesburg, 1969) is a thorough, unofficial, and reliable source on the reserves. *The Discarded People* by Cosmas Desmond, O.F.M. (Christian Institute of South Africa, Johannesburg, 1970) provides excellent descriptions of resettlement camps.

Chapter 8

The two outstanding books in the field are *The South African Economy*, by D. Hobart Houghton (Oxford University Press, London, 1967) and *The Political Economy of South Africa*, by Ralph Horowitz (Praeger, New York, 1967). Horowitz's book is more detailed and analytical, and is perhaps the most important book to be published on South Africa in the past decade. Houghton's work gives a highly readable overview of the South African economic scene.

Annual Reports for the Chamber of Mines of South Africa, 1968, 1969, and 1970, and several other Chamber promotional publications, were of great use, as was John Sackur's extensive analysis of the South African economic boom published in *The Times* of London, April 26, 1971. Annual surveys on South Africa published by *The Financial Times* of London for 1969, 1970, and 1971 were also consulted.

For a view opposite to mine, see *The Green Bay Tree*, a survey published June 29, 1968, by *The Economist* magazine of London.

Chapter 9

Two recent books that compliment each other nicely are *Rhodesia* by Frank Clements (Praeger, New York, 1969) and *Rhodesia: The Road to Rebellion* by James Barber (Oxford University Press, London and New York, 1967). Barber's view is more comprehensive and detailed, Clements' more analytical of the white population.

Chapter 10 and Chapter 11

James Duffy's *Portugal in Africa* (Penguin African Library, Baltimore, 1963) remains the best available work on this subject. *Portuguese Africa, A Handbook*, edited by D. M. Abshire and M. A. Samuels (Praeger, New York, 1969) provides more recent detail. Of special note is John Marcum's *The Angolan Revolution: Anatomy of an Explosion: 1950–62* (MIT Press, Cambridge, 1969). *The Liberation of Guinea* by Basil Davidson and *The Struggle for Mozambique* by Eduardo Mondlane, both published in 1969 by Penguin Books, London, are also useful. *The Third World* by

Franco Nogueira (International Publishers Service, New York, 1968) provides another view.

Chapter 12

J. D. Omer-Cooper's *The Zulu Aftermath* is especially good on the fragmentation of tribes that produced the three enclave states. *Africa Today*, Vol. 18, No. 2, April 1971, contains two articles of note, Henry Chipembere on Malawi and Richard F. Weisfelder on Lesotho. Recent political history of the B-L-S countries is best covered in Jack Halpern's *South Africa's Hostages* (Penguin African Library, Baltimore, 1965). For contrasting views on the outward policy, see *Vision of the Seventies*, an address by Piet Cillié, reprinted by the South African Department of Information; and *Africa and South Africa*, by Robert Molteno, a pamphlet published by The Africa Bureau, London, 1971. Between these two is Allister Sparks' speech on Lesotho, Botswana, and Swaziland, distributed by the South African Institute of Race Relations, January 1967. *Malawi: A Political and Economic History* by John G. Pike (Library of African Affairs, Praeger, New York, 1969) covers that country, and the Malawi official handbook, published annually by the government, is an unusually informative and well-done volume.

Chapter 13

The following cover portions of the subject of this chapter: *The Great Powers & Africa* by Waldemar A. Nielsen (Praeger, New York, 1969); *Against the World* by Douglas Brown (Doubleday & Co., Inc., Garden City, N. Y., 1968); *S. Africa, Crisis for the West*, by Colin and Margaret Legum (Pall Mall Press, London, 1964); *The White Tribes of Africa* by Richard West (Macmillan, New York, 1965); *Southern Africa and the United States*, William A. Hance, editor (Columbia University Press, New York and London, 1968); *Economic Priorities Report*, Vol. 1, No. 5, October–November 1970, Washington, D.C.; *Africa Today*, January 1966, New York.

Index

Abe Bailey Institute, 385
Activists, in U.S., 345–353, 373; universities, 346–347; and pressure from labor movement, 377
Addis Ababa, 311
Affluence, 6, 21, 28, 30, 186, 208–209; of Indians, 120; and protection of white economic privilege, 188–189; and Rhodesia, 235
African Advisory Committee, U.S., 365
African Explosives company, 73
African National Congress (A.N.C.), 120, 129–130; Defiance Campaign (1952), 131–132; and Communists, 143–144
African Party for Independence of Guinea and Cape Verde (PAIGC), 300–304, 309–310, 381; Russian aid, 305
Africans, 3, 13, 75–100; political rights, 7, 17, 18, 39; interest in politics, 7, 31–32, 77–78, 80, 121, 129; in Johannesburg, 11; and the power structure, 32, 36; and Dutch Reformed Church, 47; restrictions on wages and employment, 73–74, 189–190; government's term, Bantu, 76; lack of political leadership, 77–78; population, 78–79; urbanized, 79–89; and tribalism, 79–80, 92–94; bourgeoisie, 92–95; education for, 92–93, 181; Westernization of, 94; and alcohol,

95–97; and the Coloreds, 108–109; and labor unions, 113; political movements, 121; and the police security network, 121–122, 124–128, 134; and Defiance Campaign of 1952, 131; depersonalization of, 158–159; and Group Areas Act, 161; tribal governing bodies, 169; emergence of new leadership, 180–183; and economic aspects of apartheid, 184–215 passim; Rhodesian, 228–233, 236–242, 243, 244–251; in Portuguese Africa, 252, 254, 262–263, 265–266, 275, 277, 278, 279
Africa Today, American magazine, 180, 183
Afrikaans (language), xxiv, 5, 24, 75; and Afrikaner cultural nationalism, 29; in the economy, 30; universities, 47; and Coloreds, 102, 109. See also Newspapers, Afrikaans-language
Afrikaners, xiv, 3–4, 11–53, 214–215, 264, 392; urban, 5; and race, 7, 157 (see also Apartheid); and Johannesburg, 11–12; and English-speakers, 13, 27, 31, 32; rejection of integration, 17; and 1970 elections, 18, 19; history and sociology of, 20–27; and tribalism, 21–22, 28; isolation of, 22–23, 24, 370; and the African tribes, 23–24; and the Church, 24; ascension